# PRIVITY

## PRIVATE JUSTICE OR PUBLIC REGULATION

# Privity

## Private justice or public regulation

*Edited by*
PETER KINCAID
*Macquarie University*
*Sydney*

**Ashgate**

DARTMOUTH
Aldershot • Burlington USA • Singapore • Sydney

Published by
Dartmouth Publishing Company
Ashgate Publishing Limited
Gower House
Croft Road
Aldershot
Hants GU11 3HR
England

Ashgate Publishing Company
131 Main Street
Burlington, VT 05401-5600 USA



Ashgate website: http://www.ashgate.com

**British Library Cataloguing in Publication Data**
Privity : private justice or public regulation
1. Breach of contract 2. Actions and defenses 3. Third parties (Law)
I. Kincaid, Peter
346' .02

**Library of Congress Cataloging-in-Publication Data**
Privity : private justice or public regulation / edited by Peter Kincaid.
p. cm.
Includes bibliographical references and index.
ISBN 0-7546-2089-1
1. Breach of contract 2. Actions and defenses. 3. Third parties (Law) I. Kincaid, Peter.

K877 .P75 2001
346.02'2--dc21

00-54334

ISBN 0 7546 2089 1

Printed and bound by Athenaeum Press, Ltd.,
Gateshead, Tyne & Wear.

# Contents

# Contributors

**Roger Brownsword** Professor of Law and Head of Department, Faculty of Law, University of Sheffield

**J.L.R. Davis** Professor of Law, Australian National University

**Melvin Aron Eisenberg** Professor of Law, University of California, Berkeley

**Robert Flannigan** Professor of Law, University of Saskatchewan

**John Gava** Senior Lecturer in Law, University of Adelaide

**Dale Hutchison** Professor and Head of Department of Private Law, University of Cape Town

**Peter Kincaid** Visiting Fellow, Macquarie University, Sydney

**The Hon. Sir Anthony Mason, A.C., K.B.E.** Former Chief Justice of the High Court of Australia

**Catherine Mitchell** Lecturer in Law, Law School, University of Hull

**Stephen A. Smith** Professor of Law, McGill University, Montreal

**John Swan** Stikeman Elliott (Barristers and Solicitors, Montreal) and McGill University, Montreal

**Anthony Jon Waters** Visiting Professor of Law, University of Oregon School of Law; Professor of Law, University of Maryland School of Law

**Simon Whittaker** St. John's College, Oxford

# Preface

The idea of privity in contract means that only a party to a contract may sue on it. An application of the idea is the third-party rule: a third-party beneficiary of a contract cannot sue to enforce the promise in its favour. This rule has been subjected to criticism. It has been urged that a third-party beneficiary *should* be able to sue the promisor.

The third-party rule is only one small part of the law of contract. Yet the way the question of reform of this rule is approached indicates answers to a number of quite fundamental questions concerning the common law.

It is perhaps an exaggeration to say that privity of contract has been a burning issue for the past sixty years. But since 1937 there has been a steady stream of articles, now probably numbering in the hundreds, devoted to the question: should a third-party beneficiary of a contract be able to sue the promisor to enforce the contract made for its benefit? In that year, 1937, the Law Revision Committee in England recommended that the common law rule denying a right in third parties should be overturned. The rule had been settled (not to say established) by *Tweddle v. Atkinson* in 1861.[1]

Even before 1937 the rule had been subject to much criticism. The bulk of writing since then has supported reform. In 1996 the Law Commission in England published its final report,[2] recommending reform of the third-party rule by legislation. Those recommendations were substantially given effect in the Contracts (Rights of Third Parties) Act 1999, which was passed in November 1999 and came into full force in May 2000. A person not a party to a contract may now sue to enforce a contract if either the contract contains an express term to that effect, or the contract purports to confer a benefit on the third party, in which case it will rebuttably be presumed that the parties intend to confer a right to sue.

The common law rule has been subject to judicial criticism as well. Lord Denning argued that *Tweddle v. Atkinson* was wrong.[3] Although his

---

1 (1861) 1 B. & S. 393; 121 E.R. 762.

2 Law Commission (U.K.), *Privity of Contract: Contracts for the Benefit of Third Parties*, Law Com 242, H.M.S.O., London, 1996. For a summary, see Andrew Burrows, "Reforming Privity of Contract: Law Commission Report No. 242" [1996] L.M.C.L.Q. 467.

3 *Beswick v. Beswick* [1966] Ch. 538 at 553.

interpretation of the law was not approved by the House of Lords in *Beswick v. Beswick*,[4] Lord Reid was unsympathetic to the rule and warned that if Parliament did not do something about it, the House of Lords might have to.[5] Lord Diplock has described the third-party rule as "a reproach to English private law".[6] Its most powerful recent critic in England is Lord Steyn.[7]

In New Zealand,[8] Queensland,[9] and Western Australia,[10] acts have been passed to confer a cause of action on third-party beneficiaries of contracts. There has been judicial nibbling at the rule in Canada[11] and direct if limited assault on it in Australia.[12] In the United States the rule was judicially reformed in New York in 1859.[13] Other states gradually followed suit, and the right of third parties is now recognised in all jurisdictions.[14]

Despite the clamour for reform, some small voices have made themselves heard in defence of privity. The tenacity of privity in the face of criticism may be a sign that some of the points made by its unfashionable defenders cannot convincingly be brushed aside by appealing to the "obvious injustice" of the third-party rule.[15]

The following notes (Chapter One) on what I thought were the theoretical issues raised by the privity question were sent to all prospective new contributors to the book when I invited them to contribute. I wanted to encourage writers from both sides of the debate to address those issues.

*Peter Kincaid*
*Mad Dog Acres*
*Sydney*
*August 2000*

---

4 [1966] Ch. 538.
5 [1968] A.C. 58 at 72.
6 *Swain v. Law Society* [1983] 1 A.C. 598 at 611.
7 *Darlington Borough Council v. Wiltshier Northern Ltd.* [1995] 1 W.L.R. 68 at 76 per Steyn L.J.
8 Contracts (Privity) Act 1982.
9 Property Law Act 1974 s. 55(1).
10 Property Law Act 1969 s. 11.
11 *London Drugs Ltd. v. Kuehne & Nagel International Ltd.* (1992) 97 D.L.R. (4th) 261, 340-370.
12 *Trident General Insurance Co. Ltd. v. NcNiece Bros. Pty. Ltd.* (1988) 165 C.L.R. 107.
13 *Lawrence v. Fox* (1859) 20 N.Y. 268.
14 Second Restatement of the Law of Contract s. 304.
15 A not-so-small voice is that of Brennan J. in *Trident General Insurance Co. Ltd. v. McNiece Bros. Pty. Ltd.* (1988) 165 C.L.R. 107, esp. at 127, 132, and 138.

# Acknowledgments

I wish to thank the following:

The Law Quarterly Review and Robert Flannigan for permission to re-publish the article which appears as Chapter 3.

Butterworths and the Journal of Contract Law for permission to re-publish the article which appears as Chapter 4a.

The Law Quarterly Review for permission to re-publish the note which appears as Chapter 4b.

The Oxford Journal of Legal Studies, Oxford University Press, and Stephen Smith for permission to re-publish the article which appears as Chapter 8.

I also wish to thank Macquarie University and its Division of Law for generously providing me with facilities which helped me to complete this project.

# 1 Theoretical Issues Raised by the Privity Question

PETER KINCAID

## Private or Public Justice

It has frequently been said that if A and B have made a contract in which A promises B that it will confer a benefit on C, it is unjust if C cannot sue A to enforce the promise. The first issue raised by this criticism of the privity rule concerns the nature of justice in contract. Is it a private matter or a public one? And what do these terms themselves mean?

Contract as a matter of private justice can be seen as concerned with balancing the interests of the plaintiff with those of the defendant according to some criterion. The ideas of promise (invoking the trust of the promisee) and consideration (paying a requested price in exchange for a promise) are ideas which can be used to justify making the defendant promisor responsible for realising the expectations of the plaintiff promisee according to the model of contract as a matter of private justice. The rules of contract then reflect the private nature of the relationship between the parties. But private justice need not be confined to the relationship constituted by promise or exchange. An alternative is provided by estoppel: detriment suffered in reliance on an expectation of performance where the defendant has unconscionably induced the plaintiff to rely. (There is a division of opinion as to whether this is private justice *in contract*.[1]) There may be difficulty in justifying a right in a third party as a matter of private justice because of the difficulty of defining a relationship between the third party and the promisor.[2]

But the idea of justice in contract may not be concerned exclusively with private interests. The public may be said to have an interest in the efficient functioning of the economy. If so, there is a public interest in seeing contracts in general carried out. It is uncontroversial that public interests can exceptionally override private ones to deny contractual rights,

1 See *Waltons Stores (Interstate) Ltd. v. Maher* (1988) 164 C.L.R. 387.

2 *Trident General Insurance Co. Ltd. v. McNiece Bros. Pty. Ltd.* (1988) 165 C.L.R. 107, 132.

as in the case of contracts in restraint of trade. But should public interests be recognised as having a legitimate positive role in contract, not merely a negative one? A right in a third party to sue to enforce could be justified not by any qualification by the third party in its relationship of trust, expectation, reliance, or exchange to the promisor, but by the public interest in seeing the contract carried out. Of course the public interest might be in the performance of contracts generally, or in the performance of particular types of contracts, such as insurance contracts where the promisor promises to indemnify a third party.

What is, or has been, or should be the attitude of the common law in the Commonwealth to this question of contract as a matter of public or private justice?

A related question is whether the philosophy of contract law on this issue is different in different systems. Critics of the privity rule sometimes point impatiently to the civil law of France, Germany, or Scotland, or to American law. If those systems recognise third-party rights, surely it is obvious that we should do so too. But if the nature and purpose of contract in the justice system are seen as essentially private in English law, but a mixture of public and private in other systems, it is less obvious that the rules of other systems would accord with our ideas of justice if grafted onto ours.

**Flexible v. Formal Reasoning**

The above discussion assumed that a right in a third party would need to be "justified" by a process of coherent reasoning. The next issue is whether that assumption should stand. Is it instead sufficient or desirable that rules be devised and supported by a less precise, less transparent, more intuitive method of reasoning? The third-party rule is frequently described as unjust to the third party. But what this means in terms of the relationship with the promisor is usually not explained. The law commission purported to justify its proposed rule by saying that it would give effect to the intentions of the parties. What is the role of intention in contract? Is giving effect to the intentions of the parties meant to do private justice by balancing private interests, or is it meant to advance public interests?

The issue here is do those questions need to be answered? Or is it undesirable to impose a rigid requirement of reasoning from premises to conclusions to support legal rules? It may on the other hand be enough to identify a number of factors, public and private, which are thought to be relevant, without explaining precisely the role of any one of them. So it may be said (as the law commission and the High Court of Australia have done) that the third party may reasonably have expected the contract to be performed, and may even have relied on this happening. In addition, it has been said, allowing the third party to sue gives effect to the intention of the parties. A certain fuzziness in just how these factors are relevant is not necessarily bad, if the object is simply to help the intuition of "honest men"[3] to recognise what is fair, reasonable, and just.

Another version of the same issue concerns the relevance of theoretical structure in the law. If a third-party beneficiary can be given rights indirectly by the devices of trust or agency, is it legitimate to by-pass those structures and give the third party direct rights? This is what Mason C.J. and Wilson and Toohey JJ. favoured in the *Trident Insurance Case*.[4] Agency and trust use private-law concepts to explain and justify legal relationships which can include the third party. Are these forms a sophisticated waste of effort, time, and money, or are they fundamental to rational justice?

Another issue arises from the distinction between intuitive and formal reasoning. Judges, law reformers, and writers often give the impression that they are impatient with the limitations of formal reasoning, but instead of acknowledging this impatience, they pay lip-service to formal reasoning by weak or unconvincing arguments. Is this impression correct and, if so, why is there this pretence at formal reasoning?

An example concerns the relationship between consideration and privity. Critics of privity say that privity can be removed as a requirement for a plaintiff without affecting consideration. This is because, it is explained, consideration identifies the sort of promises that can be enforced, not who can enforce them. But this explanation raises a further question (referred to above) which is seldom answered. Is contract about private justice? If it is, it has to be explained how payment of a price by the promisee does anything to justify the third party's claim against the promisor. If contract is about public justice (if such a phrase is appropriate), then it may well make sense to promote the public interest in seeing bargain exchanges carried out.

## Pragmatism v. Principle

Another issue concerns the extent to which the rules of contract, and the rules concerning third parties in particular, should be motivated by broad questions of principle or, conversely, by practical questions of what is

---

3 Lord Steyn "Contract Law: Fulfilling the Reasonable Expectations of Honest Men" (1997) 113 L.Q.R. 433.

4 (1988) 165 C.L.R. 107 at 121.

needed to make the economy and its institutions work efficiently. An attempt could be made to justify a rule allowing third parties to sue according to principles of private justice (such as unconscionably-induced detrimental reliance). Or an equally broad principle of public interest could be used to justify the rule. The public interest in the morality of promise-keeping is an example. On the other hand, such a rule could be defended merely because it works. It makes insurance policies cheaper, for example, by reducing the number of policies and the number of actions needed for enforcement. Or it stimulates business by making easier the protection of various participants such as sub-contractors.

A related issue is whether any reform of the privity rule should be by a general rule allowing all third parties conforming to certain limitations to sue, or whether it should be by special rules peculiar to certain sorts of contract such as insurance contracts or construction contracts. If the driving force behind the reform movement is really economic pragmatism, then does that suggest that special rules should be adopted? Or can it be assumed that the practical advantages of allowing third parties to sue are the same regardless of the type of contract in question?

The law commission recommended a general rule. Did this recommendation imply a requirement of logical coherence? If so, can the recommendation be justified by reference to general principle? If not, why make a general rule? Special rules could perhaps fit in with a predominantly private-law view of contract as cases where, exceptionally, public interests override private ones.

## Nature and Source of a Third-Party Right

A number of issues arise from how a direct third-party right to enforce a contract should be characterised.

First, is it contractual or non-contractual? The question itself is slippery because it assumes that contract has an agreed meaning. If contract is defined to mean all the legal rights and duties attaching to anyone affected by an exchange transaction, then the question is answered. A third-party right would be contractual. Even those within the "circle of persons to whom the protective effect of a contract extends"[5] as recognised by German law, though not third-party beneficiaries of the primary obligations of the contract, would be exercising contractual rights.

But if contractual rights are thought to be defined and assumed by

[5] B. Markesinis, "An Expanding Tort Law - The Price of a Rigid Contract Law" (1987) 103 L.Q.R. 354, 363.

the parties, then the answer is not so clear. Is it necessary for a relationship between the third party and the promisor to be identified which justifies treating the third party as part of the exchange? Or is it sufficient that the parties to the contract have intended to confer a legal right upon the third party? The last question leads to another: Given doubts as to whether intention to create legal relations is necessary for a valid contract, is such an intention sufficient for their creation? The "intention of the parties" is often appealed to as a justification for third-party rights. What has been the role of intention in contract, and what should it be? The issue behind these questions concerns the role of the state in defining contractual rights.

If third-party rights are treated as non-contractual, then what is the justification for their recognition? If they are considered a matter of private justice outside contract, then, as mentioned above, the reliance of the third party may be a justifying factor. But can reliance stand alone, or must it be combined with legally relevant behaviour by the defendant, such as unconscionable inducement?

Another private-justice factor which has been used to justify third-party rights is the acceptance by the third-party of the promise made for its benefit.[6] Can acceptance alone be used to justify a third-party right within the idea of private justice?

If third-party rights are to be justified as a matter of public justice, then, as discussed above, the public policies supporting the rights may be moral, such as the desirability for the public in encouraging the keeping of promises, or practical, such as economic efficiency.

## Rights and Duties: the Question of Focus

Whether contract in general, or third-party rights in particular, are to be considered a matter of private or public justice, another issue concerns the relative importance of right and duty in the relationship between the plaintiff third-party and the defendant promisor.

The first possibility is to focus upon the duty of the defendant alone. The canon law was generally concerned with the promisor's duty. The attitude is reflected in the judgment of the majority in *Lawrence v. Fox*,[7] where it was said that the fact that the defendant had been paid for his promise made it his duty to pay the third party. The facts that the promise was not made to the third party, and neither had the third party provided consideration, were irrelevant. There are echoes of this approach in the

6 See C. Fried, *Contract as Promise* Harvard U.P., Cambridge, Mass., 1981, pp. 44-45; Queensland Property Law Act 1974 s. 55(1).

7 (1859) 20 N.Y. 268.

judgment of Gaudron J. in *Trident*.[8]

A second possibility in the right-duty balance is to focus upon the duty of the defendant, but to combine that with a "legitimate interest" in the plaintiff in seeing the promise performed. It might be said that the expectation of the third-party that the contract will be performed makes its interest in seeing it done legitimate. This raises the question of the defensibility of using expectation as a criterion justifying a cause of action.

The third possibility is to require a correlation between right and duty by requiring the plaintiff to show a legally relevant relationship between it and the defendant sufficient to justify causing the state to coerce the defendant into realising the interests of the plaintiff.

Which of these three points of view as to the relationship between rights and duties should be adopted in justifying third-party rights? And to what extent does the answer depend upon the distinction between public and private justice?

## Remedies

A final, more down-to-earth, issue concerns the remedies of the promisee (not the third party) for breach of the promise to benefit the third party. Conventional law has it that just as the right belongs to the promisee, so does the remedy. The result is that the promisee can only recover damages for losses suffered by the promisee, not those suffered by the third party.[9] The issues here are two. First, is it theoretically consistent with the nature of the relationship between right and remedy for the cost to the promisee of conferring the promised benefit on the third party to be considered a loss to the promisee?[10] Second (a further-reaching idea), should the consequential losses to the third party be able to be recovered by the promisee?

---

8 (1988) 165 C.L.R. 107 176. She says that the promisor who has been paid consideration is unjustly enriched.

9 *Coulls v. Bagot's Executor and Trustee Co. Ltd.* (1967) 119 C.L.R. 460 at 501-502 per Windeyer J.

10 As suggested by Lord Griffiths in *Linden Gardens Trust Ltd. v. Lenesta Sludge Disposals Ltd.* [1994] 1 A.C. 85.

# 2 Summaries of Essays

PETER KINCAID

## Chapter 3: Robert Flannigan, "Privity – The End of an Era (Error)"

An effect of the doctrine of privity is that it disallows enforcement of a contract by a third party whom the original parties intended should receive a benefit. Robert Flannigan sets out to show why this is wrong.

His thesis is that the privity rule is not supported by reason. Its continued existence is attributable solely to the force of precedent. In support of his thesis, he looks at the historical foundation of the doctrine, the substantive arguments for and against it, and, the core of his article, the consistency of the doctrine with various theories of contract. He concludes that it is not consistent with any theory and that its creation was an error.

In the seventeenth century the law was unambiguous in allowing third parties to sue to enforce contracts made for their benefit. The basis was the interest of the third party in having such a right. However, towards the end of that century some contradiction of the right emerged, on the ground that the promise had not been made to the third party or that he had given no consideration.

The next two hundred years saw contradictory cases being cited for and against the right of the third party, with no satisfactory resolution, although as late as 1823 a new case was decided affirming the right, which by then had substantially more weight of authority in favour of it than against it. However, in 1833, a firm if unreasoned decision was made against such a right.

The ascendancy of the view that a third-party beneficiary could not sue came about in 1861 in *Tweddle v. Atkinson*. However, the author points out that the actual reasoning in that case focused on the fact that the plaintiff third party had not provided consideration for the promise. It has, however, been treated as though it were based on the third party's lack of privity. Without careful analysis, it has been assumed that the case is authority for the proposition that privity is a rule distinct from consideration, whereas the reasoning and the result in the case are more consistent with the idea that privity is merely an application of the requirement of consideration.

The focus on consideration, conceded by counsel for the third party, led the court to treat some of the old pro-third-party cases as depending upon an exceptional sort of consideration – the "near relationship" idea – and to overlook the fact that a clear line of authority had supported a third-party right with no requirement for additional consideration. In any case, no reasons were given in *Tweddle v. Atkinson* for denying the third party a right to sue on a contract made for his benefit merely because he had provided no consideration. A fundamental reason in favour of the third party was overlooked. That is, the promisor got what he bargained for from the promisee. Having got it, it was wrong that he should be able to ignore his own promise.

The main brake on the abolition of privity is a widespread belief in the idea that it is a theoretically fundamental part of the law of contract. The author looks at several theories to see whether that is so.

The will theory provides that a contract should be enforced because to do so gives effect to the demonstrated intention of the parties. There is a public interest in seeing contracts performed. However, public and private interests must coincide in order to give a person standing to sue. Both the promisee and the third party have a relevant private interest in the performance of the contract so as to give them standing. The will theory thus supports a third-party right.

The bargain theory is built on the idea of a contract consisting of the exchange of a promise for consideration. But the author sees the function of consideration not as an element qualifying the plaintiff in his relationship with the defendant, but as evidence of serious intention. Since in a third-party situation consideration has passed from the promisee to the promisor, the cautioning function of consideration has been served and there is no reason not to allow the third party to enforce the contract.

In Fried's promise theory, respect for the promisor's autonomy as a person requires taking his promise seriously. Robert Flannigan sees no room for privity here. We show respect for the promisor by allowing the third party to insist upon the benefit the promisor has promised to bestow upon him.

As to relational contract law, American neo-classical law recognises the complexity of contract relationships and therefore allows third-party rights.

In an economic analysis of law, the third-party rule is clearly inefficient as it requires more transactions to achieve the same result as could be achieved by allowing a third party to sue directly.

A critical analysis of law also has a public focus and is concerned with the state's interest in planning. That interest encourages the fulfilment of promises. Allowing third parties to sue advances that objective.

In none of these theories, nor in an analysis of liability based on reliance or unconscionability, does the author find theoretical support for denying a right to a third-party beneficiary of a contract. The doctrine of privity is an historical and theoretical error. Effect should be given to the intention of the contracting parties to confer a benefit on the third party by allowing him to sue to enforce it.

## Chapter 4 (Part A): Peter Kincaid, "Privity and Private Justice in Contract"

In earlier articles I had asked those supporting reform of the privity rule to demonstrate how it was unjust to the third party to deny it a right of action on a promise, when the promise was not made to it and it had not paid for the promise. I had argued that the common law approach to private law liability required the plaintiff to demonstrate why, according to some criterion of justice, the defendant should be responsible for realising the plaintiff's interests. I had assumed that justice required coherent reasoning from principle to rule. Merely to relax the privity rule would satisfy none of these requirements of justice.

Very few people thought the point worth arguing, and the progress towards reform in England continued with, on the whole, enthusiastic support. This progress culminated, just before the present article, in the Law Commission's final report, the substance of which was enacted into law three years later, in the Contracts (Rights of Third Parties) Act 1999.

My thesis in this article is that the indifference by the Law Commission and many others to these requirements of private justice indicates that contract is increasingly seen not as a matter of private justice but of public regulation. I develop this thesis by analysing the justifications offered by the commission for giving a third party a right to sue on a contract. They are intention, expectation, and reliance.

The commission say that giving effect to the intentions of the contracting parties is the general justifying theory of contract. Therefore if the parties intend that the third party be able to sue, it is inconsistent with contract theory to deny it this right. I argue, however, that this mistakes the role of intention in traditional contract. The law's concern with intention is to see if the parties have bound themselves, and according to what terms, in a relationship that the law has defined. If they have, the law invests the parties with the legal right to enforce each other's promises. Their right to sue is not created by their intention. It is attached by the law.

Private justice is about a balancing of the interests of the participants in a legally-defined relationship according to criteria of justice. Third parties are not part of any relationship. To allow them to sue on the basis of the intention of the parties suggests that there is a public interest in upholding the bargain, an interest separate from the interests of the parties and the third party.

The lack of a defined relationship between the reasonable expectations of or reliance by the third party and the conduct of the promisor by way of private justification further suggests that the central concern of the commission is with the public good of allowing third parties to sue, and not with private justification for allowing the third party to interfere with the liberty of the defendant promisor.

The general lack of concern with a coherent justification at the private level for a third-party right against the promisor suggests that law in private areas like contract has become less concerned with individual rights and more concerned with public interests such as efficiency. The presumption in private law that private interests are paramount has gone.

Not only does this approach indicate changed ideas about contract and private law generally, but it also suggests a change in the nature of legal reasoning. There is less concern with rigorous defensible reasoning from principles to rules. A fuzzy mixture of partly-articulated reasons for a rule is seen as satisfactory justification, although a pretence at logical reasoning is maintained.

## Chapter 4 (Part B): Peter Kincaid, "Privity Reform in England"

This short piece was published just after the new Act became law in November 1999. It is a development of the theme in my article "Privity and Private Justice in Contract" set out above.

I begin by identifying the chief causes of the perceived injustice of the third-party rule of the privity doctrine which led to the passing of the Act. They were that the rule frustrated the intentions of the contracting parties and disappointed the expectations of the third party.

Why did it take so long to pass an Act to correct those injustices? I offer the explanation that the conception of justice has changed. The leading nineteenth century cases settling classical contract law doctrine represent a view that justice in contract derives from the relationship between the plaintiff and the defendant constituted by their participating together in a bargain. The emphasis on consideration and privity can be seen as requiring the plaintiff to establish links in his relationship with the defendant promisor, in one case that he has paid a price demanded, and in the other that the promise in question was made to him.

But this pattern of defining private justice through a relationship between the plaintiff and the defendant is not peculiar to contract. It characterises other private law causes of action in areas such as tort, unjust enrichment, equitable estoppel, etc. If the state is to coerce one individual to realise the interests of another they must be linked by a relationship of causation and fault, the transgression of some value. In contract, the legally-defined justifying relationship is based upon the value of promise and the wrongfulness of breaking one for which a price has been extracted from the promisee.

The Contracts (Rights of Third Parties) Act 1999 departs from this general pattern of private law liability. It does not define a justifying relationship between the plaintiff third party and the defendant promisor. The justification relied on for this cause of action is that it gives effect to the intentions of the contract parties. But those intentions are not relevant, in the private law scheme of legally-defined relationships, to a cause of action by the third party.

I conclude that the Act represents a shift in contract from a concern with private justice to a concern, even in actions previously thought of as private, with public goods.

## Chapter 5: Sir Anthony Mason, "Privity – A Rule in Search of Decent Burial?"

Sir Anthony Mason has two objects in his essay. The first is to examine the nature and purpose of the privity rule and its relation to consideration, and the second to assess the functional utility of the rule in light of its deficiencies.

He says that the privity rule gives expression to the idea of contract as a bargain between the parties which creates rights and obligations only between those parties. However, the rule rests on a legal conception rather than on any functional or policy consideration.

He addresses the question whether the requirement of consideration is a rule that goes to the validity and enforceability of the contract or whether it, like the privity rule, goes to the standing of the plaintiff to sue. He concludes, as did the Law Commission, that consideration goes to validity, not standing, and that the rule should thus be stated as, "consideration must move from the promisee", not "consideration must move from the plaintiff". This conclusion is important because, he says, the displacement of the privity rule would then leave the contract (which would create the third-party right) intact and valid. It also disposes of the fear that alteration of the privity rule would undermine the central conception of contract.

He discusses a number of practical and policy objections to allowing third parties to sue, but dismisses them as having little weight. The principal justification for the third-party rule, he says, is unquestionably conceptual: the idea of contract as a bargain creating rights and duties only in the parties to it.

He notes that the third-party rule has been criticised in common law jurisdictions and legislatively or judicially modified in some, and also that third-party rights exist in civil law systems.

He notes with approval the justification for departing from the third-party rule offered by Lord Steyn and picked up by the Law Commission. It is that to allow the third party to sue gives effect to the intention of the contracting parties, protects the expectations of the third party, and, as a supplementary reason, protects reliance by all three.

He discusses other reasons for reform. They include limitations on the promisee's remedies in damages and specific performance, and practical limitations in chains of construction contracts.

He then discusses criticisms of the case for reforming privity and departing from the third-party rule. He acknowledges the objection that allowing a third party to sue is difficult to reconcile with the bargain theory of contract. However, it is consistent with the will theory, which is every bit as respectable as the bargain theory and does not require privity. Under this theory a contract is binding because the intention of the parties creates the liability. And he agrees with Robert Flannigan that there is a clear public interest element in such an approach: "every citizen has an interest under the will theory in the enforcement of the agreement."

Sir Anthony Mason welcomes the prospect of a shift from a theory of contract based wholly on a balance of private interests, to one which takes account of public interests as well. However, he says that even if one focuses on the question of a private justifying relationship between the third party and the promisor, there clearly is one. It arises from the generation of expectations in the third party by the contractual expression of intention, in an exchange of promises, by the parties that the third party should have a cause of action. It is hardly to the point, he argues, to harp on inconsistency of the reforms with the bargain theory when it is deficiencies in that theory which are driving the reforms.

He acknowledges that the provisions of the new Act concerning variation and rescission raise some problems concerning theoretical coherence. However, the reforms are just and practical. Practicality rather than theoretical coherence has been the hallmark of the development of the common law.

**Chapter 6: Catherine Mitchell, "Searching for the Principles behind Privity Reform"**

Catherine Mitchell assumes that the law of contract ought to manifest coherence, which she defines as consistency in relation to the value the rules represent. The requirement of coherence is that the rules together have some purpose and that they pull towards it, although this says nothing about whether the values advanced are good.

She analyses the rules establishing third-party rights under the Contracts (Rights of Third Parties) Act 1999 and the rationale for those rules offered by the Law Commission. Her object is to see whether the new rules demonstrate coherence with the values in the rationale.

She observes that the Law Commission purports to create the new third-party right without disturbing the foundations of the orthodox or classical law of contract. A central idea of that law is that effect should be given to the intention of the contracting parties. Since the Act requires the parties, actually or by implication, to intend the third party to have a right to enforce in order for him to have one, the new right is offered by the Commission as an application of orthodox contract law.

She focuses on two elements of contract law supposedly preserved by the Law Commission's scheme. The first is consideration. The contract between the parties must obey the rules as to consideration in order to create the right in the third party. But she concludes that this adherence to consideration is an illusion. The real object of the reforms is not to protect the expectations of the contracting parties, but those of the third party. That is, the concern is with turning the interests of the third party into rights. But the third party need provide no consideration, and it is not apparent what the relevance of that provided by the promisee is to the third party's claim. So consideration is not necessary. Nor, she observes, is it sufficient. If the third party has "accepted" the right created by the contract, no bargain between the parties is sufficient to erase or modify the right. The new third-party rule, then, is incoherent with a central idea of orthodox contract: consideration.

The second element purportedly preserved by the new scheme is the distinction between tort and contract. The author examines the new right and compares it with equitable estoppel, which at least in its Australian form is now analysed as a non-contractual right. She concludes that the new third-party right, with its emphasis on realisation of the third party's expectation and enforcement of the promise, is contractual.

The result is that the Act is not coherent with the orthodox account of contract. And yet the right it creates is contractual in nature. The Act represents a radical departure from traditional contract, despite the Law

Commission's assertion that it does not. The Commission has really adopted a modern account of contract, where "reasonable expectations" of the plaintiff are given effect for a variety of reasons.

Whether those reasons are exclusively concerned with private justice between the parties, or whether public interests are also relevant, is a question which might be answered by the analysis of the new model which Catherine Mitchell invites at the end of her paper.

## Chapter 7: Roger Brownsword and Dale Hutchison, "Beyond Promissory Principle and Protective Pragmatism"

The object of Roger Brownsword and Dale Hutchison is to see what legal provisions concerning variation and rescission of contracts say about the underlying theory of two contract regimes that allow for third-party claims, namely South Africa and now England.

Their discussion is in three parts. First, an examination of the question, can the logic of promise cope with a tri-partite situation? Second, an examination of how South African law has been based on the idea that promises should be kept, and yet it has long allowed third-party claims. And third, an examination of the new English regime which is based not on promises as such, but upon respect for the contractors' intentions coupled with protection for third-party reliance.

Their conclusion is that neither the promissory principle of South Africa nor the pragmatic view of the new English law satisfactorily explains third-party rights. Behind both lies the deeper principle of meeting reasonable expectations. This principle needs to be more explicitly recognised in order to provide a coherent framework for developing the law of the creation and rescission or variation of third-party rights in contracts.

They look at the promissory model in a tri-partite situation. Where a promise is made by A to B to confer a benefit on C, but no promise is made to C, they suggest that there are three possible answers to the question when does the right vest in C. They are, 1. When A makes the promise to B and C becomes aware of it; 2. When C accepts the promise made by A to B; and 3. When C relies on the promise. They assume that B as the direct promisee must take priority over C, until something happens to make C's interests prevail. By that reasoning, only reliance by C makes sense because only then does the principle of estoppel provide a reason for preferring C's interests over B's. But, they say, the theory of promise cannot alone explain C's priority.

South African law is based upon the civilian notion of a legal bond or relationship creating rights and duties for and against the parties to it.

The notion of privity is thus attractive to South African law. However, the system has long felt the need to help third-party beneficiaries of contracts. It did this by converting the trilateral relationship into two bilateral ones. A's promise to B is construed as an offer to C which, upon acceptance by C, becomes an enforceable promise by A to C, as well as a promise by A to B.

South African law treats acceptance as governing creation of the third-party right *and* loss of the right to vary, in much the way that acceptance works in a bilateral bargain situation at common law. This is different from the English statutory position, where the third-party right comes into existence upon expression of the necessary intention in the contract, but it is liable to be varied by the parties up to acceptance or reliance by the third party. The insistence on acceptance by the third party is the dominant feature of South African law. It has the theoretical effect of creating a separate bilateral contract between the third party and the promisor. This is to be distinguished from the new English position, where the right in the third party is created directly by the contract between the principal parties; its creation requires no input from the third party. The authors prefer what they see as the conceptual clarity of the new English approach (also followed in Germany). They see the conceptual construct of South African law as an old-fashioned fixation with the notion of privity.

Turning to the new English Act, they note that, in the form adopted, the test gives effect to the intentions of the parties to create an enforceable right in the third party. But they observe that although the Law Commission saw itself as creating a new right consistent with the basic principles of traditional contract law, the intentions of the parties according to that law are relevant to the interests of the parties, not to the interests of those outside the relationship. Nor is the existence of the third-party right based upon reliance by the third party. If it is not based on intention or reliance, then what is the basis of the obligation of the promisor to the third party?

They note that reliance is adopted as part of the crystallisation test. Reliance may be seen as estopping the promisee from releasing the promisor, but why does this principle now take precedence over "the hitherto governing idea of giving effect to the joint intentions of A and B"?

The authors offer the idea of reasonable expectation as the answer and the link between third-party rights under the Act and the common law of contract as it has now evolved. This is now the basis of contractual obligation at common law. And, within a relativistic culture, reasonableness can only be assessed by observing currently accepted practice and conduct of fair dealing, rather than looking for some objective and abstract idea. So a contract between A and B may create an expectation in C that the law in the circumstances will regard as reasonable. The rules established by the Act for the creation and crystallisation of third-party rights are an application, within a more certain framework, of this broad and modern idea of the protection of reasonable expectations.

What does the analysis of Roger Brownsword and Dale Hutchison reveal about the public-private debate? First, it might be noted that although the South African law of third parties involves a factual fiction, it is consistent with the idea of private legal rights depending upon a justifying relationship between the plaintiff and the defendant. The authors prefer the direct approach to third-party rights, of which the English Act is an example. They propose the idea of reasonable expectations as a key to understanding the treatment of third-party rights in modern regimes of contract law. Whether they see contract as a matter of private justice between the plaintiff and defendant, or a matter of public regulation must depend on the range of factors permitted in their flexible notion of what is "reasonable". It seems to me that only if the expectations of the third party can be sheeted home to something the promisor has done can their notion of contract be treated as purely a matter of private justice.

## Chapter 8: Stephen A. Smith, "Contracts for the Benefit of Third Parties: in Defence of the Third-Party Rule"

Stephen Smith's article challenges the widespread view that the third-party rule is an indefensible anachronism. The rule is a fundamental part of contract law. The results in "privity cases", where a contract between A and B is intended to benefit C, are often unsatisfactory not because of a defect in the third-party rule but because of other problems in the law of obligations. These problems concern the proper protection of the three basic private law interests: expectation, reliance, and restitution.

He defends the third-party rule by treating contractual obligations as personal. They are undertaken voluntarily by one person to another. If a contract is made between A and B whereby A promises B that he will benefit C, A's duty to perform is owed to B, not to C. Thus C cannot sue A to enforce the duty because it is not owed to C. Promisees are in a different moral position from non-promisees. And the difference of their position is not explained by whether or not they have provided consideration.

One reason for this personal nature of contractual rights and duties is that they are typically positive, rather than just negative. Non-voluntary obligations like torts are duties *not* to do something, whereas contractual obligations are duties to *do* something. It is crucial that individuals be able to control the scope of such obligations.

This analysis assumes, as Stephen Smith acknowledges, that contract rights and hence contract remedies are different in kind from those in tort. But a view that contract is a species of tort does not justify allowing third parties to enforce a promise *as such*, with expectation damages. Rather it points to denying anyone such a right to enforce a promise.

Even if the parties intend to benefit the third party or that the third party should be able to sue, a third-party right cannot be justified on the ground that the object of the law of contract is to give effect to the intentions of the contracting parties. That argument mistakes the role that intention plays in the creation of contractual obligation. It determines the content of the obligations in the contract but, more importantly, it determines whether or not a person has undertaken an obligation to another. In the typical tri-partite situation, where A promises B that A will confer a benefit on C, an examination of A's intention shows that he does not undertake an obligation to C, only to B.

The real problem in privity cases, then, is not the third-party rule, but other deficiencies in the law of obligations that manifest themselves in third-party situations. The expectation interest of the promisee is not adequately protected because he may often recover only nominal damages. The problem is exacerbated in cases where the promisee has died and it is his estate that is seeking to enforce the promise to benefit a third party. But in both instances the problem is not caused by the third-party rule.

A "third party" may in fact be a promisee as where A promises both B and C that he will confer a benefit on C. C in this case has an expectation interest of his own. But evidentiary and doctrinal problems distinct from the third-party rule make it difficult to assert that interest.

A third party may have a tort or tort-like cause of action against the promisor arising from the promisor's breach, in making the promise to B, of a duty not wrongfully to induce detrimental reliance in C. This is the basis of Australian equitable estoppel. Limitations on such a cause of action in English law, for example the "shield and not a sword" limitation, are instances of the reliance interest of the third party not being adequately protected, because of shortcomings in rules other than the third-party rule.

The restitution interest of promisees and third parties is also inadequately protected, but the cause is shortcomings in the law of unjust enrichment, not the third-party rule.

Stephen Smith then looks at the Law Commission's proposals, which later resulted in the present Act. He concludes that a confusing mixture of party intention and assent or reliance by the third party, coupled with contractual remedies depending on those of the promisee, together make it unclear what the basis of the new third-party right is. The result is an ad hoc balancing of different interests. This confusion supports his thesis that it is not obviously the third-party rule, an exclusively contractual rule, that needs reforming.

Even from a practical point of view, the anomalies likely to be thrown up by an ad hoc approach to reform suggest that in the long run a principled approach is best. In some third-party situations, even under reformed principles no interest of the third party may be infringed - in expectation, reliance, or restitution. In such a case it is hard to see why, even if the result is contrary to the intentions of the contracting parties, it is unjust that C, the "third party", should have no rights against the promisor in contract.

## Chapter 9: Melvin Aron Eisenberg, "The Third-Party Beneficiary Principle"

The purpose of Melvin Eisenberg's essay is to develop a normative principle which will determine when a third-party beneficiary should be able to bring suit under a contract. He illustrates that principle with reference to the American experience of this problem. He defines "third-party beneficiary" to mean a person who is not a party to a contract but who would benefit from its performance. From the middle of the nineteenth century American law developed a right in certain third-party beneficiaries to sue.

At the outset he disposes of the objection in principle that the third party has not given consideration as being irrelevant. The purpose of consideration is not to qualify a plaintiff to sue but to distinguish enforceable promises from unenforceable ones. The whole question of a third-party claim assumes the existence of an enforceable contract. The issue is the third party's qualification to sue on it, but that issue is not determined by the criterion of consideration.

The normative purpose of contract law is to facilitate the power of self-governing parties to further their own interests by contracting. A normative as opposed to a technical objection to allowing third-party suits is that they can interfere with the interests of the parties and the freedom that contract gives them. So not all third-party beneficiaries should be able to sue. The problem is to formulate a principle to identify which ones should. He reviews three tests which have been developed respectively by the American courts and the two Restatements of the law.

The courts have filled a void in the First Restatement test by adopting intention to benefit the third party as the test of entitlement to sue, although the meaning of intention is ambiguous. The ambiguity is not cured by the intention test of the Second Restatement.

He regards the Contracts (Rights of Third Parties) Act 1999 as an enormous improvement in English contract law, although it suffers from the same ambiguities concerning intention as does the test of the Second Restatement.

To overcome the essential meaninglessness of the intention test, he proposes a test based primarily on the performance objectives of the contract. That is, a third-party beneficiary should be able to enforce a contract if such a power is necessary or important to achieving the performance objectives of the contract as manifested in the contract read in the light of surrounding circumstances, or if there are independent reasons of policy or morality for enforceability by the third-party and it would not conflict with the contracting parties' performance objectives.

The proposed test is based on a mixture of private and public interests. Performance objectives, the primary part of the test, reflect the private interests of the contracting parties, while policy and morality, the secondary and dependent part of the test, reflect public interests. The test does not focus on the private interests of the third party. All this is consistent with the view that the primary purpose of contract law is to further the "self-regarding" interests of the contracting parties. But if that primary purpose is not infringed, public interests may provide a separate secondary reason for third-party enforcement.

Melvin Eisenberg then looks at categories of situations where third-party beneficiary problems have arisen in American law and seeks to show that the results of most modern American cases are explained by his proposed third-party beneficiary principle. His categories are: 1. donee beneficiaries; 2. creditor beneficiaries; 3. cases where the parties have dealt explicitly with whether or not the third party should be able to enforce the contract; 4. suits by would-be legatees against lawyers drafting wills; 5. suits by subcontractors against sureties who have given bonds to owners; and 6. suits between multiple prime contractors.

## Chapter 10: John Gava, "Is Privity Worth Defending?"

John Gava assumes for the purposes of his essay that the attack on privity is part of a larger attack on classical common law contract. His object is to examine whether that law is worth defending.

The attack on privity is part of a perceived need to make the rules of contract law reflect the needs and practices of business. Contrary to the arguments of people like Horwitz and Danzig, he says, contract law historically has not developed changes directly in response to changes in the economy or the needs of business. Instead economic changes have thrown up problems which necessitated the development of existing principles to solve new problems. Those basic principles and their underlying values such as the moral force of a promise have not changed.

The supposed need to make legal rules reflect changing business practices assumes that contract law is central to those practices. However, studies have shown that many factors beside law govern business practices. Contract law is part of the context of doing business, but not the major part. It also serves as an available last resort when business relationships break down. In both those roles, certainty of rules is probably more important to businessmen than constantly changing rules.

Even if it were desirable for judges to alter contract law to reflect business practices, judges do not have sufficient knowledge of those practices to fashion rules accurately.

Having argued from a practical perspective against a functionalist approach to the reform of contract law, John Gava turns to issues of principle and philosophy. While business may want rules to be certain and not care much what the content of the rules is, the law as a general social institution is meant to reflect the values of the society as a whole. The central moral values present in the classical law of contract are those concerned with the making and keeping of promises. The common law of contract reinforces the ideas of the worth and autonomy of individuals and thus provides a valuable counter weight to the overbearing influence and power of today's relatively unbridled capitalism. Not only will a functionalist approach not work, but it risks destroying a social institution which is valuable in its own right.

## Chapter 11: John Swan, "The Rights of Third Parties to Contracts: A Suggested Basis for Recognition"

John Swan's purpose is to take up the challenge offered by me in several articles and to suggest a rationale for third-party rights which does not subvert the fundamental principles of the law of contract or the values of the common law.

He describes three situations where rights of third parties are commercially important and where they have been judicially recognised. The first is the extension of the coverage of insurance contracts to sub-contractors in construction projects, where two broad reasons have been used in Canada and Australia to extend rights to third parties: advancing commercial efficiency and giving effect to the intention of the parties, since the benefit of the policy was expressed to extend to the third parties.

The second is waiver in an insurance contract of rights of

subrogation of the insurer against third parties such as the charterer of a vessel owned by the insured. Allowing the third party to enforce the waiver was based squarely upon the intention of the parties.

The third situation involves extending the protection of an exclusion clause to the employees of the protected contracting party. Again a mixture of commercial efficiency and intention of the parties appears to be the reason for the extension.

The author argues that the bargain principle has not in practice been applied in the pure way in which it is stated. Consideration, for example, has not infrequently been conjured up to allow an otherwise gratuitous promise to be enforced. The courts have been more pragmatic than my argument against third-party rights, based upon the coherence of the bargain principle, supposes.

As to the argument that to allow third parties to sue, when they have not provided consideration and cannot show privity, would logically require allowing gratuitous promisees to sue, he says there are many reasons of convenience and policy to distinguish the situation of a gratuitous promisee from that of a third party.

It may be recognition rather than enforcement of a third-party right that is required, as in the case of the employee seeking to rely on an exclusion or limitation clause to which he was not a party. He is not seeking to recover anything from the promisor, only to be able to mount a defence to a claim by the promisor.

Tackling my objections head on, he says that I argue that even where the parties to an insurance contract have explicitly agreed that a sub-contractor be covered by the policy, the bargain principle requires the court to permit the insurer to deny coverage to the sub-contractor. Considering that the parties and the sub-contractor have organised risk around this contract, the application of the bargain principle achieves a result that can only be described as bizarre. Not to enforce such a contract is to ignore the very purpose of the contract. Giving effect to that purpose is the justification for recognising or enforcing the third-party rights contemplated by the contract. And if that is inconsistent with the bargain principle, so much the worse for the principle.

However, to enable the third parties in a common enterprise such as a construction project to enforce their intended rights under the contract consistently with the bargain principle, John Swan suggests drawing on the *Coulls* case and treating the contracting parties and the third parties in such an arrangement as an "entity". It was this analysis which allowed Windeyer J. in that case to regard the consideration supplied by Mr. Coulls as having been supplied by the entity consisting of him and his wife as joint promisees. By this analysis the "third party" in a common enterprise such as a construction project can be seen in fact to be a party. The court can then avoid the bizarre result whereby liability would be imposed on the only people in the enterprise who do not and would not be expected to have insurance.

The existence of such an "entity" is to be deduced, not from the words of the contract, but from an objective assessment of the relationships that underlie it. For example, in the context of protection of employees as in *London Drugs*, companies which make contracts of the type in question "can only act or operate with officers and employees and it distorts the nature of the transaction to regard either party for this purpose as an entity separate from those who make its decisions and operate it".

John Swan's conclusion indicates that he thinks commercial reality, or the needs of business, must take precedence over purity of principle, although in this instance a reinterpretation of the facts can achieve reconciliation between the two.

## Chapter 12: Simon Whittaker, "Reciprocity Beyond Privity"

Simon Whittaker notes that reciprocity has long been a feature of English contract law, from the requirement of quid quo pro on. The dual principle of privity is that in general only the parties may bear the burdens and enjoy the rights arising from a contract. However, the principle should be thought of as susceptible to exception where this can be justified. His article is about the role of the principle of reciprocity in this justification.

He sees contract not as sets of promises backed by consideration, but as agreements triggering a set of legal consequences, some arising directly from the agreement and others arising from its regulation by law. Reciprocity is thus reduced from being the defining element of contract (as bargain) to a threshold condition for recognising an effective agreement which can trigger legal consequences.

If the reluctance in adherents of the classical law of contract to recognise rights beyond privity derives from a concern to preserve reciprocity, then this concern may be used to argue for reciprocal exceptions to privity rather than no exceptions, as Crompton J. does in *Tweddle v. Atkinson*.

His object is then to see whether English law in some instances recognises reciprocity beyond privity of contract. He identifies four areas of law where it does. They are, 1. leasehold covenants, 2. the undisclosed principal, 3. rights of employees on the transfer of undertakings, and 4. transfer of a package holiday. Should these instances be developed into a broader principle of reciprocity beyond privity?

Simon Whittaker looks at consideration and notes that the reciprocity in it does not require an exchange of duty for right, as in a bilateral contract, but merely a giving up of something of value, as in a unilateral contract where the promisee does the requested act rather than making a requested promise.

He then examines the law concerning applying the benefits and burdens of contracts to people not privy to the original contract in two types of situation. They are the assignees of leasehold covenants (that is, the assignees of the lessor and of the lessee) and of employment contracts. A common characteristic of the legal recognition of the transfer of these contractual rights is that they continue to be reciprocal. So rights and duties which start off as affecting only those privy to the contract have been extended in these two areas to those not privy, but only if each person acquires both a benefit from and burden towards the other. Although, he says, reciprocity beyond privity can never be a justification for an exception to privity, the idea of reciprocity may properly shape the incidents of particular examples of exceptions to privity.

In his third category, he points out that the anomalous rights and duties of an undisclosed principal can be seen to have evolved as an application of the principle of reciprocity: for pragmatic reasons (i.e., for reasons other than reciprocity) the principal was allowed to sue. Since he could, it was only just that he be liable to be sued. Here, then, an exception to privity was allowed by reference to a view of practical convenience, but its incidents were shaped by the idea of reciprocity.

His fourth category is package holidays. E.U.-originated legislation in England permits the buyer of a package holiday to transfer the benefits and burdens to a third party. He characterises this as an example of reciprocity beyond privity.

The position of the executor of a deceased estate is not a true example of reciprocity beyond privity, but is rather the continuation of the legal personality of one of the parties privy to the contract.

The law of restrictive covenants allows the burden of certain covenants affecting land to bind a sub-purchaser. However, he says that although the doctrine started as an extension of contractual rights beyond privity, it is now conceived entirely in terms of limited property rights.

Simon Whittaker finishes by discussing Megarry's proposed "pure principle of benefit and burden" by which he who takes the benefit of a transaction must bear the burden. This "principle" has not been accepted, a rejection which the author agrees with, for, I think, two reasons. One is that privity must continue to be the default principle: benefits and burdens should in general affect only those who participate in (are privy to) the making of the contract. There are special reasons for extending rights and duties beyond privity, as in the four categories that he discusses. And reciprocity reinforces those special reasons.

His concern is not with other possible justifications for exceptions to privity, such as the Law Commission's use of the intention of the parties. His thesis is that Crompton J.'s objection, in *Tweddle v. Atkinson*, that an exception to privity would necessarily produce a lack of reciprocity was wrong, as illustrated by the several examples in the essay of situations where reciprocity has been preserved although privity has been abandoned.

## Chapter 13: J.L.R. Davis, "Privity and Exclusion Clauses"

Jim Davis's thesis is that the doctrine of privity need not be relevant to the question of whether a person may take the benefit or bear the burden of an exclusion clause contained in a contract to which he is not a party.

The *Elder Dempster* case in 1924 put forward the principle of vicarious immunity: anyone who performs any part of the obligations in a contract is entitled to the benefit of any exclusion clause in it. However, that idea has been repudiated in England, Australia, and Canada, and replaced by the principle that no one can claim protection of an exclusion clause in a contract unless he is a party to it.

However, he points out that the cases establishing this proposition were ones in which the person seeking protection was not, by the terms of the clause, protected by it. And he says that exclusion clauses can be regarded in two different ways: first as limiting or providing a defence to a liability which has arisen, and second as preventing any liability from arising in the first place. He concedes that privity is relevant to the first type.

But as to the second type, liability may be excluded by the prospective tortfeasor giving notice to the person to whom the duty is owed, as long as that person may be said to assent. This is the doctrine of assumption of risk, and it depends on consent, not contract. It is, he says, irrelevant that A (a potential victim) communicates to C his assumption of risk of injury to C by means of a clause in a contract between A and B.

In practice, courts have been willing to give effect to an exclusion clause in favour of someone who is not a party to the contract containing that clause. Because of what the author regards as misconceived doubts about the principle of voluntary assumption of risk, they have used two devices to avoid privity. The first is the *Himalaya* clause, which uses the principles of agency to make a stevedore a party to the contract and thus able to enforce the exclusion clause. The second is direct exceptions to the requirements of privity, as in the *London Drugs* case.

He regrets that the new Act in England will reinforce the assumption that a "contract analysis" is necessary to solve problems of non-parties taking the benefit of exclusion clauses. Attention is further deflected from what he regards as the elegant, relevant, and correct approach, namely to ask has the plaintiff assented, before a cause of action can arise, to assume some or all the risk of damage by the defendant? As contract is irrelevant to the relationship between plaintiff and defendant in this analysis, so is privity.

He then goes on to consider applying the burden of an exclusion clause to a non-party, a subject not dealt with by the new Act. There are two sorts of situation where the law has allowed a non-party to bear the burden. The first is the consignee of a bill of lading and the second is a sub-bailment on terms. In the first case, the consignee is bound by an exclusion clause in favour of the shipper, and in the second, the owner is bound by a clause in favour of the sub-bailee. In both situations, he says, where the issue is the imposition of the burden of an exclusion clause, the solution depends, and depends solely, upon whether the (non-party) plaintiff had sufficient notice of the clause and may thereby be taken to have assented to it. Assent is easier to infer in the case of the assignment of a bill of lading than in that of a sub-bailment on terms.

Jim Davis thus sees support for the proposition that extension of the benefit or the burden of an exclusion clause to a non-party is dependent upon the principle of assumption of responsibility, which in every case requires knowledge of and assent to the exclusion (or limitation) by the person bearing the burden.

His justification for holding a person to a responsibility that he has assumed has two parts. First, if the exclusion or limitation is in a contract, the general desirability of upholding and enforcing bargains is a reason for giving effect to the term, even if in the dispute in question, the other person affected is not a party to the contract. Second, if the limitation or exclusion is contained in a non-contractual notice, the justification for enforcing the assumption of responsibility is the moral precept that a person should not be permitted to resile from his undertakings.

These justifications give insight into Jim Davis's view as to the choice between private justice and public regulation in civil liability in general and contract in particular. His justifications do not depend upon the characteristics of the relationship between the plaintiff and the defendant, but upon a public interest in moral behaviour, on the one hand, and in seeing contracts adhered to, on the other.

## Chapter 14: Anthony Jon Waters, "Privity, Property, and Pragmatism"

Tony Waters subtitles his essay, "Can American Law Answer Kincaid's Questions?". He sets himself the task of addressing four questions raised by me. Those questions concern:

1. Whether there is need for a general rule allowing third party enforcement, given the many devices for avoiding the rule.
2. Whether recognition of a third-party right requires a departure from coherent reasoning.
3. Whether recognition of a third-party right shifts the focus of contract law from private grievances to public interest.
4. How the recognition of a general third-party right of enforcement would change the nature of contract.

He sets out to consider those questions with reference to American common law which does permit the enforcement of a contract by an "intended beneficiary".

Before proceeding to address those questions, he gives an analytical account of the adoption of the American rule. It began in 1859 with the New York case *Lawrence v. Fox*, where the third-party intended beneficiary of a contract was allowed to succeed against the promisor, despite the promise not having been made to him and his having provided no consideration. However, Holly, the promisee, owed money to Lawrence, the third party. Holly had lent the amount of that debt to Fox in return for a promise by Fox to pay Lawrence. Thus Lawrence was a creditor of the promisee, a "creditor beneficiary". It appears, though, that the debt arose from gambling and thus was not enforceable, making it difficult theoretically to base the third party's right upon the credit relationship.

I think Tony Waters's point here is that neither the original judicial rule, nor its reflection in the First Restatement, rested on a clear theoretical foundation. Was the third party enforcing a contractual right as such, or was it a species of property right, or was it based on unjust enrichment?

The Second Restatement replaced the creditor beneficiary test with the "intended beneficiary" test. A public flavour was given to the law of third parties in the 1970s and 1980s by an attempt to allow the intended beneficiaries of public schemes set up by government to sue the independent agency charged by the government with responsibility for administering the scheme and conferring the benefits.

Turning to the first question, the need for a general rule, he points out that analytical devices such as agency, trust, or *Dutton v. Poole's* "blood tie" amounting to consideration, did not allow a third party to sue. Rather they exploited established legal principles either to allow the plaintiff a cause of action outside contract or to make the plaintiff a party to the contract. The third-party beneficiary rule established in *Lawrence v. Fox* "involved another dimension altogether". It contradicted fundamental contract doctrine and had no doctrinal moorings of its own.

But law, at least in the American experience, is simply a product of the political system. So whether or not a right in third parties is theoretically tidy, there is a case for having one if it is needed. But is it? Towards the end of his paper, Tony Waters reports his surprise at the results of his survey of the 131 cases in the United States in the first six months of 2000 in which a third-party right was "germane to the issue". Eighty-five percent were roughly commercial in nature. And in about 85% of those cases, the third-party right was refused recognition. It seems from this that in bargain-type contractual situations, some mechanism rejects third-party rights even in a system where a rule of law makes them available. This observations suggests that a general rule allowing third-party rights may not be necessary in America, which has one, or in other countries which do not or until recently did not.

As to the question of coherence and fuzziness, the author says that the sort of coherence that Stephen Smith and I appear to revere in classical contract law is achieved only by confining "contract" to an unrealistically narrow range of transactions. Anyway, there is nothing inherently fuzzy about a third-party right. It can be justified by the conduct of the promisor in inducing reliance by the third party, and by the promisee's giving something up in return for the promisor's promise. The same pattern of justice can be achieved in a third-party right while breaking free of the anachronistic bonds of traditional contract law. The justification need not come from contract reasoning; a third-party right need not be seen as contractual. Instead it may be looked at from the point of view of property or unjust enrichment and be perfectly coherent.

In other words, much of the confusion caused by the American third-party rule is the result of its having been labelled "contract".

# 3 Privity – The End of an Era (Error)*

ROBERT FLANNIGAN

The doctrine of privity applies to prevent strangers from enforcing a contract. There is no real quarrel over this. But the doctrine also applies to disallow enforcement by a third party whom the original parties intended should receive a benefit. This is wrong. What follows is an attempt to explain why.

It has been said that when "a rule is well established by decisions, it is not necessary to give any reasons in its support, or to say anything to show it to be a good and useful one".[1] Unfortunately, this gibe is all too descriptive of what has been the modern approach to the doctrine of privity. Indeed, a dogmatic approach has been necessary for the continued survival of the privity doctrine in its present form because, as will become apparent, there is precious little to support the doctrine or to show it to be a "good and useful" rule.[2]

Criticism of the privity rule has been prominent in contract discussions for the greater part of this century. As yet, however, neither the courts nor legislatures have acted to abolish the general rule. So now, prompted by recent judicial calls for its reconsideration,[3] it seems appropriate to once again make the case against the doctrine. In pursuing that end, it is first convenient to closely examine the historical foundation of the doctrine. Then the substantive arguments for and against the

---

* This article was published in (1987) 103 L.Q.R. 564. It is reproduced here with the kind permission of the author and the Law Quarterly Review. Original page numbers are shown in **[square brackets]**.

1 *Emmens v. Elderton* (1852) 4 H.L.Cas. 624, 658 *(per* Maule J.).

2 According to Lord Wright ("Ought the Doctrine of Consideration to be Abolished from the Common Law?" (1936) 49 Harv.L.R. 1225, at 1226):

> The rules of law are required to justify themselves by their fitness to satisfy the practical requirements of justice, as well as to be self-consistent and rational. Criticism comes from historical studies, from logical analysis, from comparative law, from sociological ideals.

3 *Woodar Investments Developments Ltd. v. Wimpey Construction U.K. Ltd.* [1980] 1 All E.R. 571, at 588-589 and 591 (H.L.) (*per* Lord Scarman and Lord Keith).

doctrine are reviewed. Lastly, and this is perhaps the primary contribution of this article, the theoretical consistency of the doctrine is assessed. As most readers will know, there are a number of descriptive and normative theories advanced to conceptualise contract law. The doctrine of privity is analysed for its consistency with these various theories. It is determined that the doctrine cannot be justified on any theory of contract law. It is concluded that the creation of the doctrine of privity was an error and it is time now to end the era of its operation.

## The Early Cases

In the seventeenth century[4] the courts did not doubt the proposition now (sometimes virulently) denied in our modern law. Third parties were allowed to enforce contracts made for their benefit. [565]The judgments were neither ambiguous nor equivocal on this point. In *Provender v. Wood* the recorded words of the court were "[a]nd the party to whom the benefit of a promise accrews, may bring his action".[5] There was in fact an extended series of cases prior to 1669 that confirmed or were consistent with the view that a third party could take action to enforce the promise.[6] The implicit rationale was that the third-party beneficiary had a clear interest which entitled him or her to an enforcement action.[7] The law, it would seem, was settled; one might have thought firmly settled! But one would be wrong. Counsel in subsequent cases right up to and including the twentieth century apparently failed to find these cases or to cite them in sufficient quantity to indicate that the issue was already resolved.[8]

---

4 A few cases at the end of the sixteenth century had refused a third party on the ground that the promise had not been made to him. See *Jordan v. Jordan* (1595) Cro. Eliz. 369, 849; *Taylor v. Foster* (1600) Cro. Eliz. 776, 807.

5 (1630) Het. 30, 124 E.R. 318.

6 *Manwood and Burston's Case* (1587) 2 Leon. 203, 74 E.R. 479; *Rockwood's Case* (1589) 1 Leon. 193, 74 E.R. 177; *Levett v. Hawes* (1599) Cro. Eliz. 619, 652, 78 E.R. 891 *sub. nom.; Lever v. Heys,* Moore, K.B. 550; *Rippon v. Norton* (1602) Cro. Eliz. 881, Yelv. 1, 78 E.R. 1106; *Provender v. Wood* (1630) Het. 30, 124 E.R. 318; *Hadves v. Levit* (1631) Het. 176, 124 E.R. 433; *Oldham* v. *Bateman* (1637) 1 Rolle Abr. 31; *Bafeild v. Collard* (1646) Aleyn 1, 82 E.R. 882; *sub. nom. Anon* Sty, 6; *Disborne v. Denabie* (1649) 1 Rolle Abr.31 ; *Starkey v. Mill* (1651) Sty. 296, 82 E. R. 723; *Thomas v. ?* (1655) Styl 461, 82 E. R. 863; *Sprat v. Agar* (1658) 2 Sid. 115, 82 E.R. 1287; *Bell v. Chaplain* (1663) Hard.321 145 E.R. 478. Also see *Cores Case,* referred to in *Hadves v. Levit,* above and the *Physician's Case,* referred to in *Bourne v. Mason, infra,* note 11.

7 Indeed, some courts went even further and would allow an action only to the third-party beneficiary. See *Levett v. Hawes; Rippon v. Norton; Sprat v. Agar;* all *supra,* note 6.

8 The first case in which more than only a few of the early decisions were cited appears to be the Australian High Court case of *Coulls v. Bagot's Executor and Trustee Co. Ltd.* [1967] A.L.R. 385, at 408; 119 C.L.R. 460, at 497.

The complete reversal of this position took time.[9] The first significant contrary decision[10] was that in *Bourne v. Mason*.[11] The court in this 1669 case referred to only two earlier decisions.[12] Distinguishing features for those cases were fabricated and then, not unexpectedly, they were distinguished.[13] For the case at hand, it was said that the third party "did nothing of trouble to himself, or benefit to the defendant, but is a mere stranger to the consideration".[14] In other words, since the third party had given no consideration for the promise, he had no right to maintain an action to enforce it. This, it will be appreciated, is a proposition opposed by the numerous previous but uncited cases.

**[566]** Following hard on the heels of *Bourne v. Mason* were a number of cases which returned to the established rule that the third party would have an action.[15] But, oddly, it was only the case of *Dutton v. Poole*[16] which thereafter became significant. *Dutton v. Poole* was an unfortunate case for third-party beneficiaries. Unlike any of the earlier decisions supporting the third party's right of action, several of which were cited, the judgment qualified the third-party right of action by linking the availability of the action in this case to a familial nearness of relationship between the third party and the promisee.

*Dutton v. Poole* is usually cited as the major case[17] on the side of third parties in the historical debate over the third-party action.[18] This is curious, however, because in fact the case contributed substantially to the demise of the third-party beneficiary action. As qualified, the decision

---

9 The approximately 200 years between *Bourne v. Mason* (1669) 1 Vent. 6, 86 E.R. 5 and *Tweddle v. Atkinson* (1861) 1 B. & S. 393.

10 The earlier contrary decision in *Ritler v. Dennet* (1606) 1 Rolle Abr. 30 was never a factor in the process. It was never cited in any court until the doctrine was firmly entrenched in the common law by other cases. Another earlier decision, *Norris v. Pine* was disapproved of in *Dutton v. Poole,* where it is first referred to (without a citation).

11 (1669) 1 Vent. 6, 86 E. R. 5.

12 The two cases were *Sprat v. Agar, supra,* note 6, and a case for which there is no citation which I have called the *Physician's Case, supra,* note 6.

13 The third party in *Sprat v. Agar* was said to have been properly entitled to his action because he did the "meritorious act" of marrying the daughter of the promisor. But that was not the consideration. The two fathers had exchanged the giving of the hand of the daughter, on the one side, for a settlement of land on the other.

14 *Supra,* note 11 (at Vent. or E. R. 6).

15 *Hornsey (Administrator of Jane Lane) v. Dimocke* (1672) 1 Vent. 119, 86 E.R. 82; *Corny and Curtis v. Collidon* (1674) 1 Freeman 284 , 89 E.R. 205; *Dutton v. Poole* (1678), *infra,* note 16; *Chamberlaine* v. *Chamberlaine of Mangersbury* (1678) 2 Freeman 34, 22 E.R. 1041; *Yard* v. *Eland* (1698) 1 Raym 368, 91 E.R. 1143.

16 (1678) 2 Lev. 210, 83 E.R. 523.

17 Again, it seems that the bulk of the earlier cases were simply lost.

18 *E.g.* Treitel, G. H., *The Law of Contract* (6th ed.), Stevens & Sons, London, 1993, at 458-59.

essentially accepted the reasoning in *Bourne v. Mason* although the latter case was not cited. The two cases could thereafter be reconciled with one another. The general rule would then be that a person who gives no consideration will have no action. But there would be, as counsel would subsequently argue, a *Dutton v. Poole* exception to the effect that a third party related to the promisee could participate in or benefit from the promisee's consideration to the promisor. As it turned out, when the issue was eventually squarely addressed some two hundred years later, the solitary authority of *Dutton v. Poole* was explained away on the basis that "natural love and affection are not a sufficient consideration".[19]

The matter attracted relatively little attention in the eighteenth century. In 1724, the court in *Crow v. Rogers*[20] was referred to both *Bourne v. Mason* and *Dutton v. Poole.* "[W]ithout much debate", the third-party plaintiff was refused an action because he was "a stranger to the consideration".[21] In 1776, in an *obiter* **[567]** comment in *Martyn v. Hind*,[22] Lord Mansfield expressed his surprise as to "how a doubt could have arisen in *Dutton v. Poole*".[23] This remark has been taken to be an approval of the general right of a third party to bring an action.[24] Then, in 1797 in *The Master, Wardens and Commonality of Feltmaker v. Davis*,[25] Eyre C.J. refers to the unrecorded judgment in *Marchington v. Vernon*[26] where the right of a third-party beneficiary to maintain an action on the promise was approved.[27]

---

19 *Tweddle v. Atkinson* (1861) 1 B. & S. 393, at 399. This dealing with *Dutton v. Poole* has been approved by others. Windeyer J. in *Coulls v. Bagot's Executor and Trustee Co. Ltd.* put it this way:

> The case really turned, however, upon the expansive views of consideration then held, arising from close relationship and from the moral claims of a daughter to her portion. It is not at all surprising that Lord Mansfield warmly approved the decision. It accorded with his view that a moral obligation provided consideration for a binding promise, a notion not finally dispelled from the law until *Eastwood v. Kenyon* (1840) 11 Ad. & E. 438.

20 (1724) 1 Str. 591, 93 E.R. 719.

21 *Ibid.*, at Str. 592. E. R. 720.

22 (1776) 2 Cowp. 437, 98 E.R. 1174.

23 *Ibid.*, at Cowp. 443, E.R. 1177.

24 Lord Mansfield's approval was in fact the kiss of death for *Dutton v. Poole.* His view that a moral obligation or natural love and affection could constitute consideration became associated with *Dutton v. Poole* and, as we have seen *(supra,* note 19), that was the basis on which *Dutton v.Poole* was eventually discarded.

25 (1797) 1 Bos. & Pul. 98, 126 E. R. 799.

26 *Ibid.*, at Bos. & Pul. 101 (footnote c), E.R. 801.

27 In his judgment, Eyre C.J. makes the following curious statement: "As to the case put at the bar, of a promise to A for the benefit of B and an action brought by B, there the promise must be laid as being made to B and the promise made actually to A may be given in evidence to support the declaration". This is pure wishful thinking if it is

The nineteenth century began with *Pigott v. Thompson*[28] where, in a footnote, the court affirmed the "rights of a third person to sue upon a parol promise made to another for his benefit".[29] Thereafter, various of the contradictory cases were paraded before a number of courts without there being any satisfactory determination of the issue.[30] Then, in the 1823 decision in *Carnegie v. Waugh*,[31] it was accepted once again without any qualification that a third party may maintain an action on a contract for his or her benefit.[32]

To this point in time the historical case for the privity doctrine is extremely modest. The assertions of the judges in the few cases claiming a doctrine of privity were unsupported and were made in ignorance of an established line of authority. Support for a third-party right of action, in comparison, is both voluminous and continuous. This fact was apparently not fully developed before the court in *Price v. Easton*[33] After considering only a few previous cases, and without any real inquiry into or discussion of the issue, the court upheld an objection to a third-party action.

This brings us to *Tweddle v. Atkinson.*[34] It is this 1861 case that has been taken to be the one which finally ended the uncertainty **[568]** and confirmed that a third party cannot sue on a contract between two others even though it was made for the benefit of the third party. We shall examine this case to see what reasons there could be for such a result. But before doing so it is useful to momentarily investigate the nature of the principle that is being created in this process.

## Privity or Consideration?

There is an issue as to whether privity is a distinct doctrine or merely an aspect of the doctrine of consideration. On the one hand, it is said that there is both a rule that a person who is not a party to a contract cannot sue on it

supposed to be the explanation for the cases where third parties were allowed to maintain their actions.

28 (1802) 3 Bos. & Pul. 147, 127 E.R. 80.

29 *Ibid.*, at Bos. & Pul. 148 (footnote (a)), E. R. 83.

30 *Philips v. Bateman* (1812) 16 East 356, 104 E.R. 1124; *Barford v. Stuckey* (1820) 2 Brod. & B. 333, 129 E. R. 995.

31 (1823) 1 L.J. (K.B.) 89.

32 *Ibid.*, at 90.

33 (1833) 4 B. & Ad. 433, 110 E.R. 518. *Cf. Hill v. Gomme* (1839) 5 My. & Cr. 250, 41 E.R. 366.

34 (1861) 1 B. & S. 393.

and a separate rule that consideration must move from the promisee.[35] On the other hand, it is argued that the two rules are but different ways of saying the same thing.[36] The latter view may be the more plausible one. To say that a person is not a party to the contract is just another way of saying that he or she is not one of the reciprocating promisors. That is, he or she is not a person who gave a promise (i.e. consideration) in exchange for another. On that view, the "privity" rule (that a non-party cannot sue) is just a description of the result supposedly demanded by the doctrine of consideration. The rule, then, is that a third party cannot sue on the contract *because* he or she has not provided consideration.[37] Certainly the cases we have considered to this point have proceeded on this basis. The third party was disallowed an action by reason of being a "stranger to the consideration".[38]

The creation of a separate "privity" rule may have come about as a result of later judges taking loose and truncated language in the nineteenth century at face value.[39] Thus, in the often cited 1833 **[569]** case of *Price v. Easton*, Chief Justice Denman decided against the third party because there was no "consideration for the promise moving from the plaintiff [i.e. the

35 *Dunlop Pneumatic Tyre Company Limited v. Selfridge* [1915] A.C. 847, at 853; Statute of Frauds and the Doctrine of Consideration, *Sixth Interim Report of the Law Revision Committee,* 1937, Cmd. 5449, at 22; Treitel, *supra,* note 18, at 457-58; Atiyah, P. S., *Consideration in Contracts: A Fundamental Restatement,* Aust. Nat. Univ. Press, Canberra, 19711971, at 39-40.

36 Furmston, M. P., *Cheshire and Fifoot's Law of Contract* (11th ed.), Butterworths, London, 1981, at 74-75; Furmston, M. P., "Return to *Dunlop v. Selfridge*" (1960) 23 M.L.R. 373, at 382-84; Samuels, G., "Contracts for the Benefit of Third Parties" (1968) 8 U.W.A.L.R. 378, at 393.

37 The rule that consideration must move from the promisee, it should be pointed out, would actually be irrelevant in the present context if it were not simply another way of saying that a person is debarred from an action because he or she has given no consideration. This is because, when considering a third-party beneficiary right of enforcement, we are already dealing with an existing and admittedly valid contract between the original promisors. Each of the original promisors (who are both each promisees), have provided consideration for the promises made to them so that consideration does "move from the promisee" on either side.

38 *Bourne* v. *Mason* (1669) 1 Vent. 6, 86 E.R. 5; *Crow v. Rogers* (1724) 1 Str. 591, 93 ER. 719; *Price v. Easton* (1833) 4 B. & Ad. 433, 110 E. R. 518.

39 There appears to have been little talk of "privity" prior to the nineteenth century. And what there was rejected a "privity" requirement as an additional requirement to consideration. In *Dutton v. Poole (supra,* note 16, at Lev. 211, E.R. 524) it is recorded that initially two justices thought the daughter ought not to be able to sue because she was "not privy to the promise nor consideration". Of course, as the case was decided, any requirement to be a "party" to the contract was ignored and thereby implicitly rejected. The same analysis is applicable to *Yard v. Eland* (1698) 1 Raym. 368, 91 E.R. 1143.

third party] to the defendant".[40] But Littledale J. gives his judgment in these words:

> No privity is shown between the plaintiff and defendant. This case is precisely like *Crow v. Rogers* (1 Str. 582) and must be governed by it.[41]

Recalling that *Crow v. Rogers* was decided on the basis that the third party was a "stranger to the consideration",[42] that is what Littledale J. must have meant when he stated that "[N]o privity is shown...". Arguably, this looseness of language was a primary cause in the subsequent bifurcation of what had been a single rule.[43] A contributing factor may have been the use of shorthand or truncated descriptions of the original rule in turn-of-the-century textbooks. An example of such a description is that "[T]he agreement of contracting parties cannot confer on a third person any right to enforce the contract".[44] The failure to mention the reason for this result, the need to provide consideration, would make it easier for some body, such as the House of Lords, to assert the existence of two separate rules. We shall see that this very event came to pass[45] as we next review how the privity rule was cemented into the common law.

## The Entrenchment of the Doctrine of Privity

It has been pointed out that, contrary to popular legal opinion, *Tweddle v. Atkinson*[46] really does not stand as an authority for an independent privity

---

40 (1833) 4 B. & Ad. 433, 110 E.R. 518.

41 *Ibid.,* at B. & A. 434, E. R. 519.

42 *Supra,* note 21.

43 If the twentieth century is any example. See Treitel, *supra,* note 18, at 457 (footnote 38).

44 Pollock, F., *Principles of Contract* (4th ed.), Stevens and Sons Limited, London, 1888, at 260 (para. 200). The same text is carried through to the 8th edition published in 1911 only a few years before the House of Lords decision in *Dunlop Pneumatic Tyre (supra,* note 35). Compare Paine, W., *Chitty's Law of Contracts* (16th ed.), Sweet and Maxwell, London, 1912, at 38-39 where it is stated that it is "clearly settled at common law, that a mere stranger to the consideration cannot enforce performance of the contract, by an action thereon in his own name, although he be the party avowedly intended to be benefited thereby". This is clearly the consideration rule and there is no mention at all of a separate "privity" rule. Perhaps the House of Lords in *Dunlop Pneumatic Tyre* had access to the Pollock treatise but not to Chitty's. Also see Leake, S. M., *Law of Contracts* (6th ed.), Stevens & Sons Limited, London, 1912, at 297, 439 where there is a similar truncation.

45 *Dunlop Pneumatic Tyre Company Limited v. Selfridge, supra, note* 35.

46 *Supra,* note 19.

doctrine.[47] The case was one decided exclusively on the absence of consideration moving from the third party. That this mistaken view of the decision should exist is curious for the judgments themselves are straightforward. But let us look to the **[570]** judgments and consider just how the matter of the third-party beneficiary was dealt with.

It is apparent that the court in *Tweddle v. Atkinson* was not in possession of all the relevant authorities. Wightman J. had this to say:

> Some of the old decisions appear to support the proposition that a stranger to the consideration of a contract may maintain an action upon it, if he stands in such a near relationship to the party from whom the consideration proceeds, that he may be considered a party to the consideration. The strongest of those cases is that cited in *Bourne v. Mason* (I Ventr. 6), in which it was held that the daughter of a physician might maintain assumpsit upon a promise to her father to give her a sum of money if he performed a certain cure. But there is no modern case in which the proposition has been supported. On the contrary, it is now established that no stranger to the consideration can take advantage of a contract, although made for his benefit.[48]

The fact is that, apart from *Dutton v. Poole*,[49] the old decisions were not qualified on the "near relationship" basis. Moreover, whatever may have been the ultimate fate of the "near relationship" proposition, the proposition that a third party could enforce a contract had been supported in modern cases.[50] Lastly, prior to this decision it had hardly been satisfactorily established that "no stranger to the consideration can take advantage of a contract, although made for his benefit". To have "established" this principle, presumably, the authorities would be consistent and good reasons for the rule would be recorded. It is obvious in this regard, that Justice Wightman's remarks contain no *reasons*. Nothing about the general right of a third party to take action is decided here. The lack of a general right, premised on a lack of consideration, is simply assumed.

Crompton J. does purport to give one reason for debarring the third party. According to him, it would be a "monstrous proposition to say that a person was a party to the contract for the purpose of suing on it for his own advantage, and not a party to it for the purpose of being sued".[51] That the described proposition is "monstrous", however, is doubtful. The contract,

---

47 Atiyah, P. S., *The Rise and Fall of Freedom of Contract,* Clarendon Press, Oxford, 1979, at 413-414.

48 *Supra,* note 19, at B. & S. 398.

49 *Supra,* note 16.

50 *Supra,* note 26, 29, 31.

51 *Supra,* note 19, at B. & S. 398.

it will be immediately appreciated, does not seek performance of any kind from the third party. There is a promise made to benefit the third party; but there is no promise of performance made *by* the third **[571]** party which could be enforced against him or her. The original parties were obviously aware of this at the time they contracted. Is the original promisor somehow prejudiced by being compelled to perform? Most decidedly not. The promisor got what he bargained for from the promisee or, if not, he is entitled to get it in an action against the promisee. Then consider the alternative. Is it not markedly more "monstrous" that, having received performance, the promisor could ignore his or her own promise?

If we look at Justice Blackburn's judgment it is made patently clear that, in fact, the court wasn't even being asked to choose between generally allowing or disallowing third-party actions. Apparently on the authority of *Price v. Easton*,[52] counsel for the third party had conceded the general rule and sought only to argue a *Dutton v. Poole* "near-relationship" exception:

> Mr. Mellish admits that in general no action can be maintained upon a promise, unless the consideration moves from the party to whom it is made. But he says that there is an exception; namely, that when the consideration moves from a father, and the contract is for the benefit of the son, the natural love and affection between the father and son gives the son the right to sue as if the consideration had proceeded from himself. And *Dutton and Wife v. Poole* (a) was cited for this.[53]

It seems entirely unsatisfactory that the general third-party right of action should be lost on an unnecessary concession. Yet this is what happened if *Tweddle v. Atkinson* is the decisive case. The result of the concession, of course, was to allow the court to forgo any penetrating analysis of the issue.

*Tweddle v. Atkinson* was subsequently treated as having decided that a third party had no right of action.[54] As we have seen, it was actually an assumption by the court rather than a decision. Nevertheless, the court's assumption was based on a supposed need for consideration. There was no talk of an independent "privity" rule here.

In 1915, in the House of Lords decision in *Dunlop Pneumatic Tyre*

---

52 *Supra,* note 33.

53 *Supra,* note 19, at B. & S. 399.

54 See *Gandy v. Gandy* (1883) 30 Ch.D. 57, at 69 where Bowen L.J. confidently states that: "It was supposed at one time in the history of our common law, that there was an exceptional class of cases, in which where a contract was made for the benefit of a person who was not a contracting party, that is to say, a stranger, it could be enforced by that person at law. It would be mere pedantry now to go through the history of that idea: it is sufficient to say that in the case *of Tweddle v. Atkinson* (1), to which we were referred, the true common law doctrine has been laid down."

*Company Limited v. Selfridge*,[55] the bifurcated rules were **[572]** simply assumed. It is Viscount Haldane's judgment that is usually quoted to describe the final nail in the third party's coffin:

> My Lords, in the law of England certain principles are fundamental. One is that only a person who is a party to a contract can sue on it. Our law knows nothing of a jus quaesitum tertio arising by way of contract. Such a right may be conferred by way of property, as, for example, under a trust, but it cannot be conferred on a stranger to a contract as a right to enforce the contract in personam. A second principle is that if a person with whom a contract not under seal has been made is to be able to enforce it consideration must have been given by him to the promisor or to some other person at the promisor's request. These two principles are not recognized in the same fashion by the jurisprudence of certain Continental countries or of Scotland, but here they are well established.[56]

Once again there were no *reasons* given; there was no attempt to justify either of the separate rules. Nor was there here even an attempt to examine the previous authorities. Clearly there would have been difficulty in finding satisfactory cases to support an independent "privity" rule. And, in fact, the case was decided solely on the basis of no consideration.[57] Nevertheless, now the authority of the House of Lords was put on the scale. From this day forward the two rules, the "privity" rule and the consideration rule, were cemented into the common law as two separate rules.[58]

It is interesting to note that the creation of a "privity" rule independent of the consideration rule had the effect of further buttressing the consideration rule. Why would any third party now argue that further consideration (i.e. beyond that given by the promisee) was not required if, granted that, the third party still couldn't enforce the promise because he or she wasn't a "party" to the contract? In any event, if the separate "privity" rule is just the result of loose language or simply an alternative formulation

---

55 [1915] A.C. 847.

56 *Ibid.*, at 853.

57 Obviously, given the inadequate fashion in which the court dealt with the law, the case is far from being a monolithic authority. Relevant in this regard are Lord Dunedin's remarks (at 855) about the doctrine of consideration as applied in this case:

> My Lords, I confess that this case is to my mind apt to nip any budding affection which one might have had for the doctrine of consideration. For the effect of that doctrine in the present case is to make it possible for a person to snap his fingers at a bargain deliberately made, a bargain not in itself unfair, and which the person seeking to enforce it has a legitimate interest to enforce.

58 *Vandepitte v. Preferred Accident Insurance Corporation of New York* [1933] A.C. 70, at 79.

of the consideration rule, it would seem that the two rules should stand or fall together.

## The Modern Cases

One might have thought the authority of the House of Lords would have been enough to end any further debate over the right of a third party to enforce a contract. For a while it did. But in a **[573]** series of cases beginning in 1949, the case for the third party was made again. Lord Denning took up the issue in *Smith and Snipes Hall Farm LD. v. River Douglas Catchment Board*[59] and further pressed his views in *Drive Yourself Hire Co. (London) LD. v. Strutt*[60] *and Adler v. Dickson.*[61] His remarks in the first-mentioned case included these:

> Mr. Nield says that the plaintiffs cannot sue. He says that there is no privity of contract between them and the board, and that it is a fundamental principle that no one can sue upon a contract to which he is not a party. That argument can be met either by admitting the principle and saying that it does not apply to this case, or by disputing the principle itself. I make so bold as to dispute it. The principle is not nearly so fundamental as it is sometimes supposed to be. It did not become rooted in our law until the year 1861 (*Tweddle v. Atkinson* (1)), and reached its full growth in 1915 (*Dunlop v. Selfridge* (2)). It has never been able entirely to supplant another principle whose roots go much deeper, I mean the principle that a man who makes a deliberate promise which is intended to be binding, that is to say, under seal or for good consideration, must keep his promise; and the court will hold him to it, not only at the suit of the party who gave the consideration, but also at the suit of one who was not a party to the contract, provided that it was made for his benefit and that he has a sufficent interest to entitle him to enforce it, subject always, of course, to any defences that may be open on the merits.[62]

Lord Denning has been reprimanded for his views in a number of areas,[63] but in this context it is difficult to find fault with him. At the time, however, his views were not generally adopted. While he received some

---

59 [1949] 2 K. B. 500.

60 [1954] 1 Q.B. 250, at 272-75.

61 [1955] 1 Q.B. 158, at 193.

62 *Supra,* note 59, at 514.

63 As to "fundamental breach" see *Photo Production Ltd. v. Securicor Transport Ltd.* [1980] A.C. 927 and as to "inequality of bargaining power" see *National Westminster Bank plc v. Morgan* [1985] A.C. 686.

judicial support,[64] his historical arguments were soon questioned by commentators[65] and, later, in the courts.[66] It is worth noting, however, that none of these latter writers offered any *reasons* for the retention of the doctrine.

**[574]** For a while it seemed that Lord Denning's efforts[67] would become famous as the last futile attempt[68] to establish the right of a third-party beneficiary to enforce the promise.[69] This, however, was not to be the case. A number of law lords have since called for a reconsideration of the ban on third-party actions. First Lord Reid[70] and then, very recently, Lords

---

64 *Pyrene Co. Ltd. v. Scindia Navigation Co. Ltd.* [1954] 2 Q.B. 402, at 422; *Rayfield v. Hands* [1960] Ch. 1, at 6-7. And see Dowrick, F. E., "A Jus Quaesitum Tertio By Way of Contract in English Common Law" (1956) 19 M.L.R. 374.

65 (Casenote) (1954) 70 L.Q.R. 467; Scamell, E. H., "Privity of Contract" (1955) 8 C.L.P. 131.

66 *Green v. Russell* [1959] 2 Q.B. 226; *Coulls v. Bagot's Executor and Trustee Co. Ltd.* [1967] A.L.R. 385; 119 C.L.R. 460.

67 Lord Denning made a further effort to terminate the privity doctrine in his Court of Appeal judgment in *Beswick v. Beswick* [1966] Ch. 538, affd. at [1968] A.C. 58. On this occasion his argument was that the doctrine was a mere rule of procedure. For another procedure argument see Street, T. A., *The Foundations of Legal Liability,* Edward Thompson Company, Long Island 1906, Vol. 2, at 155-56.

68 One commentator (Hanson C.J., [1959] C.L.J. 153, at 155) on the case of *Green v. Russell* (*supra,* note 66) stated that "*Green v. Russell* evidences an apparently very firm intention on the part of the Court of Appeal to have nothing to do with third-party-beneficiary rights despite Lord Denning's recent advocacy of them". Also commenting on the same case, another writer (Unger, J. (1959) 22 M.L.R. 519, at 520) had this to say:

> There remains, however, as a matter of general interest the fact that the court unanimously refused to accept the view repeatedly expressed by Lord Denning that a person interested can sue on a contract expressly made for his benefit. It would seem doubtful whether the observations on this point can be dismissed as *obiter dicta,* significant chiefly as further indication that the force of the movement for reform of the common law from within, which had achieved some spectacular successes during the decade after the war, has now been spent and that the current trend is towards caution and orthodoxy.

It is worth noting that Unger (at 520-21) did not think that the Court of Appeal in *Green v. Russell* had made a "decisive contribution to the solution of this problem".

69 The independent "privity" rule was reiterated by the House of Lords in *Scruttons Ltd. v. Midland Silicones Ltd.* [1962] A.C. 446 and by the Privy Council in *New Zealand Shipping Co. Ltd. v. A. M. Satterthwaite & Co. Ltd.* [1975] A.C. 154. In neither case are any *reasons* given to justify the rule. In both cases the rule is framed as an independent "privity" rule even though Lord Reid in the former case *presumes* that the rule "crystallised" in *Tweddle v. Atkinson.* There is no mention in either case of consideration being the reason for the rule or even of a separate consideration rule. In any event, by this time, the independent "privity" rule is foremost in the minds of the judges.

70 *Beswick v. Beswick* [1967] 2 All E.R. 1197, at 1201; [1968] A.C. 58 at 72.

Scarman and Keith,[71] have spoken out. Lord Scarman's statement was this:

> I respectfully agree with Lord Reid that the denial by English law of a jus quaesitum tertio calls for reconsideration. In *Beswick v. Beswick,* Lord Reid, after referring to the Law Revision Committees' recommendation that the third party should be able to enforce a contractual promise taken by another for his benefit, observed: "If one had to contemplate a further long period of Parliamentary procrastination, this House might find it necessary to deal with this matter". The committee reported in 1937; *Beswick v. Beswick* was decided in 1967. It is now 1979; but nothing has been done. If the opportunity arises, I hope the House will reconsider *Tweddle v. Atkinson* and the other cases which stand guard over this unjust rule.[72]

These are marching orders. The legislative bodies have not acted; it is now up to the judiciary. There is, of course, nothing to [575]prevent the House of Lords or the Supreme Court of Canada[73] today rectifying the error made in the creation and continuation of the doctrine of privity.

## Privity Pro and Con

Arguments offered to justify the doctrine of privity only rarely get beyond the level of axiomatic assertion. Indeed, the infamous[74] Professor Langdell thought the mere recitation of the privity phrase was sufficient. In his view, "this latter proposition [i.e. privity] is so plain upon its face that it is difficult to make it plainer by argument".[75] Argument, as it turns out, is not something to which the doctrine stands up well.

Another American commentator, writing at a time when the United States was in the middle of a process of ridding itself of the privity bar, argued for the doctrine in this way:

> A perfect, well rounded contract requires not only a promise and a consideration, but a participation by each party in both of these elements. Possibly a privity as to only one might not always be fatal, though even this

71 *Woodar Investment Development Ltd. v. Wimpey Construction U.K. Ltd.* [1980] 1 All E.R. 571, at 588-89, 591 respectively. Also see *Swain v. The Law Society* [1983] A.C. 598, at 611 (Lord Diplock).

72 *Ibid.*, at 591.

73 *Greenwood Shopping Plaza Limited v. Beattie* [1980] 2 S.C.R. 228.

74 See Gilmore, G., *The Death of Contract,* Ohio State University Press, Columbus, 1974, at 12-13. Cf. Birmingham, R. L., "Holmes on *'Peerless': Raffles v. Wichelhaus* and the Objective Theory of Contract" (1985) 47 U. Pitt. L. R. 183.

75 Langdell, C. C., *A Summary of the Law of Contracts* (2nd ed.), Little, Brown and Company, Boston, 1880, at s.62.

is doubtful; but a want of privity as to both the promise and the consideration certainly seems to be an insuperable obstacle to an action, upon the strict principles of the common law. If no other reason existed, the fact that the person who furnished the consideration, and to whom the promise was made, could always maintain an action upon it, seems to be a sufficient reason why another person could not, even though interested in the performance. To allow two actions by two disconnected persons, having opposite interests, upon the same promise, would indeed be anomalous.

That a plaintiff cannot maintain an action when the whole consideration moves from a third person to the defendant, and the defendant's promise is made wholly to such third person, has been the law of England for over two centuries.[76]

Once beyond the question-begging appeal to "the strict principles of the common law", we find in these lines two arguments for privity. The first argument, presumably, is that otherwise the promisor would be subject to a double performance liability.[77] **[576]** This, of course, is preposterous. There is only one promise and once it is enforced by the promisee *or* the third party the promisor has fulfilled the promise and is subject to no further liability. The second argument offered by this American writer (in 1895) was that the doctrine had been the law of England for the previous two centuries.[78] We have already examined how accurate that historical argument is.

A modern summary of the arguments advanced to justify the privity rule is given by Professor Treitel. As is apparent, he is reluctant to confirm or endorse any one of these arguments:

> One possible reason for it [*i.e.* the doctrine] is that a contract is a personal affair affecting only the parties to it; but this is rather a restatement of the doctrine than a reason for its existence. Another possible reason is that it would be unjust to allow a person to sue on a contract on which he could not be sued; but the law enforces unilateral contracts, to which the same argument applies. A third possible reason is that, if third parties could enforce contracts made for their benefit, the rights of contracting parties to rescind or vary such contracts would be unduly hampered: this reasoning has certainly been influential in limiting the development of one of the exceptions to the doctrine. Yet a fourth possible reason is that the third

76 Bennett, E. H., "Considerations Moving From Third Persons" (1895) 9 Harv. Law Rev. 31, at 31-32.

77 This may not be the double liability argument but, if it isn't, it is even less tenable (i.e. the mere existence of two actions). The double liability argument was definitely advanced by Professor Langdell, *supra*, note 75.

78 The authorities cited were *Bourne v. Mason, Crow v. Rogers* and *Price v. Easton, supra.*

> party is often a mere donee. A system of law which does not give a gratuitous promisee a right to enforce the promise is not likely to give this right to a gratuitous beneficiary who is not even a promisee.[79]

Professor Treitel himself dismisses the first argument and the second has been addressed in our earlier discussion of *Tweddle v. Atkinson.*[80] The third reason or argument is one occasionally brought forward as a supposed disadvantage in the use of the trust device to circumvent the doctrine of privity.[81] But the reason is quite irrelevant as a concern with respect to third-party actions if the original parties can always rescind or vary their contract[82] or **[577]** even if they can only do so prior to a certain event such

---

79 *Supra*, note 18, at 458.

80 See text at note 51, *supra.*

81 See authorities cited at notes 92-93, *infra.*

82 There have been different suggestions as to the point at which a third-party benefit ought to crystallise so that the original parties can no longer vary or rescind the contract (see notes 9, 39 *infra).* The objection to such suggestions, whatever their intrinsic merit, is precisely that acceptance of any particular crystallising event (e.g. third-party acceptance, reliance) does involve preventing the original parties from varying or rescinding their contract. This objection can be met in one way with the argument that the original parties are not at all prejudiced once a crystallising event becomes incorporated into the law. The parties may then be presumed to have contracted with knowledge of what the law is.

But, whatever the case for crystallising events, the objection evaporates completely if the original parties remain free to vary their contract. If such were the case, the position of the third party would be as follows. The third party could enforce the original contract only if it remained unvaried. If the original parties vary the benefit the third party can only enforce the contract as varied. But if the original parties do not vary the contract, if they do not change their minds, then the original contract (or a variation of it) still exists and could be enforced by the third party if the promisor failed to perform when the time for performance arrived. The position of the third party is reduced to dependence on the will of the promisee. If the promisee no longer wishes to see the benefit conferred, he or she will make a new contract with the promisor. But if the promisee does still intend the benefit, then he or she will do nothing, the contract will remain, it will be enforced by the third party, and no person will be abused by reason of not being able to change their mind. In the absence of the concurrence of the promisee, of course, the promisor has no more right to change his or her mind than the promisor in the case of a simple contract.

This dealing with the objection allows for third-party enforcement when the original parties have not changed their minds. It takes care of those situations where the promisee is dead or absent or, although still wanting to benefit the third party, does not wish to incur the time, money and other costs of pursuing enforcement. Any substance to the objection is completely overcome because the parties remain free to contract out of their contract. A third party who wanted to act on the benefit in advance of its receipt would have to secure that benefit in some way if concerned that the original parties might, in fact, change their minds.

as third-party acceptance or reliance.[83] It is worth noting, in any event, that no case involving a third-party complaint that the original parties rescinded or varied the contract ever came before a court when third-party actions were maintainable. Usually it is because of the death or disappearance of the original promisee, or because the promisee (while still intending the benefit) does not wish to incur the litigation or other costs of enforcing the contract, that the third party is or would be forced to bring an action to compel the promisor merely to do what he or she had promised to do and was paid to do. The substance of this argument, in the end, is illusory. The fourth reason or argument is no more significant. It is in fact quite misleading to point out that the law does not give a "gratuitous promisee" a right to enforce a promise. Consider, rather, that what the law *does do* is enforce promises which are paid for. As Professor Furmston points out:

> It is one thing to say that a gratuitous promise will not be enforced; it is quite another to say that a promise seriously made and bargained for may be repudiated because the person who bought the promise is not the person who seeks to enforce it.[84]

In the third-party beneficiary situation, the promise was paid for and there is both a promisee and a third party who expect and have an interest in its performance. This is quite different from the "gratuitous promisee" situation.

A sustainable legal argument for the doctrine of privity has yet to surface. Perhaps because of that fact a variety of sociological explanations for the creation, continuation or utility of the doctrine have been advanced. Professor Atiyah's guess is economic:

> **[578]** There is a sense in which the new doctrine of privity was an important development in the law at a time of increasing complexity in multilateral commercial relationships. The appearance of middlemen in all sorts of commercial situations served to separate the parties at either end of the transaction, and it was generally accepted that no privity existed between them. Economically, this may have served a useful purpose, in that it encouraged the development of a more market-based concept of enterprise liability. But on some occasions the results were not only economically dubious but socially disastrous.[85]

83 Whether third-party reliance would or should be sufficient to crystallise third-party rights to the promise is a question that presumably could only be settled after it was determined generally whether or not the "reliance interest" is to be protected by contract law.

84 Furmston, M. P., "Return to *Dunlop v. Selfridge*" (1960) 23 M.L.R. 373, at 376.

85 Atiyah, *supra,* note 47, at 414.

Another writer describes the theory that it was actually the *Vandepitte* case[86] which established the privity rule and that it did so in order to close what were wide-open floodgates:

> Perhaps *Vandepitte v. Preferred Accident Insurance Corporation of New York*, [1933] A.C. 70 (P.C. (Can.)); aff'g., [1932] S.C.R. 22; rev'g., [1930] 4 D.L.R. 654 (B.C.C.A.), aff'g., [1930] 2 D.L.R. 562 (B.C.S.C.), established the rule, not *Dunlop Tyre*. *Vandepitte* cited *Dunlop Tyre* simply to tie into precedent, but *Dunlop Tyre* came to be perceived as the authority itself. Thus the views about the law effected in *Vandepitte* became seen as current when *Dunlop Tyre* was decided.
>
> A speculative explanation for this theory goes like this. Sometimes as the law gives, the law ensures that not too much is taken. The seminal case is *Donoghue v. Stevenson,* [1932] A.C. 562 (H.L.(Sc.)). In those days, eliminating privity as a requisite, particularly according to Lord Atkin's formula, would have been seen as leading to a horrifying flood of litigation. *Vandepitte* ensured that *Donoghue v. Stevenson's* uncertain impact was limited to tort. The Privy Council cited precedent for this position, as any competent court would; its precedent was *Dunlop Tyre.*[87]

Yet another explanation sometimes advanced is that judges have consciously retained the privity doctrine as a device to combat the scope and operation of third-party exculpation clauses, for example, clauses in retail sales contracts that seek to exclude the liability of third-party manufacturers. But if this were true, we would be paying a very high third-party price for what amounts to modest consumer protection. Moreover, for other clauses of the same variety there is a different view of the utility of the privity **[579]** doctrine.[88] Thus, it is complained that it is wrong for a third-party exculpation clause which attempts to exclude the liability of the servants, agents and independent contractors of one of the contracting parties to be rendered ineffective by the doctrine. Such a result is said to be inefficient and commercially unexpected.[89]

These sociological explanations are, for the most part, pure conjecture. As such, they provide no real basis for excusing the continuation of the doctrine's application. Moreover, and more

---

86 *Supra,* note 58.

87 Arymowicz, C. M., (Case Comment) (1982) 60 Can. Bar Rev. 467, at 470 (footnote 12). The theory is attributed to Professor Gilmore.

88 *E.g. New Zealand Shipping Co. Ltd. v. A. M. Satterthwaite & Co. Ltd.* [1975] A.C. 154 at 169 *(per* Lord Wilberforce).

89 Proponents of this view expect insurance cost savings if these clauses were to be effective. It may perhaps be doubted that third parties (e.g. stevedores) would refrain from obtaining the same liability insurance if the privity rule was abolished.

significantly, nothing in any of them provides a compelling justification for the doctrine. In the end, there just doesn't seem to be a satisfactory historical, legal or other argument to support the doctrine. Perhaps the most that can be argued is that to change the rule would upset the status quo. But this is hardly an acceptable basis for continuing to allow the pernicious consequences of the application of the doctrine. If we are concerned with retaining the status quo in order to protect the planning interest, it is well to point out that those who plan on the basis of the rule are those who contract with the knowledge that they will not have to perform the contract, a very odd position for the common law to support.

In addition to historical criticism,[90] the case *against* the doctrine of privity has been made in a variety of ways. Firstly, it is commonly argued that there are a number of other legal concepts that are inconsistent with or have the effect of displacing or subverting the doctrine.[91] Thus, it is noted that finding a trust relationship[92] is a simple and, for a while, an often-used procedure for overcoming a privity bar.[93] It is also pointed out that agency principles can be used to create a direct relationship between the third party and the promisor so as to thereby avoid the doctrine.[94] These are the major concepts proffered but others enlisted for this **[580]** argument include assignment,[95] collateral contract, attornment and tortious liability.[96]

A second line of attack involves listing the various statutory

---

90 See above and Dowrick, *supra,* note 64.

91 See, generally, the Law Revision Committee Report (1937) *supra,* note 35, at 27; Atiyah, P. S., An *Introduction to the Law of Contract* (3rd ed.), Oxford University Press, 1981, c.20; Guest, A. G., *Anson's Law of Contract* (26th ed.), Oxford University Press, 1984, c.10; Furmston (*Cheshire & Fifoot's Law of Contract*), *supra,* note 36, c.14; Waddams, S. M., *The Law of Contracts* (2nd ed.), Canada Law Book Inc., Toronto, 1984, c.9.

92 The usual formulation is to identify the promisee as the trustee of the promise. It perhaps might be a more defensible formulation to identify the promisor as the trustee. That is, in return for the consideration forthcoming from the promisee, the promisor agrees to constitute himself a trustee of the benefit to the third party.

93 See Corbin, A. L., "Contracts for the Benefit of Third Persons" (1930) 46 L.Q.R. 12; Williams, G., "Contracts for the Benefit of Third Persons" (1944) 7 M.L.R. 123.

94 See *New Zealand Shipping Co. Ltd. v. A. M. Satterthwaite & Co. Ltd.* [1975] A.C. 154. This case is problematic for a number of reasons, one of which is that the agency approach wasn't really necessary at all once the court decided to find a unilateral contract.

95 Atiyah, *supra.* note 91, at 271 states that:

> The fact that the law is thus prepared in principle to accept the simple assignability of contractual rights makes the doctrine of privity particularly anomalous, and hard to justify on rational grounds. Since the law is perfectly prepared to allow a contracting party to transfer his rights, once created, to a third party, there can hardly be any valid objection to his creating the rights for the benefit of the third party in the first instance.

96 As to the latter three, see Waddams, *supra,* note 91, at 204. 206.

exceptions to the application of the rule.[97] The point of doing so is to show just how unfair or inconvenient the doctrine has appeared to the legislature. It is a useful exercise, in this respect, because many would not otherwise appreciate the iniquitous consequences of the common law rule. Indeed, but for the statutory exceptions, the doctrine of privity would undoubtedly have been abolished long ago upon it having become widely appreciated that, for example, third parties had no right to the proceeds of life insurance policies taken out for their benefit.

Another argument involves pointing out that there is clearly no objection to the third party actually getting the benefit promised since the original promisee is allowed to obtain specific performance of the promise.[98] The third party will get the benefit notwithstanding that he or she gave no consideration.

Added to this are the "joint promisee" cases where persons were allowed to enforce contracts even though they gave no consideration.[99] Creditor compensation agreements[1] and the payment of the debts of third parties[2] are other instances where the third party, without having provided any consideration, is still able to insist on the benefit of the contract. It is sometimes said that these latter cases were decided on the basis that it would otherwise be a fraud on the promisee but, of course, there is no "fraud" here that would be any different than the "fraud" on the promisee in the ordinary third-party beneficiary situation. So, if "privity" is really only another name for consideration, the foregoing cases appear to show that it is only necessary that consideration be provided by somebody. It is not necessary that the beneficiary of the promise should have given further consideration to be able to enforce the promise directly or indirectly. There are yet other cases **[581]** that are equally inconsistent with a supposed fundamental and inviolable rule that third parties cannot take advantage of contracts made for their benefit.[3] The mere existence of all of these cases is highly problematic for the doctrine of privity.

---

97 See Treitel, *supra,* note 18, at 485-90: Law Revision Committee Report (1937), *supra,* note 35, at 25-26; Scamell, *supra,* note 65, at 140-43; Waddams, *supra,* note 91, at 204.

98 As in *Beswick v. Beswick, supra,* note 70.

99 The cases are cited in Coote. B., "Consideration and the Joint Promisee" [1978] C.L.J. 301 where it is sought to explain them on the basis that all of the promisees had in fact promised. The judgments, however, do not show this in any explicit way.

1 See Furmston (*Cheshire & Fifoot's Law of Contract*), *supra,* note 36, at 101-102.

2 *Hirachand Punamchand v. Temple* [1911] 2 K.B. 330. The third-party beneficiary neither gave consideration nor was a "party" to the contract.

3 *See Neale v. Willis* (1968) 19 P. & C. R. 836; *Killoran v. Monticello State Bank* (1921) 61 S.C.R. 528, 57 D.L.R. 359; *Re Spike and Rocca Group Ltd.* (1980) 107 D.L.R. (3d) 62; *Trans Canada Credit Corp. Ltd. v. Royal Insurance Co. of Canada* (1983) 149 D.L.R. (3d) 280; *Snelling v. John G. Snelling Ltd.* [1973] 1 Q.B. 87.

It has also been noted that the doctrine is not found in many jurisdictions.[4] The English rule was actually in place in the United States well into the last century but was then widely rejected.[5] This point is lost on those who remain confident that English common law is singularly fastidious and not prone, as might be the case in other jurisdictions, to allowing concessions from theoretical rigour. But raising this fact does lead one to the conclusion that our legal system is unlikely to come crashing down around our ears if we were to allow third parties to pursue performance of the promise made for their benefit.

There are other arguments,[6] but what is perhaps the most compelling reason for jettisoning the doctrine of privity is the continuous parade of judges, law reformers and commentators in this century who are of the opinion that the doctrine generates hardship and injustice and ought to be either abolished or at least reconsidered. It is undoubtedly because of this unrelenting effort on the part of these authorities that the issue continues to remain, essentially, an open one. The Law Revision Committee which reported on the doctrine of consideration in 1937[7] included amongst its members such persons as Lord Wright,[8] Lord Romer and Professor Goodhart. This committee recommended that the doctrine be statutorily abolished subject to certain provisos.[9] Among the others[10] who have condemned the doctrine or called for its **[582]** reconsideration are Lords

---

4 *E.g.* The United States and the civil law jurisdictions.

5 See Waters. A. J., "The Property in the Promise: A Study of the Third Party Beneficiary Rule" (1985) 98 Harv. Law Rev. 1109, de Cruz, S. P., "Privity in America: A Study in Judicial and Statutory Innovation" (1985) 14 Anglo-Amer. L.R. 265.

6 Having to do with, for example, commercial credits and restrictive covenants (see Guest, *supra,* note 91, Treitel, *supra,* note 18. c.15). Also note the arguments that privity is a procedural matter (at note 67, *supra*).

7 *Supra,* note 35.

8 Lord Wright independently recorded his disapproval. See his book review of *Williston on Contracts* at (1939) 55 L.Q.R. 189, at 208.

9 The Committee's provisos were the following:

> The first and most important provision ought to be that no third-party right can be acquired unless given by the express terms of the contract. A third-party right ought not to be acquired by implication, e.g. merely because the performance of the contract will benefit the third party. Secondly, the promisor should be entitled to raise against the third party any defence, such as fraud or mistake, that would have been valid against the promisee. Thirdly, the right of the promisor and of the promisee to cancel the contract at any time ought to be preserved unless the third party has received notice of the agreement and has adopted it either expressly or by conduct.

10 See Dowrick, *supra,* note 90; Waddams, *supra,* note 91; Hamson, C. J., "The Reform of Consideration" (1938) 54 L.Q.R. 233, at 236; Catzman, M. A., "Recent Developments in the Law of Third Party Contracts" [1975] L.S.U.C. Spec. Lec. 305; (Casenote) (1933) 49 L.Q.R. 474.

Reid,[11] Denning[12] and Scarman[13] and Professors Corbin,[14] Scamell,[15] Furmston[16] and Atiyah.[17] Professor Guest summarises some of the objections to the privity rule when he states that "[I]t is said that it serves only to defeat the legitimate expectations of the third party, that it undermines the social interest of the community in the security of bargains and it is commercially inconvenient."[18] It is time that the objections of these distinguished persons were taken seriously.

## Privity and Contract Theory

Confidence in the soundness of the doctrine of privity appears to be founded, in large part, on the belief that it is a necessary or fundamental construct of contract law.[19] It is this appeal to contract theory that may have been the most effective brake on the movement to abolish the rule. Yet the case for the theoretical necessity of privity has never been made; it is only alluded to.[20] What follows, then, is an examination of the theoretical support for the doctrine. The question is whether the doctrine of privity is required by or even consistent with any of the various theories or approaches which purport to describe or expose either the existing or the ideal state of contract law.

### *(1) Will Theory*

The analysis may appropriately be initiated with a consideration of the oldest general theory of contract, the "will theory".[21] According to this theory, an "agreement" will be enforced for the single reason that to do so

11 *Supra,* note 70, at 1201.
12 *Supra,* notes 59-61.
13 *Supra,* note 71.
14 *Supra,* note 93.
15 *Supra,* note 65.
16 *Supra,* note 36.
17 *Supra,* note 91.
18 *Supra,* note 91.
19 And, therefore, it might be feared, trashing the doctrine of privity would bring into question the whole theoretical superstructure of contract law!
20 See quotes at notes 75-76, *supra.* See Furmston (*Cheshire & Fifoot*), *supra,* note 36, at 438 where it is simply asserted that the doctrine is "a natural inference from a strict theory of contract". Cf. Dowrick, *supra,* note 64. Dowrick's express analysis (at 390-91) finds that theory *supports* a third-party right of action.
21 See Atiyah, *supra,* note 47, at 212-216. See A. W. B. Simpson's historical introduction to *Cheshire & Fifoot, supra,* note 36, at 12.

gives effect to the demonstrated intention of the parties. Professor Atiyah gives this picture of the model:

> The contract is binding because the parties intend to be bound; it is their will, or intention, which creates the liability. . . . The whole model is suffused with the idea that the **[583]** fundamental purpose of contract law is to give effect – within limits of course – to the intentions of the parties. It is their decision, and their free choice, which makes the contract binding, and determines its interpretation, and its result in the event of breach.[22]

The will theory does not require a doctrine of privity.[23] The theory requires, rather, that the prior convergence of the wills of the contracting parties be given effect to by the law. If intentions are to be perfected, the agreement must be completed. It follows that a third-party beneficiary should be able to enforce the agreement. This can be confirmed upon an analysis of the various interests involved.

There is a public interest, implicit in will theory, in seeing to the enforcement of individual agreements in order to maintain the integrity of the contracting process. As this interest is a general one, it might seem that every citizen should be permitted to seek enforcement of any particular incomplete agreement. But there are other factors which oppose a general social freedom to pursue enforcement. In fact, this combination of factors identifies only two persons who should be allowed to enforce the promise – the promisee and the third-party beneficiary.

We start with every citizen having an interest in enforcement under the will theory. This interest (i.e. in the integrity of the process) is indirect in the sense that, because we will all eventually become involved in the contracting process, each of us will be presently concerned that the process be made dependable. But circumscribing the individual enforcement of this indirect public interest are a number of direct interests. Firstly, while both the promisee and the third party have the same general interest in the integrity of the process, they each have an additional positive interest that is not shared with the public. The promisee is directly concerned that his own will be respected. The third party is directly concerned that he or she receive the benefit that was promised. These positive interests do not stand alone. The promisee and the third party have other interests which in combination with their positive interests establish their right to enforce the

---

22 Atiyah, P. S., "Contracts, Promises and the Law of Obligations" (1978) 94 L.Q.R. 193, at 195.

23 Atiyah, *supra,* note 47, at 413 states that the decision in *Tweddle v. Atkinson* was "a very late example of a refusal to recognise the autonomy of private contracts". He sees the decision as "a revision to the idea of a fair exchange".

promise exclusive of the rest of society. Other persons are excluded by reason of the will of the promisee and the third party. If it has come to the point where an ordinary citizen would have to enforce the agreement, it is because neither the promisee nor the third **[584]** party, for whatever reason, wishes to enforce the contract. If others are thereafter allowed to enforce the contract, the result would be to compel the third party to accept the benefit and thereby to disregard the direct interests of the promisee and the third party. This latter consideration, of course, does not apply to the third party who must therefore be entitled to enforce the promise in order to protect both a personal and a shared public interest. Thus, the will theory is opposed to a rule which prohibits the enforcement of promises by third-party beneficiaries.

### *(2) Bargain Theory*

In neoclassical contract theory, the will theory is incorporated into what is called the bargain theory of contract. According to bargain theory, it is only "bargains" which are justifiably enforced by the law.[24] Bargains are agreements between parties in which the promise of each is purchased by the other. A bargain is something more than a simple agreement where, for example, two or more persons may agree that something shall be done without one of the parties having to do or pay anything. For a bargain, the parties must exchange or promise to exchange value. The value forthcoming from either party is what is called "the consideration". The negotiated exchange of value is what is called the bargain (i.e. an agreement to exchange value).

Since bargain theory is a combination of will theory and the concept of consideration, it is only necessary to analyse the theoretical basis of consideration in order to assess whether or not this theory is at all supportive of the doctrine of privity. Specifically, it is necessary to determine what purpose consideration purportedly serves.

There have been serious differences of opinion over the utility of the consideration requirement.[25] Many would not agree with its present scope of operation.[26] Others see it as a blunt but useful concept. Although the debate is an important one, its prior resolution one way or the other is not critical to dealing with the doctrine of privity. If it can be shown that the

---

24 Furmston (*Cheshire & Fifoot*), *supra,* note 36, at 60-61; Waddams, *supra,* note 91, at 17-18. Dowrick, *supra,* note 64, at 390-91, analyses the privity rule for its consistency with bargain theory.

25 Atiyah, *supra,* note 35; Treitel, *supra,* note 18, at 121-123; Guest, *supra,* note 91, at 108-9.

26 Law Revision Committee, *supra,* note 35; Wright, *supra,* note 2.

ostensible purpose served by consideration is satisfied without a privity rule, the question of whether or not we should retain a consideration requirement generally would be irrelevant. If no purpose is served **[585]** by the consideration requirement, of course, no privity rule is required if it is only an aspect of consideration.

Of the different purposes that consideration might have[27] there is perhaps only one that is forcefully argued.[28] In response to the Law Revision Committee's recommendations about consideration, one commentator spelled out its function in notifying the parties that they were undertaking "legal" rather than merely "good faith" obligations:

> If it were clear when a party has formed an intention to incur legal obligation, if a person did commonly define the obligation he desired to assume in terms which left little doubt as to its nature, it would be unnecessary, and indeed merely foolish, to require an additional test of that intention. It is because persons commonly do not so define their intention, and because the common law recognizes that fact, that the common law requires a test. . . .
>
> Now bargain, or the form of bargain, is an extremely good practical test. The most uneducated layman today understands that if he makes a bargain he is binding himself in a way in which he does not conceive that he is binding himself if he gratuitously promises to do the same thing. . . .
>
> The legal obligation attaching to an enforceable promise according to English law today is far closer to the obligation arising from a warranty that something shall be in any event than to the obligation which would attach to a gratuitous and informal promise according to normal good faith. The obligation attached by English law, though great, is not unreasonable in the case of a bargain or of a formal promise: the fact of the bargain or the formality is calculated to put the parties on their guard and strictness of construction (especially the general rule that if an exception were intended it must be stated) make for certainty. But the same obligation attached to a gratuitous and informal promise would be plainly unreasonable: to put such an obligation upon such a promise would be to construe the promise in a manner normally not intended by the promisor and known by the promisee not to be so intended. . . .
>
> When a man promises gratuitously and informally, he promises in good faith. He expects, and is understood to expect, a benign construction of his promise. The construction which English law puts upon legally enforceable promises is not benign: it is strict. To catch a man up and to put

---

27 See Fuller, L., "Consideration as Form" (1941) 41 Col. Law Rev. 799; Chloros, A. G., "The Doctrine of Consideration and the Reform of the Law of Contract" (1968) 17 I.C.L.Q. 137. Also see Professor Fried's summary of the Fuller article, *infra,* note 32, at 38-39.

28 By both Hamson, *supra,* p.581, note 10 and Fuller, *supra.*

> upon his informal and gratuitous promise the strict construction possibly [586] appropriate to a formal promise or to a bargain is unreasonable and unwarranted by any system of law.[29]

It should be emphasised that this "notice" or cautionary function of consideration operates on the parties themselves at the time of contracting. We are not here concerned with another possible function of consideration which would be to show the seriousness of the contracting parties to other parties (*i.e.* court) at a later date (*i.e.* the trial of a contract claim).[30]

If this is the function of a consideration requirement, a function which focuses on the promisor, it should be immediately apparent that no doctrine of privity is necessary to implement or to further this function. The original parties gave consideration to each other and were thereby notified that a "legal" obligation was being created. There is clearly no need for a third party to also provide consideration to redundantly perform the same function again. The promise was paid for, and in the course of and by reason of the purchase, the promisor was given notice that the promise was a legally binding one. The notice function of consideration is fully performed without any notion of privity.

*(3) Promise Theory*

Bargain theory has been the generally-accepted theoretical basis for contract law in this century. The theory has not escaped criticism, however, and alternative models have been proposed. The most recent significant proposal,[31] oddly enough, is one which is just a reformulation or rehabilitation of bare will theory.[32] According to Professor Charles Fried, the "promise" principle or theory is his "version of the classical view of contract proposed by the will theory".[33] The "promise" is the "central conception of contract"[34] while consideration is of no substance or significance because it "offers no coherent alternative basis for the force of contracts."[35]

Fried's theory is built on the notions of autonomy and trust. Self-

---

29 Hamson, *supra,* note 109, at 242-247.

30 An evidentiary function that is already performed by a variety of other doctrines.

31 As to recentness, see Eisenberg, M. A., "The Responsive Model of Contract Law" (1984) 36 Stan. L.R. 1107 and Levin, J. and McDowell, B., "The Balance Theory of Contracts: Seeking Justice in Voluntary Obligations" (1983) 29 McGill Law J. 24.

32 Fried, C., *Contract as Promise,* Harvard University Press, Cambridge, Mass., 1981.

33 *Ibid.,* at 6.

34 *Ibid.,* at 5-6.

35 *Ibid.,* at 38.

actualisation and self-determination for ourselves and others requires that we have full freedom or autonomy except to the extent that our autonomy would detract from that of others. But to reach some goals of our own we must voluntarily co-operate with **[587]** others, and in doing so, we trust that the co-operation expected will be forthcoming. It is legitimate to expect such co-operation upon a promise because we have utilised a convention that is recognised as creating the expectation.[36] To invoke that convention and then to repudiate one's promise is to abuse a confidence.[37] If we allow this to occur, we are not taking the promisor seriously as a person. Holding a promisor responsible for the obligation assumed is only to respect his or her status as a free and rational person.[38]

It is evident that promise theory has no requirement for a doctrine of privity and Professor Fried acknowledges this.[39] We only show respect for the promisor in allowing the third party to pursue the promised benefit. We incidentally maintain the convention and the expectations created by its use. There is no theoretical justification here for the doctrine of privity.

### *(4) Relational Contract Law*

Professor Ian MacNeil is the most well known proponent of a relational approach to contract law.[40] He advocates recognition in contract theory of the reality of relationships, in particular, that contracts are not always

---

36 *Ibid.*, at 13.

37 Professor Fried explains as follows (at 16):

> The obligation to keep a promise is grounded not in arguments of utility but in respect for individual autonomy and in trust. Autonomy and trust are grounds for the institution of promising as well, but the argument for individual obligation is not the same. Individual obligation is only a step away, but that step must be taken. An individual is morally bound to keep his promises because he has intentionally invoked a convention whose function it is to give grounds—moral grounds—for another to expect the promised performance. To renege is to abuse a confidence he was free to invite or not, and which he intentionally did invite. To abuse that confidence now is like (but only like) lying: the abuse of a shared social institution that is intended to invoke the bonds of trust.

38 *Supra,* p.586, note 32, at 20-21.

39 *Supra,* p.56, note 32, at 44-45. Professor Fried specifically discusses the issue of for how long the original contracting parties remain free to vary this agreement. He notes that one solution is to allow any variation prior to an "acceptance" of the promise by the third party. Other conceivable solutions might be actual third-party reliance or whether the original parties "intended" the benefit to be irrevocable. See the Law Revision Committee's provisos at p.581, note 9 *supra.* Also see note 82, *supra.*

40 See MacNeil, I. R., *The New Social Contract, An Inquiry into Modern Contractual Relations,* Yale University Press, New Haven, 1980. Also see the *Law, Private Governance and Continuing Relationships* symposium papers published at [1985] Wis. L. Rev. 461-615.

accurately characterised as discrete transactions.[41] Many, if not most, transactions arise out of, are maintained or are otherwise affected by the prior and ongoing relationships amongst the various parties. The features of these relationships should be taken into account in a fuller and more explicit way than is the case at present.[42] In his view: **[588]**

> The characteristics of entirely discrete transactions, if they could occur at all, deprive them of any utility as social tools of production and distribution of scarce goods and services. That fact by no means, however, renders the construct useless as a tool of economic or legal analysis, because some discreteness is present in all exchange transactions and relations. One must simply not forget that great modification is required before the model can represent a reasonably accurate picture of actual economic life. . . . When so modified, the construct will no longer represent an entirely discrete transaction, but will retain substantial discreteness while nevertheless remaining relatively realistic.[43]

Professor MacNeil tells us how *classical* contract law reinforces the discrete transaction view of a contract by its own enhancement of discreteness and "presentiation":[44]

> Any contract law system necessarily must implement certain norms. It must permit and encourage participation in exchange, promote reciprocity, reinforce role patterns appropriate to particular kinds of exchange relations, provide limited freedom for exercise of choice, effectuate planning, and harmonize the internal and external matrixes of particular contracts. A contract law system reinforcing discrete contract transactions, however,

---

[41] The nature of a "discrete" transaction is described by Professor MacNeil in his article "Contracts: Adjustment of Long Term Economic Relations Under Classical, Neoclassical, and Relational Contract Law" (1978) 72 Nw. U. Law Rev. 854, at 856.

[42] Fried's view is that neoclassical contract theory is based on the discrete transaction with some (inadequate) relational concessions. *Supra*, note 40, at 72.

[43] *Supra*, note 41, at 856.

[44] The concept of "presentiation" is defined by Professor MacNeil in the following way *(supra,* note 41, at 863):

> Presentiation is a way of looking at things in which a person perceives the effect of the future on the present. It is a recognition that the course of the future is so unalterably bound by present conditions that the future has been brought effectively into the present so that it may be dealt with just as if it were in fact the present. Thus, the presentiation of a transaction involves restricting its expected future effects to those defined in the present, *i.e.,* at the inception of the transaction. No eternal distinctions prevent treating the contract norm of enhancing presentiation as simply an aspect of the norm of enhancing discreteness. It is, however, such an important aspect of the projection of exchange into the future in discrete contracts – to say nothing of microeconomic theory – that separate treatment aids analysis significantly.

must add two further goals: enhancing discreteness and enhancing presentiation. . . .

A classical contract law system implements these two norms in a number of ways. To implement discreteness, classical law initially treats as irrelevant the identity of the parties to the transaction. Second, it transactionizes or commodifies as much as possible the subject matter of contracts, e.g., it turns employment into a short-term commodity by interpreting employment contracts without express terms of duration as terminable at will. Third, it limits strictly the sources to be considered in establishing the substantive content of the transaction. For example, formal communication (e.g., writings) controls informal communication (e.g., oral statements); linguistic communication controls nonlinguistic communication; and communicated circumstances (to the limited extent that **[589]** any circumstances outside of "agreements" are taken into account at all) control noncommunicated circumstances (e.g., status). Fourth, only limited contract remedies are available, so that should the initial presentiation fail to materialize because of nonperformance, the consequences are relatively predictable from the beginning and are not open-ended, as they would be, for example, if damages for unforeseeable or psychic losses were allowed. Fifth, classical contract law draws clear lines between being in and not being in a transaction; e.g., rigorous and precise rules of offer and acceptance prevail with no half-way houses where only some contract interests are protected or where losses are shared. *Finally, the introduction of third parties into the relation is discouraged since multiple poles of interest tend to create discreteness-destroying relations.* (emphasis added)[45]

The foregoing describes what Professor MacNeil understands to be *classical* American contract law. He goes on to point out that *neoclassical* contract law remains founded on the discrete transaction but has adopted some techniques and fictions to lessen the rigidity of the classical model. In the United States, of course, neoclassical contract law has abandoned the privity doctrine.[46] That fact presumably represents a significant improvement on the classical position. We simply do not have to pursue the discrete transaction model to the extent that we prevent a third-party beneficiary from protecting his or her real interest in the contract. Professor MacNeil's view, at any rate, is clear. To him, the privity rule is quite "unrelated to social needs".[47] There is no support in the relational contract approach for the doctrine of privity.

---

45 *Supra,* note 41, at 862-864.

46 See note *5, supra.*

47 MacNeil, I. R , *Contracts: Exchange Transactions and Relations* (2nd ed.), Foundation Press, Mineola, N.Y., 1978, at 333.

### *(5) Economic Analysis*

If there is nothing offensive about a third-party beneficiary actually receiving the promised benefit, and the availability of an action by the promisee for specific performance confirms that there isn't, it becomes a relevant question whether or not the privity rule is an efficient one.[48] If there are results which are socially acceptable, the obtaining of those results in the least costly way is a desirable social goal.

An efficiency analysis of the privity rule is straightforward. The rule, it will be appreciated, is not one which can be contracted out **[590]** of.[49] The third party in *Tweddle v. Atkinson* had been expressly authorised by the contracting parties to pursue an action on the promise but was prevented by the court from doing so. The effect of the rule, therefore, is to require one extra transaction in order to obtain an accepted result. If A wishes to provide C with an enforceable benefit from a contract with B, A must first contract with B and then contract again with C (and C must give nominal consideration). B will be required to perform in the same way in either case, but A and C must engage in this extra transaction in order that the benefit can be enforced by C. The extra transaction between A and C will have transaction costs that would otherwise not have to be incurred. Thus, other things being equal, a privity rule is unnecessarily costly and results in the misallocation and wasting of resources. The additional costs incurred to achieve the same economic result simply cannot be justified. Economic theory, for this reason, opposes the doctrine of privity.[50]

### *(6) Critical Analysis*

A critical analysis of contract law[51] might proceed along these lines. The

---

48 Generally, see Kronman, A. T. and Posner, R. A., *The Economics of Contract Law,* Little, Brown and Company, Boston, 1979; Polinsky, A. M., *An Introduction to Law and Economics,* Little, Brown and Company, Boston, 1983.

49 This aspect of the doctrine is utterly indefensible. There is no justification whatever for preventing the original parties from expressly agreeing that the third party may enforce the promise.

50 The effect of a refusal to allow just anyone to enforce the promise is to close the class of persons who have rights in the particular contract. But the class is more efficiently closed if it includes identified third-party beneficiaries. The foundation for exchange created in this closed class is superior because of the reduction in transaction costs. See Holderness, C. G., "A Legal Foundation For Exchange" (1985) 14 J.Leg.St. 321.

51 The epistemology of critical legal studies is not precisely defined. Several approaches and traditions appear to constitute the movement. See generally Feinman, J. M., "Critical Approaches to Contract Law" (1983) 30 U.C.L.A, Law Rev. 829, Presser, S. B., "Some Realism About Orphism" (1984-85) 79 Nw. U. L. R. 869; Standen, J. A., "Critical Legal Studies as an AntiPositivist Phenomenon" (1986) 72 Va. L.R. 983;

fact of the matter is that the state enforces contracts for its own reasons. It does not make its very substantial weight available to a complainant merely because his or her intention or will was not respected or because a confidence has been abused. The state is interested in protecting social planning, whether commercial or otherwise. Doing so directly maintains public order and promotes an efficient economy. And it is only incidental that individual planning is also protected in this process.

The state is concerned to see that transactions proceed. This concern is due to an awareness that not only the immediate parties rely on a given transaction. Other persons rely, and they do so even though they have no "legal" basis for their reliance. The duty to mitigate one's damages is evidence of this state concern. The party not in breach must do what is possible to reduce the impact of a contract breach. This duty to mitigate exists so that commerce **[591]** generally is not stalled whenever a transaction breaks down. Society cannot afford to wait until each dispute is resolved. The measurement of contract damages by the "expectation" standard is further evidence of the state concern with planning. The "expectation" is granted to put the party not in breach in the position he or she would have been in if the contract had been performed. Giving damages in this amount discourages breaches by the promisor on the one hand, and, even though breach occurs, encourages the completion of the planning of the promisee, on the other. This protects planning generally because, if the promisee completes his or her plan, subsequent related or dependent planning by others can be completed.

The reality of contract law is perhaps not this one-sided. An action for enforcement, after all, is initiated by a private person. Individual will, in this and other respects, is a part of the content of contract law. Still, the utility of a critical analysis is that it focuses on the contradictory elements that can and do exist in our law. And an awareness of the interaction or competition between "individual" and "community" goals does aid one in putting contract law in a proper perspective.[52]

In any event, if we do consider the "community" or state goal in contract enforcement, it is once again apparent that there is no requirement for a privity rule. If social planning is the underlying basis for contract enforcement, there can be no complaint about the third-party action. An

---

Collins, H., "Contract and Legal Theory", in *Legal Theory and Common Law* (ed. W. Twining) Basil Blackwell Ltd., Oxford, 1986.

52 From a Marxist perspective, if legitimating the existing social order is a function served by the law, that function is better advanced by a rule less patently opposed to social needs than is the privity rule. Further, if it is a function of current law to facilitate the objectives of the ruling class, that function is obviously poorly performed by the maintenance of a rule that is opposed to the interests of the ruling capitalist class.

arrangement between A and B to benefit C is only a more sophisticated plan than the simple two-party contract. Undoubtedly other persons rely on this transaction proceeding just as they would for any other transaction. In this situation, there is simply another arm to the transaction. If general social reliance beyond the promisee is protected by contract enforcement initiated at the promisee's request, general social reliance beyond the third party should similarly be protected by enforcement at the behest of the third party.

Finally, a critical analysis involves recognising that law is neither autonomous nor absolute. Existing legal rules are in fact the result of choices. In a perfect world the contract rules in force at any time would be those which meet the particular needs of the whole community at that time. If this is accepted, there can be no excuse for continuing the bad choice made in the creation of the rule which bars third-party actions. If suits no interest and satisfies no needs. Critical theory provides no support for the doctrine.

**[592]**

*(7) Detrimental Reliance*

It has been suggested that detrimental reliance is or should be the basis for contractual liability.[53] The argument is that the enforcement of a promise really involves compensating the promisee for the injury suffered as a consequence of relying on the promise. On this view, contractual liability is assimilated to tort liability. As in tort, contractual liability is only justified in order to deter or compensate some harm to the interests of another person.

A detrimental reliance theory, it has been pointed out, "suppresses rules about privity".[54] The foreseeable reliance and the subsequent injury alone found the liability. No privity excuse is contemplated by or consistent with this basis for contractual obligation.

*(8) Unconscionability*

A generalised doctrine of unconscionability is the device some would favour to control contract abuse and injustice.[55] If an unconscionability theory were to become the foundation for contract law, it would be most unlikely that there would be a doctrine of privity. Virtually everyone

---

53 See Collins, *supra,* note 51, at l40-141; Fried, *supra,* note 32, at 4.

54 Collins, *supra*, note 51, at 140.

55 Waddams, *supra,* note 91, c.9 and 14. Also see Eisenberg, M. A., "The Bargain Principle and Its Limits" (1982) 95 Harv. Law Rev. 741, at 799-800.

agrees that the doctrine is productive of unfairness and hardship. Moreover, so long as privity remains, the promisor will be reaping a windfall benefit. There is simply no reason in "fairness" or "justice" why the doctrine should be maintained. The promisor would hardly be in a position to complain if this windfall were no longer available to be snapped up. He or she would find it most difficult to argue against the apparent unconscionability of it all.

## Conclusion

A satisfactory justification for the disallowance of third-party actions has not been forthcoming. The reason for this is not hard to find. The doctrine is an historical and theoretical error that cannot be justified.[56] On any theoretical basis, a third party ought to be able to enforce the bargain to the extent of the defined benefit. The way to explain this in traditional terms is that contractual obligation is extended to the third party by reason of the terms of the agreement and in order to give effect to the intentions of those who made it. The beneficiary is a "party" to this contract because he or she is expressly identified in it as one **[593]** who is to benefit. No argument to the contrary is tenable unless it follows from theory. Bare assertions do not determine the meaning of the term "party" or who it is that may enforce the contract. Reasons do.

---

56 For other theories offered to support the third party, see Corbin, A. L., *Corbin on Contracts,* West Publishing Co., St. Paul, 1951, Vol. 4, sec. 790 and de Cruz, *supra,* p.581, note 5.

# 4a Privity and Private Justice in Contract

*The U.K. Law Commission's Final Report on Third Parties**

PETER KINCAID

## Introduction

In *Darlington Borough Council v. Wiltshier Northern Ltd.*[1] Steyn L.J. said that it is unjust to deny effectiveness to a contract for the benefit of a third party. It is, he said, unnecessary to struggle with the point, "since nobody seriously asserts the contrary".[2]

In a series of articles published after the High Court's decision in the *Trident Insurance Case*,[3] I showed that I was such a "nobody".[4] The point I tried to make was this. Most people assumed that justice required reform of the privity rule. That rule denies third parties the right to sue on contracts, whether intended to benefit them or not. However, it was not satisfactorily explained how it was unjust to the third party to deny it a right of action on a promise when the promise was not made to it and it had not paid for it. The privity and consideration rules were coherent applications of the idea of contract as bargain, the two elements of which were promise and exchange. If the idea of contract as bargain were abandoned, and a new idea of contract adopted, then still, I argued, the common law approach to private law liability required the plaintiff to demonstrate why, according to some criterion of justice, the defendant should be responsible for realising the plaintiff's interests. I argued that justice required coherent reasoning from principle to rule. Merely relaxing the privity doctrine to

* This article was published in (1997) 12 J.C.L. 47 and is reproduced here with the kind permission of Butterworths and the Journal of Contract Law. Original page numbers are shown in **[square brackets]**.

1 [1995] 1 W.L.R. 68.

2 [1995] 1 W.L.R. 68, 76.

3 *Trident General Insurance Co. Ltd. v. NcNiece Bros. Pty. Ltd.* (1988) 165 C.L.R. 107.

4 "Third Parties: Rationalising a Right to Sue" [1989] C.L.J. 243; "The Trident Insurance Case: Death of Contract?" (1989) 2 J.C.L. 160; "Privity and the Essence of Contract" (1989) 12 U.N.S.W.L.J. 59; and "The U.K. Law Commission's Privity Proposals and Contract Theory" (1994) 8 J.C.L. 51.

allow third parties to sue satisfied none of these requirements.

There has been some half-hearted refutation of the thesis in these articles[5] but they have failed to change many minds. Certainly the Law Commission was not deflected from its tentative recommendation[6] that the privity rule should be modified in England to allow third parties a cause of action in contract. Its final proposal[7] sticks to this recommendation.

**[48]** My object in this article is not to re-argue the thesis of my earlier articles. It is instead to assess the significance of the fact that no one cares about that thesis. I assumed that everyone was concerned about justice to the parties. If so, I thought that a cause of action by the third party in contract needed to be *justified* by coherent reasoning according to the principles of private law liability. My assumptions seem to have been wrong, or at least my idea of what justice and justification meant were not shared by others. The attitudes revealed by the Law Commission and its many supporters[8] indicate things about modern attitudes to the nature of contract, the nature of private law, and the need for logical coherent reasoning in law.

## The Law Commission's Proposals

One of the Law Commissioners, Andrew Burrows, has recently written a thorough summary of the commission's final proposals in which he makes a plea for their support.[9] A very brief summary will suffice here.

The commission proposes[10] that a third party be able to enforce the contract in its own right if either the contract contains an express term to that effect, or the contract purports to confer a benefit on the third party. In the latter case it will be presumed that the parties intend the third party to be able to enforce the contract, unless the presumption is rebutted by construction of the contract. The effect of this proposal is that a right to enforce may be expressly conferred on someone who is not even a

5 H. Beale, "Privity of Contract: Judicial and Legislative Reform" (1995) 9 J.C.L. 103, 113; Law Commission (UK), *Privity of Contract: Contracts for the Benefit of Third Parties*, Law Com 242, H.M.S.O., London, 1996, p. 39 fn. 2.

6 Law Commission, *Privity of Contract: Contracts for the Benefit of Third Parties*, Consultation Paper No. 121, London, H.M.S.O., 1991.

7 Law Com 242, 1996.

8 "The Consultation Paper attracted 102 replies. A clear majority accepted the validity of our arguments in favour of reform." Law Com 242, 1996, para.1.6.

9 Andrew Burrows, "Reforming Privity of Contract: Law Commission Report No. 242" [1996] L.M.C.L.Q. 467. See also N.H. Andrews, "Reform of the Privity Rule in English Contract Law: The Law Commission's Report No. 242" [1997] C.L.J. 25.

10 Law Com 242, 1996, Draft Bill, cl. 1, and para. 3.29.

beneficiary of the contract such, perhaps, as the guardian of a beneficiary.[11] The third party must be expressly identified by name, class, or description.[12]

The third party is to have all remedies which would have been available to it had it been a party to the contract.[13] Enforceability by the third party will not prejudice the promisee's right to sue: the duty to perform is owed to both.[14]

The third party's right to sue would accrue immediately the contract was made, but the parties proper as creators of the contract would have the right to vary or cancel it up to the time the third party had communicated its assent to the contract to the promisor, or had relied on the contract and the promisor either knew about this reliance or could reasonably be expected to have foreseen it.[15] Alternatively, the parties could specify some other test governing **[49]** loss of the right to vary or cancel,[16] or could preserve the right indefinitely.[17]

The recommendations are similar to those of the Law Revision Committee in 1937.[18] The latter required an express term conferring a benefit on the third party, preserved the promisor's defences against the promisee for use against the third party, and allowed cancellation by the parties before adoption expressly or by conduct by the third party. The significant difference is that the new proposals allow the parties expressly to create in the third party a right to sue, even without conferring a benefit on that person. The 1937 recommendation required an express intention to confer a benefit. If that was present, a right to sue would be given by law.[19]

---

11 Law Com 242, 1996, paras 7.6 and 7.16. This test is different from any in the consultation paper (Consultation Paper 121, 1991, para. 5.8). The new proposals are different in that if the intent to create enforceability is express, intent to bestow benefit is irrelevant.

12 The judicial reform of *London Drugs Ltd. v. Kuehne and Nagel International Ltd.* [1993] 1 W.W.R. 1 goes beyond the Law Commission recommendations, because it allowed an employee, even though not expressly identified in the exclusion clause, to rely on it. See Law Com 242, 1996, para. 2.67, fn. 178.

13 Law Com 242, 1996, Draft Bill cl. 1(4), and para. 10.4.

14 Law Com 242, 1996, paras 11.4-11.6.

15 Law Com 242, 1996, Draft Bill cl. 2.

16 Para. 9.42.

17 Para. 9.40.

18 Law Revision Committee, Sixth Interim Report, *Statute of Frauds and the Doctrine of Consideration*, (1937) Cmd 5449.

19 See Consultation Paper 121, 1991, para. 4.30.

## The Law Commission's Justifications

The commission offers three justifications for giving a third party the right to sue on a contract. They are intention, expectation, and reliance. These justifications are summarised in the judgment of Steyn L.J. in *Darlington Borough Council v. Wiltshier Northern Ltd.*,[20] from which the commission quotes at the beginning of its report:

> The case for recognising a contract for the benefit of a third party is simple and straightforward. The autonomy of the will of the parties should be respected. The law of contract should give effect to the reasonable expectations of contracting parties. ... [T]here is no doctrinal, logical, or policy reason why the law should deny effectiveness to a contract for the benefit of a third party where that is the expressed intention of the parties. Moreover, often the parties, and particularly third parties, ... rely on the contract. It is therefore unjust to deny effectiveness to such a contract. I will not struggle with the point further since nobody seriously asserts the contrary.[21]

### *Intention*

The Law Commission's principal justification for a third-party right in contract is that it would give effect to the intentions of the contracting parties:

> If the theoretical justification for the enforcement of contracts is seen as the realisation of the promises or the will or the bargain of the contracting parties, the failure of the law to afford a remedy to the third party where the contracting parties intended that it should have one frustrates their intentions, and undermines the general justifying theory of contract.[22]

The issue raised by this quotation is whether the "justifying theory of contract" requires allowing the parties to create legal rights in people outside their relationship. I would say that the bargain theory of contract, based as it is on promise, does not include this role for intention. Briefly, the law of contract is about the enforcement of promises. A promise is a voluntary **[50]** undertaking to another to do something in the future. All promises have moral force, but the law defines those which will have legal force, namely those exchanged for something.

The law's concern with intention has two aspects. The first is to see

---

20 [1995] 1 W.L.R. 68.

21 [1995] 1 W.L.R. 68, 76, quoted in Law Com 242, 1996, para. 1.1.

22 Law Com 242, 1996, para. 3.1.

if the alleged promisor has indeed intended to promise, that is to bind itself to future conduct by relinquishing the opportunity to change its mind. The second is to find out, assuming that the person is apparently willing to be bound, what terms it is willing to be bound to.[23] If there are sufficient terms to make a contract, and if there is a manifest willingness by both parties to be bound to them, the law *invests* the parties with the legal right to enforce each other's promises. The law has defined the necessary relationship, namely that of promise within bargain. Attention is paid to intention to see if it exists and what its content is. But intention does not create the right to sue. That is attached by the law.

Third parties are not part of any relationship. The commission would treat the intention of the parties that the third party should have a right to sue as the justification for giving it that right. The commission says, "The overall coherent policy may be presented as the enforcement of bargains, the upholding of the intentions of those who have provided consideration, not the enforcement of gratuitous promises".[24] This is **[63]** in effect treating the bargain as an abstract thing worth upholding for its own sake, not a way of explaining the plaintiff's relation to the defendant and justifying holding the defendant responsible to the plaintiff. In conventional contract law, intention is relevant to the fact and content of the contract, not to the creation of a right outside contract.

To treat intention as worth giving effect to for its own sake suggests that there is a public interest in upholding the bargain. This must be the case unless the third-party plaintiff can point to a causal effect upon it and a criterion of justice sufficient to warrant recognising a legal relationship between it and the defendant. In other words, if a focus on the private interests of the plaintiff and defendant does not provide a legal reason for allowing the plaintiff a cause of action, the reason must be provided by public interest. This is how Robert Flannigan sees contractual intention. "There is a public interest, implicit in will theory, in seeing to the enforcement of individual agreements in order to maintain the integrity of the contracting process."[25]

It is clear that this is now a widespread view. The Law Commission quotes the New Zealand committee responsible for reform of the privity rule there: "We have looked in vain for a solid basis of policy justifying the frustration of contractual intentions ..."[26] I argue below that this abstract view of the importance of intention and agreement signifies a particular

23 See H.K. Lucke, "Striking a Bargain" (1962) 1 Adelaide L. Rev. 293.

24 Law Com 242, 1996, para. 6.15.

25 R. Flannigan, "Privity - The End of an Era (Error)" (1987) 103 L.Q.R. 564, 583.

26 Law Com 242, 1996, para. 4.9, quoting New Zealand Contracts and Commercial Law Reform Committee, *Privity of Contract* (1981), para. 6.2.

view of the nature of contract. **[51]**

*Expectations*

The Law Commission generalises its second justification as "injustice to the third party".[27] It identifies the injustice as constituted by "reasonable expectations" engendered in the third party by the contract, expectations "of having the legal right to enforce the contract".[28] The injustice constituted by disappointed expectations is increased where the third party has acted in reliance,[29] although not necessarily to its detriment.[30] The quote from Steyn L.J.[31] mentions expectations by the parties and reliance by the parties and the third party.

As to expectations, the reasoning of the Law Commission and Steyn L.J. suggests that either or both of the expectations of the contracting parties and of the third party may be relevant in justifying a cause of action in the third party.

Let us first consider the expectations of the promisee. If the contractual promise were simply to confer a *benefit* on the third party, then it could be said that the expectations of the promisee are protected by allowing it to sue to enforce the promise.[32]

However, suppose that the relevant term of the contract is that the third party should have a *right to sue* to enforce one of the obligations in the contract. How is this to be interpreted? There are two possibilities. The first is a promise by the promisor to the promisee to allow the third party to sue the promisor in the case of breach. The second is a mere expression of intention of both parties that the third party be able to sue.[33]

The mere fact that expectations have been raised creates an interest in the person in question, but expectations alone do not justify a cause of action. J.H. Baker makes this point:

> The disappointment of an expectation cannot by itself be a cause of action. ... If the law is to make one man answerable for another's disappointments, there must be some nexus between them which creates an obligation.[34]

---

27 Law Com 242, 1996, para. 3.2.

28 Law Com 242, 1996, para. 3.2, and see Burrows [1996] L.M.C.L.Q. 467, 468.

29 Law Com 242, 1996, para. 3.2.

30 Law Com 242, 1996, para. 9.19.

31 [1995] 1 W.L.R. 68, 76; see above.

32 See below for a discussion of the promisee's range of remedies.

33 The latter possibility is contemplated by Law Com 242, 1996, draft bill cl. 1(2).

34 J.H. Baker, "From Sanctity of Contract to Reasonable Expectation?" [1979] C.L.P. 17, 24.

In the case of expectations raised by a promise in the promisee, the invoking of trust in the promisee justifies turning the interest into a right, and the giving up of consideration by the promisee justifies making it legal. If there is a promise, as in the first possibility, there is a justification for giving the promisee a cause of action for its disappointed expectations. But what justifies giving the third party a right because of its expectations? If there is no promise, as in the second possibility, then it is hard to see how either the promisee or the third party can justify a cause of action. All this is equal to saying that expectations in the absence of privity or consideration do not serve as a justification for giving a cause of action to anyone. **[52]**

*Reliance*

The Law Commission says that a justification for giving the third party a cause of action is "the injustice to the third party where a valid contract, albeit between two other parties, has engendered in the third party reasonable expectations of having the legal right to enforce the contract particularly where the third party has relied...".[35]

The commission views reliance as evidence of expectation. The object is to protect the third party's expectation interest, not its reliance interest. It is for this reason that mere reliance, not detrimental reliance, would be required. "Reliance serves to indicate that expectations have been engendered in the third party. To require the reliance to be detrimental tends to shift the focus away from protecting the plaintiff's expectation interest to protecting the plaintiff's reliance interest."[36] "[A]n insistence that the reliance be detrimental makes it very difficult ... to explain why the third party is entitled to performance of the promise, or its monetary substitute in the form of expectation damages, rather than damages for reliance loss (as, for example, for tortious misrepresentation)."[37]

I argued above, however, that expectation alone is not strong enough to qualify a plaintiff: cf. the gratuitous promisee. If expectation will not do, the only criterion of justice relevant to the third party is reliance. But reliance in the absence of privity (that is, from the point of view of the third party, in the absence of promise) can only entitle the third party to reliance damages.

Two uses can be made of reliance, or the likelihood of it. First, reliance can be a criterion justifying a right to enforce a promise (an

---

35 Law Com 242, 1996, para. 3.2.
36 Law Com 242, 1996, para. 9.19.
37 Ibid.

assumed obligation). Second, it can be a criterion justifying the imposition of an obligation outside contract.

If reliance is a criterion for the enforcement of a promise, then the object is to protect the plaintiff's expectation. This is because in the case of a promise made to the plaintiff, it is the trust invoked by the promisor in the plaintiff promisee which is the primary criterion of justice. That trust creates the obligation.[38] Expectation is a manifestation of that trust and its measure. The right is then to have one's expectations realised, and damages would be what is necessary to do so. Reliance, like consideration, would only be a device for distinguishing legal from merely moral obligations. The degree of reliance would then not control the remedy. Reliance would be an alternative to consideration. Just as adequacy of consideration is irrelevant, so the degree of reliance, or the degree of detriment suffered in reliance would be irrelevant. The threshold would be simply that a price had been paid, or that the plaintiff had relied. Once over that threshold, it could enforce the promise.

If reliance is a criterion justifying the imposition of an obligation outside contract, then reliance (not promise) is the justification for shifting "the risk of ill consequences away from the party relying".[39] It would follow that the **[53]** remedy, like the right, would depend upon reliance and would be designed to rectify the harm caused by the reliance. It would not be to realise the plaintiff's expectations.

A difficulty with the Law Commission's approach is that it mixes up these two uses of reliance. The commission would use the bare fact of reliance to justify allowing the third party a right to sue on the promise, that is, to realise its expectations. But the promise was not made to the third party. Unlike the promisee, it cannot point to the trust invoked by the making of a promise as a justification for realising its expectations. On the other hand, the cause of action is not *based* on reliance, as evidenced by the fact that the remedy is not linked to reliance.

It may be worth reiterating that neither expectation nor reliance would need to be proved to *create* the right in the third party. All that would be necessary is intention.[40]

## *Practical Benefits*

The Law Commission lists a number of practical benefits of reform of the third-party rule. They include:

---

38 Charles Fried, *Contract as Promise*, Harvard University Press, Cambridge, Massachusetts, 1981, pp. 1-17, esp. 8 and 16.

39 P.S. Atiyah, *Essays on Contract*, Clarendon, Oxford, 1986, p 82.

40 Law Com 242, 1996, Draft Bill cl. 1.

(a) Subsequent purchasers or tenants can be given rights to enforce a builder's contractual obligations without the cost, complexity, and inconvenience of separate contracts.[41] The High Court has given such people the right to sue in tort,[42] although Brennan J. thought that such an extension of tort liability was an unwise intrusion in an area better left to contract.[43]

(b) Named beneficiaries (such as employees and sub-contractors) of insurance contracts could sue.[44]

(c) Limitation clauses designed to protect a third party from liability could be enforced by that third party.[45]

These advantages suggest that an important consideration for the commission is economic efficiency and convenience – making the economy work better. Justice in terms of a balance of the interests of the individual parties is not necessarily paramount.

The commission says, "the existence of so many legislative and common law exceptions to the rule demonstrates its basic injustice".[46] This is an example of their equating convenience with justice. At common law there are **[54]** no true exceptions to the privity rule.[47] But even if one regards a specific common law device like a Himalaya clause as an exception, it could be seen as a response, like statutory exceptions, to specific practical commercial problems. It does not follow that you can extrapolate from that to say that there is a general injustice in the third-party rule. In fact, you could say that the third-party rule *is* about justice, and the exceptions are about commercial convenience or efficiency. In other words, individual justice and the smooth functioning of the economy do not necessarily yield the same rules. The commission acknowledges its focus when it says that the elaborate structures necessary to circumvent the

---

41 Law Com 242, 1996, para. 1.2. See also Burrows [1996] L.M.C.L.Q. 467, 470.

42 *Bryan v. Maloney* (1995) 182 C.L.R. 609.

43 A conclusion also reached by the House of Lords, which held that a builder was not liable in tort to a subsequent purchaser in respect of the cost of repair of defects in a building. *D&F Estates Ltd. v. Church Commissioners for England* [1989] A.C. 177.

44 Law Com 242, 1996, para. 1.2. See also Burrows [1996] L.M.C.L.Q. 467, 471. This was the focus in *Trident General Insurance Co. Ltd. v. NcNiece Bros. Pty. Ltd.* (1988) 165 C.L.R.107, and was the effect of the Commonwealth *Insurance Contracts Act* 1984 s. 48.

45 Law Com 242, 1996, para. 1.2. This is the problem addressed by "Himalaya clauses" and by *London Drugs Ltd. v. Kuehne & Nagel International Ltd.* (1992) 97 D.L.R. (4th) 261, 340-370. See Law Com 242, 1996, paras 2.19-2.35.

46 Law Com 242, 1996, para. 3.5, and see Burrows [1996] L.M.C.L.Q. 467, 469.

47 *Trident General Insurance Co. Ltd. v. NcNiece Bros. Pty. Ltd.* (1988) 165 C.L.R. 107, 135 per Brennan J.

third-party rule produce uncertainty and "such uncertainty is commercially inconvenient".[48] Also, it says, it would be convenient to harmonise U.K. law with that of continental Europe, where the law does recognise third-party rights.[49]

The Law Commission displays an impatience with the unwillingness of theorists to recognise direct third-party rights. In *Junior Books Ltd. v. Veitchi Ltd.*[50] a subcontractor was liable for expectation loss to the owners in tort. The commission says that in this case the "owners' claim can again be viewed as being one by a third-party beneficiary of a contract ... to enforce the benefit which was contracted for".[51] Rather than disguising the cause of action as tort, it says, "it should be straightforwardly possible for contracting parties to confer on third parties the right to enforce the contract".[52]

The commission has the same attitude to assignment. "The effect of assignment is that the promisor is faced with an action brought on the contract by a person whom he did not regard as a party and whom he may not have intended to benefit."[53] "If an immediate assignment is valid, there can hardly be fundamental objections to allowing the third party to sue without an assignment."[54]

The desirability of cutting through technicalities and allowing a direct third-party right was recently recognised by the House of Lords.[55]

*Remedies*

The orthodox view of contract damages is that even though a promisee may have bargained for a benefit to be conferred upon a third party, the promisee can recover only what *it* has suffered.[56] The failure to pay the third party may cause loss to the promisee, as where the object of the third-party contract was to have the promisor pay a debt owed by the promisee to the third party. But **[55]** the mere frustration of the promisee's purpose to confer a benefit on the third party was not recognised as a loss warranting

48 Law Com 242, 1996, para. 3.6.
49 Law Com 242, 1996, para. 3.8.
50 [1983] 1 A.C. 520.
51 Law Com 242, 1996, para. 2.14.
52 Law Com 242, 1996, para. 3.28.
53 Law Com 242, 1996, para. 2.16.
54 Law Com 242, 1996, para. 2.17. Flannigan (1987) 103 L.Q.R. 564, 580, fn. 95, and P.S. Atiyah, *An Introduction to the Law of Contract*, 5th ed, Clarendon, Oxford, 1995, p. 364, have the same attitude.
55 *The Mahkutai* [1996] 3 W.L.R. 1, 12 per Lord Goff.
56 *Coulls v. Bagot's Executor and Trustee Co. Ltd.* (1967) 119 C.L.R. 460, 502 per Windeyer J.

compensation.

The result is that the third party cannot sue because of want of privity, but the promisee may not be able to demonstrate loss. As it is the promisee's right, so it is the promisee's remedy. It is true that this inability of damages to do justice will often warrant specific performance,[57] but the contract will not always lend itself to specific performance.[58]

In *Linden Gardens Trust Ltd. v. Lenesta Sludge Disposals Ltd.*,[59] Lord Griffiths proposed allowing the promisee to recover as damages an amount sufficient to enable it to carry out the frustrated purpose of benefiting the third party. In other words, the promisee's loss in such a situation would be seen as substantial. This idea was supported by Steyn L.J. in *Darlington Borough Council v. Wiltshier Northern Ltd.*[60] as consistent with the idea of compensating the promisee, not the third party, for "the loss of bargain or of expectation interest".[61] Steyn L.J. did not agree with a limitation proposed by Lord Griffiths, namely that the promisee show that it is likely to carry out the purpose of benefiting the third party. The new principle is a recognition that the promisee has not got what it bargained for, and that it should be compensated for that lost expectation. But, "it is no concern of the law what the plaintiff proposes to do with his damages".[62]

It is arguable that if the object of damages is to provide just compensation for disappointed expectation then it is justifiable to look more closely at what the promisee contracted to achieve. If it is benefiting a third party, then failure to do it disappoints the promisee's expectations. The compensation should be what is necessary to allow the promisee to achieve the contracted-for object. So Lord Griffiths's change, as extended by Steyn L.J., would bring the law of damages more into line with principle.

The Law Commission supports these changes to the law of damages,[63] but is in favour of going further and allowing the third party a cause of action. Its proposals **[56]** would allow the parties to a contract to create legal causes of action at will in a person who has nothing to do with the contract even to the extent of being a beneficiary of it.[64] The remedies

---

57 *Coulls v. Bagot's Executor and Trustee Co. Ltd.* (1967) 119 C.L.R. 460, 503 per Windeyer J.

58 Law Com 242, 1996, para. 3.3.

59 [1994] 1 A.C. 85.

60 [1995] 1 W.L.R. 68.

61 [1995] 1 W.L.R. 68, 80.

62 [1995] 1 W.L.R. 68, 80.

63 Law Com 242, 1996, paras 5.4 and 5.15. See also H. Beale, "Privity of Contract: Judicial and Legislative Reform" (1995) 9 J.C.L. 103, 108.

64 Law Com 242, 1996, para. 7.16.

available to such a person could be limited as it may, like the promisee in a third-party situation, not be able to show damage. However, specific performance could still be available on the theory that the object of relief is to give effect to the intentions of the parties. Such a person "will be in no worse position that a contracting party suing for a third-party beneficiary under the present law".[65] And if the third party's expectations are to be compensated, it appears that the *Linden Gardens* reform would allow the third party to recover as damages the cost of conferring the benefit on the fourth party.[66]

## Issues Raised by Justifications

### *Nature of Contract*

The commission argues that although its proposed reform "departs from a long-established common law rule, we hope that it will not be seen as cutting across the underpinning principle of the common law".[67] Flannigan, similarly, scoffs at the idea that "trashing the doctrine of privity would bring into question the whole theoretical superstructure of contract law!".[68]

It has to be acknowledged that there is debate about the nature of the classical law of contract. Some argue that consideration need not be provided by the plaintiff as long as some one has paid for the promise.[69] Others say that privity is an arbitrary rule limiting the ability to acquire rights under a contract to those who have made it.[70]

I have argued elsewhere[71] that the coherent view of the classical law is that contract is bargain. The essential characteristics of bargain are promise and exchange. A promise is a voluntary undertaking, in which the promisor defines both the content of the promise and to whom it makes its undertaking. "Privity" simply expresses the idea that a promise is a private and voluntary relationship resulting in rights and duties which have been defined by the promisor. You cannot have a right under the promise unless the promisor has chosen to make the promise to you.

The law has chosen to add legal to moral right and duty if the

---

65 Law Com 242, 1996, para. 7.16.
66 Law Com 242, 1996, para. 3.32.
67 Law Com 242, 1996, para. 1.10.
68 Flannigan (1987) 103 L.Q.R. 564, 582, fn. 19.
69 J. Beatson, "Reforming the Law of Contracts for the Benefit of Third Parties: A Second Bite at the Cherry" (1992) 45 C.L.P. 1, 5.
70 Flannigan (1987) 103 L.Q.R. 564, 576, quoting Treitel.
71 "Privity and the Essence of Contract" (1989) 12 *U.N.S.W. Law Journal* 59.

promise has been exchanged for a price demanded of the promisee. Thus although privity and consideration are distinct ideas, only the promisee can show consideration. Consideration and privity qualify a plaintiff to enforce a promise according to the bargain theory of contract. Since the third party can show neither that it gave consideration, nor that the promise was made to it, clearly the third party cannot qualify to sue under the bargain theory. If the "underpinning principle" of the common law of contract is bargain, the commission is not warranted in hoping that its reform will not cut across that principle.

Viewed as bargain, contract is a private, facilitative affair. It is private because the moral relationship constituted by promise is confined to the parties. The purpose of the law is to allow parties to make their own contracts and to enforce the promises they contain provided there is no reason of equity or public policy for not doing so. The law's concern is with justice between the parties. It is concerned with the interests of the parties and not to any substantial degree with public interests.

**[57]** The significant thing about the commission's view of the nature of contract as revealed by its proposals is that the focus of contract law is shifted from private interests to public ones.

The commission's chief justification is giving effect to the intentions of the parties. This looks at first sight like concern with private interests. But a closer look suggests otherwise. The contracting parties have every right to sue each other to give effect to their intentions.[72] If they do, the job of the court will be to balance their interests as plaintiff and defendant according to the ideas of justice expressed by the relationship of contract. But surely the third party is not suing to protect the private interests of the contracting parties. It is suing to realise its own interests. The intentions of the contracting parties alone do not explain the justice of preferring the interests of the third party (in having the contract performed) to those of the promisor defendant (in not doing so). If the action by the third party cannot be justified by a balancing of private interests, one is left with the conclusion that it is in the interests of the public or community to give effect to the intentions of the contracting parties.

If you look at the list of practical benefits of reforming the third-party rule,[73] giving effect to the intention of the parties starts to look like public interest. It is a good idea to do it because it has practical benefits for the economy and the judicial system. Contract becomes a regulatory scheme. The state has an interest in regulating transactions and one aspect

72 Assuming that any shortcomings as to remedies are addressed in the way suggested by Lord Griffiths and Steyn L.J.

73 Law Com 242, 1996, para. 1.2.

of its interest, as suggested by Steyn L.J.,[74] is in giving effect to the will of the parties. As Flannigan says, there is "interaction or competition between 'individual' and 'community' goals" in the enforcement of contracts.[75]

A view of the nature of contract is revealed that is fundamentally different from that of the bargain theory. First, contract as bargain sees obligations as privately assumed, not imposed by the law. The role of the court is to enforce those obligations, or to reduce them as required by equity and public policy, but never to add obligations of its own. The relationship constituted by the exchanging of promises defines both the rights and duties and their holders. Second, contract as bargain sees an action in contract as a balancing and realisation of *private* rights, not public ones. Third, contract is no longer just a private relationship created by the parties but a relationship which includes other people who are affected by the formation of the relationship between the promisor and the promisee.[76]

*Nature of Private Law*

The proposals challenge not only the nature of contract, but the traditional common law view of the nature of a private law suit.

Private law is about making one person, the defendant, responsible for **[58]** realising the interests of another, the plaintiff. The approach of the common law in private law actions has been that the defendant is free of responsibility for the disappointments or injuries of the plaintiff unless the plaintiff can show how a principle of law establishes a relationship between the two to justify responsibility. The defendant must have done something which has had an effect on the plaintiff. But a causal link is not enough. The defendant's behaviour vis-à-vis the plaintiff must have transgressed some value. In other words, the approach has been to require the plaintiff to demonstrate why, according to a defined criterion of justice, the defendant should take responsibility for realising the plaintiff's interests.

According to the bargain theory, privity and consideration provide the reasons. The defendant promisor in a bargain has induced the plaintiff promisee to trust him and raised the promisee's expectations. The promisor has done this by making a promise to him, and the promisee's trust and expectations have been disappointed by the defendant's breach. The plaintiff promisee has also given up something by way of the price of the promise, as the result of a request by the defendant promisor.

The proposed rule does not fit the pattern of justification according

---

74 In *Darlington Borough Council v. Wiltshier Northern Ltd.* [1995] 1 W.L.R. 68, 76.

75 Flannigan (1987) 103 L.Q.R. 564, 591.

76 See B. Markesinis, "An Expanding Tort Law - The Price of a Rigid Contract Law" (1987) 103 L.Q.R. 354, esp. at 363.

to a relationship between the plaintiff third party and the promisor. First of all, what has happened to the plaintiff? In the simplest situation, where the parties have not changed their minds, all that has happened is that its expectations have been raised. And what need the defendant have done? Expressed an intention (not necessarily by way of promise, and in any case not made to the plaintiff). The connection between the plaintiff and the defendant is so weak as to suggest that the plaintiff's cause of action against the defendant cannot be justified on that basis. The plaintiff has not demonstrated that it is deserving, nor that the defendant should be responsible.

The requirement that the plaintiff *justify* the defendant's responsibility shows a concern with the defendant's liberty. The attitude of the Law Commission and its supporters to establishing a third party's cause of action in contract is evidence of a lessening concern for personal liberty and autonomy.[77]

One writer, Beale, discusses the criticism that allowing a third party a cause of action weakens the doctrine of consideration. But, he says, allowing the third party a cause of action "would be so convenient that I would be prepared to see the doctrine of consideration 'weakened' to this extent".[78] The fact that the plaintiff third party cannot justify its attempt at state coercion of the defendant by showing that it gave consideration does not matter. It only matters that it is convenient, not whether it is just. Beale agrees that to allow the third party to sue shifts the "burden of justification" to the promisor since the third party has no "strong claim to justice". But, he says, so what? "The beneficiary of a deed under seal or of a promise for nominal consideration has **[59]** no stronger claim."[79] It does not matter that nothing legally relevant has happened to the plaintiff.

Another commentator, Beatson, explains that giving effect to the intention of the parties "promotes the idea of agreement as a source of obligation".[80] The trouble with that is that it looks at duty divorced from right. Causes of action in contract are not just about sources of obligation; they are about a relationship. What is the third party's relationship to the

---

77 P.S. Atiyah, *Essays on Contract*, Clarendon, Oxford, 1986, p 146.

78 H. Beale, "Privity of Contract: Judicial and Legislative Reform" (1995) 9 J.C.L. 103, 113.

79 Beale (1995) 9 J.C.L. 103, 113. I am here concerned with approach. But his specific argument is unsound. If by the beneficiary of a deed, he means the person to whom the promise is made, that person can at least show privity. As to nominal consideration, to be enforceable the promise must have the form of an exchange, but the very idea of the individual liberty contained in the concept of bargain is that the promisor can state his own price. The promisee of a promise for nominal consideration has paid that price. In addition he can show privity.

80 (1992) 45 C.L.P. 1, 4.

promisor?

This approach, shared by the Law Commission and by most commentators on its proposals, shows that many people no longer care about justification at this personal level. They are happy to see the promisor held liable in a private action without a satisfactory justification. Law in private areas like contract becomes less concerned with individual rights and more to do with efficiency. So if reform will prevent a multiplicity of contracts, or of suits, then the fact that the plaintiff third party can show neither a change in its condition nor a link to the defendant to justify a private right against the defendant does not matter the way it once seemed to. "Intention" and "injustice to the third party" are imprecise, partly-formed ideas that are put on the scales along with public ideas like efficiency and convenience to tip the scales in favour of reform.

The commission's main reason why the defendant should be liable at the suit of the plaintiff is that the parties intended it. Intention alone seems like a feeble reason, because the parties can always carry out their own intention. If the promisor changes its mind and the intention was expressed in a promise, the promisee can sue to enforce it.

If there was a mere joint expression of intention that the third party be able to sue,[81] with no promise to confer a benefit, then the promisee would have no cause of action. There is no promise to enforce. The third party can sue if it wants to. Whether its standing is recognised or not will depend upon a rule of law. If the court gives effect to the term, or intention, the third party *will* be able to sue. The proposed rule would allow the parties, merely by expressing an intention, to confer a cause of action on somebody.

Generally the *law* defines a cause of action, not the parties. It says, if you people *do* something, a cause of action will be created. And the "something" has been defined in terms of balancing the interests of the parties by defining a relevant relationship and a criterion of justice. But here we would be allowing the parties to create a cause of action by intention, without the limit of a defined just relationship.

This is comparable to the treatment of domicile in *Re G.*[82] Domicile is a status defined by the law in which intention (as to where the person is to live) plays a part. In *Re G*, a mother sent her retarded daughter to live permanently **[60]** in Scotland. The judge decided that the daughter remained domiciled in New Zealand because the mother intended the daughter's *domicile* to be New Zealand. By allowing a person to define his domicile by applying his intention directly to the *legal* issue of domicile,

---

81 Law Com 242, 1996, Draft Bill cl. 1(1)(a).

82 [1966] N.Z.L.R. 1028.

the law abdicates control over what constitutes justice.

The job of the law is to lay down rules which control the outcome of a legal question according to an idea of justice. If the outcome of the legal question is handed without control to the intention of a person or people, the law is giving up its ability, and duty, to determine outcomes according to justice. A plaintiff has a cause of action against a defendant because what the defendant has done has created a relationship between them. The law defines this relationship as legally relevant according to criteria of justice for altering the existing balance of interest between the parties or, in other words, for requiring the defendant to realise the plaintiff's interests.

To say that the defendant must realise the plaintiff's interests because the defendant (in a contract with someone else) has *intended* that this be the case is an abdication of the state's control over the definition of justice, unless it can be demonstrated that that intention, *independently of the intention that the plaintiff be able to sue*, creates a factual relationship which justifies a cause of action.

The commission favours general reform of the third-party rule by way of a detailed legislative scheme, over further exceptions in specific instances. "To create further situation-specific exceptions misses the point that the third-party rule is generally flawed."[83] My argument is that it has not demonstrated that. Intention and expectation are the ideas it uses in its attempt, but those ideas fail to justify a cause of action by the third party.

How do existing legislative exceptions to the third-party rule, such as that constituted by s. 48 of the Commonwealth *Insurance Contracts Act*, tie in with the idea that private law is about private interests? They can be seen as limited instances of public interests exceptionally outweighing private interests. This is analogous to the weighing process that goes on in a particular case whenever it is argued that public policy considerations should override private interests. Public policy is applied subject to what Kahn-Freund calls the principle of the "relativity of public policy".[84] By this he means that the public harm in the particular case in giving effect to private rights, such as contractual ones, has to be sufficiently great to warrant overriding those rights. This process requires a balancing of the public harm in the individual case against the injustice to the parties in overriding their private interests.

An example is *St. John Shipping Corporation v. Joseph Rank Ltd.*,[85] a case of an allegedly unlawful contract. A cargo owner argued that its duty in the contract of carriage to pay the freight could not be enforced

---

83 Law Com 242, 1996, para. 5.3.

84 Kahn-Freund "Reflections on Public Policy in the English Conflict of Laws" (1953) 39 Trans. Grot. Soc. 39, 57.

85 [1957] 1 Q.B. 267.

against it because, in the course of performing the contract, the shipowner had broken the law by overloading the ship. The public interest in upholding shipping law had to be weighed against the private interests of the shipowner as a contractor. **[61]** Although Devlin J. purported to decide the case by looking for statutory intention, it is apparent that he was applying the weighing process described by Kahn-Freund. Devlin J. quoted Lord Wright in *Vita Food Products Inc. v. Unus Shipping Co.*:[86] "[T]he rule by which contracts ... are ... nullified for disobedience to a statute is a rule of public policy only, and public policy ... may at times be better served by refusing to nullify a bargain ...".[87] In the *St. John* case it was held that the public interest had been adequately protected by the fine already levied against the shipowner. The presumption that private interests in a contract matter should prevail was not rebutted.

Specific statutory exceptions to privity are consistent with the idea that private interests as a rule govern in contract. The *Insurance Contracts Act* represents a legislative assessment that in a particular commercial *class* of case, namely insurance contracts, a public interest, perhaps in the shape of commercial convenience or efficiency, should outweigh the absence of justification for recognising the third party's private interests. But the public interest reasons present in one commercial class of contract are not necessarily present in contracts generally. The piecemeal and exceptional nature of reform so far suggests that private interests are still presumed to be paramount. It has been necessary that for each given class of contract, a public interest be demonstrated sufficient to rebut the presumption. It may be that the process of demonstration is not very convincing or complete, but the *approach* is that there have to be exceptional reasons to override private interests.

The Law Commission's proposals for a general exception in favour of third parties[88] amount to an acknowledgment that in all cases of third-party contracts, public interests are sufficient to outweigh private ones. A more extreme conclusion, which I suggest is the right one, is that the proposals represent not merely an evidentiary finding, but a change of philosophy. The old presumption in private law that private interests are paramount has gone.

To summarise, the commission's proposals reveal three changes in attitudes to the nature of private law. First, it is no longer necessary for the plaintiff to justify its claim against the defendant in terms of a relationship with the defendant. Second, justice in private law need no longer be defined by the state. And third, private interests are no longer presumed

---

86 [1939] A.C. 277.

87 [1939] A.C. 277, 293.

88 To the extent that they represent coherent ideas. See below.

paramount over public ones in contract law.

*Coherence of Reasoning*

The approach shared by the Law Commission with its many supporters suggests that changes have occurred in thinking about contract and private law. It also suggests a lessening concern with rigorous defensible reasoning from principles to rules.

There are two aspects to this changed attitude to legal reasoning. The first is that the "justification" for a legal rule or a cause of action becomes less strictly logical and more impressionistic. A fuzzy mixture of reasons, only partly articulated, is seen as satisfactory. The second is that despite clear evidence of this movement from logic to impression, the commission still **[62]** thinks it necessary to seem to be abiding by the rules of coherent and logical reasoning.

The commission purports to think it important to justify its proposal according to the tradition of reasoning from principles to rules. So it addresses the questions whether privity is essential to the idea of contract and whether principle requires the rule that consideration must move from the plaintiff.[89] It also tries to present intention, expectation, and reliance as justifying the creation of the right in the third party.

I have tried to demonstrate that its reasoning is either faulty or insufficiently explained so that there are doubts about it. But most of the defects in its reasoning were pointed out by my earlier articles, two of which[90] the commission refers to in its reports.[91] My criticisms are not effectively refuted, just ignored. This suggests that the commission members do not really attach much importance to coherent reasoning.

Private law can be seen as a selection of values of justice concerning the relationships between people which in turn lead to the articulation of principles of responsibility from which specific rules are developed consistent with those principles. But the attitude revealed in the report is that the rules for determining liability between individuals are a mixture of pragmatism and justice. What is efficient and economically convenient becomes as much a factor in deciding rules of liability as does the notion of justice between the parties. And justice becomes an impressionistic thing.

Previously the defendant was entitled to ask "*why* should I be responsible for realising the plaintiff's interests?". Justice meant that it was entitled to expect an answer defensible both in terms of consistency of the

89 Law Com 242, 1996, paras 6.4 and 6.8.

90 "Third Parties: Rationalising a Right to Sue" [1989] C.L.J. 243, and "The U.K. Law Commission's Privity Proposals and Contract Theory" (1994) 8 J.C.L. 51.

91 Consultation Paper 121, 1991, pp. 2, 11, and 49; Law Com 242, 1996, pp. 35 and 39.

rule with the underlying principle and of the value behind the principle.

The commission tries to deal with the problem of why the third party, who is not privy and who has not provided consideration, should have better rights than a gratuitous promisee.[92] In the end, it does not really answer this, except to say that a relaxation of consideration is not necessarily a bad thing, since there are other exceptions, including letters of credit, compositions with creditors, and the doctrine of promissory estoppel.[93]

The commission is thus prepared to "relax" the rule that consideration must move from the plaintiff.[94] Consideration would no longer be a clear criterion which qualifies the plaintiff to sue because it has participated in a bargain.[95] As the commission explains, "The overall coherent policy may be presented as the enforcement of bargains, the upholding of the intentions of those who have provided consideration, not the enforcement of gratuitous promises".[96] This is in effect treating the bargain as an abstract thing worth upholding for its own sake, not a way of explaining the plaintiff's relation to the defendant and justifying holding the defendant responsible to the plaintiff.

The commission and its supporters[97] do not see coherence as essential to justice. Or perhaps it is that convenience is more important than justice. Beale gives a further illustration of this approach when he comments on one of my articles.[98] He writes, "to say that a promise is never to be enforceable in contract by anyone but the promisee but that a third party who relies on it can enforce it in tort strikes me as unnecessarily conceptual".[99] To that it might be answered that concepts, like the distinction between tort and contract, are important to rational justice.[100] Another example of support for an impressionistic approach to legal

---

92 Law Com 242, 1996, para. 6.13.

93 Law Com 242, 1996, para. 6.17. The last cannot be seen to be an exception to consideration in Australia, because *Waltons Stores (Interstate) Ltd. v. Maher* (1988) 164 C.L.R. 372 treats it as not the enforcement of a promise.

94 Law Com 242, 1996, para. 6.8.

95 See K.O. Shatwell, "The Doctrine of Consideration in the Modern Law" (1954) 1 Syd. L. Rev. 289.

96 Law Com 242, 1996, para. 6.15.

97 E.g., Beale (1995) 9 J.C.L. 103, 113.

98 "The U.K. Law Commission's Privity Proposals and Contract Theory" (1994) 8 J.C.L. 51.

99 Beale (1995) 9 J.C.L. 103, 114.

100 In any case, I did not say that a third party should be able to enforce the promise in tort. I said that any cause of action based on reliance would have to be "*outside contract*", in other words, not the enforcement of a promise. (1994) 8 J.C.L. 51, 63.

reasoning comes from the Supreme Court of Canada. McLachlin J. says,[101] "[T]he incremental approach of *Kamloops*[102] is to be preferred to the insistence on the logical precision of *Murphy*.[103] It is more consistent with the incremental character of the common law. It permits relief to be granted in new situations where it is merited."

Does it matter whether there is a theoretically coherent basis for private law? If private interests and personal liberty are the paramount concerns, it does. But if contract is just a pragmatic series of adjustments to make the economy work better, perhaps it does not. In earlier articles I tried to demonstrate the lack of coherence in writing on third-party rights. I thought people might not have appreciated this lack. But the truth is that no one seems to be very worried by it. The Law Commission sidesteps my objections. It writes,[104] "Kincaid ... argues that the promise theory underpinning contract dictates that only the promisee can enforce the promise: in our view, this is to take an unnecessarily narrow view of the morality of promise-keeping where a promise is intended to benefit a third party."[105]

## Conclusion

The Law Commission proposes to allow a third party to sue on the contract if that is the intention of the contracting parties. It would justify this by the need to give effect to the intentions of the parties and the expectations of the third party. It does not show how intention and expectation justify a right-duty relationship between the third party and the promisor in the way that privity and consideration do between the promisee and the promisor.

The absence of this justification indicates that the commission and its many supporters view contract not as a private affair concerning only its originators, **[64]** but as a matter of public concern. Duties in contract are not simply those assumed by the promisor. They will be imposed by the state where a mixture of private interests and public interests (prominently including convenience and efficiency) warrant doing so.

The goal of the law in an area of private law like contract ceases to be doing justice between the parties according to a coherent scheme for

---

101 In *C.N.R. v. Norsk Pacific Steamship Co. Ltd.* [1992] 1 S.C.R. 1021at 1149, quoted with approval by Toohey J. in *Bryan v. Maloney* (1995) 182 C.L.R. 609, 661.

102 *City of Kamloops v. Nielsen* [1984] 2 S.C.R. 2.

103 *Murphy v. Brentwood District Council* [1991] 1 A.C. 398.

104 Commenting on "The U.K. Law Commission's Privity Proposals and Contract Theory" (1994) 8 J.C.L. 51.

105 Law Com 242, 1996, para. 3.1 fn 2.

balancing their private interests. Private law becomes instead an area where public and private interests compete. In the particular topic of a general right of third parties in contract, the absence of private justification for the third party means that public interests govern.

The requirement of coherent logical reasoning in terms of values, principles, and rules as they rationalise balancing the interests of the plaintiff and the defendant with reference to the relationship between them has not just been an attempt to make legal rules look pre-ordained and immutable, like the rules of science. It has been seen as part of the protection of the liberty of the individual according to the rule of law.[106] The Law Commission displays an attitude to legal reasoning that is more fluid, less precise, and less concerned with justification at the private level.

106 See Kincaid, "Justice in Tort Choice of Law" (1997) 18 Adelaide L. Rev. 191, 193-194.

# 4b Privity Reform in England

*The Contracts (Rights of Third Parties) Act 1999**

PETER KINCAID

The rule preventing third-party beneficiaries of a contract from suing has been criticised for the injustice it causes. Not only does it frustrate the intentions of the contracting parties, but it also disappoints the legitimate expectations of the third party.

In 1996 the Law Commission recommended that the third-party rule be abolished in England and Wales. The resulting Contracts (Rights of Third Parties) Act 1999 provides that a third party will be able to enforce a term of the contract in its own right if either the contract expressly provides that it may or the term purports to confer a benefit on the third party. In the latter case, there is a rebuttable presumption that if the parties confer a benefit on the third party, they intend that it be able to enforce the term creating the benefit. The test is thus two-pronged. The parties to a contract can create a right to enforce their contract in someone who is not a party to it by expressing an intention that the third party should have that right. Alternatively, they can confer a benefit on the third party, in which case the intention will be presumed. It should be noted that the Act has broadened the meaning of "third party". In this context the expression has meant "third-party beneficiary". The privity rule has been criticised for its injustice chiefly to such beneficiaries. But the new ability of the parties directly to confer a right to enforce on a non-party means that they can confer it on someone who is neither party nor beneficiary such, perhaps, as the guardian of a beneficiary.

The Contracts (Rights of Third Parties) Act may be seen as calculated to achieve the objects of justice in contract by giving effect to the intentions of the contracting parties and the legitimate expectations of the third party created by the contract. To explain the effect and purpose of the Act like this gives point to Lord Irvine L.C.'s closing speech in the second reading in the House of Lords: "The one question … about the Bill is not **[44]** why it has been introduced, but why it has not been introduced

* This short essay was published as a note in (2000) 116 L.Q.R. 43. It is reproduced here with the kind permission of the Law Quarterly Review. Original page numbers are shown in **[square brackets]**.

before". If the reform seems so obviously right and just, why has it taken so long to be achieved?

The explanation may well be that the conception of justice has changed. I contend that leading mid-nineteenth century cases, at least in retrospect, represent a coherent decision that justice in contract derives from the relationship between the plaintiff and the defendant constituted by their participating together in a bargain. *Eastwood v. Kenyon*[1] may be seen as a conscious choice about the meaning of consideration. It was not enough that there was a moral reason to make the defendant pay. To succeed the plaintiff needed to show that it had paid the price demanded by the promisor for the promise. Similarly, *Tweddle v. Atkinson*,[2] as confirmed in later cases such as *Dunlop Pneumatic Tyre Co. v. Selfridge & Co. Ltd.*,[3] was a further important step towards the theory that the justification of contractual liability was participation in the exchange relationship. Just as *Eastwood v. Kenyon* emphasised that aspect of the relationship concerned with the price, so *Tweddle v. Atkinson* emphasised another aspect of the same relationship: the promise sued on must have been made to the plaintiff.

Contract is only one sort of civil cause of action by which one individual, the plaintiff, may single another individual, the defendant, out of the mass of society, and seek to have the state apply its coercive power to the defendant. The plaintiff's object is that the defendant realise the plaintiff's interests, typically by paying money to the plaintiff. The plaintiff's cause of action may be based on contract, or it may be based on tort, unjust enrichment, equitable estoppel, etc. In every case something disadvantageous has happened to the plaintiff and, to confine the discussion to the typical remedy, the plaintiff wants the defendant to pay for it. What has happened to the plaintiff may, for instance, be a disappointed expectation, a personal injury, deprivation of property, detrimental reliance on another's conduct, or something else.

The approach of the law in all areas of private civil liability seems to obey the same pattern. It is one thing for the law to take property from everyone, or broad classes of people, for public purposes, in the way that tax laws do, and transfer that property to the state. No detailed justification is needed. The reasons can be many, and vary from vague to precise. They will depend on the political views of the government of the day. They may be seen as unfair, but provided the democratic process is adhered to, it will be hard to characterise them as unjust.

It is a different matter when the power of the state is to be used to

---

1 (1840) 11 Ad. & El. 438; 113 E.R. 482.

2 (1861) 1 B.& S. 393; 121 E.R. 762.

3 [1915] A.C. 847.

force the transfer of property from one individual to another, usually by ordering the payment of damages. Then the object of the civil law has been to do justice between the parties by balancing the interests of the plaintiff and the defendant. The defendant has been regarded as entitled to ask why it should **[45]** take responsibility for realising the plaintiff's interests. A positive rule of law has not been regarded as sufficient answer. Until now, the common law has required the plaintiff to justify its claim against the defendant. The pattern of justification in all civil causes of action is such that the plaintiff must demonstrate a relationship between it and the defendant which warrants singling the defendant out from all others. More specifically, the relationship must consist of some behaviour (action or occasionally inaction) by the defendant, some effect on the plaintiff giving rise to an interest in redress, and crucially a link between the two. As J.H. Baker says, "If the law is to make one man answerable for another's disappointments, there must be some nexus between them which creates an obligation."[4]

The link or nexus between the plaintiff and the defendant in a civil cause of action joins their otherwise independent acts and aspirations to make them related. It consists of what may be called fact and fault. There must first be factual causation. So a fraudulent misrepresentation which has not induced the plaintiff to make the contract, even though the plaintiff knew about it, gives no cause of action. The factual connection is lacking. Conversely, an innocent misrepresentation (neither fraudulent nor negligent) gives no cause of action in tort even though it induces the plaintiff to act to its detriment. The "fault" connection is lacking. The fault connection is the transgression of some value which, in the eyes of the law, justifies making the defendant legally responsible for the harm it has factually caused the plaintiff.

I have argued that *Eastwood v. Kenyon* and *Tweddle v. Atkinson* together had the effect of settling the nature of contract. But they do not just confirm that its essence is bargain; they also represent a realisation that civil liability in contract, as in other areas of civil liability, must be based on a justifying relationship. In contract, the behaviour by the defendant is making a promise and demanding a price. The effect on the plaintiff is the invoking of his trust and his payment of the price. The factual link consists in the plaintiff's trust being invoked by the defendant's making a promise to him, and by the plaintiff paying the price (typically by making another promise) in response to the defendant's request. The "fault" link, or criterion of justice, is the wrongfulness of invoking the convention of trust constituted by making a promise and then breaking it, combined with the

---

4 [1979] C.L.P. 17 at 24.

added wrongfulness of having extracted a price from the plaintiff for the promise, and then breaking it.

In the tort of negligence, the defendant's act causes an injury to the plaintiff. The foreseeability of the result and the carelessness of the defendant provide the criterion of justice.

In unjust enrichment, the defendant has been enriched by the plaintiff, as where the plaintiff has transferred property to the defendant. It is the lack of justification for the defendant holding this property, as where it has been **[46]** paid under a mistake or under a contract since repudiated, which provides the criterion of justice.

In Australia the doctrine of equitable estoppel has been refined and altered so that it, unlike estoppel in pais, now provides a separate cause of action in equity's independent, not supplementary, role. To establish the cause of action, the plaintiff must show that the defendant has induced in the plaintiff a two-fold belief: that the defendant will do something, such as make a contract, and that the defendant is not free to withdraw. The plaintiff relies on this belief to its detriment. The criterion of justice completing the relationship and justifying a cause of action is the defendant's unconscionability. The unconscionability lies in the defendant inducing a belief in the plaintiff, knowing about the plaintiff's detrimental reliance, and doing nothing to prevent it.[5]

These representative examples of different categories of civil liability indicate that until now there has been a remarkable consistency in the underlying philosophy of civil liability. It has been seen as a matter of private justice. If P is to single out D from the mass of the population and seek the coercive power of the state to force D to realise P's interests, the state (the law) has required P to show that they have both participated in a relationship which justifies making D responsible to P. The law, as the arbiter of justice, defines the elements of the various relationships which will justify a cause of action.

The new scheme for third-party rights established by the Contracts (Rights of Third Parties) Act departs from that pattern of civil liability. The contract relationship cannot justify the third party's claim, as he is not part of it. The promise sued on was not made to him, and nor did he provide the consideration.

A new relationship with a new criterion of justice could be fashioned in the traditional pattern. A deliberate breach by the defendant causing detriment because of the third party's reasonable reliance could be characterised as unjust by recognising a positive duty to act where it is foreseeable that failure to do so will cause damage to someone else. One

5 *Waltons Stores (Interstate) Ltd. v. Maher* (1988) 164 C.L.R. 387 at 427-429.

might or might not agree with the criterion of justice so defined. But the underlying idea of private justice, of private justification in civil causes of action, would be maintained.

The primary justification of the Law Commission for the creation of a third-party right is that the object of contract is to give effect to the intentions of the contracting parties. This would not serve as a justification under the traditional pattern for two reasons. First, the intentions of the contracting parties do not establish or define a relationship between the promisor and the third party. Their intentions are relevant to their relationship with each other. Those intentions enable one to work out whether they are willing to be bound to each other and if so according to **[47]** what terms. And second, it is the law's job to define what is just. The justice of the plaintiff's claim is not determined by the intentions of the parties that it should have a cause of action. The old law has defined the relationship of bargain and said that if you participate in such a relationship, it is just that you should have a cause of action. The Act allows the contracting parties to create a cause of action in the third party by intending that it should have one. By the standards of the old law with its private-interests orientation, the new law amounts to an abdication of the law's duty to define justice between parties. The new law is equivalent to the law's saying, "Justice is whatever you, the parties, say it is."

It might be argued that the flaw in such a criticism of the new law is that it is based on a now out-moded assumption. That assumption is that in a civil cause of action, the law is concerned with a just balance between the private interests of the plaintiff and the defendant. The new concern to give effect to the intentions of the parties is irrelevant to that balance. It reflects instead a public interest in seeing contracts carried out. Similarly, the expectations of the third party could be used as part of a relationship on the old civil cause of action model. But in the absence of any defined relationship between the third-party plaintiff and the promisor defendant, the law's concern with those expectations can only be prompted by the public interest in seeing those expectations realised. Giving effect to the intentions of contracting parties and realising the expectations of third parties will be efficient and be good for business and the economy. The significance of the new law is that it marks a shift from concern with narrow matters of individual liberty and justice to a broader more public-spirited concern with the good of the community at large.

It is, then, somewhat ironical that Lord Diplock should have described the privity rule as "a reproach to English private law".[6] The privity rule was justified if contract law was seen as a matter of private law.

---

6 *Swain v. The Law Society* [1983] A.C. 598 at 611.

The essence of Lord Diplock's objection was that the third-party question was not treated as a matter of public law.

# 5 Privity – A Rule in Search of Decent Burial?

SIR ANTHONY MASON

My object in this essay is first, to examine the nature and purpose of the privity rule and its relationship with the doctrine of consideration and, secondly, to review the deficiencies of the rule as an element in assessing whether the rule has sufficient functional utility to justify its retention. Because abolition of the rule will result in direct enforcement by a third party of a third-party promise, it will be necessary to consider whether the expressed intentions or expectations of the parties are a sufficient justification of direct enforcement. It will also be necessary to consider the conditions according to which direct enforcement will be permitted and the consequences of such enforcement.

## The Nature of the Privity Rule

There are two broad elements in the concept of privity in the common law of contract. One element, which is not of present concern, is the rule that a contract cannot impose obligations or liabilities on a person who is not a party to the contract. The second element, which is of present concern, is the principle which prevents a third party from obtaining a right or benefit under a contract. This element involves denying to a stranger not only a right to sue on the contract, but also a right to take advantage of a clause in a contract excluding or limiting liability.[1]

## The Purpose of the Privity Rule

The privity rule, namely that only a party to a contract can sue on the contract, was not embedded in the common law until 1861 when *Tweddle*

1 See *London Drugs Ltd. v. Kuehne & Nagel International Ltd.* (1992) 97 D.L.R. (4th) 261 at 343.

*v. Atkinson*[2] was decided. The antecedents of the rule, as well as the doctrine of consideration and the relation between the two are obscure and complicated.[3]

> [L]awyers in the sixteenth and seventeenth centuries simply did not think of the action of assumpsit as an action between parties to a contract.[4]

Initially, it seems, the common law permitted third parties to enforce contracts made for their benefit.[5] In 1669, however, in *Bourne v. Mason*,[6] the third party, who failed in his action on the contract, was described as "a mere stranger to the consideration".[7] In the next two hundred years, although the law was not settled either way, it was moving towards the position adopted in *Tweddle v. Atkinson*.

On one view, the basis of the decision in that case was that the plaintiff third party failed because no consideration moved from him. But high authority subsequently made it clear that the decision established the rule that a stranger to the contract cannot sue on it and that there are two principles, namely the privity rule and the consideration rule.[8] At the same time, the two principles, though distinct, are inter-related. With the development of the doctrine of consideration, the plaintiff's right to sue in assumpsit was related to the existence of a sufficient reason for his enforcing the promise and consideration played a part in showing that.[9] Certainly a review of the old cases suggests that this was so.[10]

The recognition of the distinct character of the privity rule stems in all probability from the emergence of the law of contract out of the action

---

2 (1861) 1 B. & S. 393; 121 E.R. 762.

3 See A.W.B. Simpson, *A History of the Common Law of Contract*, Clarendon Press, 1987, 475 et seq.

4 Ibid. at 476.

5 See Flannigan, "Privity – The End of an Era (Error)" (1987) 103 L.Q.R. 564 at 564-565, esp. fn 6. The article is reproduced in this book.

6 (1669) 1 Vent 6; 86 E.R. 5.

7 (1669) 1 Vent 7; 86 E.R. at 6.

8 *Dunlop Pneumatic Tyre Co. Ltd. v. Selfridge & Co. Ltd.* [1915] A.C. 847 at 853; *Vandepitte v. Preferred Accident Insurance Corporation of New York* [1933] A.C. 70 at 79; *Midland Silicones Ltd. v. Scruttons Ltd.* [1962] A.C. 446 at 467-468, 473-494; *Beswick v. Beswick* [1968] A.C. 58; *Kepong Prospecting Ltd. v. Schmidt* [1968] A.C. 810 at 826; *Wilson v. Darling Island Stevedoring & Lighterage Co. Ltd.* (1956) 95 C.L.R. 43; *Coulls v. Bagot's Executor & Trustee Co. Ltd.* (1967) 119 C.L.R. 460.

9 *Dutton v. Poole* (1677) 2 Lev. 210; 83 E.R. 523 (where the third-party donee, who was a daughter of the promisee, was held entitled to sue the promisor her brother). Lord Mansfield said of this case "it is a matter of surprise how doubt could have arisen in that case": *Martyn v. Hind* (1776) 2 Cowp. 437 at 443; 98 E.R. 1174 at 1177.

10 See A.W.B. Simpson, *A History of the Common Law of Contract*, Clarendon Press, 1987, 475 et seq.

in *assumpsit* and the development of the classical law of contract in the nineteenth century. This development led to the conception of the contract as a bargain between the parties to it, a conception which was expressed by Professor Anson in his "Principles of the English Law of Contract" in this way:

> A contract is an agreement between two or more persons, by which an obligation is created, and those persons are bound together thereby. If the obligation takes the form of a promise, by A to X to confer a benefit on M, the legal relations of M are nonetheless unaffected by that obligation. *He* was not a party to the agreement. *He* was not bound by the *vinculum juris* which it created and the breach of that legal bond cannot affect the rights of a party who was never included in it.[11]

The general rule therefore is that a contract cannot confer rights or impose obligations on any person except the parties to it.

The privity rule accordingly gives expression to the notion that the legal conception of a contract is that it is a bargain between the parties to it and that it creates rights and obligations only as between the parties to it. The rule rests primarily on a legal conception rather than on any functional or policy consideration, the legal conception itself embracing the idea that a person who makes a promise is accountable at law to the person to whom it is made and not to anyone else. Stephen Smith has expressed the conception in this way:

> Contractual obligations are voluntary obligations. Voluntary obligations are obligations undertaken to, and extending only to, particular persons. In the case of a promise, that person is the promisee. Third parties, by definition, are not promisees, and hence should not be able to enforce promises made to others.[12]

It is doubtful whether any larger purpose lay behind the legal conception, though the conception was well adapted to the common law requirement of a contract that the parties should intend to create legal relations. Such an intention is apparent as between the parties to the contract; it is not so clear in the case of a stranger to the contract.

The legal conception gained added strength from the principle that consideration must move from the promisee. The consideration is "the

---

11 1st ed., 1879, p. 195.

12 Stephen A. Smith, "Contracts for the Benefit of Third Parties: In Defence of the Third-Party Rule" (1997) 17 O.J.L.S. 643 at 649, reproduced in this book.

price for which the promise is bought".[13] That principle embodies the idea that the person to whom a promise is made must do something to merit reception of the benefit promised to him. Ordinarily that will occur when he is a party to the contract.

There is a question as to the character of the rule that consideration must move from the promisee. Is it a rule that goes to the validity and enforceability of the contract? Or is it, like the privity rule, one which goes to the standing or entitlement of the promisee to sue? If the answer to the first question is in the affirmative, then the two rules are different and not merely different ways of expressing the same principle. An affirmative answer to the first question conforms to the statement of the consideration rule which speaks of "the promisee", that is, someone who is a party to the contract. This is how the Law Commission has understood the rule[14] and, with respect, the view is correct.[15]

This conclusion is important because it means that the displacement of the privity rule not only leaves the consideration rule in place but also leaves the contract on foot as a valid contract. This consequence is of added importance because it is possible that an influential reason for the retention of the privity rule was a strong conviction on the part of judges and lawyers that it was an integral element in the basic English conception of a contract and that its abolition would undermine that conception. This uncertainty surrounding the relationship between the two rules and the lack of clarity in the precise legal consequence or sanction attaching to the privity rule would have reinforced rather than diminished the belief that the two rules went to the very heart of the common law conception of a contract.

## Suggested Justifications for the Rule

Additional reasons, however, have been offered as justifications for the rule. Professor Treitel has mentioned, without endorsing (1) the injustice of allowing a person to sue on a contract when that person could not be sued on the contract; (2) the effect on the rights of contracting parties to rescind or vary their contract of a third party's right to enforce a promise made for its benefit; and (3) the lack of symmetry in allowing a third party donee to

---

[13] *Chitty on Contracts*, 27th ed, 1994, para. 3-007.

[14] The Law Commission – Privity of Contract: Contracts for the Benefit of Third Parties, Law Com. No. 242, 1996, par. 6.7.

[15] Note, however, that there is some support for the contrary view; see *Dunlop Pneumatic Tyre Co. Ltd. v. Selfridge & Co. Ltd.* [1915] A.C. 843 at 853 per Viscount Haldane ("only a person who has given consideration may enforce a contract").

sue when the law does not give a gratuitous promisee a right to enforce the promise.[16]

These suggestions have little weight. Unilateral contracts are enforceable by a party who cannot be sued. The second suggestion has been more influential but there are various ways in which the impact upon the parties' right to rescind or vary can be protected. The suggestion ignores the fact that there is consideration for a promise to a third party which is unenforceable by the third party only because that party is a stranger to the contract.[17] Professor Atiyah has expressed the view that the rule "encouraged the development of a more market-based concept of enterprise liability".[18] Another suggested justification, which may well have appealed to judges, is the apprehension that actionability by third parties may have resulted in a flood of litigation.

The justifications which have been advanced, or some of them, may well have played a part in inducing judges to adopt or to retain the rule. It is proper to regard them as reasons or possible reasons for the adoption or retention of the rule. It is, however, difficult to regard any of them as having sufficient weight to constitute a justification for the rule.

The principal justification is unquestionably conceptual, arising from the bargain exchange theory of contract and the apparent attraction of the idea that only a person to whom a promise is made can sue on it. The attraction of the idea is enhanced by the simplicity of the rule and its capacity to provide a clear solution to a variety of problems. Its capacity to provide a clear solution amounts to a functional justification. To that justification we can add the second point which I have attributed to Professor Treitel, namely that the rule avoids any impairment of the contracting parties' right to rescind or vary the contract which might arise from enforceability of a promise by a third party. In other words, the rule has an advantage in avoiding what otherwise would be the necessity of resolving a difficult question. As we know, abolition of the rule brings a number of problems, not easily resolved, in its train.

To the extent to which the rule is associated with the consideration principle, it may be said that the rule also draws upon the justifications which are urged in support of the consideration principle. But if they are two distinct, even if inter-related principles, as I consider them to be, the purpose of the privity rule must be ascertained on the footing that it stands apart from the consideration principle.

---

16 *The Law of Contract*, 6th ed, 1983 at 458.

17 See Flannigan, "Privity – the End of an Era (Error)", (1987) 103 L.Q.R. 564 at 576-577; M. Furmston, "Return to *Dunlop v. Selfridge*?" (1960) 23 M.L.R. 373 at 376.

18 *The Rise and Fall of Freedom of Contract*, Clarendon Press, 1979, 414.

## The Rule is not Accepted or has been Modified Elsewhere

The privity rule is not a rule which is necessarily inherent in the idea of contract.[19] It accords with Roman law but not with the modern civil law of France, nor with the law of Quebec.[20] In Australia[21] and Canada,[22] the rule has been significantly modified by judicial decision. Scotland recognises the right of a third party to sue on a contract so long as an intention to confer a benefit on the third party can be ascertained from the terms of the contract or the conduct of the parties. In the United States, the rule did not become entrenched as it did in England. Indeed, in 1859, two years before *Tweddle v. Atkinson*, the New York Court of Appeals in *Lawrence v. Fox*[23] recognised that a third-party beneficiary could enforce various contractual stipulations made for its benefit.[24]

The rule has been legislatively modified in various jurisdictions. They include New Zealand,[25] Western Australia,[26] Queensland[27] and England.[28] These legislative modifications follow in the wake of widespread criticisms of the rule and of recommendations by Law Reform Commissions and Committees for its abolition as well as judicial criticisms of the rule. Of the judicial criticisms it is sufficient to mention the criticism made by the High Court of Australia in *Trident General Insurance Co. Ltd. v. McNiece Bros. Pty. Ltd.*,[29] the Supreme Court of Canada in *London Drugs Ltd. v. Kuehne & Nagel International Ltd.*[30] and the English criticisms reviewed by Steyn L.J. (as he then was) in *Darlington Borough Council v. Wiltshier Northern Ltd.*[31] In his judgment in that case, Steyn L.J. referred also to criticism of the rule by academics and lawyers.[32] His Lordship went on to make the point that the civil law systems of the members of the European Union recognise such contracts, leaving England at a disadvantage in a single commercial market.

---

19 *Olsson v. Dyson* (1969) 120 C.L.R. 365 at 393 per Windeyer J.
20 *London Drugs Ltd. v. Kuehne & Nagel International Ltd.* (1992) 97 D.L.R. (4th) 261 at 351.
21 *Trident General Insurance Co. Ltd. v. McNiece Bros Pty. Ltd.* (1988) 165 C.L.R. 107.
22 *London Drugs Ltd. v. Kuehne & Nagel International Ltd.* (1992) 97 D.L.R. (4th) 261.
23 20 N.Y. 268 (1859).
24 See also *Choate, Hall and Stewart v. S.C.A. Services Inc.* 392 N.E. 2d 1045 (1979).
25 *Contracts (Privity) Act* 1982.
26 *Property Law Act* 1969.
27 *Property Law Act* 1974.
28 Contracts (Rights of Third Parties) Act 1999.
29 (1988) 165 C.L.R. 107.
30 (1992) 97 D.L.R. (4th) 261.
31 [1995] 1 W.L.R. 68 at 77-78.
32 Ibid. at 77.

## The Justification for Departing from the Rule

The principal arguments in favour of abolition of the rule were stated by Steyn L.J. in these terms:

> The autonomy of the will of the parties should be respected. The law of contract should give effect to the reasonable expectations of contracting parties. Principle certainly requires that a burden should not be imposed on a third party without his consent. But there is no doctrinal, logical or policy reason why the law should deny effectiveness to a contract for the benefit of a third party where that is the expressed intention of the parties. Moreover, often the parties, and particularly third parties, organise their affairs on the faith of the contract. They rely on the contract. It is therefore unjust to deny effectiveness to such a contract.[33]

At first glance, it might seem that to say, as his Lordship did, that there is no doctrinal, logical or policy reason to support the privity rule where there is an expressed intention to benefit a third party, might be thought to be rather sweeping in the light of the foregoing discussion of the suggested justifications. They may not be all that persuasive but they do not deserve to be dismissed as if they did not exist. But it is important to note what his Lordship really said, namely that the justifications for the privity rule do not provide a doctrinal, logical or policy reason in the case of expressed intention to benefit a third party. In such a case they provide no reason for overriding the parties' intention.

The Law Commission's main justification for recommending a departure from the rule was expressed this way:

> If the theoretical justification for the enforcement of contracts is seen as the realisation of the promises or the will or the bargain of the contracting parties, the failure of the law to afford a remedy to the third party where the contracting parties intended that it should have one frustrates their intentions, and undermines the general justifying theory of contract.[34]

The Commission's next justification for the departure, in conformity with Lord Steyn's remarks, was "injustice to the third party",[35] arising from

---

33 Ibid. at 76. See also *Trident General Insurance Co. Ltd. v. McNiece Bros. Pty. Ltd.* (1988) 165 C.L.R. 107 at 168 per Toohey J. (the privity rule "is based on shaky foundations and, in its widest form, lacks support in both logic and jurisprudence").

34 Law Com. No. 242, 1996, par. 31.

35 Ibid, par. 3.2.

"reasonable expectations" generated in the third party, that is, expectations of having the right to enforce the third-party promise.[36] The injustice is increased when the third party acts in reliance on the promise.[37]

## Other Reasons for Departing from the Rule

There are other reasons for departing from the rule. One reason is the inability of the promisee under the contract to recover, at least in all cases, substantial damages for the promisor's failure to perform the promise in favour of the third party. Other reasons relate to deficiencies in alternative remedies and problems which have arisen in relation to other principles of law when they have been applied in an endeavour to remedy injustice attributable to the privity rule.

### *(a) Recovery of Damages*

The governing principle has been that a contracting party can only recover by way of damages the loss that it has suffered. There is authority which supports the proposition that, under a contract between A and B by which B promises to pay a sum certain to C, A can only recover nominal damages from B if B fails to honour his promise.[38] But the cases on the point are by no means one way, as Windeyer J. noted in *Coull's v. Bagot's Executor & Trustee Co. Ltd.*[39] And, as his Honour pointed out, A would be entitled to recover more than nominal damages if the promise was to pay an amount which was owing by A to C or was otherwise for A's benefit.[40] Moreover, A may be entitled to specific performance of the contract, in which event the restriction on recovery of damages will be of no consequence except in so far as it may be a ground for granting specific performance, there being no adequate remedy in damages.

Had the law as to damages developed along the line that A was entitled to recover the amount which B promised to pay and was under an obligation to pay the amount recovered to C, opposition to the privity rule may have abated. The only such case in which A can recover from B and is clearly under an obligation to pay the amount recovered to C is where the contract, on its true construction, creates a trust of the benefit of the promise in favour of the third party.

---

36 Ibid.
37 Ibid.
38 *West v. Houghton* (1879) 4 C.P.D. 197; *Viles v. Viles* [1939] S.A.S.R. 164.
39 (1967) 119 C.L.R. 460 at 501.
40 Ibid. at 501-502.

However, in *Linden Gardens Trust Ltd. v. Lenesta Sludge Disposals Ltd.*,[41] Lord Griffiths suggested that, so long as the plaintiff established that, if successful, it would be likely to benefit the third party, then damages should be awarded in an amount sufficient to enable it to confer on the third party the benefit contracted for. In *Darlington Borough Council v. Wiltshier Northern Ltd.*,[42] Steyn L.J. favoured a more radical approach, namely that the plaintiff should be awarded substantial damages on the basis that it had not obtained what it bargained for – in other words, that it should be compensated on the basis of lost expectation. His Lordship rejected the notion that expending the damages recovered on securing the benefit to the third party was a condition of recovering substantial damages because the law is not concerned with what the plaintiff does with his damages. But, as things presently stand, the cases in which the promisee can recover the third party's loss are exceptional.[43]

If, as seems to be the case, the law is moving towards the recovery of damages for breach of contract on the basis of lost expectation or restriction,[44] that development would eliminate some of the injustice alleged to be occasioned by the privity rule. It would not, however, eliminate the injustice arising from the disappointed expectations of the third party because the third party would be dependent on the contractual promisee for enforcement of the promise and the promisee would, as things stand, be under no general enforceable obligation to account to the third party for any part of the fruits of a judgment recovered against the promisor.

*(b) Specific Performance*

The traditional reluctance to award specific performance of contracts to pay a sum of money is no longer as strong as it was. The modern principle is that

---

41 [1994] A.C. 85 at 97.
42 [1995] 1 W.L.R. 68 at 80-81.
43 *The Albazero* [1977] A.C. 774; *Linden Gardens Trust Ltd. v. Lenesta Sludge Disposals Ltd.* [1994] 1 A.C. 85; *Darlington Borough Council v. Wiltshier Northern Ltd.* [1995] 1 W.L.R. 68; *Alfred Macalpine Constructions Ltd. v. Panatown* [1998] C.L.C. 636; 88 B.L.R. 67.
44 Compare *Ruxley Electronics & Construction Ltd. v. Forsyth* [1996] A.C. 344; *Alfred Macalpine Constructions Ltd. v. Panatown* [1998] C.L.C. 636 ; 88 B.L.R. 67; *Attorney-General v. Blake* [1998] 1 All E.R. 833.

> [e]quity will grant specific performance when damages are inadequate to meet the justice of the case.[45]

Because contracts to pay money or transfer property to a third party are often contracts for breach of which damages are an inadequate remedy, such contracts should usually be susceptible of specific performance, unless there are aspects of the particular contract which render it incapable of specific performance.[46] In such cases the incapacity of the third party results in the law giving less protection to the promisee and third party than the promisor.[47]

## Trust of the Third-Party Promise

Despite criticism of the uncertainties surrounding the circumstances in which the courts will recognise a trust in contracts for the benefit of a third party,[48] the principle is sufficiently clear – it is a matter of ascertaining whether there is an intention to create a trust from the language employed, the nature of the transaction and the circumstances. Even applying that principle, there are many cases of contracts involving a promise for the benefit of a third party in which no trust will be brought into existence.

## Complexity, Artificiality and Uncertainty

The principal example offered of complexity and artificiality is the use of a unilateral contract to enable enforcement of an exclusion clause ("the Himalaya clause") by a person who otherwise would have been regarded as a stranger to the contract between the parties to it.[49] In *London Drugs Ltd. v. Kuehne & Nagel International Ltd.*,[50] the Supreme Court of Canada preferred to relax the doctrine of privity by applying a limitation of liability or exclusion clause to the employees of a contracting party rather than extend any artificial exception to the rule. An illustration of uncertainty is the way in which further exceptions are being developed to the principle

---

45 *Beswick v. Beswick* [1968] A.C. 58 at 102 per Lord Upjohn; *Trident General Insurance Co. Ltd. v. McNiece Bros. Pty. Ltd.* (1988) 165 C.L.R. 107 at 119-120 per Mason C.J. and Wilson J.

46 See, for example, *Jackson v. Horizon Holidays Ltd.* [1975] 1 W.L.R. 1468.

47 See Collins, *Law of Contract*, 1986, 107.

48 Corbin, "Contracts for the Benefit of Third Parties" (1930) 46 L.Q.R. 12 at 17.

49 *New Zealand Shipping Co. Ltd. v. A.M. Satterthwaite & Co. Ltd. (The Eurymedon)* [1975] A.C. 154; *The Mahkutai* [1996] 3 W.L.R. 1.

50 1992) 97 D.L.R. (4th) 261.

that a party to a contract can only sue to recover the loss which it has suffered, though this development is occurring for reasons not confined to the enforcement of promises for the benefit of third parties.[51]

## Adverse Consequences for Commercial Activities

The Law Commission identified two areas where the privity rule caused practical difficulties which should be avoided.[52] The first was construction contracts where, without entering into separate contracts, the duties of the architect and the main contractor do not extend to subsequent purchasers, tenants or financiers and the benefit of exclusion clauses does not extend to employees,[53] sub-contractors and others. And, in the case of insurance contracts, the benefit is unenforceable by dependants, sub-contractors[54] and others who are not parties to the contract, even though they are included in the class to benefit.

## Criticisms of the Case for Departing from the Rule

It is said that the stated justifications for the reform proceed on a view of contract which differs from the bargain and exchange theory of contract under which promises are exchanged between the parties to the bargain.[55] The third party who gives no consideration and is not a contracting party cannot sue under the bargain theory. So enabling him to sue works a departure from the bargain theory. Instead, by giving effect to the intention of the parties, the reform appears to conform to a will theory of contract. Not that this matters very much. Although the bargain theory, like the doctrine of privity, has informed the development of the common law of contract, the common law of contract can survive even if the bargain theory is compromised.

The bargain theory of the common law of contract contends for acceptance with other theories. The "will theory" has the most ancient lineage. Under this theory, a contract is binding because the will or

---

51 See, for example, *Ruxley Electronics & Construction Ltd. v. Forsyth* ]1996] A.C. 344.

52 See A. Burrows, "Reforming Privity of Contract: Law Commission No. 242" (1996) Lloyd's Maritime & Commercial Law Quarterly 467 at 470-471.

53 But cf. *London Drugs Ltd. v. Kuehne & Nagel International Ltd.* (1992) 97 D.L.R. (4th) 261.

54 But cf. *Trident General Insurance Co. Ltd. v. McNiece Bros. Pty. Ltd.* (1988) 165 C.L.R. 107.

55 P. Kincaid, "Privity and Private Justice in Contract" (1997) 12 Journal of Contract Law 47, reproduced in this book.

intention of the parties creates the liability.

> It is their decision, and their free choice, which makes the contract binding, and determines its interpretation, and its result in the event of breach.[56]

The will theory does not mandate the privity rule.

According to Flannigan, as the will theory calls for perfection and completion of the agreement, the third-party beneficiary (using that term in a non-trust sense) should be able to enforce the agreement.[57] This proposition is based on the view that every citizen has an interest under the will theory in the enforcement of the agreement. This does not mean that every citizen can enforce the agreement but that a contracting party and a third-party beneficiary have direct positive interests, not shared by other members of the public, which entitle them to enforce the agreement.

Another theory of the common law conception of contract, one even more opposed to the privity rule than the will theory, is the "promise theory" advocated by Professor Charles Fried. Fried sees the promise as the central conception of contract and dismisses consideration as having no significance.[58]

Other theories of contract law are the relational theory and those deriving from economic and critical analysis. None of them, as Professor Flannigan has demonstrated, necessitates the adoption of the privity rule.[59] According to Professor MacNeil, the advocate of the relational theory, the privity rule is "unrelated to social needs".[60]

The viability of other theories of contract law and the fact that none of them mandates the privity rule are significant. It is equally significant that the foundation for the opposition to the elimination of the privity rule rests substantially, if not wholly, on the bargain/exchange theory of contract which is itself subject to contention and was re-invigorated by the decision in *Tweddle v. Atkinson.* It was that decision which strengthened the bargain/exchange theory vis-à-vis the will theory.[61]

It follows that discarding the privity rule is at variance with only one of the competing theories of contract law, that being the very theory which is centred on the privity rule and its close relationship with the consideration rule.

---

56 P.S. Atiyah, "Contracts, Promises and the Law of Obligations" (1978) 94 L.Q.R. 193 at 195.

57 R. Flannigan, "Privity – The End of an Era (Error)" (1987) 103 L.Q.R. 564 at 583.

58 C. Fried, *Contracts as Promise*, Harvard, 1981 at 5-6, 38.

59 R. Flannigan, "Privity – The End of an Era (Error)" (1987) 103 L.Q.R. 564 at 587-592.

60 I.R. MacNeil, Contracts: Exchange Transactions and Relations (2nd ed), 1978 at 333.

61 Ibid. at 56-61; and see R. Flannigan, "Privity – The End of an Era (Error)", (1987) 103 L.Q.R. 564 at 583.

## Other Criticisms of Reform

Critics also assert that the reform moves the focus of contract law away from the private interests of the contracting parties to public interests as well. Central to this criticism is the idea that the Law Commission's justification that the reform gives effect to the intentions of the parties is an incomplete statement of the position. By permitting the third party to sue, a new dimension is added. The third party sues not to give effect to the private interests of the parties, but to realise his interests.[62]

In this respect, there is a departure from the concept of a contract as a bargain under which obligations are privately assumed, not imposed by law. So the contractual relationship ceases to be simply a private relationship created by the parties and becomes a larger one including others who are affected by the relationship created by the parties to the agreement. This change is not inconsistent with the will theory.

As already mentioned,

> there is a public interest, implicit in will theory, in seeing to the enforcement of individual agreements in order to maintain the integrity of the contracting process.[63]

In other words, there is a public interest in seeing that a promise to a third party is enforceable by the third party.

The criticism that the reform moves contract law from the sphere of private interests into the realm of public interests is once again based on the bargain/exchange theory. The criticism assumes, mistakenly in my view, that the theory has been and continues to be an indispensable core element of English contract law.

That assumption also underlies the criticism that the reform, by giving effect to the intentions of the contracting parties, does not define a justifying relationship between the promisor and the third party.[64] The answer is that the relationship is one in which the third party is the intended beneficiary of a promise made by the promisor, the promise being intended by the contracting parties to be enforceable, thereby generating expectations in the third party. It is not to the point to say that thejustice of the third party's claim is not determined by the intentions of the parties that

---

62 P. Kincaid, Ibid. at 57.
63 R. Flannigan, Ibid.
64 P. Kincaid, "Privity Reform in England" (2000) 116 L.Q.R. 43 at 45, reproduced in this book.

it should have a cause of action. It is rational that the law should define what is just by reference to the intentions of the contracting parties on the footing that it will generate expectations in a third party which should not be disappointed. It may well be that the reform indicates a shift from a restricted focus on the private interests of contracting parties to a broader public interest perspective of contract law. If so, this would not be the first such shift.

Critics of the reform have also drawn attention to suggested inadequacies in the justification based on expectations and reliance. The point is that

> expectations in the absence of privity or consideration do not serve as a justification for giving a cause of action.[65]

Disappointed expectations without more cannot be a cause of action.[66] If, however, the disappointed expectations arise from non-performance of a promise which was intended to be binding, even if it is a promise made to a person who is a stranger to the contract and to the consideration, there is a justification for allowing the right to sue, at least when the parties make their intention in that respect clear. The argument that the expectations of a third party who is not a party to the contract and provides no consideration are not a justification for creating a cause of action in the third party stems from the view that bargain and exchange are central to our thinking about contract. As the deficiencies in the consequences of that conception are driving the reform, it is scarcely to the point to criticise the reform by reference to the conception unless departure from it has other detrimental consequences.

The Law Commission regards reliance on a third-party promise as evidence of expectation:

> Reliance serves to indicate that expectations have been engendered in the third party. To require the reliance to be detrimental tends to shift the focus away from protecting the plaintiff's expectation interest to protecting the plaintiff's reliance interest.[67]

The Law Commission made it clear that the justification for making a promise enforceable by a third party was expectation not reliance, and that it was using reliance simply as evidence of expectation. Reliance was not

---

65 P. Kincaid, "Privity and Private Justice in Contract" (1997) Journal of Contract Law 47 at 51.

66 J.H. Baker, "From Sanctity of Contract to Reasonable Expectation?" (1979) C.L.P. 17 at 24.

67 Law Com. No. 242, 1996, par. 9.19.

advanced as an alternative to expectation.

In any event, even if reliance were advanced as an alternative justification to expectation, it would not necessarily follow that a remedy by way of damages should take the form of recouping reliance loss, as distinct from protecting the plaintiff's expectation interest. In the area of promissory estoppel, there is an on-going debate as to whether remedies should protect the reliance or the expectation interest.[68] There is growing support for the view that, in cases of estoppel by representation, relief should be granted with a view to protecting the expectation interest. In view of this development, the Law Commission's reference to reliance is not vulnerable to criticism. The reference, in any event, treated reliance as no more than evidence of expectation on the part of the third party.

## Conditions According to which Third-Party Enforcement is Permitted

The Contracts (Rights of Third Parties) Act 1999 adopts a test of enforceability by a third party which contains two elements. The third party has the right (a) where it is given to him by an express term of the contract or (b) where the provision to be enforced purports to confer a benefit on the third party and the third party is expressly identified as a beneficiary of that provision by name, class or "particular" description provided that in that case there shall be no right of enforceability where, on the proper construction of the contract, it appears that the contracting parties did not intend the third party to have that right.[69] In the absence of the contract expressly conferring a right to sue, the statutory right rests on a presumption that the parties intended that there should be such a right where the contract purports to confer a benefit on the third party. The cases in which the presumption will be rebutted should be rare. The third party can enforce limitation or exception clauses.[70]

The consequences of third-party enforcement on variation or cancellation have always been thought to be a problem. Under the Act, the parties cannot vary the contract so as to alter the third party's rights without the third party's consent once the third party communicates his assent to the express term to the promisor, or if the promisor is aware, or reasonably could have foreseen, that the third party has relied on the term.[71]

No doubt there will be some questions of interpretation which will

---

68 See *Commonwealth v. Verwayen* (1990) 170 C.L.R. 394. Compare 415-416 per Mason C.J. and 429-430 per Brennan J. with 441-443 per Deane J.

69 S. 1.

70 S. 1(6).

71 S. 2.

require clarification by judicial decision.[72] But if the New Zealand experience of the *Contracts (Privity) Act* 1982 is any guide, these questions will not constitute a major difficulty. Nor does it appear that the statutory régime will generate practical difficulties.

## Conclusion

Because the reform of the privity rule has been carefully tailored to leave the consideration rule in place, the reform is unlikely to have a radical or detrimental impact on the operation of the common law of contract. Indeed, the reform is likely to remedy injustice and to overcome substantially some existing complexities in the law. At the same time, the reform, based as it is on the intentions and expectations of the parties (as well as of the third party), is consistent with the will theory of contract law. On the other hand, the statutory régime, notably in restricting the rights of the parties to vary and rescind the contract, has generated an element of complexity into the theory underlying contract law. In this respect, the reform has subtracted from the conception of contract as the autonomous creation of the parties, imposing new rights and obligations on that construct and, in that way, altering the rights, obligations and liabilities that have hitherto arisen from that construct. What consequences that alteration will have remains to be seen. It is unlikely that the law of contract will unravel, though it may become less theoretically coherent. After all practicality, if not pragmatism, rather than theoretical coherence, has been the hallmark of judicial development of the common law of contract.

72 See D. Dyer, "Pulling the privity thread: will contract law unravel?" [1999] I.T.L.Q. 105.

# 6 Searching for the Principles Behind Privity Reform

CATHERINE MITCHELL

## Introduction

The Contracts (Rights of Third Parties) Act, which received royal assent in November 1999, has finally conferred on certain third parties a general right to enforce a contractual term, thus ending the tenacious hold of the doctrine of privity of contract on English contract law. The Act follows the recommendation of the U.K. Law Commission in their 1996 report that third parties be given rights to enforce contracts in circumstances when the contract expressly provides that the third party may enforce or when the contract confers a benefit upon the third party.[1] Importantly, the Act implements the report's recommendation as to when the third-party right will "crystallise", that is, the point at which the contracting parties cannot alter or revoke the third party's right to enforce without the third party's consent.[2] Although there had been signs in case law that the English judiciary were gearing up to make an assault upon privity, legislative reform makes judicial intervention unnecessary.[3] The advantage of the legislative route to reform is that a novel principle can be imposed onto the

---

1 Privity of Contract: Contracts for the Benefit of Third Parties Law Com No. 242 Cm 3329 (London: HMSO, 1996), hereafter Law Com 242, para. 7.6. The test of enforcement is enacted in s.1(1) of the Act. The attempt to reform privity in English law has a long history. Commentaries on the history of the doctrine and previous attempts at reform can be found in J. Beatson, "Reforming the Law of Contracts for the Benefit of Third Parties: A Second Bite at the Cherry" (1992) 45 C.L.P. 1 and R. Flannigan, "Privity – The End of An Era (Error)" (1987) 103 L.Q.R. 564.

2 Law Com 242, para. 9.26 and s. 2(1) of the Act.

3 See, for example, the comments of Lord Goff in *The Mahkutai* [1996] 3 All E.R. 502 at p. 512 and Steyn LJ (now Lord Steyn) in *Darlington B. C. v. Wiltshier Northern Ltd.* [1995] 1 W.L.R. 68 at p. 76. In this regard, English judges have been inspired by judicial relaxation of the privity rule elsewhere, notably by the Supreme Court of Canada in *London Drugs Ltd. v. Kuehne & Nagel International Ltd.* (1993) 97 D.L.R. (4th) 261 and by the High Court of Australia in *Trident General Insurance Co. Ltd. v. McNiece Bros. Pty. Ltd.* (1988) 165 C.L.R. 107.

discrete area of third-party rights in contract.[4] The great weakness of the common law on privity was that while much judicial ingenuity was demonstrated in creating ways to circumvent the third-party rule in specific cases, the question of whether any general principle justified these departures from doctrine was never satisfactorily answered. Instead, the judicial approach to privity was a rather *ad hoc* affair, most of the so called exceptions being based upon the operation of other principles and legal rules, such as agency, trusts and the law of tort.[5] The common law thus represented a pragmatic approach to the question of third-party rights in contract: judges sought to avoid the rule when circumstances of justice or commercial expediency appeared particularly compelling, but denied that any general third-party right to enforce contracts existed (however critical they were of this state of affairs).

The aim of this chapter is to identify the extent to which, given the pragmatic character of the common law response to privity, the new statute adopts a more principled approach to the treatment of third parties in English contract law. This is done by noting the justificatory arguments for reform that were advanced by the Law Commission in their 1996 report, and which are reflected in the current Act, and examining whether the principles that justify reform fit within our current understanding of the nature of contractual obligations or if the advent of third-party rights requires a reassessment of that understanding. R. Flannigan, amongst others, doubts that any reassessment is necessary.[6] My reasons for thinking this may be a matter of some importance are set out below. The issue is complicated by the lack of academic consensus on the underlying principles that explain the theoretical foundation of specifically *contractual* obligations.[7] Given this difficulty, all that is done here is to examine two broad accounts of the nature of contractual obligation – called orthodox and

---

4 "We see our draft Bill as achieving at a stroke and with certainty and clarity what a progressive House of Lords might well itself have brought about over the course of time." Law Com 242, para. 1.10.

5 Thus it could be doubted that these are "exceptions" at all: P. Kincaid, "Privity and Private Justice in Contract" (1997) 12 J.C.L. 47 at p. 54 and Brennan J. in *Trident General Insurance Co. Ltd. v. McNiece Bros. Pty. Ltd.* (1988) 165 C.L.R. 107 at p. 135.

6 He clearly demonstrates some impatience with the notion that "trashing the doctrine of privity would bring into question the whole theoretical superstructure of contract law": Flannigan, "Privity – The End of an Era (Error)" at p. 582 (n.19). Issues of principle are clearly an important matter for Kincaid: "Privity and Private Justice in Contract" at pp. 47-48 and also S. Smith, "Contracts for the Benefit of Third Parties: in Defence of the Third-Party Rule" (1997) 17 O.J.L.S. 643 at pp. 645-649.

7 The problems with the law of contract in this regard have been expressed in pithy terms by P. Atiyah: "contract law works well enough in the great mass of cases, but its theory is in a mess." *Pragmatism and Theory in English Law* (London: Stevens, 1987) at p. 173.

modern – and explore how different aspects of privity reform can be reconciled with each account. This approach tests the Law Commission's claim that the proposals are modest and do not "cut across the underpinning principles of the common law".[8] It may also provide some clue as to how third-party rights might develop in the future, given that the statute is only the first step in reform, not the last word. The judicial influence on the development of third-party rights will be important, not only because of their role in interpreting the Act, but also because the Act is not comprehensive. Section 6 of the Act contains a list of exceptions and, in addition, section 7(1) preserves the common law responses to the privity doctrine: legislation and common law on third-party rights will exist side by side. In attending to these matters of principle more specific questions are raised: Is the prime motivation for reform that the privity rule causes injustice to the third party or to the contracting parties? Does widening the categories of persons entitled to sue have any implications for other classes of plaintiffs that were taken to be outside the scope of reform?

Attention to these sorts of questions, and a belief in their relevance, is based on an assumption that the law of contract ought to manifest the value of coherence. In other words, the rules, whether of statutory or common law origin, should make sense when taken together. Not everyone may agree on the relative importance of coherence, particularly in relation to a doctrine so heavily criticised as privity, but I share the view expressed by Stephen Smith in his contribution that the principled approach to reform is usually preferable in the long run.[9] As a lack of consistency in application is one of the chief criticisms of the privity doctrine, it seems safe to assume that this is also one of the concerns of the supporters of privity reform.[10] Coherence in the development and application of rules is partly, but not completely, a matter of being consistent. Coherence is consistency in relation to the values the rules represent, rather than in relation to the rules themselves. Thus the requirement of coherence is satisfied when, from a set of rules, we can detect the value, policy or principle that the rules pursue.[11] Broadly, it is the requirement of the rules "pulling in one direction" towards a particular goal, or state of affairs. Although rules may satisfy this requirement of coherence, this does not entail that the values, principles or goals the legal system pursues are good, or right, or worth advancing. What it does tell us is that the rules have

---

8 Law Com 242, para. 1.10.

9 Smith at p. 662.

10 See Law Com 242, paras. 3.5 and 3.6; A. Burrows, "Reforming Privity of Contract: Law Commission Report No. 242" [1996] L.M.C.L.Q. 467 at p. 469; Flannigan, at p. 580.

11 N. MacCormick, *Legal Reasoning and Legal Theory* (Oxford: O.U.P. 1978) chapters V and VII.

some overall point, value or purpose - they are not just a group of random rulings, but together they comprise an *intelligible system.*[12] The importance of coherence in a common law system should not be underestimated. It demonstrates that the system has a rational basis and it acts as a constraint upon judges when deciding cases apparently not covered by existing laws. By the development and application of the wider general principles that underlie the rules, precedents can be extended to cover novel situations, seemingly without violating the precepts against judicial creativity.[13] It might be wondered whether the same considerations can apply to statutory reform, given that statutes can deal with discrete matters and can single out sections of the community for special protection or treatment.[14] The requirements of coherence must still be an important factor here. The question of general entitlement to enforce a contractual obligation cannot be regarded as a minor, discrete issue but must be a central, if not definitive, concern for the law of contract. Although the statute neither repeals the previous law nor precludes further judicial expansion of third-party rights it will undoubtedly form the foundation for the future development of such rights. It therefore seems a fitting object of inquiry to uncover the principles that lie at the heart of reform and the effect they will have on the nature and scope of contractual obligations.

Although the privity rule has relevance to a number of situations, not just where the contract expressly confers a benefit upon the third party, my main concern is with the general operation of the privity rule and the simplest case where reform will be relevant. I am not concerned with the technical details and practical effects of reform. The paradigm and simplest example of the third-party rule is probably that occurring in the classic case of *Beswick v. Beswick.*[15] In this case a nephew promised his uncle that he would pay his aunt £5 a week for the rest of her life in return for the uncle promising to transfer his coal business to the nephew. The nephew defaulted on his contract with his uncle. Could his aunt, a third-party beneficiary of the contract, enforce it in her personal capacity? The answer was no.[16] Whilst each case concerning the privity rule raises different practical problems the underlying issue of principle is the same – why should a third party be able to enforce a promise not made to him and for which he has provided no consideration? Therefore, the general

---

12 MacCormick, *Legal Reasoning and Legal Theory* at p. 106-107.

13 MacCormick gives the example of the development of the neighbour principle in Lord Atkin's speech in *Donoghue v. Stevenson* [1932] A.C. 562: MacCormick, at p. 124-128.

14 H. Collins, *The Law of Contract,* 3rd edn. (London: Butterworths 1997) at p. 39.

15 [1968] A.C. 58.

16 The aunt was also the administratrix of the uncle's estate and, in that capacity, she obtained a decree of specific performance of the contract, enabling her to receive the promised benefit.

principle behind reform, if there is one, should be applicable to all the cases, regardless of practical import.

## The Proposals for Reform

Under section 1(1) of the Act a third party (who must be expressly identified by name or as a member of a class) may enforce a term of the contract in one of two situations: (a) when the contract expressly provides that he may; or (b) if the term purports to confer a benefit on him. Section 1(1)(b) does not apply if it appears, on proper construction of the contract, that the parties did not intend the term to be enforceable by the third party.[17] All remedies for breach of contract are available to the third party as if he were a party to the contract.[18] The third party is thus entitled to claim protection for his expectation interest. The third party also has the right to take advantage of a promised exclusion or restriction of the promisor's rights as if a party to the contract.[19] The Act also states that no right is conferred upon the third party otherwise than subject to and in accordance with any other relevant terms of the contract.[20] Importantly, the parties may not vary or cancel the contract in such a way as to extinguish or alter the third-party right, without the consent of the third party if (a) the third party has communicated his assent to the term to the promisor; or (b) the promisor is aware that the third party has relied on the term; or (c) the promisor can reasonably be expected to have foreseen that the third party would rely on the term and the third party has in fact relied on it.[21] In an action by a third party under the contract the promisor has available any defences that would have been available had the action been brought by the promisee.[22] In their report the Law Commission maintained that the third party's rights are additional to, and not at the expense of, the promisee's rights, and the promisee thus retains the right to enforce the contract.[23]

---

17 S. 1(2) of the Act and Law Com 242, para. 7.6 and Part VII generally.

18 S. 1(5) of the Act and paras. 3.30 - 3.33 of the report.

19 S. 1(6) of the Act.

20 S. 1(4) of the Act.

21 S. 2(1) of the Act and Law Com 242, Part IX. The contracting parties may expressly reserve the right in the contract to vary or cancel the third-party right irrespective of the third party's reliance or acceptance: s. 2(3)(a) of the Act. The parties may also expressly stipulate a different test for the crystallisation of the third-party right: s. 2(3)(b) of the Act.

22 S. 3 of the Act.

23 S. 4 of the Act.

## The Law Commission Proposals and the Orthodox Account of Contractual Obligation

The orthodox, or classical, account of contractual obligations is well known and only briefly described here.[24] This account is characterised by a fairly rigid scheme of doctrine that is concerned with such matters as how contractual obligations are created, the remedies available for breach, who is entitled to such remedies and the limited circumstances in which a party can escape contractual liability. This model is supplemented by a theoretical foundation that relies upon the will and (objective) intention of the contracting parties as justification for enforcing the obligation: contract is essentially a form of self-imposed liability. Two particular ideas are taken to be paramount – sanctity of contract and freedom of contract. Thus, under the orthodox account, contract law is comprised of a distinct set of rules that can easily be separated from other parts of the law of obligations, such as restitution and tort. Although it must be doubted that this model can completely explain contractual obligations, even historically,[25] the power and influence of the model cannot be ignored – its legacy is still evident today in the arrangement and subject matter of most contract law textbooks.[26] The emphasis in contract law on the voluntariness of the undertaking, resulting in a binding obligation, naturally gives rise to the idea that promise lay at the root of contract with the inherent implication that the obligation to perform the promise is owed only to that individual to whom the promise is made - the arguable origin of the privity rule. This is subject to an important limitation: the law will not enforce gratuitous promises, but only bargains or exchanges. This requirement leads to an elaborate set of rules relating to consideration and also provides a further reason for the exclusion of a third party from a contractual relationship: he

---

24 For brief narratives on the main features of the orthodox model of contract see P. Atiyah, "Contracts Promises and the Law of Obligations" in *Essays on Contract*, (Oxford: O.U.P. 1986) at pp. 10-16 and *An Introduction to the Law of Contract,* 5th ed. (Oxford: O.U.P. 1995), at pp. 7-15; Collins, *The Law of Contract,* 3rd edn. at pp. 3-7. Chapter 2 of J. Adams and R. Brownsword, *Key Issues in Contract*, (London: Butterworths, 1995) contains a brief review of the basic doctrines of contract law.

25 The model is stretched to breaking point in a case like *Carlill v. Carbolic Smoke Ball Co. Ltd.* [1893] 1 Q.B. 256. The limitations of the model have been recognised by the judiciary. Lord Wilberforce famously remarked"... English law having committed itself to a rather technical and schematic doctrine of contract, in application takes a practical approach, often at the cost of forcing the facts to fit uneasily into the marked slots of offer, acceptance and consideration": *New Zealand Shipping Co. Ltd. v. A.M. Satterthwaite & Co. Ltd.* [1975] A.C. 154 at p. 167.

26 P. Atiyah *The Rise and Fall of Freedom of Contract* (Oxford: O.U.P. 1979) at pp. 681-687; J. Adams and R. Brownsword, *Understanding Contract Law* 2nd edn. (London: Fontana Press, 1994) at pp. 30-39.

takes no part in an exchange. The prime interest protected by the law of contract is the expectation interest: in a suit for breach of contract the innocent party is entitled to be placed in the position they would have been in had the contract been performed. Thus the orthodox model has four distinct hallmarks: the discrete nature of contract law; the defining importance of exchange or bargain; the foremost protection offered to the expectation interest; the importance of the will theory as justifying the imposition of contractual liability.

Commitment to a broadly orthodox account of contractual obligation is evident both in the Act and in the Law Commission report. It is clear from the report that the Law Commission's aim is to create a third-party right with as little disturbance as possible to the main tenets of the orthodox account of contractual obligation. Indeed the orthodox will theory provides the main justification for giving third parties the right of enforcement: the third-party right is essentially the creation of the contracting parties.[27] The Commission argue that the realisation of the intentions of the contracting parties is the first argument in favour of reform and that the lack of a third party remedy frustrates the intentions of the contracting parties and undermines the general justifying theory of contracts.[28] On this interpretation the injustice of the privity rule is primarily visited on the contracting parties, rather than the third party: they chose to confer a right to enforce, or a benefit, upon the third party and the object of their agreement (at least insofar as it affects the third party) is thwarted by the operation of the privity rule. In this way, one of the main aims of the reform is to make contractual obligations more effective between the parties. This attempt to work within the orthodox account is reflected in the Act by the requirement that the *terms of the contract* expressly confer a right to enforce or confer a benefit upon the third party. It is only these terms that the third party is entitled to enforce. Similarly, some of the provisions have the effect of keeping ultimate control of the agreement with the parties. The third-party right will be denied if the contract cannot be interpreted as intending to confer any right upon him. The parties can expressly deny the third-party right, put forward a different crystallisation test or maintain that the third-party right is not to crystallise. Thus, under the legislative scheme, the third-party right can only arise from the contract; there is no mechanism for the third-party right to arise independently of the agreement between the parties, as a tortious or restitutionary claim might.[29]

While the third-party right is, in a sense, parasitic on the contract, at

27 Law Com 242, para. 1.8.

28 Law Com 242, para. 3.1.

29 As the Act does not repeal any of the common law developments relating to privity, it would not preclude a third-party right arising in this way under the common law.

no point do the Law Commission engage in any extended discussion of what a "contract" is. Instead, contractual obligations are understood in the straightforward orthodox sense of a voluntary agreement between the parties, supported by consideration moving between them.[30] It is through *this mechanism* that the parties can confer a right of enforcement upon the third party. Difficult problems that indicate the substantial overlap between contract and tort, or that otherwise bring into question the explanatory force of the orthodox account in relation to third-party rights, are left to be determined by the common law: the position of a joint promisee who does not provide consideration,[31] the remedies available to the promisee in a contract enforceable by a third party[32] and the position of a beneficiary under a negligently drafted will.[33] Because the third-party right is rooted in the terms of the contract and cannot arise independently from it, the Law Commission can keep faith with two important facets of the orthodox account: the retention of consideration and exchange as the hallmarks of contractual obligation and the commitment to a meaningful distinction between contract and tort.

### *(i) Commitment to Consideration as Test of Enforceability*

The Law Commission state that they regard the coherent policy behind reform as the enforcement of bargains, rather than gratuitous promises.[34] The orthodox view of contractual obligations would maintain a commitment to exchange as the test of legal enforceability of agreements. A further advantage of the orthodox view of the third-party claim is that it avoids, on a practical level at least, the possible difficulties posed by lack of consideration moving from the third party. Just as the third-party claim is, in a sense, parasitic on the promise, it is also parasitic on the consideration that supports that promise and converts it into an enforceable bargain. The Law Commission admit that their proposals may have the effect of weakening the requirement for consideration, but this much is conceded only in relation to third parties, not the contracting parties.[35] They therefore

30 "The Commission's proposals broaden the range of eligible plaintiffs who may enforce a contract; they do not redefine *what counts* as a contract": J. Adams, D. Beyleveld and R. Brownsword, "Privity of Contracts - The Benefits and Burdens of Law Reform" (1997) 60 M.L.R. 238 at p. 248.

31 Law Com 242, paras. 6.9 - 6.12.

32 Law Com 242, para. 5.17.

33 Law Com 242, paras. 7.19 - 7.27. See below.

34 Law Com 242, para. 6.15.

35 Law Com 242, para. 6.17: "while formally, our reform does not affect the requirement of consideration, at a deeper policy level, *and within the area of third-party rights*, it may represent a relaxation of the importance attached to consideration." (Emphasis added.)

determine that the rule that consideration must move from the promisee is amended to the extent necessary to ensure the effectiveness of the proposed reforms to privity.[36] However, between promisor and promisee, the requirement for a bargain (and hence consideration) is ostensibly unchanged by the Law Commission proposals. This mirrors other schemes of privity reform where the third party is not required to provide consideration because it is judged to have *already been provided* by the promisee.[37] This concession to the bargain theory, outwardly at least, maintains a distinction between a third-party beneficiary and a gratuitous promisee. In the case of a gratuitous promisee, there is no consideration moving from anywhere to support the promise – the element of bargain or exchange is completely lacking. In relation to the third-party beneficiary on the other hand, the exchange theory of contract is not undermined because, although the third party has not provided any consideration for the promise, the contract which is the source of his right *is* supported by consideration. The third party is thus upholding a bargain, although in relation to him it is a gratuitous promise.

*(ii) Commitment to the Distinction between Contract and Tort*

By justifying the third-party right within a broadly orthodox account a distinction can also be maintained between contract and tort. Whatjustifies the third-party enforcement is the terms of the promise between promisor and promisee: the *contract* must expressly confer either a right of enforcement or a benefit upon the third party. This gives the third party an expecion of performance which he is entitled to have satisfied. As we have seen, the Law Commission frame the third-party right as one created and defined by the contract between the parties and protection of the third party's expectation interest is the Law Commission's paramount concern. This approach is significant because it allows the Law Commission to maintain a crucial distinction between a third-party beneficiary, who will gain rights to sue under the proposals, and a stranger to the contract, who does not. In turn, this exclusion allows the Law Commission to draw a neat dividing line between third-party claims arising in contract, and those arising in tort. The Law Commission can therefore maintain the orthodox division between contract and tort and ignore the difficult questions of the

36 Law Com 242, para. 6.8 and Part VI generally.

37 The Commission quotes the New Zealand Contracts and Commercial Law Reform Committee *Privity of Contract* (1981) at para 8.2.4:"...the consideration necessary to support the contract ought not to have to be provided by the third party; it should be sufficient, we think, that the consideration for the promise be supplied by a party to the contract": Law Com 242, para. 6.17.

interrelationship between these two in the realm of third-party rights.

The distinction between third-party beneficiaries and strangers to the contract can be made clearer by comparing the positions of the third parties in the cases of *Beswick v. Beswick*[38] and *White v. Jones.*[39] The facts of *Beswick* have already been related. *White* concerned a negligent solicitor who had been instructed by his client (the testator) to draw up a revised will containing legacies for his two daughters. The daughters had been cut out of the testator's original will following a family dispute. The testator died two months after giving instructions for the new will but before the solicitor had drawn it up. As a result, the legacies to the two daughters failed to take effect. The failure of the solicitor to draw up the revised will which reflected the new wishes of the testator was, of course, a breach of his contract with the testator, but the testator could not sue for the breach for two reasons; firstly, he was dead and so it would be up to his personal representatives to take the necessary action; secondly, and more importantly, there had been no tangible loss to the estate. There was no diminution in the testator's assets, they simply did not end up with the right people. The disappointed beneficiaries had of course suffered a lost expectation, but they could not sue for breach of contract because they were not party to the relevant contract between the testator and the solicitor, nor had they provided any consideration. They successfully sued the solicitor in the tort of negligence, however, and recovered damages equal to the sum of their lost legacies. In effect, the law of tort enabled the beneficiaries to claim damages for their disappointed expectations.

*White* is given over to lengthy discussion in the report and the Law Commission maintain that their proposals would not afford the beneficiaries a direct right to sue the solicitor for breach of his contract with the testator.[40] Firstly, the beneficiaries are not expressly recognised in the contract as having the right to sue and secondly, neither is a benefit conferred upon them *by the terms of the contract between the testator and the solicitor.* The subject matter of the contract is that the solicitor will draw up the will. Nothing is conferred on the third parties by this contract, only what *results* from it – the new will. While the solicitor impliedly promised to carry out the contract with reasonable care and skill, and had he done so the beneficiaries would have received their expected benefit, it was no part of his promise to the testator to *confer* that benefit on the third parties.[41] The beneficiaries' claim in *White v. Jones* is not parasitic on the

---

38 [1968] A.C. 58.

39 [1995] 1 All E.R. 691; [1995] 2 A.C. 207.

40 Law Com 242, paras. 7.19 - 7.27.

41 This point was recognised by some of their Lordships in *White v. Jones*. See in particular the dissenting judgment of Lord Mustill [1995] 1 All E.R. 691 at p. 723. See

promise but completely independent of it. To make this clearer, contrast the case of *Beswick*. In that case the subject matter of the promise (or part of the subject matter) was to confer a direct benefit upon the third-party aunt - it was part of the necessary content of the contract, not a mere contingency. Thus the Law Commission can safely leave the *White v. Jones*-type cases to the common law to determine – they are beyond the scope of their proposals for reform. In turn, this exclusion allows the Law Commission to draw a neat dividing line between third-party claims arising in contract, and those arising in tort. The discrete nature of contractual obligations is thereby preserved. Part of the Law Commission's reasoning in leaving cases of negligent will drafting to the determination of the common law is that the decision in *White* has given such plaintiffs a tortious remedy, and as such there is no pressing practical need to bring such plaintiffs within the scope of reform. However there can be no doubt that one of the reasons why the plaintiffs resorted to a tort action was precisely because privity of contract barred any possible contractual claim against the solicitor.[42] If privity of contract is now to be reformed, is it not right to ask whether such claims properly belong within the law of contract rather than tort, given that the effect of the action in tort is to enforce the promise between the contracting parties and to confer the expected benefit upon the third parties? As in relation to the third-party right, the action in tort has the effect of making the contractual obligation between the parties more effective.[43] The Law Commission seem tacitly to recognise this with the cryptic remark that they regard the beneficiaries' claim as belonging more properly within contract rather than tort.[44] Of course, the Law Commission prefer that these two causes of action are differentiated by the distinct way in which the *obligation arises* in each case, rather than assimilated by their comparable outcome and practical effect. The plausibility of the exclusion from the reform of *White v. Jones*-plaintiffs depends on the extent to which this differentiation can be maintained. We will see below that, in relation to the scheme of third-party reform, some doubt arises as to this.

## Can the Orthodox Account Justify Third-Party Rights in Contract?

The Law Commission's orthodox approach raises a number of questions

---

also K. Barker, "Are We Up To Expectations? Solicitors, Beneficiaries and the Tort/Contract Divide" (1994) 14 O.J.L.S. 137 at p. 142.

42 Lord Goff rejects a contractual approach in *White* precisely because it circumvents the doctrines of privity and consideration: [1995] 1 All E.R. 691 at p. 708.

43 Per Lord Goff [1995] 1 All E.R. 691 at pp. 702 and 710.

44 Law Com 242, para 7.27.

about the scheme of privity reform. It is often noted that the main reason why the privity rule causes so much difficulty is unrelated to the general desirability of third parties being able to enforce contractual obligations, but concerns the lack of adequate redress for the promisee when a contract to benefit the third party is breached.[45] If the promisee cannot demonstrate any personal loss in such a contract, his entitlement is limited to the payment of nominal damages. As *Beswick* so amply demonstrates, a remedial scheme that prioritises the promisee's right to performance of the contract, rather than just damages for his own losses arising on breach, is one way out of the difficulties presented by the privity rule. The question of the proper protection to be afforded to the promisee's performance interest is one that has recently come to the fore in the law of contract, and not just because of frustration over the privity doctrine. In the House of Lords case of *St Martin's Property Corp. Ltd. v. Sir Robert McAlpine & Sons Ltd.*, reported with *Linden Gardens Trust Ltd. v. Lenesta Sludge Disposals Ltd.*,[46] the defendant breached a building contract with the plaintiff after the building had been transferred to a third party. The question was whether the plaintiff was entitled to recover substantial damages for the breach, notwithstanding that it no longer owned the property and that it was in fact a third party that had suffered financial loss. The defendant argued that the plaintiff could recover only nominal damages at best – since the plaintiff no longer owned the property, it could not have suffered any loss. Some members of the House of Lords were sympathetic to the argument that a plaintiff may suffer a loss in not getting what he bargained for, although this support did not harden into acceptance of the proposition as a legal principle, and the case was resolved on an alternative ground. Lord Griffiths expressed the opinion that the plaintiff had suffered a financial loss because it did not receive the bargain for which it had contracted. The measure of damages was the cost of securing the bargain: "the person who places the contract has suffered financial loss because he has to spend money to give him the benefit of the bargain which the defendant promised but failed to deliver".[47] The wider significance of the *St Martin's* decision

---

45 Smith, "Contracts for the Benefit of Third Parties: in Defence of the Third-Party Rule" at p. 650.

46 Reported with *Linden Gardens Trust Ltd. v. Lenesta Sludge Disposals Ltd.* [1994] 1 A.C. 85.

47 [1994] 1 A.C. 85 at p. 97. Lord Keith also expressed some sympathy with this view at p. 95 and Lord Bridge was attracted by the argument at p. 96. Lord Steyn agreed with the principle in *Darlington B. C. v. Wiltshier Northern Ltd.* [1995] 1 W.L.R. 68 at p. 80. In the recent decision of *Alfred McAlpine Construction Ltd. v. Panatown Ltd.* (1998) 88 B.L.R. 67 the Court of Appeal preferred the view that the promisee can recover *on behalf of* the third party for the third-party loss, rather than on his own behalf for his own loss and that, ultimately, the existence of the promisee's right depends upon the

is that it attempts to place a value on the plaintiff's interest in*performance* of the contract, rather than the *benefits* of performance.[48] Similarly, in the recent case of *Attorney General v. Blake,* which concerned a breach of contract which resulted in a gain for the defendant, but no loss to the plaintiff promisee, the problem identified by Lord Woolf was the deprivation of an effective remedy for the promisee because of failure to attach a value to his legitimate interest in performance.[49] These cases suggest that as it is the promisee who provides the consideration, he is the only one who has taken part in a bargain and, arguably, he suffers a loss if the bargain is not upheld. Thus the Law Commission's appeal to the "enforcement of bargains" as the coherent basis for reform does not provide complete justification for why specifically the third party, rather than the promisee, should be able to enforce the contract and be awarded substantial damages.

Given the present difficulties over this question of the promisee's loss in third-party cases, it might be thought prudent to confer a direct right of enforcement on the third party beneficiary. Nevertheless, one could still interpret the third-party right as a device designed to ensure increased protection for the *promisee's* performance interest in the contract. On this interpretation, the role of the third-party right is to support the contractual relationship and, in the process, the institution of contracting by giving a further avenue of redress in the case of breach. While the third party Act thus constitutes an expansion of persons who may enforce, it is an expansion that is sought to be contained within an orthodox account of contractual obligation. The advantage is that, while the range of persons entitled to enforce a contract is expanded, this seemingly requires no

---

terms of the contract. As an explanation of Lord Griffiths approach in *St Martins* it is submitted that it is not consistent with what Lord Griffiths actually said, which is that the promisee is recovering for *his own loss*. See also the comments on this issue by G. Treitel "Damages in Respect of a Third Party Loss" (1998) 114 L.Q.R. 527 at p. 530. S. 5 of the Act protects the promisor from liability to both promisee and third party in respect of the same loss. If a contract is enforceable by a third party and the promisee has already recovered damages from the promisor representing (a) the third party's loss, or (b) the promisee's loss in making good the performance owed to the third party then the court can, in any proceedings brought by the third party, reduce the award to the third party.

48 B. Coote, "Contract Damages, *Ruxley*, and the Performance Interest" [1997] C.L.J. 537 at p. 550. Coote distinguishes between bargained-for contractual rights (benefits in law) and enjoyment of the fruits of performance (benefits in fact). The problem is the court's ascription of value to the benefits in fact only, not the benefits in law. This analysis suggests that in third-party cases there is the possibility of two different kinds of losses: loss of the benefits in law (the promisee's loss) and loss of the benefits in fact (third party's loss). S. 5 of the Act would seem to have no applicability under this analysis as the promisee would be recovering his own loss, not that of the third party.

49 [1998] 1 All E.R. 833 at p. 845.

fundamental reassessment of the nature of contractual liability. The Law Commission do not consider the nature of the obligation owed to the third party, whether it is contractual or some other kind of obligation. They state that they do not regard their reforms as giving the third party full contractual rights, nor should it be interpreted that the third party becomes a party to the contract under their proposals,[50] although this is subject to some exceptions.[51] This suggests that although the third-party right arises from the contract the Law Commission do not regard the right itself as being contractual in nature. This would fit with the orthodox view that genuine contractual rights and obligations can only arise from an exchange relationship. The question that emerges is whether it is possible to expand the range of enforcement without changing the nature of contractual obligations. This obviously depends upon what the terms contract, contractual obligation and contractual liability are taken to mean. Certainly if contractual obligations are understood in the orthodox sense as arising from agreement supported by consideration then the third-party right is not "contractual". Rather, the third-party right is an exceptional measure lying just outside the core of contractual obligations exemplified by the orthodox account. On this basis, one might argue that the third-party right is loosely analogous to the doctrine of promissory estoppel, which is often interpreted as a method of enforcing promissory obligations extraneous to the realm of orthodox contract law. But this is surely too simple an assertion as there is in fact great debate over how the relationship between estoppel and contract is to be understood. This impinges on the issue of whether the orthodox account still has any explanatory force in relation to contractual obligations.

At its inception, the modern doctrine of promissory estoppel was considered to be a limited exception to the consideration rule operating within an already established contractual relationship, rather than a way of bringing persons into a contractual relationship on the basis of reliance on an otherwise gratuitous promise. In *Central London Property Trust Ltd. v. High Trees House Ltd.*[52] the basic principle suggested by Lord Denning was that a promise could be binding, notwithstanding the absence of consideration, if it was intended to create legal relations and if, to the knowledge of the person making the promise, it was going to be acted on

---

50 Law Com 242, para. 13.2.

51 Law Com 242, para. 13.4. The provisions relate to the remedies available to the third party, defences and set offs available to the promisor, and the operation of exclusion clauses. The report states that for the purposes of these provisions the third party is to be treated *as if he were* a party to the contract, not that he becomes a party to the contract. These provisions are reflected in the Act. See, for example, ss. 1(5) and 3(6).

52 [1947] K.B. 130 and [1956] 1 All E.R. 256.

by the person to whom it was made, and was in fact so acted upon.[53] As Lord Denning later confirmed in *Combe v. Combe*,[54] the doctrine did not give a cause of action in damages for the breach of such a promise, rather its relevance was that it prevented a party later acting inconsistently with such a promise. In popular parlance, the doctrine of promissory estoppel was "a shield not a sword". The effect of this was that the requirement for consideration to support the initial promise was seemingly undiminished and promissory estoppel was not regarded as a way of protecting a plaintiff's expectation interest. However, in *Crabb v. Arun District Council*[55] the plaintiff's detrimental reliance on the representation of the Council that he would be granted a point of access onto the Council's road was sufficient to grant him the right of way. The effect of the remedy was to satisfy his expectation interest, even though no contract in the orthodox sense had been entered into with the Council. The remedy was justified by the need to satisfy the "minimum equity" to do justice to the plaintiff.[56] The suggestion here is that, although the defendants are required to honour the terms of the representation, the basis for the liability is equitable rather than contractual: contractual liability can only arise by way of exchange.[57] Similarly, in *Walton Stores (Interstate) v. Maher* the view was taken that the function of estoppel was not to enforce the promise and gain the expected benefit, but to avoid the *detriment* that the promisee suffered because of his reliance on a promise that the promisor had unconscionably reneged on. Even if the detriment could only be avoided by enforcing the promise, this did not mean that estoppel, at its foundation, was a means of enforcing gratuitous promises.[58] On this analysis, estoppel is a response to the unconscionable behaviour of the defendant and the remedy is variable depending on the detriment that is caused to the plaintiff as a result.[59] Thus, although estoppel may occasionally protect the expectation interest, this

---

53 Per Lord Denning [1956] 1 All E.R. 256 at p. 258. Lord Denning was following dicta of Lord Cairns in *Hughes v. Metropolitan Railway Co.* (1877) 2 App. Cas. 439.

54 [1951] 2 K.B. 215 at p. 220.

55 [1976] 1 Ch. 179.

56 Per Scarman LJ [1976] 1 Ch. 179 at p. 198.

57 Collins, *The Law of Contract,* 3rd edn. at pp. 72-73.

58 Per Brennan J in the decision of the High Court of Australia in *Walton Stores Interstate v. Maher* (1988) 164 C.L.R. 387 at 429. See also A. Robertson, "Reliance and Expectation in Estoppel Remedies" (1998) 18 L.S. 360. Robertson argues that estoppel is wider than contract, protecting against harm resulting from reliance, rather than upholding the bargain: pp. 364-365.

59 "Thus the line between promissory estoppel and consideration does not parallel the line between reliance protection and expectation protection.": P. Atiyah, "Consideration: A Restatement" in *Essays on Contract*, (Oxford: O.U.P. 1986) at p. 240. For Atiyah, this leads to doubt that there is any significant difference between contractual obligations and those arising under promissory estoppel.

fact alone does not elevate the doctrine into a means of creating contractual obligations. The latter is the preserve of exchange relationships and the enforcement of promises *qua* promises. Of course, the other interpretation is that this is a distinction without a difference and that there is no meaningful way to discriminate between obligations arising under contract and those arising under promissory estoppel: reliance can constitute good consideration for an otherwise gratuitous promise;[60] or it is an alternative to exchange as a badge of enforceability of a promise.[61] Alternatively, the fact that the expectation interest is occasionally protected by promissory estoppel is evidence that the doctrine is about enforcing promises and so forms part of contract law. [62]

This debate over whether promissory estoppel is part of contract law, or a species of equitable/reliance-based obligation lying outside, mirrors the third-party reform because both raise the question of the distinguishing characteristics of contractual obligation. For some commentators the issue of whether promissory estoppel is a contractual doctrine is not resolved by simply assimilating contractual obligation with exchange: rather, the existence of promissory estoppel raises the question of whether exchange (and the orthodox account more generally) provides an exhaustive account of the conditions under which promises are legally enforceable. Even if promissory estoppel is viewed as a general exception to the orthodox account, one can ask how many exceptions can be tolerated before the account loses most of its explanatory force. The issues that are relevant to the debate over promissory estoppel may therefore be relevant in isolating the nature of the third-party right: Is the plaintiff's performance interest protected?; Is he required to show reliance (detrimental or otherwise) upon the promise?; Is the main motivation for the remedy to enforce the promise, rather than avoid any detriment? In relation to the third-party right, the expectation interest is the paramount right protected,[63] the operation of the right does not require any acts in reliance on the promise[64] and it follows that the main motivation behind the third-party right is enforcement of the promise in his favour. The Law Commission is content to confer upon the third party the "one genuine contractual interest": the right to performance and satisfaction of his expectation interest.[65] If there can be debate over whether promissory estoppel is a species of contractual obligation there

60 Atiyah, "Consideration: A Restatement" at p. 240.

61 Collins, *The Law of Contract*, 3rd edn. at p. 71.

62 S. Smith, "Rights and Remedies" (1997) 113 L.Q.R. 424 at p. 432.

63 S. 1(5) of the Act and Law Com 242, paras. 9.19 and 9.33.

64 The least that can be done to crystallise the right is acceptance by the third party: s. 2(1)(a) of the Act and Law Com 242, para. 9.20.

65 D. Friedmann "The Performance Interest in Contract Damages" (1995) 111 L.Q.R. 628 at p. 632.

must be even less room for doubt in relation to the third-party right, which has more of the features of a contractual right. The sticking point remains that the third party does not provide any consideration. But even here we can doubt the commitment of the Law Commission to the exchange model of contractual obligations, at least as the basis for the third-party right. This doubt arises because of the provision for crystallisation of the third-party right.

## The Crystallisation Test

As we have seen, the contracting parties will not be able to rescind or vary the third-party right if the third party accepts the term or relies upon it to the promisor's knowledge.[66] On the orthodox account, the only limitations on the contracting parties changing the bargain are those stipulated by the general law of contract – chiefly, ensuring the provision of consideration and avoiding economic duress. Yet under the proposals, notwithstanding that the contracting parties may agree to a variation in the third-party right, and even provide consideration for it, protection of the third party's expectation interest takes precedence if the third party does not agree to the variation. This suggests that the orthodox account cannot do all the justificatory work required in relation to the third-party right. Instead, there are independent grounds justifying the third-party right, viz., the third party's own legitimate expectation of performance, manifested by his acceptance of, or acts of reliance on, the promise. In this context it should be noted that reliance simply constitutes evidence that the third party has an expectation of performance: it is not the third party's reliance *interest* but his expectation interest that is primarily sought to be protected by the proposed reform.[67] Thus the reforms give the third party a right to the promised benefit.

Given the crystallisation test, one might now question the precise significance of the third party's expectation arising from *an exchange between the parties*, rather than just a bare promise to confer some benefit upon him. A person in the latter position is a gratuitous promisee rather than a third-party beneficiary, but, as one is left wondering what the exact role of consideration is in this reform, it may be doubted that this distinction really matters. Although seemingly rooted in an orthodox account of contractual obligation, the third-party right in the end undermines that account. The fact that the contracting parties provide

66 S. 2(1) of the Act.
67 Law Com 242, paras. 3.32, 9.19 and s.1(5) of the Act.

consideration confers no special status upon them. It does not prevent the crystallisation of the third-party right. The Law Commission seemingly regarded the status of "contracting party" as having some importance – it provided the initial justification for the inception of the third-party right – only to empty it of any substantive content for the purpose of crystallisation. These difficulties concerning consideration are all avoided once it is recognised that justification for a third-party right to enforce the contract can be based solely upon the injustice caused to a third party by the disappointment of his expectations.[68] This is an argument to which the presence or absence of consideration is an irrelevance, because it is an argument that is unrelated to any particular features of the agreement between the parties: there is no necessity for either an agreement between two other parties or consideration. All that is required is some trigger to generate the legitimate expectations of an individual – the simple act of giving a promise could be sufficient. The core of contractual obligations would not be identified within the strict doctrines of the classical account, but in the explication of the wider circumstances in which voluntary undertakings to another are legally enforceable. In the light of the crystallisation test, the third-party right is better interpreted as a further development in the relaxation of the strict confines of the orthodox model in favour of a more flexible modern account of contractual obligations.

## The Law Commission and the Modern Account of Contractual Obligations

The orthodox account has faced increasing competition from other accounts that doubt orthodoxy's explanatory force in relation to the modern day law of contract and put forward alternative explanations of the nature of contractual obligations. While the exact content of the modern accounts varies with each exponent, some broad themes and trends can be identified, even if a completely accurate classification eludes us. On a general level, the modern account identifies the need for values of flexibility and justice in contract, and it requires that contract law be sensitive, as the classical model is not, to differences in bargaining power, status, circumstances and situation between contractors.[69] For some modern accounts the existence of greater flexibility, particularly in relation to how such obligations arise, calls into question whether there is any meaningful distinction to be drawn

---

68 Law Com 242, para. 6.15.

69 See, for example, chapter 1 of Adams and Brownsword, *Key Issues in Contract.*

between elements of the law of obligations.[70] Atiyah, for example, while not doubting the force of the orthodox account in contract law, regards it as fundamentally misleading as an explanation of the entirety of circumstances in which "contractual" obligations can arise. On his account, whenever acts of reasonable reliance take place and whenever benefits are rendered, obligations (of whatever type) may be imposed. There is not necessarily any requirement for a *promise* either to pay for benefits received or make good the acts of reliance, for the obligation to be created, nor for there to be an exchange of promises.[71] On another modern account, the basis for contractual obligation is sought not only within a strict formula of agreement supported by consideration, but also in the protection of the legitimate expectations of individuals that promises seriously made will be honoured.[72] Of wider ambit is the work of Hugh Collins. He broadly identifies the themes of what he calls the "transformation thesis". The transformation thesis, according to Collins, describes a movement in contract law away from the classical ideas of freedom and justice in exchange towards a more flexible, responsive law of contract built around the themes of control of unjustifiable domination, fairness in exchange and cooperation between contractors. One of the ways in which this transformation manifests itself is in a loosening of the conditions under which contractual obligations may be imposed.[73] He also argues that the modern law cannot decide whether individual reliance or more communitarian ideals of trustworthy conduct and loyalty to contracting partners lie at the root of contract.[74]

In terms of doctrinal changes the modern approach to contract is evident in, amongst other things, the growth in legislation aimed at greater consumer protection,[75] and in the cautious relaxation of some of the strict doctrines of contract law, such as consideration.[76] In *Williams v. Roffey* the Court of Appeal advocated a flexible approach to the requirement for consideration where the promisee was carrying out an existing contractual

---

70 For example, Grant Gilmore in *The Death of Contract* (Columbus: Ohio State University Press, 1974).

71 Atiyah, "Contracts, Promises and the Law of Obligations", at p. 22.

72 Adams and Brownsword, *Key Issues in Contract*, especially chapters 4, 5 and chapter 10.

73 Collins, *The Law of Contract*, ch. 2.

74 "The Transformation Thesis and the Ascription of Contractual Responsibility" in *Perspectives of Critical Contract Law* ed. T. Wilhelmsson (Aldershot: Dartmouth, 1993) at pp. 306-307.

75 Contained, for example, in the Unfair Contract Terms Act 1977 and the Unfair Terms in Consumer Contracts Regulations (SI 1999 No. 2083).

76 For example, in the doctrine of promissory estoppel, discussed above, and in the case of *Williams v. Roffey Bros & Nicholls (Contractors ) Ltd.* [1991] 1 Q.B. 1.

duty to the promisor. In particular it was ruled that performance of a contractual obligation already owed to the promisor could nevertheless constitute a practical benefit to the promisor. This practical benefit would then be sufficient consideration moving from the promisee to support a fresh undertaking by the promisor to the promisee. This approach is significant in that it marks a shift away from one of the hallmarks of the orthodox account of contract: the strict exchange model of consideration, as evident in the classic case of *Stilk v. Myrick*.[77] Instead, it seemingly endorses one of the ideas of the modern account that contractual obligations can be created by furnishing some requested benefit on the promisor, even if the promisee suffers no corresponding detriment.[78] Lest it be thought that these developments are limited to cases of contractual variation, there is also the case of *Blackpool & Fylde Aero Club Ltd. v. Blackpool B.C.* in which the English Court of Appeal ruled that contractual obligations may arise on the basis of the reasonable expectation of the promisee that the promisor will honour his promise, even in the absence of reliance by the promisee.[79] Lord Steyn, writing extra-judicially, has recently remarked that "in contract law effect must be given to the reasonable expectations of honest men".[80] Interpreted in the light of these developments, the third-party right is justified because there are compelling reasons why the third party *in his personal capacity* should be able to enforce the agreement. The prime injustice of the privity rule is visited on the third partywho has relied upon or had legitimate expectations raised by the contract which, hitherto, he has been unable to convert into an enforceable right. The existence of the modern account of contractual obligations perhaps provides an answer to the riddle of why, after so many years of criticism but little progress, privity reform is finally a reality. Given the weakening of the doctrine of consideration, the development of exceptions such as promissory estoppel and the sympathy of judges to the protection of reasonable expectations, the time appears right for privity reform. But privity reform is not just a product of this increasingly flexible approach to the creation and enforcement of contractual obligations, it is also an important development of it. The possibility of crystallisation of the third-party right must bring into question whether the notion of exchange or bargain can still be considered as lying at the core of contractual obligations. Given that not all

---

77 (1809) 2 Camp. 317.

78 J. Adams and R. Brownsword, "Contract, Consideration and the Critical Path" (1990) 53 M.L.R. 536 at p. 536.

79 [1990] 3 All E.R. 25 at p. 30. J. Adams and R. Brownsword, "More in Expectation than Hope: The Blackpool Airport Case" (1991) 54 M.L.R. 281 at p. 285.

80 "Contract Law: Fulfilling the Reasonable Expectations of Honest Men" (1997) 113 L.Q.R. 433.

promises can be enforceable, it is difficult to see what will replace it. Certainly, the existence and crystallisation of the third-party right does not depend on any acts of reasonable or detrimental reliance on the promise. In addition, given the protection of the third party's performance interest, it is difficult to resist the conclusion that the third party is owed a contractual obligation to have his expectations satisfied and compel the promised performance.

## Conclusion

The orthodox justification for the third-party right ultimately does not succeed. The protection of the legitimate expectations of the third party must be seen as the dominant motive behind the proposals for reform. What are the implications of this for a coherent law of contract? The possibility of crystallisation suggests that consideration is a superfluous requirement to the legitimate expectations of a third party. In that case, it must also be superfluous to the position of a gratuitous or joint promisee. Expectations can arise from a simple unilateral promise to benefit a plaintiff. If the law's concern is to protect the expectations of persons who reasonably rely on promises to benefit them then the law is incoherent if it grants a remedy to third parties, but not other categories of gratuitous promisees. This development can be viewed as following the modern trends in contract law, where expectations and reasonable reliance of parties are more important to determining the nature and scope of contractual obligations than the notion of agreement supported by consideration. In its report, the Commission does no more than hint at the possibility that consideration may need reform,[81] but its explicit proposals go no further than relaxing this requirement in relation to third parties. It might be argued that the orthodox account of contract is not undermined at all because the parties still retain ultimate control over their agreement. The contracting parties can expressly stipulate that the third party is not to have the right of enforceability, or that the right is not to crystallise, or the parties may lay down a different test of crystallisation.[82] In other words, the proposals apply only by default in the situation where the contracting parties have made no express provision. Although the parties can make their own provision for crystallisation of the third-party right, the "default position" tells us much about the kinds of claims, and the justification for those claims, that the law will uphold. The argument presented here is that,

[81] Law Com 242, para. 6.17.
[82] S. 1(2), 1(4), 2(3) of the Act.

contrary to the view of the Law Commission that their proposals are modest, reform of the third-party rule necessitates a re-examination of the fundamental nature of contractual obligations.

# 7 Beyond Promissory Principle and Protective Pragmatism

ROGER BROWNSWORD and DALE HUTCHISON

## 1. Introduction

The two cornerstone provisions of the Contracts (Rights of Third Parties) Act, 1999, that recently made its way through the United Kingdom Parliament, are sections 1 and 2, the former setting out the test(s) of enforceability[1] and the latter the so-called "crystallisation" test concerning variation or rescission of the contract.[2] During the consultation leading to the legislation, most attention focused on the enforceability test(s) and, although there was some debate about the basis on which enforceability should rest, the general view was that third parties should be given a right to enforce contracts that were made specifically for their benefit.[3] In the case of the crystallisation test, however, although there was again a general consensus that some sort of balance had to be struck between the interests of the contractors (who might change their mind) and the interests of third parties (who might be prejudiced if the contractors changed their mind), no clear view emerged as to the right point at which to strike such a balance.[4] In the event, the legislation reflects the uncertainties of consultees, section 2 limiting the rights of the original contractors if:

(a) the third party has communicated his assent to the term to the promisor,

(b) the promisor is aware that the third party has relied on the term, or

---

1 For the terms of the enforceability test, see section 4 below.

2 The legislation takes forward the recommendations developed by the Law Commission in *Privity of Contract: Contracts for the Benefit of Third Parties* (Law Com Consultation Paper No 121) (1991); *Privity of Contract: Contracts for the Benefit of Third Parties* (Law Com No 242) (Cm 3329, July 1996) (hereafter the Report). For comment on the Report, see J.N. Adams, D. Beyleveld, and R. Brownsword "Privity of Contract – the Benefits and the Burdens of Law Reform" (1997) 60 M.L.R. 238.

3 See the Report, para. 1.6.

4 See the Report, para. 9.1 et seq.

(c) the promisor can reasonably be expected to have foreseen that the third party would rely on the term and the third party has in fact relied on it.

To simplify, we can say that section 2 enacts two limiting conditions, one based on assent by the third party, the other based on reliance by the third party.

The relative lack of interest or concern in relation to the crystallisation test probably indicated two judgments: first, that securing a third-party right of enforcement was by far the top priority for English law[5] (particularly bearing in mind that this was what Jack Beatson rightly called the law reformers' "second bite at the cherry");[6] and, secondly, that in practice the question of variation or rescission would arise only occasionally. Having argued strongly in favour of a relaxation of the privity rule, at least one of us must plead guilty on the first score;[7] and, the speculation that the question of variation or rescission would rarely prove an issue in practice might also be correct.

Nevertheless, in the present paper, we want to start by exploring the relatively neglected question of variation or rescission with a view to seeing what it discloses about the underlying theory of those contract regimes that allow for third-party claims. In order to earth our somewhat abstract reflections, we will track our discussion through two such legal regimes, that of South Africa (where third-party claims have been long recognised) and that now being put in place in England.

Our discussion is in three principal parts. We start, in section 2, by exploring the building blocks of a promissory regime, considering in particular the logic of such a regime when we move from a simple bilateral situation to a trilateral situation of the kind that involves a third-party beneficiary (and which might then raise the question of variation or rescission). The key issue here is whether we can protect the interests of third parties without compromising the integrity of the promissory model –

---

5 The Report opens with Steyn L.J.'s critical observations on the injustice of the privity principle in *Darlington Borough Council v. Wiltshier Northern Ltd.* [1995] 1 W.L.R. 68, 76 – particularly to the effect that "there is no doctrinal, logical, or policy reason why the law should deny effectiveness to a contract for the benefit of a third party where that is the expressed intention of the parties". For further examples of judicial calls for reform, see paras. 2.64-2.69 of the Report.

6 See J. Beatson, "Reforming the Law of Contracts for the Benefit of Third Parties: A Second Bite at the Cherry" (1992) 45 C.L.P. 1.

7 See John Adams and Roger Brownsword, "Privity and the Concept of a Network Contract" (1990) 10 Legal Studies 12; D. Beyleveld and R. Brownsword, "Privity, Transitivity, and Rationality" (1991) 54 M.L.R. 48; and J.N. Adams and R. Brownsword, *Key Issues in Contract* (London: Butterworths, 1995) Ch. 5.

or, as Holmes might have put it, the question is whether the lived experience of trilateral cases can be married to the logic of promisor/promisee relationships. In section 3, we consider how an essentially promissory model – keeping faith with the principle that promises should be kept – has been adopted in South African contract law before turning, in section 4, to the new English regime – a rather more pragmatic regime based on respect for the contractors' intentions coupled with a degree of protection for third-party reliance.

Our general conclusion is that, whether we focus on the enforceability test or the crystallisation test, we find that the basis for the legal recognition of the third-party claim needs to be clarified. A regime that adheres to a simple promissory principle can provide some protection in trilateral situations; but, so too, a regime that takes a pragmatic view can protect the interests of third parties. Beyond such promissory principle and protective pragmatism, however, lies the deeper principle of meeting reasonable expectations – and it is this principle, we suggest, that needs to be brought more clearly into view if we are to understand the basis of third-party claims (and defences) as well as the basis on which limits to the contractors' right of rescission or variation should be put in place.

## 2. From Bilateral to Trilateral Promissory Situations

If our thinking about contract hinges on the enforcement of promises and if, concomitantly, our thinking about third-party claims centres on the enforcement of promises, then we should start by differentiating between what we will call a "bilateral promissory situation" and a "trilateral promissory situation". In the bilateral promissory situation, A (the promisor) promises B (the promisee) that he, A, will confer a benefit on B. In the trilateral promissory situation, A (the promisor) promises B (the promisee) that he, A, will confer a benefit on a third-party, C. If our theory of promises gives the promisee the exclusive right to enforce the promise, then the difficulty for the promissory principle is that C seems to have no right to hold A to his promise.[8]

---

8 See e.g., Stephen A. Smith, "Contracts for the Benefit of Third Parties: in Defence of the Third-Party Rule" (1997) O.J.L.S. 643. Having said (at 644) that the third-party (privity) rule "holds that only a promisee can enforce a promise", Smith goes on to contend (at 645) that the reason why C "should not be able to enforce A's promise is the simple but profound fact that A did not make a promise to C. The promisor A has a duty to perform his promise, but the duty is owed to B, the promisee, not to C". To similar effect, see the several articles on this theme by Peter Kincaid, including "Third Parties: Rationalising a Right to Sue" [1989] CL.J. 24, "The UK Law Commission's Privity Proposals and

In a bilateral promissory situation, it is plausible to treat B (the promisee) as having the following two rights against A (the promisor):

(a) an enforceability right: that is, should A fail to carry out his promise, B has a right to enforce the promise (or, at least, to have some form of remedy against A for non-performance or defective performance); and

(b) a right against unauthorised rescission or variation: that is, a right that A should not withdraw or vary his promise (to the potential detriment of B) without B's consent. (Of course, if A has expressly reserved a right to vary or rescind, then B's right against unauthorised rescission or variation is qualified by the express terms of A's promise).

We must also assume that B has the right or power to release A from his promise – or, at any rate, we must assume this if our theory of promising allows the promisee to waive the benefit of the promise; and, whilst this is of limited interest in a bilateral promissory situation, it is of considerable importance in a trilateral promissory situation.

If we accept that B has these rights in a bilateral promissory situation, then the next question is when precisely these rights vest in B. The answer to this question is not obvious. Possible responses are:

(a) as soon as A makes the promise – or, perhaps, as soon as A makes the promise and B is aware of it;

(b) as soon as B "accepts" the promise (by communicating his assent to A); or

(c) as soon as B relies on the promise.

At this stage, we do not need to settle this question and different schools of Contract theorists would no doubt offer different answers.[9] There is also the question of whether the two rights vest at the same time. Again, the answer is not obvious. For instance, if we think that B's enforceability right vests as soon as A makes the promise (as in response (a)), we might think that B's right against rescission or variation vests only when B accepts (as in response (b)) or when B relies (as in response (c)). Again, however, at this stage, we need not settle this question: it suffices to say that there is a question and that the answer to it is unsettled.

---

Contract Theory" (1994) 8 J.C.L. 51, and "Privity and Private Justice in Contract" (1997) 12 J.C.L. 47, reproduced in this book.

9 See e.g., P.S. Atiyah, *Promises, Morals, and the Law* (Oxford: Clarendon Press, 1981) and *Essays on Contract* (Oxford: Clarendon Press, 1986) Ch. 2.

The next step is to try to map this analysis on to a trilateral promissory situation. Before we do this, however, we need a further distinction. This is the distinction between a trilateral promissory situation in which the promissory relationship between A and C is *direct* and that in which the promissory relationship is *indirect*.

Where (in a trilateral promissory situation) the relationship between A and C is *direct*, A (the promisor) promises B (the promisee) that he, A, will confer a benefit on a third-party, C; and A also promises C that he, A, will confer a benefit on C.

Where (in a trilateral promissory situation) the relationship between A and C is merely *indirect*, A (the promisor) promises B (the promisee) that he, A, will confer a benefit on a third-party, C; but A does not also promise C that he, A, will confer a benefit on C.

What immediately suggests itself in the light of this contrast is that, where the promissory relationship between A and C is *direct* then we effectively have two bilateral (albeit linked) promissory relationships, one between A and B and the other between A and C – a phenomenon well known to contract lawyers through the use of collateral contracts to reconstruct trilateral situations in bilateral terms.[10] It follows that C's rights against A (C's enforceability right and his right against unauthorised rescission or variation) must be mutatis mutandis the same as B's rights against A. Granted, we have not yet settled all questions about B's rights against A. Nevertheless, if the bilateral analysis maps straightforwardly onto the trilateral situation (where it is of the *direct* kind) then we can at least say that, whatever B's rights against A, C is basically in the same position.

However, it is not at all clear that we can apply this analysis where the promissory relationship between A and C is *indirect*. For, even if we can say that C's enforceability right against A coincides with B's enforceability right against A, we surely cannot say this about C's right against unauthorised rescission or variation (by A and B) – B, it will be recalled, has an independent power to release A from his promise in favour of C. The puzzle that is taking shape, therefore, is this: where a legal regime sets up a trilateral promissory situation in which the relationship between A and C is merely *indirect*, when does C's right against unauthorised rescission or variation vest in C? And, how does C's right stand in relation to B's power of release?

---

10 Well-known examples include *Shanklin Pier v. Detel Products Ltd.* [1951] 2 K.B. 854; *Wells (Merstham) Ltd. v. Buckland Sand and Silica Co. Ltd.* [1965] 2 Q.B. 170; *Charnock v. Liverpool Corporation* [1968] 1 W.L.R. 1498; and *New Zealand Shipping Co. Ltd. v. A.M. Satterthwaite and Co. Ltd.: The Eurymedon* [1975] A.C. 154. See the Law Commission's Report para. 2.18.

Refashioning the responses that we suggested to the equivalent question in a bilateral promissory situation, the possible answers are that the right vests in C:

(a) as soon as A makes the promise to B – or, perhaps more plausibly, as soon as A makes the promise to B, and C is aware of it;
(b) as soon as C "accepts" the promise that A has made to B (by C communicating his assent to A); or
(c) as soon as C relies on the promise that A has made to B.

Again, the selection of the appropriate response is not obvious. If one of the key elements in resolving this puzzle is the assumption that, other things being equal, B, as the direct promisee, must take priority over C, as the indirect promisee, in relation to A's promise, then it follows that B must have the right to release A from his promise up to the point where C's interests prevail. In this light, response (a) seems to give inadequate weight to B's prior position (as against C); response (b) looks like an attempt to convert the indirect relationship between A and C into a direct relationship; and response (c) seems to leave the indirect relationship as it is except that C's reliance reverses the priority that hitherto favoured B over C.

Two points of interest emerge from this analysis. First, although the practical effect of C's acceptance (as in (b)) or C's reliance (as in (c)) is to preclude unauthorised rescission or variation of the promised benefit to C, the reason why such preclusion occurs is quite different. In the case of C's acceptance, the significant impact is upon A (who now becomes directly bound to C and who cannot be released by B from this independent promissory commitment to C). In the case of C's reliance, however, the significant impact is on B (who, as it were, is estopped from exercising his otherwise prior right to release A from his promise). Secondly, whereas responses (a) and (c) retain the trilateral indirect matrix, response (b) seems to convert it to a trilateral direct matrix (which itself can be reduced to a linked pair of bilateral promissory relationships).

What do these remarks add up to? Put shortly, the upshot is that the integrity of a promissory model is challenged by a regime that allows third-party claims in trilateral situations where the relationship between A and C is indirect. A crystallisation test based on acceptance by C is in line with promissory thinking but C's prior right to enforce still needs to be explained. A crystallisation test based on reliance by C is consistent with B being estopped from exercising his power of release in favour of A. Again, though, C's prior right to enforce still needs to be explained. On the other hand, if the relationship between A and C is direct, the promissory model has a reasonably straightforward application to what starts off as a trilateral situation.[11] With this thought in mind, we can turn to the regime of third-party rights as found in the South African law of contract.

## 3. The South African Regime

The South African experience in this field affords an interesting example of how a system with a deep attachment to the notion of privity can nonetheless embrace, in a principled way, the concept of a contract for the benefit of a third party (or *stipulatio alteri*). The attachment to privity stems not so much, as one might expect, from the strong influence that English law has exerted on the South African law of contract, as on the old civilian notion of a contract as a legal bond or "*vinculum juris*" creating rights and duties only for and against the parties to it. Despite an enduring tendency to view contract in this rather dimensional way, the South African courts have from the outset shown a marked willingness to come to the assistance of third-party beneficiaries under a contract, as we shall see. Because of that tendency, however, they have adopted a construction of the *stipulatio alteri* that effectively converts a trilateral relationship into two bilateral ones founded in the usual manner upon offer and acceptance: A's promise to B is construed as an offer to C which upon acceptance by C affords the latter a right to claim the benefit from A. That construction, and the set of rules that has evolved from it, is based more on principle than on any pragmatic considerations, and despite some powerful academic criticism[12] has endured with little obvious need for modification over the years.

Before outlining the basic principles of the South African regime it might prove helpful to make some general comments about the related issues of enforceability and crystallisation of the third party's right. In any legal system that recognises contracts for the benefit of a third party there are essentially three questions that need to be addressed:

---

11 Cf Smith, note 8 above, at pp. 648-649.

12 See generally J.C. de Wet *Die Ontwikkeling van die Ooreenkoms ten behoewe van 'n Derde* (Leiden: Sijthoff's, 1940); R.G. McKerron, "The Juristic Nature of Contracts for the Benefit of Third Persons" (1929) 46 South African Law Journal 387; J. Kerr Wylie, "Contracts in Favour of Third Parties" (1943) 7 Tydskrif vir Hedendaagse Romeins-Hollandse Reg 94; L. Getz, "Contracts for the Benefit of Third Parties" (1962) *Acta Juridica* 38; D.B. Hutchison, "Unravelling the *Stipulatio Alteri*" (1974) 3 *Responsa Meridiana* 1.

(a) Is the contract truly one for the benefit of a third party? Usually this will be made to depend upon the intentions of the original contracting parties.

(b) If it is such a contract, when does the third party acquire an enforceable right to the benefit stipulated in his favour? Some systems require an act of acceptance or adhesion by the third party as a precondition for enforceability, others recognise an immediate right to enforce.

(c) Finally, up to what point may the original parties, or perhaps the stipulator alone, change their minds and revoke or vary the benefit stipulated for the third party?

It will be apparent from what we have said in section 1 above that the English legislation effectively elides the first two questions (as the test for enforceability): once the first question is answered affirmatively, the immediate existence of a right to enforce is simply assumed and the only relevance of acceptance by the third party is in relation to the issue of crystallisation. The South African law, by contrast, draws a clear distinction between questions (a) and (b), but tends to compress questions (b) and (c): until he has accepted the benefit the third party has no enforceable right, even though the contract was clearly intended for his benefit; it is considered almost axiomatic, therefore, that the benefit can be revoked prior to acceptance.[13] Given this clear difference in approach between the two systems, care should be taken, when drawing comparisons, to ensure that it is the same issue that is being addressed in each case: in a South African context enforceability usually relates to question (b) above; in an English context it usually relates to question (a).

For a proper understanding of the South African law in regard to the *stipulatio alteri* it is important to appreciate its historical origins in the old Roman-Dutch law. The evolution of the doctrine has been traced in masterly fashion by the late J.C. de Wet,[14] the hugely influential professor from Stellenbosch University whose writings have contributed enormously to the shaping of the modern South African law of contract. From this brief history it will be apparent just how far back the debate about enforceability and crystallisation of the third party's right goes.

The basic rule of the classical Roman Law was that a third party could not acquire any independent right under a contract to which he was a stranger.[15] As in English law, however, the rule sometimes proved inconvenient, with the result that in post-classical times numerous

---

13 See the discussion below.

14 See note 12 above.

15 *D* 45.1.38.17; *Inst* 3.19.19 : "*alteri stipulari nemo potest*".

exceptions to it were admitted.[16] One such exception in particular was much discussed by the medieval scholars and gave rise to a number of theories concerning the legal relations between the three parties involved. It concerned a donation of property made by B to A, with a stipulation that in due course A should transfer the property on to a third person, C.[17] The stipulation in favour of C was valid, but there was a difference of opinion as to when C acquired a right to the property, and whether or until when B could release A from the promise.[18]

One view was that immediately on conclusion of the contract between A and B, C acquired an irrevocable right to the transfer of the property at a later date; in our terminology, both the right to enforce and the right against unauthorised variation or rescission vested in C without further ado.

A second school also favoured simultaneous vesting of both rights, but only on acceptance communicated to B: the agreement was construed as an indirect offer of donation from B to C, prior to acceptance of which C acquired no right to the property, and B could release A from the obligation to pass the property on to C.

The view that attracted most support, however, lay between these two positions, and drew a distinction between the two rights as regards their time of vesting: C acquired an immediate right to the benefit, but until such time as C perfected this right by communicating acceptance to B, B could release A. Acceptance was thus a matter between the donor B and the ultimate donee alone: the promisor A could not rely on its absence to deny the right of C.

Of these three theories De Wet strongly favoured the third, on the grounds that it gave the best effect to the true intentions of A and B in concluding the contract, and was furthermore the most consistent with general contractual principle. The aim of the parties, he argued, was immediately and without the need for anything more to confer rights against the promisor A on both B and C. As a matter of principle, however, A and B should be entitled to rescind or vary their agreement before C had perfected his right by communicating his acceptance of the donation to B, the donor. That act of acceptance sealed the agreement between B and C, and precluded B from thereafter changing his mind.[19]

Central to De Wet's thesis is the idea that C's right flows directly from the contract between A and B and not from any act on his own part. It is probably correct to say that that is what the parties A and B usually have

16 See De Wet, note 12 above, at p.140.
17 See *C* 8.54.3.
18 See De Wet, note 12 above, at pp. 141-142.
19 *Ibid.*

in mind in such a situation; but to give effect to that intention within a theory that focuses upon consensus and the bilateral nature of the contractual bond presents obvious difficulties. Insistence on acceptance by C as a prerequisite for the creation of his right is far more in line with traditional contract thinking, since it creates a further bilateral relationship by bringing C in as a contracting partner with one of the other parties. But with whom is that contractual bond formed – with A or with B? Both the second and the third theories above envisage an acceptance communicated to B, perhaps because their focus is on a contract of donation, with B as donor and C as second donee. However, the intention of the parties, in this and in all other contracts for the benefit of a third party, is that the promisor A, and not B, should be obliged to make a performance to C; and, conversely, that C's right to the performance should lie against A. The envisaged *vinculum juris* is thus between A and C, not between B and C; and the easiest way of ensuring that result within traditional contract theory is to construe the agreement between A and B as constituting an offer by A to C of the intended benefit. C's acceptance should then in logic be directed to A.

This, at any rate, was the solution proposed by Grotius[20] and adopted by most of the Roman-Dutch writers who followed him.[21] As we shall now see, it was also the construction that found favour with the South African courts.

The earliest case is *Louisa and Protector of Slaves v. Van den Berg*,[22] which appears in the very first volume of law reports ever published in South Africa. The plaintiff Louisa was a slave who had borne a child by the defendant Van den Berg's son. On his deathbed, the son had extracted a solemn promise from his father, in the presence of Louisa, that he would purchase the freedom of Louisa and her child. When the father subsequently reneged on his promise, Louisa, with the assistance of the Protector of Slaves, sued for enforcement. The Cape Supreme Court had no hesitation in allowing the claim, laying down that

> a gratuitous promise made to A for the benefit of B, accepted by A and B, is binding on the promiser, and that performance thereof, if refused, may be enforced by legal proceedings, if not in its nature illegal.[23]

Interestingly, the Court emphasised that, though the promise had been

---

20 *Inleidinge tot de Hollandsche Rechts-geleerdheid* 3.3.38; *De Jure Belli ac Pacis, Libri Tres 2.11.18*; De Wet, note 12 above, at pp. 115-122.

21 De Wet, note 12 above, at pp. 125-139.

22 1830 (1) Menz. 471.

23 At 472.

made to the son, it was accepted also by Louisa, her acceptance being either taken for granted or inferred from her subsequent conduct. To whom such acceptance was communicated, if it had to be communicated at all, is not clear from the brief report; nor is it clear whether acceptance would preclude variation or rescission, the Court merely noting the absence of evidence that the son had, before his death, in any way released his father from the obligation.

The case that really laid the foundations of the South African law on the matter is *Tradesmen's Benefit Society v. Du Preez*.[24] During his lifetime Du Preez had been a member of the defendant benefit society. In terms of its rules, on the death of a member the society would contribute the sum of £20 towards the cost of his interment, the money being payable either to the member's nominated beneficiary or, failing which, to his closest relatives. When Du Preez died his widow paid the funeral expenses and thereafter sought to recover £20 from the benefit society, which refused the claim on the grounds of lack of privity. Once again, the Cape Supreme Court brushed aside this defence, holding that in accordance with Roman-Dutch law two parties could validly contract for the benefit of a third:

> If once a just cause has been established, a third person may … adopt and ratify a stipulation made on his behalf by another. From the moment such ratification being announced to the promisor, he is bound to complete his promise for the benefit of such third person, exactly as if the relation of principal and agent had subsisted between the original promisee and such third person.[25]

Although the Court employed the terminology of the law of agency, it clearly construed the promise to Du Preez as an offer to his widow which, on acceptance communicated to the promisor, established an irrevocable contractual bond between them.

Any residual doubts that might still have existed concerning this construction were dispelled by the Appellate Division when it applied the principles of the *Du Preez* case first to life insurance policies[26] and then later to pre-incorporation contracts[27] and to *inter vivos* trusts.[28] In *Mutual Life Insurance Co. of New York v. Hotz*[29] the Court regarded the principle as by now firmly established that a third party could enforce a stipulation

---

24 (1887) 5 S.C. 269.
25 At 278, per DeVilliers C.J.
26 *Mutual Life Insurance Co. of New York v. Hotz* 1911 A.D. 556.
27 *McCullogh v. Fernwood Estate Ltd.* 1920 A.D. 204.
28 *Commissioner of Inland Revenue v. Estate Crewe* 1943 A.D. 656; *Crookes N.O. v. Watson* 1956 (1) S.A. 277 (A).
29 1911 A.D. 556, at 567 (per Innes J.).

made in his favour only if he accepted it "for until he has notified his decision to the promisor, there is no *vinculum juris* between them". The stipulation might be accepted at any time while it was still open, and the circumstances of each case would determine the period for which it remained open. Prior to acceptance by the third party the stipulator and the promisor could by mutual agreement cancel their contract. In *McCullogh v. Fernwood Estate Ltd.*[30] the Court added the important rider that if the benefit offered to the third party carried with it a corresponding obligation (as is usual in pre-incorporation contracts), the two would go together: acceptance of the benefit would involve an undertaking of the consequent obligation.

It will be noted that in all the cases discussed thus far the emphasis has fallen more on the time of acquisition of the third party's right than on the prior question of whether he was intended to have a right to enforce at all. The court in each case simply assumed it was dealing with a contract for the benefit of a third party and then proceeded to grapple with the legal consequences of such an agreement. In many other cases, however, the courts have been confronted with the logically anterior problem of determining whether or not the agreement in question is a *stipulatio alteri*, when third parties have attempted to enforce contractual provisions that purported to confer some benefit on them. In one early case, a purchaser of land by public auction sought to rely on an undertaking given by the auctioneer to the seller that he would charge commission at the rate of only 2½%;[31] in another, a local authority tried to enforce a stipulation in a deed of sale that the purchaser would pay all arrear rates and taxes owing to it.[32] More recently, law firms have attempted to rely on clauses in deeds of sale drafted by themselves in which one of the parties purports to confer some benefit on the firm (e.g. appointment as conveyancer;[33] or an undertaking to pay their fees[34]); and a trade union has sought to compel an employer to continue deducting union dues from employees' wages, despite the latter's ceasing to be members of the union, on the grounds that stop order authorisations signed by the employees were contracts for the benefit of the union.[35]

---

30 1920 A.D. 204, at 206 (per Innes C.J.).

31 *Hyams v. Wolf & Simpson* 1908 T.S. 78.

32 *Baikie v. Pretoria Municipality* 1921 T.P.D. 376.

33 *Joel Melamed and Hurwitz v. Cleveland Estates (Pty.) Ltd.* 1984 (3) S.A. 155 (A).

34 *Barnett v. Abe Swersky & Associates* 1986 (4) S.A. 407 (C). Cf. *George Ruggier and Co. v. Brook* 1966 (1) S.A. 17 (N.)where a stipulation in a deed of sale that the purchaser would pay the estate agent his fee was held to be enforceable by the agent either as a *stipulatio alteri* or as a distinct collateral contract in his favour – an interesting example of what we have termed a direct trilateral promissory situation.

35 *Consolidated Frame Cotton Corporation Ltd. v. Sithole* 1985 (2) S.A. 18 (N.).

In all of these cases the claims of the third parties were denied. The courts have consistently ruled that in order to constitute a *stipulatio alteri* it is not sufficient that the contract confers some incidental benefit or advantage upon the third party; nor even that the contract is intended to benefit the third party. What is required, according to these cases, is a mutual intention to create an enforceable obligation in favour of the third party: a *vinculum juris* compelling the promisor to make a performance to the third party, and giving the latter an enforceable right to demand the performance. For, as Schreiner J.A. explained in a leading case,

> ... what is not very appropriately styled a contract for the benefit of a third person is not simply a contract designed to benefit a third person; it is a contract between two persons that is designed to enable a third person to come in as a party to a contract with one of the other two.[36]

This test comes close to the so-called "dual intention" test of enforceability originally proposed by the English Law Commission,[37] and automatically excludes a large number of claims, for example that of a disappointed beneficiary under a negligently drafted will,[38] or of an owner against a subcontractor.[39]

Assuming the existence of a true contract for the benefit of a third party, as outlined above, the legal consequences according to the case law may be summarised as follows:

(a) Until the third party C has communicated his acceptance of the benefit to the promisor A, he acquires no enforceable right under the agreement, and B may release A from his obligation, or A and B acting in concert may vary or rescind their agreement.[40]

---

36 *Crookes N.O. v. Watson* 1956 (1) S.A. 277 (A), at 291. This formulation of the test has often been cited with approval in subsequent cases: see e.g. *Joel Melamed and Hurwitz v. Cleveland Estates (Pty.) Ltd.* 1984 (3) S.A. 155 (A)at 172 and the cases cited there. See also, generally, *Jankelow v. Binder, Gering and Co.* 1927 T.P.D. 364; *Salisbury Bottling Co. (Pvt) Ltd. v. Lomagundi Distributors (Pvt) Ltd.* 1965 (3) S.A. 503 (S.R.).

37 See section 4 below.

38 Cf. Owen Rogers, "The Action of the Disappointed Beneficiary" (1986) 103 *South African Law Journal* 583, at 594. Such claims have been recognised in tort by the South African courts: see *Pretorius v. McCallum* (unreported C.P.D. case no.7173/94) ; *Ries v. Boland Bank P.K.S. Ltd.* (C.P.D. case no. 6435/98, as yet unreported).

39 Cf *Lillicrap, Wassenaar and Partners v. Pilkington Brothers (S.A.) (Pty.) Ltd.* 1985 (1) S.A. 475 (A).

40 *Mutual Life Insurance Co. of New York v. Hotz* 1911 A.D. 556 at 567; *McCullogh v. Fernwood Estate Ltd.* 1920 A.D. 204 at 215; *Commissioner for Inland Revenue v. Estate Crewe* 1943 A.D. 656 at 674, 683; *Crookes N.O. v. Watson* 1956 (1) S.A. 277 (A) at 287-288, 306.

(b) The relationship between A and B will depend upon the terms of their agreement.[41] Generally, however, B will have no right to demand performance to himself, personally; his right, pending acceptance by C, is to insist that A should do nothing in conflict with his promise.[42] Whether, after acceptance by C, B can compel performance to C is not altogether clear.[43]

(c) Once C has accepted the benefit in his favour, by communicating his acceptance to A, he acquires an independent right to enforce performance to him by A.[44] According to some cases,[45] C becomes a party "to the contract", suggesting a trilateral relationship; others[46] state that C's contract is with one of the other two parties – presumably with A, in view of the preferred construction of the *stipulatio alteri*, and the frequently encountered suggestion that on acceptance by C, B drops out of the picture altogether.[47] Again, however, it is submitted that there need not and probably cannot be any fixed pattern, for the rights and duties of the parties, and the duration of their various relationships,

---

41 *Nine Hundred Umgeni Road v. Bali* 1986 (1) S.A. 1 at 6, approving what was stated in *Gardner v. Richardt* 1974 (3) S.A. 768 (C) at 770.

42 *African Universal Stores v. Dean* 1926 C.P.D. 390; *Semer v. Retief* 1948 (1) S.A. 182 (C) at 194.

43 In principle it seems that B should have such a right, for it constitutes specific performance of the obligation which A undertook to B (i.e. to confer the benefit on C) – cf. De Wet note 12 above at 3. However in *Nine Hundred Umgeni Road v. Bali* 1986 (1) S.A. 1 (A) at 6 it was said that in the case of a pre-incorporation contract the trustee (i.e. the promisee) "is not personally entitled to exact or obliged to render the performance which is stipulated for the third party unless the contract so provides"; and in *Byworth v. Stevenson* (1902) 19 S.C. 18, where S had promised B that he would make a donation to a hospital, it was held in an action brought by B for an order compelling S to make the payment, that no such order could be granted save on application by the hospital authorities. See too *Baikie v. Pretoria Municipality* 1921 T.P.D. 376 at 380.

44 *Tradesmen's Benefit Society v. Du Preez* (1887) 5 S.C. 269; *Mutual Life Insurance Co. of New York v.* Hotz 1911 A.D. 556 at 567; *Crookes N.O. v. Watson* 1956 (1) S.A. 277 (A) at 291.

45 See e.g. *Joel Melamed and Hurwitz v. Cleveland Estates (Pty.) Ltd.* 1984 (3) S.A. 155 (A) at 172I; *George Ruggier and Co. v. Brook* 1966 (1) S.A. 17 (N.) at 23.

46 See e.g. *Crookes N.O. v. Watson* 1956 (1) S.A. 277 (A) at 291 (text to note 36 above).

47 See e.g. *Crookes N.O. v. Watson* 1956 (1) S.A. 277 (A) at 291; *Nine Hundred Umgeni Road (Pty.) Ltd. v. Bali* 1986 (1) S.A. 1 (A) at 5B; *The London Chemists and Opticians Ltd. v. Shapiro* 1926 T.P.D. 690 at 695.

will depend in the first instance upon a proper construction of the contract in question, rather than on rigid rules of law.[48]

(d) Where the benefit offered to C carries with it a corresponding obligation, acceptance of the benefit involves an undertaking of the obligation.[49] This rule requires some explanation, if not qualification. Where the promisee B has undertaken an obligation to A in return for the latter's promise – for example, the duty to pay the premiums on a life insurance policy – acceptance of the benefit by C clearly need not saddle C with B's obligation. On the other hand, where the benefit offered to C takes the form of an option to buy land, say, from A, then C clearly cannot acquire the land without incurring the duty to pay the price. But one should be careful in such cases to distinguish between the acceptance of the benefit under the *stipulatio alteri* (i.e. the offer of the option) and the acceptance of the main offer embodied in the option (i.e. the offer to sell the land to C). C can here accept the benefit of the option without necessarily electing at that stage to exercise the option. It is only once C has decided to exercise the option that he is saddled with the duty to pay the price, but that consequence flows from the conclusion of the separate contract of sale rather than from the acceptance of the benefit under the original *stipulatio alteri*.[50]

The dominant feature of the South African law is thus its insistence upon acceptance by the third party. Throughout his life De Wet remained adamantly opposed to this construction, arguing that it amounted in effect to a denial of the possibility of a true contract for the benefit of a third party, since the need for acceptance signified that the third party C acquired his right not from the agreement between A and B, but from his own,

48 See note 41 above.

49 *McCullogh v. Fernwood Estate Ltd.* 1920 A.D. 204 at 206; *Crispette and Candy Co. Ltd. v. Oscar Michaelis N.O. and Leopold Alexander Michaelis N.O.* 1947 (4) S.A. 521 (A) at 541.

50 See *Kynochs Limited v. Transvaal Silver and Base Metals Ltd.* 1922 W.L.D. 71 at 77, where Ward J. makes the following observation: " In the case where A promises B that he will confer on C the benefit of a bilateral contract, such bilateral contract is not in existence until C accepts the benefit and then A is bound to enter into the contract with C....But this contract is not the contract between A and B". See also De Wet, note 12 above, at 156-157; but cf. *Crispette and Candy Co. Ltd. v. Oscar Michaelis N.O. and Leopold Alexander Michaelis N.O.* 1947 (4) S.A. 521 (A) at 541.

separate agreement with A.[51]

It is interesting to observe in conclusion that, though unequivocally rejected in South Africa,[52] De Wet's opinion is in accordance with the new position in English law; indeed, the Law Commission seems not to have even contemplated the possibility of requiring acceptance as a precondition for the right to enforce. His view also finds strong support in modern German law, which has abandoned the earlier insistence upon a formal declaration of adhesion by the third party, and now treats the intention of the parties as being powerful enough in itself to establish the third party's right to claim.[53] The *Burgerliches Gesetzbuch* provides that one may so bargain with another for the making of a performance to a third party that the latter acquires a right to the performance "directly", that is without any declaration of acceptance.[54] Should the third party not want the right he can decline it by giving notice to the promisor.[55] However, the will of the parties is paramount: if their intention is that the third party should acquire the right only after the death of the promisee, for example, that intention will be respected, with the practical result that during his lifetime the promisee may vary or rescind the benefit aimed at the third party.[56]

German commentators commend the "conceptual clarity" of this "mature manner" of dealing with the problem of third-party contracts, and consider that it delivers more satisfactory results in practice than the earlier law which required acceptance by the third party.[57] It is sobering for a South African lawyer to read that the main obstacle that had to be cleared in arriving at the modern solution was "a rather dimensional and unabstract way of looking at the problem, of seeing a contract as a bond binding the parties, as a '*vinculum juris*'".[58] One is left with the inescapable feeling that perhaps, after all, De Wet was right, that he was ahead of his time, and that South African lawyers, more so now than their counterparts in the Anglo-American world, have become the victims of their fixation with the notion of privity of contract.

---

51 De Wet, note 12 above, at 144-145, 161; see also J.C. de Wet & A.H. van Wyk, *Die Suid-Afrikaanse Kontraktereg en Handelsreg* (Durban: Butterworths, 5th ed 1992) 105.

52 See *Commissioner for Inland Revenue v. Estate Crewe* 1943 A.D. 656 at 674-675; *Crookes N.O. v. Watson* 1956 (1) S.A. 277 (A) at 286-287.

53 See Konrad Zweigert and Hein Kötz, *Introduction to Comparative Law* (Oxford: Clarendon Press, 3rd revised ed., translated from the German by Tony Weir, 1998) 456 – 469.

54 § 328 par.I.

55 § 333 *BGB*.

56 § 331 *BGB*; Zweigert & Kötz, note 53 above, at 460.

57 Zweigert & Kötz, note 53 above, at 468.

58 Zweigert & Kötz, note 53 above, at 457.

## 4. The New English Regime

Adopting the Law Commission's recommendations, section 1(1) of the Contracts (Rights of Third Parties) Act provides that a third party (expressly so identified) may enforce a term in a contract if (a) the contract expressly provides that he may do so, or (b) the term purports to confer a benefit on him. In the latter case, however, the third party will not have such a right if, as section 1(2) puts it, "on a proper construction of the contract it appears that the parties did not intend the term to be enforceable by the third party". According to section 1(5), the remedies available to the third party (in relation to the right to enforce) are just those that would have been available to him if he had been a party to the contract. These provisions, as we have seen, are to be read alongside the qualified rights of the contractors to vary or rescind their contract. What are we to make of this regime?

Initially, the Law Commission proposed a so-called "dual intention" test of enforceability.[59] Under this test, the third party would have the right to enforce only if the contractors intended the contract to be for the benefit of that party and if they intended to create an enforceable obligation in favour of that party (if, as some commentators presented it, the contractors intended to create legal relations with the third party). These provisional recommendations were heavily underwritten by a policy of respecting the contractors' intentions. Although the final recommendations and the ensuing legislation finesse the original test somewhat, the policy of giving effect to the contractors' intentions continues to underwrite section 1.

In taking this approach, the Law Commission saw itself as respecting the spirit (and, to a considerable extent, the letter) of traditional thinking about the basis of contractual obligation. Granted, the Commission does not principally employ the terminology of promises; but the idea of effectuating the intentions (or the common will) of the contractors is in much the same vein. In both cases (promise or intention), it is the interests of the co-contractor/promisee that really matter; and, quite consistently, the Commission resisted arguments that the relaxed privity regime should be based on the protection of third-party reliance. If third parties relied on terms that the contractors did not intend to be for the benefit of the former (or did not intend to be enforceable by the former) then so much the worse for third parties who so relied. And, proponents of a promissory model of contract might say much the same. Nevertheless, the new regime is

---

59 See Law Commission, *Privity of Contract: Contracts for the Benefit of Third Parties* (Law Com Consultation Paper No 121) (1991).

different from that of a strict promissory model. As the Commission makes perfectly clear, it is unhappy that collateral contracts need to be relied on to join third parties to contractual agreements – and the outstanding feature of the reform is that, in trilateral situations, the third party C does not have to have a contractual connection with A and/or B.[60] That said, the mystery is how A's obligation to C is grounded: if it is not necessary for A to promise C and if reliance by C is not sufficient, then what precisely is the basis of C's claim?

Once we turn to section 2 of the new legislation, we find that the treatment of the contractors' right to vary or rescind is not entirely faithful to a traditional common intention approach. The acceptance test fits well enough but the reliance test is more difficult to explain. If A and B are no longer minded to confer a benefit on C, why should reliance by C override their (later) intentions? If what is essentially a gift from A and B in favour of C has not been completed, why should reliance by C preclude unauthorised rescission or variation? Of course, we can say that C's reliance estops B from releasing A from the agreed contractual performance in favour of C, but this does not explain why reliance now has this priority over the hitherto governing idea of giving effect to the joint intentions of A and B.

We have not yet found the key to the puzzle. In the modern law of contract, the basis of contractual obligation, we suggest, is not intention, promise or even reliance as such. Rather, we have to go back to the idea of reasonable expectation to put the different pieces of the jigsaw into place – for the pieces are, so to speak, framed by this principle. Clearly, a moral viewpoint is required from which we can assess whether a particular expectation (for example, the expectation of a promisee that a promise will be performed) is reasonable or unreasonable. Whether or not such a viewpoint can be objectively secured (as a matter of necessity rather than mere optionality) is moot: it is an issue about which philosophers continue to disagree. In the common law world, the sceptics, relativists, and post-modernists outnumber the moral objectivists and full-blooded rationalists, thereby encouraging the view that the reference point for the reasonableness of expectations rests on acceptance or recognition rather than any other basis. In other words, the reference point is contingent on what for the time being is accepted or recognised as the criterion of reasonableness. Copying this relativistic approach into the law of contract,

---

60 See the Report paras. 1.2 and 3.12-3.19. In the former the Commission says: "Our proposals will mean, for example, that subsequent purchasers or tenants of buildings can be given rights to enforce an architect's or building contractor's contractual obligations without the cost, complexity and inconvenience of a large number of separate contracts...."

the principle of reasonable expectations operates with three reference points: (i) at widest, expectations are relative to the community's recognised standards of fair dealing (and it is these ideas that support inter alia the idea that a promise represents a binding commitment); (ii) less broadly, where business sectors have their own local standards of fair dealing, their own customs and practices, expectations are judged reasonable or not relative to these sectoral norms; and (iii) most proximately, where the parties themselves act in ways which create certain expectations in their fellow contractors, then the signals sent between the parties (in the light of their inter-subjective understanding) serve as a reference point for the reasonableness of particular expectations.[61]

Now, when the law is framed by the principle of reasonable expectation understood in this relativistic way, there is no intrinsic obligatory magic in the promise given by A to B (in favour of C), the joint intentions of A and B (to confer a benefit on C), or reliance by C. In each case, C forms an expectation that a benefit is to be conferred, alongside which C may well form an expectation that he has a *right* to enforce performance and a *right* to veto variation or rescission on the part of A and B. However, a mere expectation falls short of a justified expectation;[62] and whether these latter expectations of *entitlement* are reasonable (or justified) has to be judged in the light of the material reference points, starting with the community's standards of fair dealing. If those standards hinge on the obligatory nature of promises or common intentions, then one might expect the law of contract to follow suit by designing its privity regime along bilateral (or *direct* trilateral) lines. However, if the community's standards of fair dealing are more pluralistic (in the sense of being multi-factored) then the law may well incorporate *indirect* trilateral elements.

Although the modern English law of contract is framed by the principle of reasonable expectation, its doctrinal particulars are not always straightforward copies of the community's standards of fair dealing. These standards are mediated by the imperatives of legal culture, in particular by the law's concern with doctrinal calculability. As is well known, English law tends to eschew general principles of fair dealing (principles such as those requiring good faith or prohibiting unconscionable conduct) and this was quite clearly one of the considerations that shaped the new English

---

61 For a fuller statement of this view, see *The Law of Contract* (Butterworths Common Law Series) (London: Butterworths, 1999) Ch. 1 passim.

62 A point well made in Peter Kincaid, "Privity and Private Justice in Contract" (1997) 12 J.C.L. 47, at 51.

privity regime.[63] The Law Commission made no secret of the fact that it wished to open up third-party rights on a narrow front, in the belief that such a cautious start would build on a solid consensus.[64] Accordingly, whilst the protection of third-party reliance might have some support in the community's sense of fair dealing, the scope of the idea is more difficult to determine (and draft) – hence the enforceability test is drafted in a way that not only taps into a strongly supported principle of fair dealing but also avoids opening up third-party rights in a way that is difficult to contain. When the Law Commission moved on to address the crystallisation test, it found that consultees lacked a clear sense of what fair dealing required, although the protection of third-party reliance was again part of the picture. At this second stage of the relaxed regime, however, the Commission could afford to allow in the idea of reliance; for third parties would be able to plead their reliance only in order to veto rescission or variation, not to generate the right to enforce in the first place. To this extent, we might characterise the English regime as somewhat "pragmatic" – but it is a pragmatism born of an approach that rests (at least implicitly) on the protection of reasonable expectation (understood in a relativistic way) coupled with a legalism that puts a premium on certainty and calculability of doctrine.[65]

## 5. Conclusion

In a privity regime centred on the protection of promisees, one would expect to find a close relationship between the test of enforceability and the crystallisation test. Similarly, one would expect to find such a close relationship (albeit a different one) in a privity regime centred on the protection of reliance. In the new English regime, however, there is a real sense of disjunction between the enforceability and crystallisation tests. By the time that we get to section 2 of the legislation, we must assume that the third party has the right to enforce (under section 1); and the use of acceptance and reliance in section 2 implies that section 1 must be organised around the ideas of promise and/or reliance. In fact, though, the

63 For a critical and comparative review of the English approach to good faith, see Roger Brownsword, Norma J. Hird, and Geraint Howells (eds), *Good Faith in Contract: Concept and Context* (Aldershot: Ashgate, 1999).

64 See the Report para. 1.9: "Our general approach has been to devise moderate reform proposals which can be expected to gain wide support."

65 Cf. Smith note 8 above (at 660) where the final result of the Commission's deliberations is described as "a sophisticated, but ultimately ad hoc, balancing of different interests" – such that (at 661): "Any support that is given to the Law Commission's proposals can only be on purely pragmatic grounds."

enforceability test in section 1 is organised around neither of these ideas. Hence, section 1 gives no direct lead in relation to the setting of the crystallisation test; and, conversely, section 2 does not help us to anticipate the terms of the enforceability test (which centre on giving effect to the parties' common intention). On the face of it, the new English regime, unlike the promise-driven South African regime, is a pragmatic welding together of a number of doctrinal strands. It is not, however, a hopeless case. The protection of reasonable expectations is the deep mission of the modern English law of contract and, provided that this is understood, then not only can some sense be made of the new third-party regime, but a jurisprudence can be developed to carry it forward in a way that goes beyond the cautious start made by the Law Commission.

# 8 In Defence of the Third-Party Rule[Ψ]

STEPHEN A. SMITH[*]

This article challenges the widespread view that the common law "third-party rule" – the rule that only the parties to a contract can enforce the contract[1] – is an indefensible anachronism. It will be argued that despite the near universal condemnation of the rule by judges,[2] academics,[3] and

---

Ψ This article was published in (1997) 17 Oxford Journal of Legal Studies 643 and is reproduced here with the kind permission of the author and Oxford University Press. Original page numbers are shown in **[square brackets]**.

* I am grateful to Nicholas McBride, Ewan McKendrick, Edwin Peel, James Penner, Michael Spence, and Simon Whittaker for their helpful comments on this article. An earlier version was presented at a seminar series on Private Law Theory at King's College London and to the Oxford Common Law Discussion Group.

1 *Tweddle v. Atkinson* (1861) 1 B. & S. 393. The third-party rule has a second limb which states that a contract cannot impose a burden on a third party. This, largely uncontroversial, limb of the rule will not be discussed.

2 See e.g. *Beswick v. Beswick* [1968] A.C. 58, 72; *Woodar Investment Development Ltd. v. Wimpey Construction U.K. Ltd.* [1980] 1 W.L.R. 277, 300; *White v. Jones* [1995] 2 A.C. 207, 262-263; *Darlington Borough Council v. Wiltshier Northern Ltd.* [1995] 1 W.L.R. 68, 76; *Trident General Insurance Co. Ltd. v. McNiece Bros. Pty. Ltd.* (1988) 165 C.L.R. 107, 118, 123, 168, 170-71; *London Drugs Ltd. v. Kuenhe & Nagel International Ltd.* (1992) 97 D.L.R. (4th) 261, 340-370.

3 The critical literature is voluminous; see e.g.: Corbin, "Contracts for the Benefit of Third Parties" (1930) 46 L.Q.R. 12; Furmston, "Return to *Dunlop v. Selfridge*?" (1960) 23 M.L.R. 373; Markesinis, "An Expanding Tort Law - The Price of a Rigid Contract Law" (1987) 103 L.Q.R. 354; Beatson, "Reforming the Law of Contracts for the Benefit of Third Parties: A Second Bite at the Cherry" (1992) 45 C.L.P. 1; Whittaker, "The Third-Party Rule of Contract and the Tort of Negligence: Future Directions" (1996) 16 O.J.L.S. 191. A notable exception is Kincaid, "Third Parties: Rationalising a Right to Sue" (1989) 48 C.L.J. 243 and "The U.K. Law Commission's Privity Proposals and Contract Theory" (1994) 8 J.C.L. 55. Kincaid's article on the Law Commission's consultation document on privity, which came to my attention after this article was accepted for publication, adopts a broadly similar approach to that defended in this article.

the Law Commission,[4] the rule is a fundamental feature of contract law. Any duties owed to third parties – and it will be suggested that in certain circumstances they may be owed duties in contract and/or tort – are not duties to perform contracts to which the third parties are strangers.

In the first part of the article, the third-party rule is defined and defended. In the second part, it is argued that the reason the results are so often unsatisfactory in what I shall call "privity cases" – cases where a contractual obligation between A and B is intended to benefit a third party C – is not because of the third-party rule, but because privity cases are a locus for a number of distinct, but general, problems in the law of obligations. The problems arise in respect of the proper **[644]** protection of each of the three basic private law interests, *viz*: (i) the expectation interest; (ii) the reliance interest; and (iii) the restitution interest.[5] In the third part of the article, the Law Commission's recent proposal[6] to reform the third-party rule is examined.

## 1. The Third-Party Rule Defined and Defended

### *A. Definition*

In this article, modern usage is followed in distinguishing between the third-party rule and the consideration rule.[7] The third-party rule is the rule that only the persons between whom a contractual offer and acceptance is made – hereafter the parties to the contract – can enforce the resulting contract. Stated differently, the third-party rule holds that only a promisee can enforce a promise. The consideration rule is the rule that only promises that have been paid for, and paid for by the promisee, are legally enforceable.

On one interpretation of the consideration rule the third-party rule is

[4] *The Third-Party Rule of Contract: Contracts for the Benefit of the Third Party* Law Com. No. 242 (1996). A draft Bill is Appendix A to the Report. The Law Revision Committee put forward a similar suggestion in 1937: Law Revision Committee, Sixth Interim Report: *Statute of Frauds and the Doctrine of Consideration* (1937) Cmd 5449.

[5] I have adopted Fuller and Purdue's terminology because, while it may not be the most accurate way of describing the interests protected by contract, tort and restitution (on which see Friedmann, "The Performance Interest in Contract Damages" (1995) 111 L.Q.R. 628; Stapleton, "The Normal Expectancies Measure in Tort Damages" (1997) 113 L.Q.R. 257; and Smith, "Rights, Remedies and Normal Expectancies in Tort and Contract" (1997) 113 L.Q.R. 426), it is familiar to most lawyers: Fuller & Purdue, "The Reliance Interest in Contract Damages" (1936) 46 Yale L.J. 52, 373.

[6] *Supra* n. 4.

[7] *Scruttons Ltd. v. Midland Silicones Ltd.* [1962] A.C. 446.

superfluous. If the consideration rule is interpreted as requiring that in order to enforce a promise a person must have provided consideration for that promise – in other words, that the *plaintiff* must provide consideration for the promise – then the consideration rule bars third parties from enforcing contracts. Consideration can only be provided by a promisee and, on this interpretation of consideration, only persons who have provided consideration can enforce a promise.[8] Thus, third parties cannot enforce promises. But even assuming this interpretation of consideration is correct, it does not establish that the third-party rule is merely one aspect of the consideration rule. The rules may, and almost certainly do (on this interpretation), overlap in their operation. For it is clear that if the consideration rule were abolished, a rule would still be required to identify who can sue upon a promise and, furthermore, that this rule would treat third parties and promisees differently. All legal systems, regardless of whether they require consideration, accept that special rules are needed to identify those persons who, while not **[645]** party to an agreement, may sue on the obligations it creates. The natural way to understand the third-party rule, then, is that it is the common law rule for determining which third parties can sue.[9] Furthermore, even if the third-party rule is just one aspect of consideration, it is important to consider whether – as this article suggests – there is another reason, unrelated to the justification for consideration, for precluding individuals from enforcing contracts to which they are strangers.

### *B. Defending the Third-Party Rule*

A simplified example is helpful in discussing the third-party rule. I will refer to the following as the "gardening contract":

A agrees with B that in return for B paying A £100, A will do C's

---

8 This interpretation is suggested by, e.g., Furmston, *supra* n. 3 and Coote, "Consideration and the Joint Promisee" [1978] C.L.J. 301. See also generally *The Third-Party Rule of Contract: Contracts for the Benefit of the Third Party* Law Com. No. 242 (1996), paras 6.1 - 6.8. In an earlier paper I also defended this interpretation, arguing that on any plausible understanding of the justification for the consideration rule that rule holds that only a person who has provided consideration for a promise ought to be able to enforce the promise: "Contract" (1995) 48 *Current Legal Problems* (Part 1) 4, 27-28. Whether or not this interpretation is correct, it is clear that the question whether consideration needs to be reformed in order to allow third parties to sue in contract cannot be answered without first determining what justification, if any, underlies the consideration rule. Until we know why consideration is necessary generally we cannot know whether consideration should be provided by anyone wishing to enforce a contract.

9 This interpretation is supported by the Privy Council's comment in *Kepong Prospecting Ltd. v. Schmidt* [1968] A.C. 810, 826 that a Malaysian ordinance stipulating that consideration need not move from the promisee did not affect the third-party rule.

gardening for one year (C is B's sister). A receives the money, does C's gardening for one month, and then goes on holiday for the rest of the year.

The effect of the third-party rule is to preclude C (the third party) from successfully suing A (the promisor) for the value (to C) of A's promise to B: in other words, the third-party rule prevents C from enforcing the contract.

How can this result be justified? The justification, it is suggested, flows from the nature of contractual obligations as voluntary obligations. The specific type of voluntary obligation (promise, agreement, consent, etc.) to which contractual obligations give rise is not important for our purposes: for ease of expression I will adopt conventional terminology and refer to contractual obligations as promissory obligations. What is important is that voluntary obligations, of whatever stripe, do not exist in the air: they are obligations undertaken to particular persons, extending to and only to those persons.[10] A promise is formed by communicating an intention to undertake an obligation. The communication must be addressed to (and received by) the person to whom the obligation is undertaken. This is a general feature of voluntary obligations. In the case of a vow the obligation is addressed to and undertaken to oneself. In the case of a promise the obligation is undertaken to the addressee of the promise. The promissory obligation thus created is an obligation between the person undertaking it, the promisor, and the person to whom the obligation was given, the promisee. Thus the reason that C in our example should not be able to enforce A's promise is the simple but profound fact that A did not make a promise to C. The promisor A has a duty to perform his promise, but the duty is owed to B, the promisee, not to C.[11]

**[646]** That promisees and non-promisees are in a different position vis a vis the enforcement of a promise is a well-recognized feature of ordinary moral reasoning. Few would dispute that there is a difference between B in our example saying "but you promised me you would do it" and C saying, "but I heard you promise B that you would do it". It is because of this difference that we get more upset, and with good reason, at promise-breakers when the promise broken was made to us than when it was made to someone else, even if the practical consequences are the same in each case. Indeed, that promisees and non-promisees are in a different position regarding the enforceability of a promise is accepted by even the

10 On the nature of voluntary undertakings see: Raz, "Promises and Obligations" in *Law, Morality, and Society* eds Hacker & Raz (London: 1977) 210; Raz, "Voluntary Obligations and Normative Powers" Proceedings of the Aristotelian Society, (1972) Supp'y Vol XLVI 59.

11 On the importance of the correlativity of rights and duties in understanding privity, see Kincaid (1994), *supra* n. 3.

strongest critics of the third-party rule. No one suggests that just anyone should be able to sue on a (legally valid) promise and no legal system allows just anyone to sue. Only some third parties should be able to sue. But if there is a difference between third parties and promisees, what is it? The difference cannot be merely that third parties have not provided consideration. As noted earlier, no one supposes that were consideration abolished then just anyone would be able to sue on a promise and in legal systems without a requirement of consideration this clearly is not the case. Nor can the difference be that promisees are more likely than third parties to rely on the promise. Reliance is discussed in more detail below, but the short response to this suggestion is that reliance is not relevant to the existence of promissory obligation. Promises may bind even when they have not been relied upon. The only possible significance of the distinction is the most obvious one: the promisee alone is the person to whom the promissory duty is owed. Thus only the promisee can complain of the promise qua promise being broken. This is what it means to be a promisee; and it is why contractual rights have always been understood, correctly, as personal rights.

Exactly why promissory obligation is personal in this way is not, strictly speaking, a question we need to answer. For our purposes it is enough to acknowledge that this is a feature of promissory obligation. Nevertheless, it may be worth mentioning that the explanation undoubtedly lies in the importance of individuals being able to control, and to control in a particular way, the scope of such obligations. Promissory obligations are obligations to benefit others, rather than merely obligations not to harm others, and as such are particularly important - and onerous - obligations. It is crucial that individuals be able to control the scope of such obligations. Moreover, because the value of promising lies largely in the way that it helps individuals to forge deeper relationships with one another,[12] the prima facie proper way of achieving such control is by holding that promissory obligations are owed only to those to whom they are addressed.

It may be helpful both in understanding the justification for the third-party rule and as an introduction to the second part of this article to consider briefly **[647]** two possible objections to the above defence.[13] The

12 See Raz, *supra* n. 10.

13 A third possible objection, not discussed below, is that civil law systems, though originally adhering to the classical Roman approach of generally denying third parties contractual rights, now all provide for third-party rights. Space limitations preclude more than the briefest comments on the civilian approach. A good case can be made that the modern civil law approach to third-party rights produces better results in practice than the modern common law approach. The question addressed in this Article, however, is whether the common law would be better served by reforming the third-party rule or by reforming other rules. On this, very different question the comparativist

first objection questions the assumption that contractual obligations are voluntary obligations, promissory or otherwise, and suggests instead that contractual obligations are obligations imposed by law, designed to protect individuals who reasonably rely on statements made by others.[14] On this, the "contract-as-tort" view of contractual obligation, the third-party rule clearly is an anachronism. If contract law is about protecting reliance, then anyone who relies on a promise has a potential claim in contract, subject only to the usual tort limitations of proximity, foreseeability, and so on. It is not possible in this article to comment generally on the contract-as-tort theory of contract (but see Part II where I explain how promises may give rise to tort obligations *in addition* to contractual obligations). It must be stressed, however, that the contract-as-tort theory of contract does not so much support giving third parties the right to enforce promises as support abolishing all rights to enforce promises. If contract is about protecting reasonable reliance, then third parties (and promisees for that matter) should be limited to suing for their reliance losses. Only if one accepts Fuller and Purdue's interpretation of expectation damages as a proxy for difficult-to-measure reliance losses can a tort approach support giving third parties expectation damages.[15] Even then, this approach to the third-party rule assumes that contract is not a distinct species of obligation. It also follows that the third-party rule is only one of a large number of contract

---

must tread carefully. As we shall see privity cases raise a number of interlocking legal issues, cutting across contract, tort and restitution. Because of the different ways in which civilian and common law systems deal with - to mention just a few - trusts, undisclosed principals, assignment, the distinction between tort (reliance) damages and contract (expectation) damages, the recovery of economic loss in tort, and consideration, any attempt to transplant a single rule - here the rule regarding third-party rights in contract - must be approached cautiously. Even the most committed common law critics of the third-party rule would hesitate, I suspect, before importing into English law the German ruling that a child who slipped and injured herself while shopping with her mother has an action in contract against the store (B.G.H.Z. 66, 51.) or the French ruling that a patient given tainted blood has an action in contract against the transfusion centre that supplied the blood to the hospital (Civ. G.P. 1955.1.54). What the civilian approach (and the reforms of the third-party rule enacted in New Zealand, America and Australia) does tell common lawyers is that it is possible in practice to operate a system granting contractual rights to third parties. Discussions of the third-party rule from a comparative perspective include Zwiegart & Kotz, *An Introduction to Comparative Law* (Oxford: 1992, 2nd ed.) ch. 41; Markesinis, *supra* n. 3; Markesinis, Lorenz & Danneman, *The German Law of Contract* (Oxford: 1997) ch 4; Whittaker, "The Third-Party Rule of Contract and the Law of Tort: the French Experience" (1995) 15 O.J.L.S. 327.

14 See e.g. Atiyah, *The Rise and Fall of Freedom of Contract* (1979) 1-7; Gilmore, *The Death of Contract* (Columbus, 1974).

15 Fuller & Purdue, *supra* n. 5.

rules that ought to be reformed.[16]

**[648]** A second possible objection is that the above defence of the third-party rule is inconsistent with the principle of respecting the intentions of the contracting parties. Surely if the contracting parties intend to benefit a third party then the law should support this intention by allowing the third party to enforce the contract. This objection misunderstands the specific role that intentions play in creating contractual obligations. There are three ways in which intention is relevant in contract law. First, in order to create a valid contract the parties must "intend to create legal relations". This little-used requirement is probably best explained as a means of excluding certain categories of agreements from legal control, regardless of the legal intentions of the parties (a person who mistakenly thinks that a contract must be in writing can still be bound by an oral agreement), but even if it is interpreted literally it does not support the objection. A mere intent to create legal relations clearly is insufficient to establish a contract and hence a contractual obligation to a third party. It is only once offer and acceptance have been established that intent to create legal relations is even considered by a court. If an acceptance fails to match an offer, the parties will not have created a contract, even if they sign a document stating "we have a legally binding contract".

Second, intentions are relevant in determining the content of the contracting parties' agreement. Such a determination, however, cannot lead to the conclusion that third parties should have the right to enforce a contract to which they are not party since the issue in privity cases is not the content of the contractual obligation owed to the promisee or to the third party. The issue is whether the third party is owed a contractual

---

16 Related to the contract-as-tort objection is the objection that since it is possible for third parties to obtain the right to enforce a promise if (i) a trust has been created in their favour or (ii) contractual rights are assigned to them or (iii) they are undisclosed principals of promisee agents or, finally, (iv) under a deed, then it must follow that voluntary obligations can extend to third parties or that contracts are not voluntary obligations. The response to this objection, in brief, is, first, that the third-party rule is consistent both with the possibility of creating a trust of the right to enforce a promise and with the possibility of assigning a right of enforcement because the third-party rule governs the creation of rights, while trust and assignment regulate what individuals can do with rights once created. It may be that the rules regarding trusts and assignment ought to be reformed so as to make it easier to create a trust of a promise or to assign a contractual right. The third-party rule, however, is not a barrier to such reform. Second, the ability of an undisclosed principal to enforce a contract does seems inconsistent with the third-party rule and with the above account of voluntary obligations, but this controversial rule is not, it is suggested, significant enough to justify jettisoning the proposed theory of contractual obligations. Third, deeds raise difficult issues because it is not clear if they are best analysed as contractual or quasi-proprietary documents, but, again, even if they are contractual they are not central enough to the modern law of contract to support an alternative general theory of contractual obligation.

obligation at all.

The third and most important way in which intentions are relevant in contract law is in establishing that the alleged contracting parties in fact undertook obligations to each other. A promise is created by communicating an intention to undertake an obligation. Thus to create a contract each party must intend (or at least appear to intend) to undertake a voluntary obligation. It is the function of the rules on offer and acceptance to establish such intentions. This third sort of intention is relevant to understanding privity cases because in some privity cases one or both of the contracting parties may have communicated to the third party an intention to undertake an obligation to that party. I discuss this possibility in more detail in Part II; for the moment it is enough to note that where such an intention has been communicated the third-party rule is not a bar to the third-party bringing an action in contract (the primary bar is consideration). This is because where one or both of the contracting parties communicate to the third party an intention to be bound to that party, the requirements for promissory obligation are satisfied. A promise has been made **[649]** to the third party. Thus, the third party is not a third party to the agreement made with her, but only to the agreement made between the other two parties. It remains to add only that it is crucial to distinguish this sort of intention (the intention to undertake an obligation) from a mere intent to benefit another or to grant another person legal rights. If X says "it is my desire and intention to give Y £100 on December 1st" no contract has been created (even ignoring consideration). The same is true if X says "I grant Y the right to cross over my property".[17] Assuming that X's words were intended to be understood in their ordinary sense,[18] the reason no contract is created is that while X has intended to do something (to pay a sum of money, to grant a legal right), he has not communicated an intention to put himself

---

[17] Similarly, if X says "I grant Y the right to sue me in contract if I do not give him £100 next week" a contractual obligation is not created. Nor has X succeeded in transferring a contractual right to Y: X is trying to alienate a right (to sue himself) that he does not own. Of course it is possible for a promisee to assign a right to enforce a contract to a third party. The third-party rule does not bar such a transfer (see *supra* n. 16) and thus there is nothing wrong with allowing promisees who have obtained a contractual right to transfer that right to a third party immediately. Clear evidence of intent to transfer is necessary and note that where the contractual right has been transferred the promisee relinquishes not only the ability to vary the original contract but also any right to enforce that contract.

[18] The caveat is necessary because while it is clear that the phrases "I promise to do Z" and "I intend to do Z" mean different things when used in their ordinary senses, in special contexts a person saying "I intend to do Z" may mean, and be taken to mean, "I promise to do Z".

under an obligation to do something for Y.[19]

To conclude: contractual obligations are voluntary obligations. Voluntary obligations are obligations undertaken to, and extending only to, particular persons. In the case of a promise, that person is the promisee. Third parties, by definition, are not promisees and hence should not be able to enforce promises made to others.

## 2. The Real Problems in Privity Cases

If the third-party rule is a fundamental feature of contract law, why are the results in privity cases so often unsatisfactory? The explanation, it is suggested, is that privity cases are a locus for a number of distinct, but general, problems in the law of obligations. The problems arise in respect of protecting each of the three fundamental private law interests: (a) the expectation interest; (b) the reliance interest; and (c) the restitution interest.

### *A. The Expectation Interest*

The first problem raised by privity cases concerns the proper protection of a person's interest – the "expectation interest" – in the performance of promises made to him or her. This problem surfaces in two different ways in privity cases: the first affecting promisees, the second affecting third parties.

**[650]**

*(i) Difficult to quantify losses* In our gardening contract, A has breached his contractual obligation to B to do C's gardening and thus B can bring an action for breach of contract against A. The difficulty for B is that under the traditional approach to damages he is unlikely to obtain more than a nominal sum.[20] The explanation given for this result is that since it was C's garden that was untended, B has not suffered a loss. If B sues for specific performance a similar response will be given: nominal damages are an adequate remedy because B has not suffered any loss.

It should be evident that the traditional rule is unsatisfactory. The rule assumes that if B has not suffered a tangible, pecuniary loss then B has not suffered a loss. But not all losses are pecuniary. I may place great

---

19 This is not to deny that it is possible to transfer legal rights other than by a voluntary undertaking. Rights can be transferred by, for example, a will or simply by giving someone a gift. The third-party rule is not concerned with such arrangements since it governs only the creation (and not the transfer) of contractual rights (see *supra n.* 16).

20 *The Albazero* [1977] A.C. 774, 846.

value on, and contract for the building of, a lurid statue in my front garden even though the statue lowers the market value of my property. In our example, B presumably attaches some value to C's gardening being done or else he would not have agreed to pay A to do it. Indeed, prima facie the value of A's gardening to B is the amount that B was willing to pay for it: £100.

There is a strong argument in principle, therefore, for courts attempting, in cases like our gardening contract, to assess promisees' true losses rather than merely awarding nominal damages. The courts' traditional reluctance to award significant damages in such cases undoubtedly stems from the evidential difficulties involved in placing monetary figures on hard-to-quantify losses. These difficulties are not limited to cases involving non-pecuniary losses. Consider the breach of a promise to accept responsibility for any damage to goods caused by the promisee's subcontractors. As with the gardening example, the promisee presumably attaches some value to the promise or else he would not have bargained for it. But to determine the financial implications of breach to the promisee entails difficult assessments about the breach's long-term effects on the promisee's reputation and on his dealings with future subcontractors.

It is submitted that courts should not let evidentiary concerns stand in the way of assessing promisees' losses in privity cases. Such assessments will often involve speculation, but a degree of imprecision is better than awarding nominal damages, as the latter is almost certain to undercompensate. In many cases the price paid for the promise will give a good idea of the value placed by the promisee on performance (although this sum must be discounted by the value of any part performance). Alternatively, an order of specific performance, where feasible, is an appropriate response to the evidential difficulty of assessing loss. Specific performance is awarded in two-party cases where the value of performance is difficult to assess (e.g., unique goods) and should in principle be available on the same grounds in privity cases.[21]

**[651]** The recent willingness of English courts to recognize non-pecuniary harm in two-party cases[22] and to allow promisees to recover for losses borne by third parties in some privity cases[23] suggests that future

---

21 In this respect the decision in *Beswick v. Beswick* [1968] A.C. 58 to grant specific performance is unimpeachable. An injunction was used for similar purposes in *Snelling v. John G. Snelling Ltd.* [1973] 1 Q.B. 87.

22 *Ruxley Electronics & Construction Ltd. v. Forsyth* [1995] 3 W.L.R. 118.

23 *Linden Gardens Trust Ltd. v. Lenesta Sludge Disposals* and *St. Martins Property Corp. Ltd. v. Sir Robert McAlpine & Sons Ltd.* [1993] 3 All ER 417 (building on *The Albazero* [1977] A.C. 774); *Darlington Borough Council v. Wiltshier Northern Ltd.* [1995] 3 All E.R. 895.

courts may increasingly be willing to award more than nominal damages to promisees in privity cases. The main point I wish to make in this section, however, is not about how the rules regarding difficult to quantify losses will or should be reformed. The point, rather, is that insofar as the promisee's interest in performance is insufficiently protected in privity cases the reason is not the third-party rule, but artificial limitations on recovery of difficult to quantify losses (or on the availability of specific performance). The problems that these limitations cause can and do arise in standard two-party contract cases. If we are willing to live with the limitations in two-party cases, then we should be willing to live with them in privity cases, and vice versa.

Before leaving the promisee's expectation interest it should be noted that there is one category of privity case which raises a further, specific difficulty in this regard. The category includes contracts of the following sort: (i) a life insurance contract between A and B to benefit C in the event of A's death; (ii) a contract whereby A sells his business to B in exchange for B paying a monthly sum to A's wife C after A has died; and (iii) a contract whereby B agrees to draw up A's will so as to benefit C, A's daughter. Regardless of whatever rights the third parties may have in such cases,[24] the promisee's expectation interest is at risk for an obvious reason: the promisee will be dead when any breach occurs (this is the fact that links the cases). Executors are of course required to enforce contracts made to the deceased, but only where enforcement would benefit the deceased's estate financially and only in order to benefit the estate. Thus an executor will normally not demand specific performance of a contract to benefit a third party (the natural remedy for the breach of such an obligation, as explained above) nor hand over any damages awarded in compensation to the third party (which sum should prima facie be the value of the contract to the third party, as explained above). That the promisee's death makes all the difference in such cases is made clear by changing the facts of our examples so that the promisee is alive – if say in the third example the gift is inter-vivos.[25] If the promisee is alive he can bring an action himself to protect his expectation interest and, assuming that interest is assessed

[24] Leaving aside the possibility of a trust, it is possible, for reasons explained below, that in some cases a third party will be able to enforce a collateral promise made to her or be able to recover her reliance loss. The third party's reliance loss may equal the value of the contract since reliance may take the form of not making a collateral contract or not obtaining, say, separate insurance.

[25] Which is why in just such a case, *Hemmens v. Wilson Browne* [1993] 4 All E.R. 826, the court held it was unnecessary to create an exception to the third-party rule. In *White v. Jones* [1993] 3 W.L.R.730 , where the gift was to take effect through a will, the court allowed the third party to recover the value of the promise (albeit in tort, thus making transparent the doctrinal inconsistency underlying the decision).

properly by the court, recover its full value. It might be thought that a promisee's interest in performance does **[652]** not survive his death, but this cannot be right. After-death interests raise interesting philosophical problems (that are outside the scope of this article),[26] but their existence seems incontrovertible. It is the primary reason we make wills – and the primary reason the law enforces wills. The same could be said of many trusts. In short, where the promisee has died in a privity case the normal mechanism by which private law allows aggrieved individuals to enforce their rights is frustrated, leaving the promisee's expectation interest at risk. The obvious, if not necessarily simple solution is to give greater recognition to after-death interests than presently afforded by the rules on wills, trusts and estates.[27] The reason such protection is inadequate at present would appear to stem not from theoretical difficulties with after-death interests, but from concerns about fraud and other essentially evidential matters. Hence the formalities involved in making a will. Whether greater protection of after-death interests is best achieved by amending the laws regulating wills or trusts or executors' duties is a question for specialists in these areas. In any event, as in the case of difficult to quantify losses, the main point I wish to make here is not about how the law ought to be amended in this area. The main point is that insofar as it is thought that a promisee's after-death interest in performance is not adequately protected in privity cases, this problem is not caused by the third-party rule.

*(ii) Third-party promisees* It is not only the promisee's expectation interest that may be inadequately protected in privity cases; the third party's

---

26 See e.g. Parfit, *Reasons and Persons* (Oxford: 1984) parts 2 & 3.

27 For a similar suggestion, offered as a way of solving *White v. Jones* [1993] 3 W.L.R. 730 (on which the will example is based), see Weir, "A *Damnosa Hereditas*" (1995) 111 L.Q.R. 357. *White v. Jones* illustrates well the difficulties attendant to giving greater protection to after-death interests. In *White* a solicitor negligently failed to revise a will with the result that when the testator died his intended beneficiaries did not benefit. The problem would have never arisen if the testator could have made a will simply by declaring or writing down his intentions. It is because the law requires certain formalities in order to make a will that the intended beneficiaries did not benefit. Thus if the law is amended so as to ensure that the beneficiaries get what the testator intended them to get, then, regardless of the means used to achieve this end, the result is to avoid the formalities required to make a will. In short, it is the rules regarding wills, not the third-party rule, that is the source of the legal quandary in *White* (which is just another way of saying that the law fails to protect after-death interests perfectly). It may well be desirable, on balance, to allow an end run around the formal requirements for wills: formalities are a pragmatic response to evidential concerns and as such can be outweighed by other pragmatic concerns (here the impossibility of making a new will that meets the formal requirements). But we must realize the price paid for such reform - in this case the loss of certainty achieved by the formal requirements for making a will.

expectation interest may also be inadequately protected. Protection may be inadequate where the third party, though a stranger to the contract between the promisor and promisee, is party to an identical, or identical in part, ("collateral") contract with the promisor. Consider the following variation on our gardening contract. Suppose that A, the promisor, does not merely make a promise to B that he will do C's gardening, but also makes the same promise to C. The promises may be made at the same time or made at different times and C may receive communication of the promise directly or indirectly (via B or some other method of communication). Can C enforce the promise made to her in order to protect her expectation interest?

At least two obstacles may get in C's way. The first is that courts normally **[653]** require clear evidence of an intent to be bound before finding that a contractual offer has been made. As a result, they are understandably reluctant to read into communications between two contracting parties a further contractual offer to a third party who is not present and who has not taken part in the communications.[28] The third party's absence from negotiations and direct communication does not mean it is impossible for her to be the offeree of an offer made by one of the parties. Many offers are communicated by strangers; for example, an offer can be placed in a newspaper.[29] It does mean, however, that the task of determining whether the purported offeror intended to make an offer to the third party is complex and that any ambiguity in the promisor's language as to whether or not he intended to undertake an obligation to the third party or merely to benefit the third party is likely to be interpreted to mean the latter.

This first, evidential obstacle to C's possible action in contract is not insuperable, as can be seen by the courts' occasional willingness to find offers to third parties within a document that was drawn up by, and created a contract between, two other parties.[30] The second obstacle to C's action is more serious. Unless for some reason it is appropriate to regard B and C as joint parties to the contract, that is, as one party albeit composed of more than one person,[31] then C is barred by the consideration rule from enforcing

---

28 See e.g. *Southern Water Authority v. Carey* [1985] 2 All E.R. 1077.

29 Another example is a communication between an individual and the secretary of a club or other unincorporated association that creates a contract with each member of the club: *Hybart v. Parker* (1858) 4 C.B. 209; *Touche Ross & Co. v. Colin Baker* [1992] 2 Lloyd's Rep. 207; Treitel, *The Law of Contract* (London: 1995, 9th ed.) 537.

30 See e.g. *The Eurymedon* [1975] A.C. 154.

31 If B and C are joint parties, then neither the third-party rule nor the consideration rule should be a bar to C suing in contract. The promise was made to B and C together and by definition the consideration paid by B was paid on behalf of B and C. The contract is in essence a standard two-party bargain, the only difference being that one of the two parties is comprised of more than one person.

the contract. No consideration was provided for A's promise to C and thus C cannot sue A in contract.

C is barred by the consideration rule even if one believes that the function of consideration is merely to identify *which* promises are legally valid, the function of the third-party rule being to identify *who* can enforce a legally valid promise.[32] The consideration paid by B does not help C because B's consideration was for a different promise. If B and C are distinct rather than joint parties, A has made two distinct (albeit identical in content) promises. This follows from the nature of promises as obligations undertaken to particular persons. It is possible to make a single promise to two joined persons (joint promisees), but it is not possible to make a single promise to two unjoined persons (separate promisees). Promises are attached to promisees, so that where the promisees are separate so too are the promises.

The above point can be illustrated by an example. Suppose a builder agrees with homeowner Y to build a pool at the end of Y's street and in return Y agrees to give the builder £1000. Later that day the builder makes the same promise to Z, another homeowner on Y's street, except this time Z gives nothing in **[654]** return. No one would suppose that in a common law regime the builder has a contractual obligation to Z to build the pool. Z's claim in contract would fail because he did not provide consideration for the builder's promise.[33] That the builder received consideration from Y for the promise to build the pool would be irrelevant because it is clear that that promise was separate from the promise given to Z. Now suppose that instead of making promises to Y and Z at different times, the builder makes both promises at the same time and in the same document. The document says that X agrees with Y and Z that he will build a pool and that Y will pay X £1000. If Y and Z are acting together, as one party, then as noted a moment ago Z should be able to enforce the promise. But if Y and Z are acting separately, the situation is indistinguishable from the previous scenario. X has made two promises and established separate relationships with Y and Z. Each promise requires separate consideration to be legally enforceable.[34]

Thus the expectation interests of third parties in some privity cases

---

32 A view proposed in the Law Commission's Consultation Paper No. 121, *Privity of Contract: Contracts for the Benefit of Third Parties* (1991) para. 2.1.

33 The problem with this agreement is not that the builder has failed to provide consideration. A promise to perform a pre-existing contractual duty owed to a third party is good consideration (*The Eurymedon* [1975] A.C. 154) and even if it were not the issue here is whether the *homeowner* provided consideration for the builder's promise.

34 Thus I disagree with the majority's reasoning in *Coulls v. Bagot's Executors* (1967) 119 C.L.R. 460.

may be protected inadequately because the consideration rule can prevent third parties from enforcing promises made to them. This is not the place to debate the merits of the consideration rule: for our purposes it is sufficient to acknowledge that the rule has been subject to more than passing criticism.[35] The point I wish to make here is that the primary barrier to third-parties enforcing collateral promises made to them stems from consideration, not from the third-party rule. Moreover, the need for consideration is clearly a general problem, or at least a general issue, in contract law. For this reason, the arguments for and against abolishing consideration apply to collateral promises and ordinary promises equally, and any proposed substitute for consideration should be the same in each case.[36] It remains only to add that even if consideration were abolished, such reforms would help only those third parties to whom a collateral promise had been made. Most third parties do not fall into this category.

### *B. The Reliance Interest*

In addition to her possible contractual action against the promisor, the third party in our gardening example may also have a non-contractual action against A.[37] If C has detrimentally relied on A's promise, then in principle C should have a possible action against A (and, in some cases, against B[38]) to recover her [655] reliance losses.[39] Whether or not the action is successful depends on various circumstances surrounding the making of A's promise.

The idea underlying C's action is that a person who induces an assumption that he will act in such and such a way has, in certain circumstances, a duty not to let the "induced" person down. The duty may be described as a "duty to insure the reliability of induced assumptions".[40]

---

35 See e.g. Fried, *Contract as Promise* (Cambridge MA: 1981) ch. 3.

36 Third-party promisees may of course fail to satisfy whatever requirement is substituted for consideration. If the substitute is communicated acceptance of the offer, the third party may fail to make such a communication.

37 For a sensitive discussion of this issue, see Kincaid (1989), *supra* n. 3, 266-268.

38 Sometimes C will have relied not (or not only) on A's representations (which C may been unaware of), but instead (or in addition) on B's representations. For example, B, an employer, may have told C, his employee, that C can rely on an exclusion of liability clause in B's contract with A. In such a case, C should normally be unable to recover from A, the necessary proximity being lacking, but C may have a potential action against B for induced detrimental reliance (subject to the provisos discussed below).

39 Note that enforcing a promise is sometimes the only satisfactory way of protecting the reliance interest.

40 Spence, "Australian Estoppel" (1997) 11 J.C.L. 1. The nature of the duty described above is explained more fully in Spence's Article. See also McBride, "A Fifth Common Law Obligation" (1994) 14 Legal Studies 35.

Whether the duty is in tort or is a distinct (and yet to be named) category of obligation is a matter for debate; for terminological convenience I shall describe it as a duty in tort. One way in which the assumption triggering the duty can be induced is by making a promise: in normal circumstances we expect people to keep their promises. If the person in whom the assumption is induced is the promisee of the promise then the duty overlaps with the duty to keep a promise. But if the person in whom the assumption is induced is not the promisee, then the duty in tort is the only duty owed to that person. Of course not all persons who act in reliance on a promise fall within the scope of the promisor's duty in tort. Identifying those individuals to whom the duty is owed in any particular case is a complex, but familiar, task. The relevant factors are similar to those that determine the scope of the duty not to make negligent misstatements.[41] They seek to establish the antecedent likelihood and appropriateness of the third party, here C, relying on the promisor's promise. Thus a court should consider questions such as whether C was present when A made the promise, whether C was named in the promise, whether C was an intended beneficiary of the promise, whether A knew that C was likely to rely on the promise, whether C was dependent on A in some way and whether C had in the past relied on A.

C's possible tort action is the least developed, in legal terms, of the three possible actions arising out of A's breach that we have considered so far. That something like a duty to insure the reliability of induced assumptions finds expression in English law seems clear. The duty is the basis of a variety of forms of estoppel and arguably the law on negligent misrepresentation.[42] It is also clear that the duty is not a contractual duty. Although the aggrieved party may be suing *on* a promise she is not suing for the enforcement of a promise, but rather for compensation for the loss caused by relying on the promisor's expression of intention.

It is unlikely that under the present English law C in our example would be able to protect her reliance interest through an action against A, however that action was labelled. In particular, although C's claim might satisfy the standard **[656]** requirements for promissory estoppel,[43] C would be barred by the rule that estoppel can be used only as a defence and not as

41 See e.g. *Caparo Industries v. Dickman* [1990] 2 A.C. 605.

42 See Spence, *supra* n. 40.

43 See e.g. *Central London Property Ltd. v. High Trees House Ltd.* [1947] K.B. 130. McKendrick defines promissory estoppel in these terms: "where, by words or conduct, a person makes an unambiguous representation as to his future conduct, intending the representation to be relied on and to affect the legal relations between the parties, and the representee alters his position in reliance on it, the representor will be unable to act inconsistently with the representation if by doing so the representee would be prejudiced": *Contract Law* (2nd ed., 1994) 93.

a cause of action.[44] It is difficult to find any justification for this much-criticized rule, aside from the considerable practical difficulties involved in fixing the scope of the duty, and it is suggested that in principle a third party ought, in appropriate circumstances, to be able to bring a tort action against a breaching promisor.[45] Recent developments, primarily in Australia, suggest the possibility of English judges moving in this direction in the future.[46] Again, however, the main point I wish to make in this section is not about how the law will or should be changed. The point rather is that the problem of third parties not being compensated for harm suffered through relying on contractual promises is not a problem caused by the third-party rule. The limits placed on recovery for induced detrimental reliance, including detrimental reliance on promises, is a general problem in the law of obligations. If we are willing to live with this problem in two-party cases then we should be willing to live with it in privity cases, and vice versa.

Before leaving liability in tort it should be noted that the arguments for allowing C, a third party, to sue A in tort for A's broken promise to B also work in the opposite direction. That is, just as contractual statements between A and B can affect A's liability in tort to C, so too contractual statements between A and B can affect C's liability in tort to A. This is how contractual exemption and limitation clauses designed to cover third parties can be given effect without infringing the third-party rule. As a number of decisions have recognized,[47] a third party ought, in appropriate circumstances, be able to rely on a contractual exemption or limitation clause as a defence to a tort action by the promisor. If the clause, properly interpreted, extends to the third party, then it is evidence that the promisor

---

44 *Combe v. Combe* [1951] 2 K.B. 215.

45 One argument put forward for protecting third parties through contract rather than tort is that it is easier to control the scope of liability in contract: Markesinis, *supra* n. 3. My comments above are not meant to deny the practical difficulties attendant to expanding the scope of protection in tort. My concern at this stage is with the arguments in principle for liability in tort. Later, when the Law Commission's reform proposals are examined, I consider whether practical difficulties associated with, inter alia, extending protection in tort might lend support to granting third parties contractual rights. It is worth mentioning, however, that in a legal system that distinguishes clearly between the measures of damages in tort and contract, switching the legal basis of the duty to the third party affects more than the ability of the courts to control the scope of liability.

46 *Waltons Stores (Interstate) Ltd. v. Maher* (1988) 164 C.L.R. 387; *Commonwealth of Australia v. Verwayen* (1990) 170 C.L.R. 394.

47 *Norwich City Council v. Harvey* [1989] 1 W.L.R. 828; *Southern Water v. Carey* [1985] 2 All E.R. 1077; *Pacific Associates v. Baxter* [1990] Q.B. 993; McLachlin J. in *London Drugs Ltd. v. Kuenhe & Nagel International Ltd.* (1992) 97 D.L.R. (4th) 261. Decisions which have refused to adopt this approach include *Scruttons Ltd. v. Midland Silicones Ltd.* [1962] A.C. 446; *The Aliakmon* [1986] A.C. 785.

accepted responsibility for all or part of the damage caused by the third party. That the limitation or exclusion of liability is given effect through a clause in the plaintiff's contract, rather than, say, through a notice on a board staked to the defendant's property is immaterial. The defendant is not **[657]** relying on the contractual effect of the exclusion clause but on its effect on his duty in tort.[48]

## *C. The Restitution Interest*

In our gardening example, as in many privity cases, a second interest of the promisee (B) is affected by the promisor's (A's) breach. B paid A £100 for one year's gardening yet A did just one month's work in return. Therefore A has been unjustly enriched at B's expense and in principle B should have a claim against A for restitution of the amount by which A was enriched. The appropriate sum is prima facie that part of the contract price for which A did nothing in return. Under the present law, however, a claim against A in unjust enrichment is far from straightforward. The most obvious possible bar is the rule that restitution is available only where there has been a total failure of consideration and not, as in our example, where the promisor did part of what he was supposed to do.[49] In my view this largely evidential obstacle should not be regarded as an insuperable barrier and in principle B ought to be able to recover in unjust enrichment for that part of the contract price for which A did nothing in return. Others agree that in principle restitution should be available[50] and recent cases suggest that the requirement of total failure of consideration is being relaxed.[51]

---

48 Other ways of giving force to a contractual exemption or limitation clause may be available in certain cases. Leaving aside the possibility that B acted as C's agent, B has an action for breach of contract against A and may, assuming his loss is assessed accurately, be able to recover significant damages (B's reputation will suffer if B's subcontractors get sued). B may also have an claim in unjust enrichment (B presumably paid for the exemption clause). Finally, it may be possible to show that A made a separate promise to C or, more likely, that C detrimentally relied on A (say by forbearing from entering a separate contract with A or by not obtaining insurance).

49 *Whincup v. Hughes* (1871) L.R. 6 C.P. 78. Another possible difficulty stems from the rule that if a breach is not repudiatory (and hence the contract is not discharged) then restitution is not possible. This rule appears to be based on the fallacy that the existence of a contract trumps all other forms of liability. The better view, adopted in our earlier discussion of exemption and limitation clauses, is that the *words* of a contract can affect, and sometimes entirely eliminate, other forms of liability, but the mere existence of a contract qua contract does not exclude other forms of liability: see Smith, "Concurrent Liability in Contract and Unjust Enrichment" (1999) 115 L.Q.R. 245.

50 See e.g. Birks, *An Introduction to the Law of Restitution* (London: 1985) 242-245; Burrows, *The Law of Restitution* (London: 1993) 259-261.

51 *Rover International Ltd. v. Cannot Film Sales Ltd. (No. 3)* [1989] 1 W.L.R. 912; *Goss v. Chilcott* [1996] A.C. 788, 798.

As with the rules limiting protection of the expectation and reliance interests, however, the main point I wish to make here is again not about how the law will or ought to be changed. The point is that the problem of promisors, in privity cases, being able to "snap their fingers at a bargain and walk away"[52] is one aspect of a general problem in the law of unjust enrichment. The problem is not caused by the third-party rule. If we are willing to live with the limits on restitution in standard contract cases, we should be willing to live with them in privity cases and vice versa.

**[658]** This completes our discussion of the overlapping problems raised by privity cases. To summarize: the reason the results in privity cases are so often unsatisfactory is that in respect of each of the basic private law interests – expectation, reliance, restitution – the present law appears to provide inadequate protection. In respect of none of these interests, however, is the third-party rule the reason the protection is inadequate. The inadequacies stem from general problems in the law of obligations, problems that can and do arise in all manner of contract cases. What makes privity cases special is that these general problems all can arise in a single fact pattern.[53]

---

[52] Lord Dunedin in *Dunlop Pneumatic Tyre Company Ltd. v. Selfridge* [1915] A.C. 847, 855. Note that although this comment is frequently cited in criticisms of the third-party rule, Lord Dunedin was discussing the effect of the consideration rule and as such his comment is consistent with the arguments of this Article.

[53] Note that even if all the reforms mooted above were undertaken the possibility of multiple law suits presents at most a minor problem. Under most scenarios the different actions are related so as to prevent either under or over compensation. Thus, if the third party recovers in contract as a collateral promisee or in tort for reliance losses, the amount that the promisee can then recover in a subsequent action against the promisor (whether for breach of contract or in restitution) is discounted by the sum of money earlier awarded to the third party. This is because insofar as the third party realizes the value of the promise, the promisee's expectation or restitution interests are protected to that extent. Although the promisee has breached a duty, by failing to perform his primary obligation, the promisee has not suffered any loss as a result. The only difficult case is where the third party sues in contract or tort *after* the promisee has recovered either in restitution or in contract. If, as was held in, e.g., *Darlington B.C. v. Wiltshier Northern Limited* [1995] 3 All E.R. 895, the promisee holds any sums recovered in trust for the third party then, as above, there is no risk of excessive liability. The amount that the third party can recover is discounted by the amount that the promisee hands over to her. If, however, it is held that the *Darlington* ruling relies on a fiction and that the promisee is not obliged to hand over any sums recovered to the third party (after all, the promisee is suing in his own name and to protect his own interests), then there is a potential problem. If the third party is awarded damages in her subsequent action, the promisee will be overcompensated since his award was based on the assumption that the third party did not and would not receive any of the value of the promise. And the promisor will end up paying twice for the same wrong. A similar problem arises under the Law Commission's Draft Bill. The Draft Bill's solution of denying the third party an action where the promisee has already recovered (Draft Bill, cl. 5) is unsatisfactory

## 3. The Law Commission's Reform Proposals

Following its earlier Consultation Document, the Law Commission in a recent Report and draft Bill has proposed that legislation be enacted granting third parties the right, in certain circumstances, to enforce contracts to which they are not party.[54] Briefly, the right arises where there is an express contractual term to that effect (the first "limb") or where the contract purports to confer a benefit on the third party unless it is clear that the parties did not intend the contract to be enforceable by the third party (the second "limb").[55] The contract cannot be varied without the third party's consent once the third party has either relied upon the contract or communicated her assent to the promisor.[56] Finally, the [659] promisor can raise against the third party any defences or set-offs arising from the contract that he could have raised against the promisee.[57]

The draft Bill is a sophisticated document that draws carefully on reforms proposed or adopted by a variety of commentators and jurisdictions. Nevertheless, it displays in its core elements an unresolved tension between at least three possible sources for the new right that it grants to third parties. The first source is contractual. This source is most clearly evident in the third party's remedy of enforcement of the promise. It is also evident in the proposal that a contract be irrevocable once the third party has assented to it. Assent is a frequently suggested substitute for consideration and, as we have seen, in order that third-party promisees consistently be able to enforce collateral promises made to them the consideration rule must be reformed.

Other features of the draft Bill seem inspired more by a concern for

---

unless it is assumed that the promisee must always hand over any damages to the third party. A better, if unorthodox solution would be to allow the promisor, once he has been found liable in the first action, to pay the damages to the third party rather than to the promisee. The idea here is that in order to prevent double liability we allow the promisor to compensate the promisee by a form of specific performance. The promisor does not actually perform the contract, but he pays the value of performance to the person to whom the promisee wanted it to go. The promisee cannot complain because if the third party is compensated then the promisee will, as explained above, also be compensated. A second alternative would be to allow the promisor to join the third party to the promisee's action and to require that the promisee's action be decided first.

54 *The Third-Party Rule of Contract: Contracts for the Benefit of the Third Party* Law Com. No. 242 (1996) (hereafter "Report"). The Draft Bill is Appendix A to the Report (hereafter "Draft Bill").

55 Draft Bill, cl. 1(1)-(2).

56 Draft Bill, cl. 2(1)(2).

57 Draft Bill, cl. 3.

the third party's reliance interest. Rather than asking courts to determine if a collateral promise was made, explicitly or implicitly, to the third party, the draft Bill asks courts to determine if the parties either intended that the third party have rights or intended to confer a benefit on the third party. These sorts of intentions are not relevant, except as indirect evidence, in establishing that a contractual obligation has been undertaken to the third party. They are relevant, however, in establishing a tort action for induced detrimental reliance. It is reasonable to rely on people's expressed intentions. (Note however that focusing on the intentions of *both* parties is inconsistent with both promissory liability and reliance based liability. It is only the promisor's intentions that matter in either case.) The rule that a promise is irrevocable once the third party has relied upon it seems, at first blush, also to be inspired by a concern for the third-party's reliance interest. However, if the promisor's liability were truly in tort then reliance by the third party would not bar variation, but merely be the measure of the promisor's liability. Furthermore, the fact that the third party's reliance need not be detrimental in order to crystallize her rights is inconsistent with her having a right in tort.[58] On the other hand, the reliance trigger cannot easily be interpreted as a proxy for assent (and hence tied to the third party's expectation interest) since it is not required that the promisor know that the third party has relied.[59] In the end, the interest that the reliance trigger seeks to protect remains unclear.[60]

**[660]** Finally, allowing the promisor to raise any defences or set-offs that could have been raised against the promisee is inconsistent with understanding the third party's rights as either in tort or in contract. Undue influence exerted by a third party is not a defence in contract (unless there is actual or constructive knowledge of the undue influence),[61] nor is misrepresentation by a third party a defence in tort. Similar provisions regarding defences and set-offs are, however, found in the rules regulating

58 Report, para. 9.19.

59 Draft Bill, cl. 2(1)(c). The draft Bill stipulates that if the promisor is unaware that the third party has relied then the third party's reliance must be reasonably foreseeable in order to preclude variation. This proviso does not bring the reliance trigger closer to assent. An uncommunicated acceptance of an offer does not become effective merely because it was likely that the offer would be accepted.

60 The explanation offered in the Report - that the reliance trigger protects "reasonable expectations" (para 9.19) - assumes what we are trying to prove. Why are the third party's expectations reasonable? The explanation cannot be that it was statistically probable that the third party would benefit under the contract. Furthermore, if the third party's expectations were reasonable, then they remain reasonable, and ought to be protected, whether or not the third party relies on the contract. An unreasonable expectation is not turned into a reasonable expectation by reliance.

61 *Barclays Bank plc v. O'Brien* [1994] 1 A.C. 180.

agency (in respect of undisclosed principals)[62] and assignment.[63] It appears that in this respect at least the draft Bill envisages a third party as something like the promisee's undisclosed principal or the assignee of the promisee's rights.

The Law Commission's proposals fail, then, to distinguish clearly between different possible sources of the third party's new right – as might be expected if the argument of this article that the third-party rule is not the problem in privity cases is correct. The final result is a sophisticated, but ultimately ad hoc, balancing of different interests. The Law Commissioners seem at times to be aware of this. They noted that no consensus could be reached amongst consultees on the pivotal question of when variation of a contract should be allowed[64] and added that their own solution to the question was as an attempt to "balance" the competing interests of the three parties.[65] Crucially, they also acknowledge that the third party's action does not fall under a recognized category of legal right and in particular that it does not fall under contract. The Commissioners write that "it is not intended that the statute should give the third party full 'contractual rights'".[66]

These observations about the Law Commission's proposals raise two fundamental questions that must be answered by any advocate of reforming the third-party rule. First, if (as seems clear) the new right that it is proposed to give third parties is not in fact a contractual right, why is the third-party rule the target of reform? The third-party rule is a contract law rule and it bars only the enforcement of a contract, not other sorts of actions. Second, if the third party does not have a contractual (or tortious, etc.) right, what sort of right does it have? It is possible, I suppose, that a third party's right is some type of *sui generis* right, not otherwise recognized in the law and combining elements of contract, tort, unjust enrichment, and so on. But it is not clear what sort of a right this could be and why, aside from a desire to get around (without directly addressing) a number of distinct problems in the law of obligations in a single move, that right has the sort of characteristics ascribed to it by the Law Commission.

What, then, is the way forward? In principle, the first step for any would-be reformer is to distinguish clearly between the different rights at stake in privity **[661]** cases. The second step is to decide what reforms are needed in order to give full expression to those rights. The final step is to decide whether legislation or judicial activism is the best means to

---

62 *Browning v. Provincial Insurance Co. of Canada* (1873) L.R. 5 P.C. 263, 272.
63 *Chitty on Contracts* (27th ed., 1994) paras 19-002.
64 Report, para. 9.1.
65 Report, para. 9.18.
66 Report, para. 13.2.

accomplish the needed reforms. Of the reforms mooted in this paper the least likely to be achieved by the judiciary is probably the granting of contractual rights to third-party promisees in cases where a collateral promise was made to them – requiring, as it would, a major reform of consideration.[67] Thus it would seem sensible for those who believe third-party promisees ought to have contractual rights to focus their legislative energies in this direction initially.

Any support that is given to the Law Commission's proposals can only be on purely pragmatic grounds. Coherence is not the only virtue of a legal system. Although the ideal legal system is a coherent one, in our imperfect world, imperfectly coherent solutions are sometimes the best that can be achieved, at least in the short run. Bluntly, it could be argued that it is too difficult in practice to achieve, within a reasonable time frame, the legitimate reforms needed in order to achieve just results in privity cases. To undertake all of the reforms mooted in this article would clearly be a daunting task. A quick glance at recent cases on duty of care in tort makes clear the difficulties attendant to any expansion in the scope of recovery for induced detrimental reliance.[68] Similarly, that some judges have hesitated to give effect in tort law to exemption clauses is not surprising in view of the complex chains of contracts (often incorporating international conventions such as the Hague Rules) that can form the background to such cases.[69] On the contractual side, determining whether a promisor explicitly or implicitly made a second promise to the third party raises similar difficulties. The problems attendant on reforming consideration are well known. In short, insofar as the common law does not provide full protection for the expectation, reliance and restitution interests in privity cases, the reason is not because of a mere oversight, but because of the genuine difficulties involved in reforming the law. Because of these difficulties, it could be argued – I would go no further than this – that in practice the best way forward at the present time is to grant third parties the type of rights proposed by the Law Commission. At a minimum, the pragmatic arguments for abolishing the third-party rule seem overwhelming in respect of certain categories of contracts (for example negotiable instruments, bills of lading, life insurance contracts – each of which is already governed by legislation[70]). If, however, the third-party rule were

67 On the other hand, the ability of the judiciary to "invent" consideration should not be underestimated.

68 See e.g. *Caparo Industries plc v. Dickman* [1990] 2 A.C. 605; *Spring v. Guardian Assurance* [1994] 3 W.L.R. 354; *White v. Jones* [1995] 2 W.L.R. 761; *Page v. Smith* [1995] 2 W.L.R. 644; *Stovin v. Wise* [1996] 3 W.L.R. 388.

69 See e.g. *The Aliakmon* [1986] A.C. 785.

70 Bills of Exchange Act 1882, s. 38(1); Carriage of Goods by Sea Act 1992, ss. 2 & 3; Married Women's Property Act 1882, s. 11.

abolished for these, essentially pragmatic reasons, abolition must be recognized for what it is – a second best solution in a still-evolving legal system. Abolition will inevitably produce anomalies and injustices. Over time, the anomalies and injustices will assume greater significance. Furthermore, the practical difficulties involved in removing **[662]** or reforming legislation introduced in order to overcome problems of a common law that has since reformed itself (consider, to mention just one example, the Misrepresentation Act 1967), suggest that the pragmatic arguments for legislative reform are not as strong as might be thought. In the long run, the principled approach is usually the most practical.

## 4. Conclusion

One way of summarizing the arguments of this article is to say that they reinterpret the standard criticisms of the third-party rule as criticisms of other legal rules. The criticism that the third-party rule fails to respect the intentions of the contracting parties is explained as a criticism of the rules regarding recovery of difficult-to-quantify loss. The criticism that the third-party rule fails to protect third parties adequately is a criticism of the scope of recovery for induced detrimental reliance and of the consideration rule. Finally, the criticism that the third-party rule allows a promisor to take the benefit of a bargain and then walk away is a criticism of the rules governing restitutionary awards for breach of contract. It should not be supposed, however, that if all the reforms mooted in this article were introduced then third parties would in the end always get what the contracting parties originally intended them to get. In our gardening contract, for example, C may have not relied on A's promise, nor be able to establish that a separate promise was made to her. Furthermore, B may refuse to sue A or, if he does sue A, neither request specific performance nor agree to hand over any money awarded to C.[71] On these facts C gets nothing. We may feel sympathy for C in such a case, but legally the result seems unimpeachable. Assuming that neither A nor B had a prior duty to benefit C, it is hard to see what right of C's has been infringed by non-performance. No promise was made to C. C was not harmed by (relying upon) A's promise. C cannot claim that A was unjustly enriched at her expense. What other source could there be of C's alleged right? C may have been looking forward keenly to receiving the benefit of A's promise, but this is different from having a right to that promise. C's position is

[71] But note that the court may hold that any damages recovered by the promisee are held on trust for the third party: *Darlington Borough Council v. Wiltshier Northern Ltd.* [1995] 1 W.L.R. 68.

similar to that of a nephew whose uncle informs him that he intends (but does not promise) to give him £1000 on his 21st birthday. Assuming the nephew does not rely on this statement, no right of the nephew is infringed if the uncle fails to deliver the money.

The justification for the third-party rule is simple and compelling: only a person to whom a promise has been made can legitimately demand that the promise, qua promise, be enforced. Privity cases, however, are complex - even when the facts are simplified as in our gardening contract example. They are complex because they raise difficult problems in respect of protecting each of the basic private law interests - expectation, reliance and restitution. The proper **[663]** protection of those interests may require a controversial expansion of promisees' rights in contract and restitution, and of third parties' rights in tort and contract. But however complex the reasoning required to decide privity cases properly, in no case is the third-party rule a bar to achieving the just result.

# 9 The Third-Party Beneficiary Principle

MELVIN ARON EISENBERG*

## Introduction

The purpose of this paper is to develop the principle that determines when a third-party beneficiary should be entitled to bring suit under a contract.

Nomenclature is important here. I will use the term *third-party beneficiary* to mean a person who is not a party to a contract, but who would benefit from its performance; the term *promisor* to mean a person who has made a legally enforceable promise, the performance of which would benefit a third-party beneficiary; and the term *promisee* to mean the person to whom this promise is made.[1] Finally, I will use the term *contract* to mean an enforceable agreement between a promisor and a promisee, the performance of which would benefit a third party; and the term *contracting parties* to refer to the promisor and the promisee, taken together.

Although this paper is largely normative, in the sense that the object of the paper is to develop the principle that should govern the law of third-party beneficiaries, I will make extensive use of existing legal materials. Because the United States has had a long history of allowing suits by third-party beneficiaries, these materials will be American. I will use American secondary materials in the course of developing the principle that should

* This paper draws heavily on my earlier article, "Third-Party Beneficiaries" 92 Colum.L.Rev. 1358 (1992).

1 This nomenclature is somewhat artificial, because in bilateral contracts each party is both a promisor and a promisee. Typically, however, a third-party beneficiary would be benefited only by the performance of one of the parties - the party I call the promisor.

The term third-party beneficiary is sometimes used by courts to mean a third party who can enforce a contract, as opposed to one who cannot. See, e.g., *Dravo Corp. v. Robert R. Kerris, Inc.* 655 F.2d 503, 510 (3d Cir.1981). However, the definition of the term in this paper, to include all third parties who would benefit from the performance of a contract, whether or not they can enforce the contract, parallels the usage of other courts and of the Restatements. See Restatement of Contracts § 133 (1932) [hereinafter Restatement First]; Restatement (Second) of Contracts § 302 (1979) [hereinafter Restatement Second].

govern the law of third-party beneficiaries. I will use American case law to illustrate the application of that principle by examining its application to some recurring third-party-beneficiary problems.

## 1. The Principle Governing Enforceability of Contracts by Third-Party Beneficiaries

For some time, recognition of the right of third-party beneficiaries to bring suit under a contract was blocked by two conceptual objections. First, a third-party beneficiary has not given consideration. Second, he is not in privity with the parties to the contract; in particular, not in privity with the promisor.

These doctrinal objections were mistaken on the substantive level, because if third-party beneficiaries, or some of them, should be allowed to enforce contracts as a normative matter, lack of consideration and privity are irrelevant.

The objections were also mistaken on the technical level.

The objection based on privity – that the plaintiff "must have some legal interest in the undertaking" – was circular, because the very question was whether a third-party beneficiary *had* a legal interest in the undertaking.

The objection based on lack of consideration was also wide of the mark. The purpose of the requirement of consideration in contract law is to screen out those promises that are legally enforceable from those that are not. A suit by a third-party beneficiary *assumes* that a legally enforceable contract is in existence. The question therefore is not whether an enforceable promise has been made – it has – but who can enforce the promise. That question may often be very difficult to answer, but it is not a question of consideration.

Despite the poverty of the technical objections, it is easy to see normative reasons why not every third-party beneficiary should be allowed to enforce a contract. The reasons for enforcing bargain promises are complex, but the most important is that bargains enhance the wealth of the contracting parties by creating value through exchange and allowing the contracting parties to shift risks and make reliable plans. At its core, therefore, contract law seeks to facilitate the power of self-governing parties to further their own interests by contracting. Allowing enforcement of contracts by third-party beneficiaries often conflicts with those interests.

For example, suppose Martial is a manufacturer of specialty toy soldiers. To manufacture the toy soldiers, Martial purchases specially crafted dies from Diemaker and special paints from Color, and employs skilled workers on an hourly basis. At a time when Martial would have otherwise had to idle her plant for lack of business, Access, a distributor, places a large order for new, highly detailed Civil War toy soldiers, to take advantage of a special surge of interest in that war. Access plans to resell the toy soldiers to large retailers, including Toys Galore. With Access's order in hand, Martial designs the toy soldiers, draws engineering plans for the necessary dies, and enters into a contract with Diemaker, who agrees to produce the dies. At the time the contract is made, Diemaker knows that Martial requires the dies to fill her contract with Access, that Access plans to resell the toy soldiers to Toys Galore and other retailers, and that Martial has no other business in prospect.

In breach of his contract, Diemaker fails to deliver the dies. As a result, Martial is in breach of her contract with Access, and is forced to idle her plant for six weeks, until new orders begin to come in. Martial sues Diemaker under their contract. Access sues Martial under their contract. Toys Galore sues Diemaker for its lost profits on resale of the toy soldiers. Color sues Diemaker for its lost profits on sales of paint to Martial. Martial's workers sue Diemaker for their lost wages.

Toys Galore, Color, and the workers are all third-party beneficiaries of the contract between Diemaker and Martial, but intuitively it seems clear that none of them should be able to bring suit against Diemaker.[2] The source of the intuition lies in considerations that might be thought of as *remedial*, that is, considerations concerning the promisor's liability and the impact of that liability on the contracting parties. In the hypothetical, Martial is entitled to expectation damages against Diemaker as a result of Diemaker's breach. These damages would be measured in part by Martial's lost profits, and also by the damages Access would collect against Martial, which were reasonably foreseeable to Diemaker. It can be assumed that the prospect of such damages affected the price Diemaker charged. If Martial had initially agreed to forgo expectation damages against Diemaker in the event of Diemaker's breach, Diemaker presumably would have agreed to a lower price. If Martial did not agree to forgo those damages, presumably that was partly because she wanted full compensation if Diemaker breached, and partly because she would have viewed the contract with Diemaker as unreliable if the contract was not backed by the sanction of expectation damages.

---

2 See Restatement Second § 302 illus. 16, 19:

16. B contracts with A to erect an expensive building on A's land. C's adjoining land would be enhanced in value by the performance of the contract. C [cannot bring suit under the contract].

19. A contracts to erect a building for C. B then contracts with A to supply lumber needed for the building. C ... and B [cannot bring suit under each other's contract]....

Suppose now that the contracting parties, Martial and Diemaker, had directly addressed the question whether to allow Toys Galore, Color, and the workers to bring suit under the Martial-Diemaker contract. If Diemaker was to be exposed to liability to the third parties, as well as liability to Martial, Diemaker would certainly have demanded a higher price from Martial. Martial, however, would almost certainly have been unwilling to pay that higher price, because she would receive an insufficient benefit in return. We can therefore be fairly confident that if Martial and Diemaker had directly addressed the issue, they would have agreed that the third parties should not be able to enforce the contract. Accordingly, if the interests of the contracting parties, Martial and Diemaker, are measured by what they would have agreed to if they had addressed the issue, allowing the third parties in the hypothetical to enforce the contract would conflict with those interests.

In short, although as I show in Part II there are often good reasons why *some* third-party beneficiaries should be allowed to enforce contracts, not *all* third-party beneficiaries should be allowed to enforce contracts. Therefore, the problem is to formulate a general principle to determine when enforcement by third-party beneficiaries should be permitted. I begin my examination of this question by reviewing three earlier formulations: the test in *Restatement (First) of Contracts*; the "intent-to-benefit" test developed by American courts; and the test in the *Restatement (Second) of Contracts*.

### *A. The Restatement First Test*

Given the poverty of the doctrinal objections to enforcement of contracts by third-party beneficiaries, it was only a matter of time, at least in the United States, until those objections eroded and then collapsed.

The erosion of the objections to the rights of third-party beneficiaries to bring suit received its single most important expression in the United States in *Restatement (First) of Contracts*, published in 1932. *Restatement First* § 133 provided:

> (1) Where performance of a promise in a contract will benefit a person other than the promisee, that person is ..:
>
> (a) a donee beneficiary if it appears from the terms of the promise in view of the accompanying circumstances that the purpose of the promisee in obtaining the promise of all or part of the performance thereof is [i] to make a gift to the beneficiary or [ii] to confer upon him a right against the promisor to some performance neither due nor supposed or asserted to be due from the promisee to the beneficiary;

(b) a creditor beneficiary if no purpose to make a gift appears from the terms of the promise in view of the accompanying circumstances and performance of the promise will satisfy an actual or supposed or asserted duty of the promisee to the beneficiary ...;

(c) an incidental beneficiary if neither the facts stated in Clause (a) nor those stated in Clause (b) exist.

Sections 135 and 136 of *Restatement First* then went on to provide that a donee or creditor beneficiary could bring suit under a contract, but an incidental beneficiary could not.

The nomenclature of *Restatement First* can be reformulated in the following terms. There are two easy, basic categories of third-party beneficiaries who can enforce contracts. In one of those categories, the object of the promisee is to bring about the payment of a legal obligation he owes to the beneficiary. This category is covered in Section 133(1)(b), and in such cases the third party is labelled a *creditor beneficiary*. The second category consists of cases in which the object of the promisee is to make a gift to the beneficiary. This category is covered in Section 133(1)(a)[i], and in such cases the third party is labelled a *donee beneficiary*. In cases falling outside these two easy categories, sometimes it is appropriate to allow the beneficiary to enforce the contract, and sometimes it is not. Under the terminology of *Restatement First*, when the purpose of the promisee is to confer a right on the beneficiary, enforcement is appropriate. Section 133(1)(a)[ii] uses the label *donee beneficiary* in these cases as well. In other cases, enforcement is inappropriate. In those cases, Section 133(1)(c) labels the beneficiary an *incidental beneficiary*.

In short, *Restatement First* did not formulate a general principle to cover all third-party beneficiary cases. Instead, it adopted three separate rules to cover three separate categories of beneficiaries – a type of scheme often referred to as a *categorical* approach. The three categorical rules were: (1) Creditor beneficiaries could enforce contracts. (2) True donee beneficiaries could enforce contracts. (3) Third-party beneficiaries who were neither creditor beneficiaries nor true donee beneficiaries could enforce contracts if, but only if, "the purpose of the promisee in obtaining the promise [was] ... to confer on [the beneficiary] a right against the promisor".

By adopting separate rules for creditor beneficiaries and true donee beneficiaries, *Restatement First* treated creditor beneficiaries and true donee beneficiaries as special cases, rather than as instances of a general principle that applied to all third-party beneficiaries. Furthermore, the *Restatement First* rule governing all other beneficiaries – which, as the residual rule, was crucial to the enterprise – was seriously defective. By labelling all third-party beneficiaries who could enforce contracts (other than creditor beneficiaries) as donee beneficiaries, *Restatement First* infected the treatment of residual cases by inviting an inquiry centred on whether a gift of a right was intended by the promisee – an unlikely finding, in a context that by hypothesis does not involve true donative intent. The focus of *Restatement First*'s residual rule solely on the promisee's purpose was also inappropriate. In determining whether a third-party beneficiary should be allowed to enforce a contract, the objectives of both contracting parties, not merely the promisee, should be determinative. After all, the contract sought to be enforced is that of both parties, not merely of the promisee.

Despite the awkward nature of its nomenclature and the unsatisfactory nature of its residual test, *Restatement First* initiated the modern law of third-party beneficiaries by taking two critical steps. First, it pushed aside, by brute force, the doctrinal objections to enforcement by third-party beneficiaries. Second, it set the stage for movement away from a rule-based body of third-party-beneficiary law, comprised of a collection of specific categories, toward a body of law in which enforceability by third-party beneficiaries would be determined by a general principle.

But what is that principle? *Restatement First* did not have much to offer in this regard. Its residual rule, which turned on whether the promisee's purpose was to confer a right on the beneficiary, provided no guidance concerning the critical question of how a court was to determine whether this purpose was present. In the end, therefore, *Restatement First*'s crucial residual test was largely empty.[3]

*B. The Intent-to-Benefit Test*

For this or other reasons, although American courts made wide use of the *Restatement First* terminology, they have tended to adopt a variation of the *Restatement First* residual test. The test in most common use is whether the promisee – or, in some formulations, the parties to the contract - intended to benefit the third-party beneficiary.[4] This test is also defective,

---

3 See David M. Summers, Note, "Third Party Beneficiaries and the Restatement (Second) of Contracts" 67 Cornell L.Rev. 880, 884 (1982).

4 See, e.g., *Buchman Plumbing Co. v. Regents of the Univ. of Minn.* 215 N.W.2d 479, 483 (Minn.1974); *Snyder Plumbing & Heating Corp. v. Purcell* 195 N.Y.S.2d 780, 783 (App.Div.1960) ; *Vogel v. Reed Supply Co.* 177 S.E.2d 273, 279 (N.C.1970); Harry G. Prince, "Perfecting the Third Party Beneficiary Standing Rule Under Section 302 of the

because the term "intent" is deeply ambiguous along at least three axes.

First, "intent" can refer either to the parties' actual subjective intent, or to the intent that is objectively manifested.

Second, "intent" can refer either to acting with a motive to achieve a given result, or to choosing a course of action with knowledge that a given result is likely to follow from the action, even if the actor is indifferent about achieving the result or indeed would prefer to avoid it. This point is exemplified in Illustration 1 to *Restatement (Second) of Torts* Section 8A:

> A throws a bomb into B's office for the purpose of killing B. A knows that C, B's stenographer, is in the office. A has no desire to injure C, but knows that his act is substantially certain to do so. C is injured by the explosion. A is subject to liability to C for an intentional tort.

Third, "intent" can refer either to the end an actor seeks to achieve or to the means that an actor uses to achieve an end. For example, suppose that A, a country at war, stages a bombing raid on the civilian population of its enemy, B. The end that A seeks to achieve by the raid may be to kill B's civilians (perhaps in retribution for the killing of A's civilians) or to induce B's surrender. Although in the first case killing civilians is intended as an end, and in the second it is intended as a means, in both cases it could be said that A intended to kill civilians.

Courts that use the intent-to-benefit test often fail to make clear what they mean by "intent" in the context of this test.[5] Certainly, the test could not be satisfied merely by knowledge that performance of the contract will benefit the third party. By definition, in every case involving a third-party beneficiary the third party will benefit from performance of the contract, and normally the contracting parties will know with substantial certainty that this benefit will result. Accordingly, if the intent-to-benefit test was satisfied merely by knowledge that performance would benefit the third party, every third-party beneficiary could enforce a contract. Many or most courts that use the test avoid this problem by effectively treating the issue as whether the contracting parties, or the promisee, had a subjective motive to confer a benefit on the third party as an end.

Indeed, unless the intent-to-benefit test has this meaning, it is largely empty. If the intent-to-benefit test is satisfied by objective intent, it provides no guidance on the issue that the test makes critical: How is it to be determined, as an objective matter, why in some contracts whose

---

Restatement (Second) of Contracts" 25 B.C.L.Rev. 919, 923 (1984); Note, "The Third Party Beneficiary Concept: A Proposal" 57 Colum.L.Rev. 406, 408-09 (1957).

5 See, e.g., *State v. Osborne* 607 P.2d 369, 371 (Alaska 1980); *Little v. Union Trust Co. of Maryland* 412 A.2d 1251, 1253 (Md.1980).

performance will benefit a third party, the benefit is "intended" within the meaning of the test, while in other contracts whose performance will benefit a third party, the benefit is not so "intended"?

Perhaps to ameliorate these difficulties, some courts patch additional formal requirements onto the intent-to-benefit test. For example, some cases impose a requirement that an intent to benefit the third party be "clear", "express", or "definite",[6] and some require that an intent to benefit the third party be found in the language of the contract itself, and cannot be established on the basis of surrounding circumstances.[7] The former type of requirement is based on the erroneous assumption that contracting parties normally have a "clear", "express", or "definite" intent on benefiting the third party. Both types of requirement are inconsistent with modern principles of contract interpretation, which do not place a thumb on the interpretative scale, by requiring a meaning to be "clear" or "definite", and do allow courts to look to surrounding circumstances. And both types of requirement are difficult or impossible to apply meaningfully and consistently, and are not so applied in fact.[8] The better-reasoned cases reject these formal requirements,[9] and so does *Restatement (Second) of Contracts*.[10]

Other courts patch an additional substantive test onto the intent-to-benefit test. Some authorities require the performance to be rendered directly to the beneficiary.[11] This requirement, however, has no rational connection with the intent-to-benefit test or, for that matter, with anything else. Not surprisingly, therefore, the direct-performance test is both over- and under- inclusive.

The direct-performance test is under-inclusive, because it would

---

6 See, e.g., *Security Mut. Casualty Co. v. Pacura* 402 So.2d 1266, 1267 (Fla.Dist.Ct.App.1981) (clear); *Donalson v. Coca-Cola Co.* 298 S.E.2d 25, 27 (Ga.Ct.App.1982) (clear); *Khabbaz v. Swartz* 319 N.W.2d 279, 285 (Iowa 1982) (express); *Snyder Plumbing* 195 N.Y.S.2d at 783 (clear); *Keel v. Titan Constr. Corp.* 639 P.2d 1228, 1231 (Okla.1981) (express); *Kelly Health Care, Inc. v. Prudential Ins. Co. of Am.* 309 S.E.2d 305, 307 (Va.1983) (clear and definite); Prince, supra note 4, 25 B.C.L.Rev. 919 at 926 (1984).

7 See, e.g., *Securities Fund Servs., Inc. v. American Nat'l Bank & Trust Co.* 542 F.Supp. 323, 329 (N.D.Ill.1982).

8 See Prince, supra note 4, 25 B.C.L.Rev. 919 at 927-30 (1984).

9 See *E.B. Roberts Constr. Co. v. Concrete Contractors, Inc.* 704 P.2d 859 (Colo.1985); *J. Louis Crum Corp. v. Alfred Lindgren, Inc.* 564 S.W.2d 544, 547 (Mo.Ct.App.1978); *Black & White Cabs of St. Louis, Inc. v. Smith* 370 S.W.2d 669, 675 (Mo.Ct.App.1963); Prince, supra note 4, 25 B.C.L.Rev. 919 at 928-29 (1984).

10 See Restatement Second § 302(1)(b).

11 See *Fidelity & Deposit Co. v. Rainer* 125 So. 55, 58-59 (Ala.1929); *Carson Pirie Scott & Co. v. Parrett* 178 N.E. 498, 501-04 (Ill.1931); Laurence P. Simpson, *Handbook of the Law of Contracts* § 117, at 246-48 (2d ed. 1965); Note, supra note 4, 57 Colum.L.Rev. 406 at 425-28 (1957).

exclude enforcement by third-party beneficiaries in certain cases in which enforcement should be and commonly is permitted. For example, when an attorney has broken a contract with a client to draft a will in favour of a designated legatee, the attorney's performance is rendered to the client, not to the would-be legatee, but the would-be legatee should be and generally is entitled to enforce the contract.[12]

The direct-performance test is over-inclusive, because there are many cases in which a contracted-for performance is to be rendered to a designated third person, but that person should not be given the right to enforce the contract. For example, suppose that A, a computer manufacturer, and B, a software producer, enter into a contract to stage a joint demonstration of their products at the San Francisco Hilton. A is to pay Hilton; B is to pay any other third parties whose services will be required.[13] Before any contract is made with Hilton, A breaks his contract with B. Here, Hilton is a third-party beneficiary, Hilton is named in the contract, and A is to render a performance (payment) directly to Hilton, but it seems clear that Hilton should not be able to enforce the contract. A *Restatement Second* illustration takes just this position on comparable facts: "B contracts with A to buy a new car manufactured by C. C [cannot bring suit under contract], even though the promise can only be performed if money is paid to C".[14]

The failure of the formal and substantive add-ons to the intent-to-benefit test only serves to illustrate that this test, like the *Restatement First* residual test to which it is intimately related, is unjustifiable. Insofar as the test is construed to require a subjective motive or an objective intent to benefit the third party as an end, it is misguided. Except in some cases involving true donee beneficiaries, the intent of the contracting parties is typically to further their own interests, not the interests of a third party. Accordingly, the question whether there is a motive or intent to benefit the third party as an end normally cannot

12 See infra part II.D. A variation of the direct-performance test is that there must be an intent to confer a "direct" benefit on the third-party beneficiary. See, e.g., *Holley v. St. Paul Fire & Marine Ins. Co.* 396 So.2d 75, 80 (Ala.1981); *Reidy v. Macauley*, 290 S.E.2d 746, 747 (N.C.Ct.App.1982); Prince, supra note 4, 25 B.C.L.Rev. 919 at 933-34, 990-91 (1984). This requirement, however, is just as empty as the intent-to-benefit test itself and leads to the same kind of conclusory reasoning.

13 This is a variant of a hypothetical posed in Gary T. Schwartz, "Economic Loss in American Tort Law: The Examples of J'Aire and of Products Liability" 23 San Diego L.Rev. 37, 42 (1986).

14 Restatement Second § 302 illus. 17; see also *Dravo Corp. v. Robert B. Kerris, Inc.* 655 F.2d 503, 510-11 (3d Cir.1981) (holding that Dravo could not enforce a subcontract in which A agreed to construct a plant for X, A subcontracted to B the installation of ventilation systems, and the subcontract between A and B provided that B would use only Dravo ventilation units).

generate a useful answer, and the intent-to-benefit test is therefore difficult or impossible to apply in a meaningful and consistent way.[15] As a result, the test is characteristically applied by the courts in a conclusory fashion, with no real analysis of the case at hand and, indeed, often without even an attempt at analysis.[16]

### *C. The Restatement Second Test*

*Restatement Second* makes still another attempt to formulate a principle to determine which third-party beneficiaries should be allowed to enforce a contract. Preliminarily, *Restatement Second* breaks with *Restatement First* by substituting, for the awkward nomenclature of *Restatement First*, a single term, "intended beneficiaries", to describe all third-party beneficiaries who are entitled to enforce contracts.

However, *Restatement Second* fails to follow up on the concept of a unified nomenclature by adopting a unified principle of enforceability; and the principles it does adopt are seriously flawed. These principles are set out in Section 302(1):

> Unless otherwise agreed between promisor and promisee, a beneficiary of a promise is an intended beneficiary if recognition of a right to performance in the beneficiary is appropriate to effectuate the intention of the parties and either
>
> (a) the performance of the promise will satisfy an obligation of the promisee to pay money to the beneficiary; or
>
> (b) the circumstances indicate that the promisee intends to give the beneficiary the benefit of the promised performance.

Under Section 302, to enforce a contract a third-party beneficiary must satisfy the requirements of the introductory clause of the Section and either Subsection 1(a) or 1(b). The introductory clause has the look and feel of an intent-to-benefit test, while Subsections (1)(a) and (b) are essentially counterparts of the *Restatement First* tests for creditor and donee beneficiaries. Accordingly, *Restatement Second* has most of the flaws of prior law.

---

15 See Prince, supra note 4, 25 B.C.L.Rev. 919 at 923 (1984).

16 See, e.g., *Buchman Plumbing Co. v. Regents of the Univ. of Minn.* 215 N.W.2d 479, 483-84 (Minn.1974); *Vogel v. Reed Supply Co.* 177 S.E.2d 273, 279 (N.C.1970) . See generally Note, "Third Party Beneficiaries and the Intention Standard: A Search for Rational Contract Decision-Making" 54 Va.L.Rev. 1166, 1170-74 (1968).

*D. The Contracts (Rights of Third Parties) Act 1999*

The Contracts (Rights of Third Parties) Act of 1999 in England adopts a dual principle to govern the issue when a third-party beneficiary can enforce a contract. Under Section 1(a) of the Act, a third-party beneficiary can enforce a contract when the contract expressly so provides. Under Sections 1(b) and 2, a third-party beneficiary can enforce a contract when the term purports to confer a benefit on him and it does not appear, on a proper construction of the contract, that the contracting parties did not intend the term to be enforceable by the third party.

The adoption of the 1999 Act is, of course, welcome. It does for the United Kingdom what the *Restatement First* did for the United States. Furthermore, Section 1(a) of the Act states a principle that is unexceptionable, as will be discussed further in Part II(C) of this paper. However, sections 1(b) and 2 essentially comprise a variation of the American intent-to-benefit and *Restatement Second* tests, with the difference that once the contract purports to confer a benefit on the third party, there is a presumption that the third party can enforce it, so that the intent-to-benefit principle under the Act is essentially negative rather than positive. Nevertheless, an intent-to benefit test it is, and while the enactment of this principle is certainly an enormous improvement in English contract law, the principle has most or all the problems of the intent-to-benefit and *Restatement Second* tests.

*E. The Third-Party-Beneficiary Principle*

The *Restatement First* test, the intent-to-benefit test, the *Restatement Second* test, and the test of the 1999 Act are all inadequate and indeed largely empty. What principle, then, should determine whether a given third-party beneficiary should be permitted to enforce a contract?

To answer this question, recall the reason why not every third-party beneficiary should have power to enforce contracts: in some cases, such enforcement would conflict with the interests of the contracting parties. The same reason points the way to the principle that should determine whether any given third-party beneficiary should have power to enforce a contract. This principle, which I will call the third-party-beneficiary principle, is as follows: A third-party beneficiary should have power to enforce a contract if, but only if:

(a) Allowing the beneficiary to enforce the contract is a necessary or important means of effectuating the contracting parties' performance objectives, as manifested in the contract read in the light of surrounding circumstances; or

(b) Allowing the beneficiary to enforce the contract is supported by reasons of policy or morality independent of contract law and would not conflict with the contracting parties' performance objectives.

The term "the contracting parties' performance objectives" needs some exegesis. Normally, a third-party beneficiary will bring suit only if the promisor has breached. Obviously, it is not an objective of the promisor at that point to perform. Furthermore, in one sense it is never an objective of a promisor to perform, but only to obtain what is promised to her if she agrees to and does perform. Such a characterisation of the promisor's objectives, however, would be too narrow, because the promisor can attain what she is promised only by joining in the enterprise that is embodied in the contract – an enterprise designed to fulfil various objectives, some shared, some dearer to the heart of the promisor, some dearer to the heart of the promisee. Accordingly, by the contracting parties' performance objectives I mean those objectives of the enterprise embodied in the contract, read in the light of surrounding circumstances, that the promisor either knew of or should have known of at the time the contract was made.

I will call the two elements of the third-party-beneficiary principle the first and second branches of that principle. The first branch of the principle reflects the concept that at its core contract law seeks to facilitate the power of self-governing parties to further their own interests by contracting. Under this branch of the principle, therefore, the purpose of allowing suit by a third party is not to ensure that the third party realises a benefit, but to ensure that the contracting parties' performance objectives are effectuated. Unlike the intent-to-benefit test, which turns on whether the contracting parties had an *other-regarding* intent to benefit the third party, the first branch of the third-party-beneficiary principle turns on whether allowing the third party to enforce the contract will further the *self-regarding interests* of the contracting parties.[17]

To put this differently, under the first branch of the third-party-beneficiary principle, the law of third-party beneficiaries is largely conceived as remedial, rather than substantive. The question addressed by the first branch of the principle is not whether the contract is intended to create a right in the third party, but whether empowering the third party to enforce the contract is a necessary or important means of effectuating the contracting parties' own performance objectives.

Under the first branch of the third-party principle, therefore, the issue

---

[17] See Robert P. Smith, Recent Case, 31 Tex.L.Rev. 210, 211 (1952).

is whether allowing the third party to bring suit is an appropriate *remedy* to further the interests of the contracting parties. Like other remedial problems, this question is seldom answered by the literal terms of the contract itself. In part, this is because it is costly to write contract terms, and it is likely to be more efficient for the parties to focus on terms that describe the performance they expect to render and receive, rather than on terms that describe the consequences that are to result if an expected performance is not rendered. Furthermore, although it is relatively easy for contracting parties to specify in advance the performances they want, it is often extremely difficult to adequately specify remedies in advance of knowing the nature of the breach and the circumstances of the world at the time of the breach.

Nevertheless, a court asked to determine a remedial problem would normally do well to ask what the parties would have provided if they had bargained under ideal conditions – that is, where foresight was perfect and negotiation and drafting were cost-free. The rules that the courts apply to fill in contracts should be both fair and efficient. Contracts negotiated under ideal conditions will be efficient, and enforcing the terms of such contracts will usually be regarded as fair. Thus, a remedial rule is fair and efficient if it corresponds to the terms that rational parties situated like the contracting parties would have reached when bargaining under ideal conditions. That determination, in turn, rests largely on whether the promisee will realise the objectives he bargained for if a suit by the third-party beneficiary is not allowed; whether the promisor's liability will be extended if the suit is allowed; and, if that liability will be extended, whether the parties have implicitly bargained for the risk that it will be extended.

To put the matter simply, the question is whether it is likely that the promisee would have made the contract on the price terms he accepted if the contract had explicitly stated that the third party would not be allowed to bring suit, and whether the promisor would have made the contract on the price terms she accepted if the contract had explicitly stated that the third party would be allowed to bring suit.

Unlike the first branch of the third-party-beneficiary principle, which focuses exclusively on effectuation of the contracting parties' performance objectives, the second branch of the principle reflects the concept that in certain cases contract law properly may give effect to policy and moral concerns that are independent of the contracting parties' performance objectives. Policy and morality have traditionally entered into contract law in a variety of ways. For example, these elements help shape the rules of contract law on such issues as what kinds of promises the law should enforce, the extent to which the law should recognise limits (such as unconscionability) on the enforcement of bargain promises, and what remedies contract law should afford when enforceable promises are broken. Policy and morality also openly figure in the interpretation of contracts. For example, *Restatement Second* Section 207 provides: "In choosing among the reasonable meanings of a promise or agreement or a term thereof, a meaning that serves the public interest is generally preferred." Similarly, *Restatement Second* Section 204, Comment d states: "[W]here there is in fact no agreement [on a matter that falls within the ambit of a contract], the courts should supply a term that comports with community standards of fairness and policy rather than analyze a hypothetical model of the bargaining process."

Given the primacy of the contracting parties' performance objectives, enforcement by the third-party beneficiary should not be permitted if it would conflict with those objectives. If, however, there is no such conflict and the interests of policy or morality would be served by allowing the third party to enforce the contract, the rules of contract law should be shaped to allow such enforcement, just as they are shaped by policy and morality in other cases. Indeed, the principle that enforcement by a third party should be allowed in such cases is even easier than the principle that policy and morality are relevant to determining such issues as the interpretation of a contract or the remedies to be afforded for breach. When policy and morality figure in those areas, the results may conflict with the contracting parties' performance objectives. In contrast, under the second branch of the third-party-beneficiary principle enforcement is allowed only when there is no such conflict.

## 2. Some Recurring Third-Party-Beneficiary Categories

Part 2 illustrates the third-party-beneficiary principle, develops its implications, and shows how it explains the results of many or most of the modern American cases, by examining the application of the principle to some commonly recurring third-party-beneficiary problems. I begin with the two paradigmatic cases: donee beneficiaries (Section A) and creditor beneficiaries (Section B). I then consider cases in which the parties have explicitly provided that a third party should or should not be allowed to enforce the contract (Section C); suits by would-be legatees against attorneys who have failed properly to execute testamentary instructions (Section D); suits by subcontractors against sureties who have given bonds to owners (Section E); and suits between prime contractors (Section F).

## *A. Donee Beneficiaries*

A third-party beneficiary is a donee beneficiary when a performance objective of the contracting parties, as manifested in the contract read in the light of surrounding circumstances, is to give effect to a donative intention of the promisee. The paradigmatic American case is *Seaver v. Ransom,* decided by the New York Court of Appeals in 1918.[18] An analysis of the facts of that case shows why a donee beneficiary should be permitted to enforce a contract under the first branch of the third-party-beneficiary principle.

The contracting parties in this case were Mrs. Beman and her husband, Judge Beman. Judge Beman had drawn a will for Mrs. Beman when she was about to die. The will left a house owned by Mrs. Beman to Judge Beman for life, with the remainder to a charity. When the will was read to Mrs. Beman, she said she wanted to leave the house to her niece, Marion. Mrs. Beman's strength was waning, and although Judge Beman offered to write another will, she was afraid that she would not hold out long enough to sign it. Judge Beman therefore promised that if Mrs. Beman would sign the original will, he would leave enough to Marion in his own will to make up the difference. When Judge Beman died, however, it was found that his will made no provision for Marion. The court held that Marion could enforce the contract against Judge Beman's estate.

The result in *Seaver v. Ransom* was justified by the first branch of the third-party-beneficiary principle. A central performance objective of Judge and Mrs. Beman, as manifested in the contract, was that a gift be made to Marion through the instrumentality of the contract. Allowing Marion to enforce the contract was an important, if not necessary, means of effectuating this objective. If the contract could not be enforced by Marion, it could be enforced only by Mrs. Beman's estate. Mrs. Beman's estate, however, would have had no economic incentive to enforce the contract, because the estate would bear all the costs of enforcement while Marion would reap all the benefits. Furthermore, the estate's expectation damages would be zero, because performance of Judge Beman's promise would not have put Mrs. Beman's estate in a financially better position than would non-performance. Perhaps the estate could have sued Judge Beman's estate for unjust enrichment, but even if Mrs. Beman's estate prevailed on that theory, the suit would not effectuate the contracting parties' performance objective because Mrs. Beman's estate, rather than Marion, would end up with the recovery, and in any event the amount by which Judge Beman was unjustly enriched (the value of a life estate in Mrs. Beman's house) might

---

[18] 120 N.E. 639 (N.Y.1918).

be less than the amount he had promised to confer on Marion (the value of the house itself). A suit by the estate for specific performance would solve these problems, but again the estate would have no economic incentive to bring such a suit, and in any event specific performance is always a problematic remedy because it so often rests in the court's discretion.

Finally, allowing Marion to enforce the contract would not enlarge the liability that Judge Beman must have expected at the time the contract was made. Judge Beman's obligation under the contract was to confer upon Marion a certain amount of money. Allowing Marion to enforce the contract would not increase his liability beyond that amount.

This analysis of *Seaver v. Ransom* holds true for donee-beneficiary cases as a class. To begin with, many donee-beneficiary cases involve promises that are likely to mature only after the promisee's death. Indeed, the most common donee-beneficiary contract is the family life insurance policy, which is analytically identical to *Seaver v. Ransom.*

Of course, in some donee-beneficiary cases the promisee will not have died before the breach. The promisee may then herself have an altruistic interest in enforcing the contract. Even in such cases, however, at the time of breach the promisee will not have an economic incentive to enforce the contract. Furthermore, the problem of remedy remains. The promisee's expectation damages will often be zero; unjust enrichment might be less than the value of the promised performance; and specific performance is a problematic remedy. And whether or not the promisee is still living, enforcement by the third-party beneficiary will not expand the promisor's liability beyond what he must have expected at the time of contract formation. Accordingly, enforcement by donee beneficiaries is always justified by the first branch of the third-party-beneficiary principle, because allowing donee beneficiaries to enforce contracts under which they will benefit is a necessary or important means of effectuating the performance objectives of the parties to such a contract.

### *B. Creditor Beneficiaries*

A third-party beneficiary is a creditor beneficiary when the promisee owed the third party a legal obligation prior to the contract, and a performance objective of the contracting parties is to arrange for the discharge of that obligation by the promisor. The paradigmatic American case is *Lawrence v. Fox*, decided in 1859 by the New York Court of Appeals.[19] An analysis of the facts of that case shows why a creditor beneficiary should be permitted to enforce a contract under both the first and second branches of

19 20 N.Y. 268 (1859).

the third-party-beneficiary principle.

The contracting parties in this case were Holly and Fox. Holly owed a debt of $300 to Lawrence. Under the contract, Holly loaned $300 to Fox, and Fox in turn agreed to pay $300 to Lawrence in satisfaction of Holly's debt to Lawrence. The court held that Lawrence could enforce the contract against Fox.

This result was justified by the first branch of the third-party beneficiary principle. A central performance objective of Holly and Fox, as manifested in the contract, was that Holly should be made economically free of his obligation to Lawrence through the instrumentality of the contract. Allowing Lawrence to enforce the contract against Fox was an important means of effectuating this objective. Furthermore, allowing Lawrence to enforce the contract would not enlarge the liability that Fox must have expected at the time the contract was made. Fox's obligation under the contract was to pay Lawrence $300. If Lawrence was allowed to enforce the contract, Fox had to pay that amount. Indeed, Fox's liability would have been $300 even if Lawrence could not enforce the contract. If Fox breached the contract, Holly could sue Fox, and Holly's expectation damages would be $300 – the difference between his debts as they actually would have been on Fox's breach and his debts as they would have been if Fox had performed.

This analysis of *Lawrence v. Fox* holds true for creditor beneficiaries as a class. Accordingly, enforcement by creditor beneficiaries is always justified under the first branch of the third-party beneficiary principle. Enforcement by creditor beneficiaries is also justified under the second branch of the third-party-beneficiary principle. Enforcement by creditor beneficiaries will not conflict with the contracting parties' performance objectives, for the reasons just examined. Enforcement is supported by an independent reason of policy, because it short-circuits multiple lawsuits. If the creditor beneficiary is not allowed to enforce the contract, two suits are required: one by the beneficiary against the promisee, under the pre-existing obligation; one by the promisee against the promisor, under the contract. If the creditor beneficiary is allowed to enforce the contract, one suit will suffice.[20]

Permitting enforcement by creditor beneficiaries also helps prevent unjust enrichment. This characteristic is brought out by considering the question: Why doesn't the creditor beneficiary sue the promisee, who by hypothesis owes him a pre-existing obligation, rather than taking the more problematic path of suing the promisor? Presumably, in most cases the reason is that the promisee is not easily subject to suit – because, for

20 See *Matternes v. City of Winston-Salem* 209 S.E.2d 481, 488 (N.C.1974).

example, he is outside the jurisdiction or has become insolvent or incapacitated. If in such cases the creditor beneficiary cannot sue the promisor, the promisor would often be unjustly enriched by the amount of the consideration he has received from the promisee.

### *C. Cases in Which the Parties Have Explicitly Provided that a Third-Party Beneficiary Should or Should Not Be Allowed to Enforce the Contract*

There is one class of third-party-beneficiary cases that is even easier to resolve than the donee- and creditor-beneficiary cases. This is the class of cases in which the contracting parties explicitly provide that a third-party beneficiary should or should not be allowed to enforce the contract. Such cases are easy because they leave no doubt whether allowing the third party to enforce the contract is a necessary or important means of effectuating the contracting parties' performance objectives: the parties themselves have explicitly spoken to that issue. For example, an American Institute of Architects (A.I.A.) form of a payment bond between an owner on the one hand, and a principal contractor and a surety on the other, provides:

> The . . . Principal and Surety hereby jointly and severally agree with the Owner that every [third-party] claimant as herein defined, who has not been paid in full before the expiration of a period of ninety (90) days after the date on which the last of such claimant's work or labor was done or performed, or materials were furnished by such claimant, may sue on this bond . . . , prosecute the suit to final judgment for such sum or sums as may be justly due claimant, and have execution thereon.[21]

In contrast, an A.I.A. form for contracts between owners and architects provides that "[n]othing contained in this Agreement shall create a contractual relationship with or a cause of action in favor of a third party against either the Owner or Architect".[22]

Under the third-party-beneficiary principle, both types of provisions should be given effect – one type to allow enforcement by third parties, and one type to deny such enforcement – because that result is required to effectuate the contracting parties' performance objectives.

### *D. Would-Be Legatees*

Another relatively easy case involves a class of third parties that I will call

---

21 Am.Inst. Architects Doc. A311, Labor and Material Payment Bond art. 2 (1970).

22 Am.Inst. Architects Doc. B141, Standard Form of Agreement Between Owner and Architect art. 9.7 (1987). See also Am.Inst. Architects Doc. A201, General Conditions of the Contract for Construction art. 1.1.2 (1987).

would-be legatees. Assume that A wishes to confer a given benefit on T at the time of A's death. B, an attorney, agrees with A to prepare a legal instrument – typically, a will – to accomplish A's objective.[23] Upon A's death, it becomes clear for the first time that A's will fails validly to confer the given benefit on T. T then sues B, the attorney, as a third-party beneficiary of the contract between B and A.

Under the first branch of the third-party-beneficiary principle, the would-be legatee should be allowed to enforce the contract against the attorney. A performance objective of the contracting parties, testator and attorney, was to make whatever legal arrangements were required to ensure that on the testator's death a given benefit would be conferred on the would-be legatee. Allowing the would-be legatee to recover against the attorney is an important and indeed necessary means to effectuate that objective.[24] The testator cannot sue the attorney, because the testator has died. The testator's estate cannot sue the attorney, because the estate has not been injured.[25] Even if the estate could sue the attorney, its damages would be measured only by the testator's disappointed expectation, which would be almost impossible to fix, and in any event the recovery would end up in the hands of the estate rather than those of the would-be legatee.

Unlike the donee- and creditor-beneficiary cases, allowing a would-be legatee to enforce the contract between the testator and the attorney exposes the attorney to a liability that is different and inevitably much wider than the performance required under the contract, which is simply to draw up a will. However, this wider liability is generally comparable to the liability to which attorneys are routinely subject in non-testamentary cases under the law of malpractice. Because an attorney's exposure to liability is greater if a would-be legatee can enforce the contract than if he cannot, the attorney's fee will presumably reflect a premium for that liability. However, testamentary clients are undoubtedly willing to pay that premium, just as non-testamentary clients are willing to pay a premium for attorney malpractice liability in all other cases.

The modern American cases generally support the conclusion that a would-be legatee should be allowed to recover against an attorney who has failed properly to execute her client's testamentary objectives. There is some conflict, however, concerning the proper theory on which the action

---

23 For ease of exposition, I will focus on would-be legatees, but the same analysis applies to other similarly situated persons, such as would-be beneficiaries under trusts that include benefits that are to take effect on the settlor's death.

24 See *Guy v. Liederbach* 459 A.2d 744, 751 (Pa.1983); *Lucas v. Hamm* 364 P.2d 685, 689 (Cal.1961).

25 See *Heyer v. Flaig* 449 P.2d 161, 165 (Cal.1970); *Liederbach*, supra, 459 A.2d at 749 (1983).

should be based. Most of the modern cases allow a would-be legatee to rest on third-party-beneficiary theory,[26] but many allow him to rest alternatively on negligence,[27] some allow him to rest only on negligence,[28] and some allow him to rest only on contract.[29]

This confusion is not surprising. Because the relationship between professionals and their clients is consensual, a suit against a negligent professional can often be conceptualised as sounding either in malpractice for non-performance of an obligation to exercise care that is imposed by law, or in breach of contract for non-performance of an obligation to exercise care to which the parties implicitly agreed.[30]

Although the importance of allowing a would-be legatee to recover overshadows the theory of recovery, the contract theory is preferable to the tort theory, in part because it sharpens the nature of the attorney's obligation in the legatee case. In contract cases, typically each contracting party obliges itself to achieve a given result. In contrast, in most malpractice cases the obligation of the professional is not to achieve a given result, but to employ an appropriate process. In the typical physician-patient case, for example, the physician's obligation is not to cure, but only to treat properly. Similarly, a litigator is typically not obliged to win a suit, or even to achieve a favourable settlement, but only to handle the suit properly. Because professionals normally do not explicitly or implicitly promise to do more than use an appropriate process, in most cases the professional's obligation could be treated under tort or contract law with essentially the same result.[31]

Different considerations apply, however, when an attorney drafts a will. In such cases, a lay client is justified in forming the expectation that unless stated otherwise, the attorney has committed herself to achieve a certain result – namely, that the client's stated objectives will be achieved. If there is doubt whether the client's stated objectives can be achieved – if, for example, the client's objectives are problematic under the Rule Against

---

26 See, e.g., *Stowe v. Smith* 441 A.2d 81, 83 (Conn.1981); *Hale v. Groce* 744 P.2d 1289, 1292 (Or.1987); *Liederbach*, supra, 459 A.2d at 753 (Nix, J., concurring) (1983).

27 See, e.g., *Lucas*, supra, 364 P.2d at 688 (1961); *Garcia v. Borelli* 180 Cal.Rptr. 768, 772 (Ct.App.1982); *Bucquet v. Livingston* 129 Cal.Rptr. 514, 518 (Ct.App.1976); *Ogle v. Fuiten* 445 N.E.2d 1344, 1348 (Ill.App.Ct.1983).

28 See *Heyer* supra, 449 P.2d at 164 (1970).

29 See, e.g., *Liederbach*, supra, 459 A.2d at 750 (1983).

30 Cf. id. at 748 (client may sue attorney for malpractice under either trespass or assumpsit theory).

31 I put aside here peripheral rules, such as differences in the statutes of limitation for contract and tort or the availability of punitive damages, that are accidental in the sense that, as applied to the malpractice case, they turn on the form of the complaint rather than on the substance of the underlying transaction.

Perpetuities – the attorney is obliged to tell the client of the doubt and lay out the risks and the options. If she fails to do so, and an unexplained risk matures, the attorney should be liable for breach of her implied promise to achieve the client's objectives. Courts that allow a would-be legatee to sue only in negligence may easily miss that point and focus instead on whether the attorney failed to use a required degree of skill.

### *E. Suits by Subcontractors Against the Sureties of Prime Contractors*

This and the next section concern cases that arise in construction settings. The rich web of contracts that are often found in these settings gives rise to a variety of recurring third-party-beneficiary problems.

In the typical construction setting, a private or public entity – an owner – makes a contract with a prime contractor who agrees to perform specified construction. The prime contractor, in turn, contracts with various subcontractors, who agree to perform portions of the construction. Because contractors are typically thinly capitalised, an owner often requires a prime contractor to provide either (i) a performance bond, under which a surety guarantees the owner that the prime contractor will perform its contract with the owner; (ii) a payment bond, under which a surety guarantees the owner that the claims of subcontractors will be paid; or (iii) both a performance and a payment bond. In this Section, I consider the question whether an unpaid subcontractor can enforce a payment bond between a surety and an owner.

In the traditional analysis of this issue, American courts distinguished between payment bonds running to public owners and payment bonds running to private owners. Subcontractors were allowed to recover under payment bonds running to public owners, but not under payment bonds running to private owners.[32] The distinction rested on an application of the intent-to-benefit test to the assumed motivations of public and private owners in requiring the prime contractor's payment obligations to be bonded.

The analysis was as follows. A subcontractor usually has a right to file a lien on a private owner's property for the value of the work it has performed. As a result, if the prime contractor fails to pay a subcontractor, a private owner may be required either to pay the subcontractor itself or to bear the impact of a foreclosure under the lien. Accordingly, the courts reasoned, when a private owner requires a prime contractor to bond the

---

[32] See, e.g., *National Sur. Co. v. Brown-Graves Co.* 7 F.2d 91, 92 (6th Cir.1925); *Maryland Casualty Co. v. Johnson* 15 F.2d 253, 254-55 (W.D.Mich.1926). For a review of the older case law, see *Cretex Cos. v. Construction Leaders, Inc.* 342 N.W.2d 135, 139-40 (Minn.1984).

prime's payment obligation to subcontractors, the private owner's intent must be, not to benefit the subcontractors, but to benefit itself, by ensuring that it will not suffer economic injury as a result of liens filed by unpaid subcontractors. Based on this line of reasoning, it was held that under the intent-to-benefit test the subcontractors could not sue the surety in a private-construction case, because the private owner did not intend to benefit the subcontractors.

On the other hand, the lien laws typically do not extend to public construction. Therefore, a public owner will typically suffer no economic injury if subcontractors are not paid.[33] Accordingly, if a public owner requires a prime contractor to bond its payment obligation, the owner's intent must be to benefit not itself, but the subcontractors. Based on this line of reasoning, it was held that under the intent-to-benefit test the subcontractors could sue the surety in a public-construction case, because the public owner must have intended to benefit the subcontractors.

In contrast to this traditional analysis, the modern American tendency is to allow subcontractors to recover against the sureties of payment bonds in both private and public cases.[34] This approach is supported by the third-party beneficiary principle. The traditional analysis of the owner's motivation was myopic, because under the intent-to-benefit test the courts looked for other-regarding rather than self-regarding objectives. Certainly, a private owner, and probably even a public owner, who secures a surety bond does so for self-regarding reasons. However, it is easy to see why both public and private owners would have self-regarding objectives that would best be effectuated by allowing subcontractors to sue a surety on a payment bond.

Begin with public construction. A public owner may reasonably believe that the cost of construction will be lower if subcontractors are afforded assurance of payment. Subcontractors will make lower bids to prime contractors if they need not impound the risk of non-payment into their costs; and if subcontractors' bids are lower, prime contractors' bids will also be lower.[35] It is true that the cost to a prime contractor for a payment bond will be higher if subcontractors can enforce it,[36] and that cost

---

33 Justin Sweet, *Legal Aspects of Architecture, Engineering and the Construction Process*, § 37.07, at 748 (4th ed. 1989).

34 See, e.g., *Socony-Vacuum Oil Co. v. Continental Casualty Co.* 219 F.2d 645, 649 (2d Cir.1955); *Daniel-Morris Co. v. Glen Falls Indem. Co.* 126 N.E.2d 750, 752-53 (N.Y.1955); *Jacobs Assocs. v. Argonaut Ins. Co.* 580 P.2d 529, 532 (Or.1978); Sweet, *Legal Aspects*, supra note 33, § 37.10(A), at 750.

35 See Sweet, *Legal Aspects*, supra note 33, § 37.07, at 748.

36 If subcontractors on a public bond remain unpaid, the public owner's loss, and therefore the surety's liability for the owner's damages, is likely to be zero. In contrast, the subcontractors' losses will be substantial. Therefore, if subcontractors can enforce the

will be passed along to the owner when the prime contractor sets its total price. However, public owners may reasonably believe that the decrease in cost if subcontractors are assured of payment will exceed the increase in cost resulting from the surety's higher premium, because subcontractors would be likely to charge more than sureties for bearing the risk of a prime contractor's insolvency. One basis for such a belief is that subcontractors are often both small and thinly capitalised, and therefore especially risk-averse. Another basis for such a belief is that subcontractors are less able than sureties to determine the creditworthiness of prime contractors, and therefore are likely to include in their calculations an extra margin for ignorance. Because a surety will be more knowledgeable about the risk of a prime's creditworthiness, and less risk-averse, than a subcontractor, the premium charged by a surety to assure payment to subcontractors often or usually will be less than the premium that subcontractors will add to their prices to cover the risk of non-payment by the prime. Since either type of premium will ultimately be passed along to the public owner, the owner may reasonably believe that his costs will be lower if subcontractors are assured of payment than if they are not.

Of course, a public owner may believe that the contrary is true. However, the fact that a public owner has required a payment bond tells us that it has adopted the performance objective of affording subcontractors assurance of payment. To effectuate this performance objective, subcontractors must be given a right to enforce the bond.

Essentially the same analysis applies to private construction. It is true that in the case of private construction, unpaid subcontractors often will not lose out completely, because they will be protected under the lien laws. Despite the lien laws, however, some risk will remain. The lien laws are not always easy to comply with, enforcing a lien can be complex and expensive, and the private owner's equity may be less than the total claims of lienholders. Even in the case of private construction, therefore, a subcontractor who is not afforded assurance of payment is likely to include a premium in his bid to cover the risk of non-repayment, and this premium may exceed the premium charged by a surety.

Professor Sweet has pointed out still another self-regarding motive that a private owner may have for affording subcontractors assurance of payment – an interest in the smooth administration of the construction process:

> [Subcontractors] should be more willing to perform properly and deliver materials as quickly as possible when they have assurance they will be paid.

---

bond, the potential liability of the surety – and accordingly, its premium – will be higher than if the surety is liable only for the public owner's damages.

> Though they have a right to a mechanics' lien, the procedures for perfecting the lien and satisfying the unpaid obligation out of foreclosure proceeds are cumbersome and often ineffective. Payment bonds are preferable to mechanics' liens.[37]

Finally, a private owner may also want to afford subcontractors assurance of payment to avoid the transaction costs involved when liens are filed.

In short, a private owner may reasonably believe that he will lower his costs if he affords assurance of payment to subcontractors by obtaining a payment bond. Allowing subcontractors to enforce a payment bond is a necessary means of effectuating that objective.

How do we know whether a given surety bond embodies that performance objective? Often, the bond tells us so. Recall that one form of the A.I.A. Payment Bond explicitly states that subcontractors can sue the surety on the bond.[38] Even when a bond is not as explicit as the A.I.A. Form, the very fact that a private owner has required a payment bond normally reveals that his objective is to afford subcontractors assurance of payment. If an owner only wants to protect himself against his own direct losses resulting from the non-payment of subcontractors, he can do so by simply requiring the prime contractor to provide a performance bond. Performance bonds protect an owner against loss caused by the prime contractor's non-performance, and therefore normally cover losses to the owner as a result of subcontractor liens. Accordingly, if an owner requires a prime contractor to provide a payment bond as well as a performance bond, the inference is compelling that the contracting parties' performance objectives include affording subcontractors assurance of payment.[39]

The case is different if an owner requires a performance bond, but not a payment bond. A payment bond explicitly provides that subcontractors will be paid. A performance bond does not. Given the wide availability and frequent use of payment bonds, the decision of an owner to obtain only a performance bond reveals that the performance objectives of the owner and the surety do not include affording subcontractors assurance of payment. Accordingly, subcontractors normally should not be allowed to enforce performance bonds.[40]

---

37 See Sweet, *Legal Aspects*, supra note 33, § 37.07, at 748.

38 See supra Part II.C.

39 See, e.g., *Socony-Vacuum Oil Co. v. Continental Casualty Co.* 219 F.2d 645, 648 (2d Cir.1955); *Fidelity & Deposit Co. v. Rainer* 125 So. 55, 58 (Ala.1929); *Jacobs Assocs. v. Argonaut Ins. Co.* 580 P.2d 529, 531 (Or.1978).

40 See *Cretex Cos. v. Construction Leaders, Inc.*, 342 N.W.2d 135, 137- 38 (Minn.1984):

> [The surety] points out that if the owner and general contractor had wished to protect third-party materialmen they could have purchased, for a separate premium, a "labor

## *F. Multi-Prime Contracts*

Another, more difficult case that arises in the construction setting involves claims among prime contractors in a multi-prime contract. Most construction contracts involve a single prime contractor who contracts directly with the owner and is responsible for the coordination of all construction, and who in turn contracts with a number of specialised subcontractors. In contrast, in multi-prime contracts an owner either contracts with several prime contractors or contracts directly with specialised contractors who normally would contract only with a prime.

An owner may enter into a multi-prime contract for business reasons – for example, because the construction is divided into semi-independent segments, such as portions of a pipeline or highway or because it is more efficient for the owner to take on the task of coordination than to pay a prime contractor for doing so. Often, however, multi-prime contracts are made because they are required by statute.[41]

Because the performances of prime contractors in a multi-prime contract tend to be closely interrelated, a delay or other breach by one prime will often lead to losses by others. Suppose Prime 1 delays or otherwise breaches its contract with the owner, and Prime 2 is injured by the breach. Can Prime 2 sue Prime 1 as a third-party beneficiary of the contract between Prime 1 and the owner? The general trend of the American cases allows such suits.[42] That result is supported by the third-party-beneficiary principle.

In some cases, Prime 1 explicitly promises the owner that it will pay

---

> and material payment bond", a bond which [the surety] also sells and which is usually issued simultaneously with the performance bond. A "payment" bond expressly provides for the surety to pay the claims of third-party subcontractors and materialmen if the general contractor fails to do so. The distinction between performance bonds and payment bonds is well recognized in the construction industry; the two bonds cover different risks and premiums are set accordingly.

*Accord Hewson Constr., Inc. v. Reintree Corp.* 685 P.2d 1062, 1066 (Wash. 1984) (bond guaranteed only performance, not payment).

41 See generally Sweet, *Legal Aspects*, supra note 33, § 21.04, at 379. Such statutes are usually adopted at the instance of subcontractors, because subcontractors on public construction prefer to be in a direct contractual relation with the governmental entity, which typically presents little or no risk of insolvency, rather than with a prime contractor, which often presents a significant risk of insolvency.

42 See, e.g., *M.T. Reed Constr. Co. v. Virginia Metal Prods. Corp.* 213 F.2d 337 (5th Cir.1954); *Hanberry Corp. v. State Bldg. Comm'n* 390 So.2d 277, 278-81 (Miss.1980); *J. Louis Crum Corp. v. Alfred Lindgren, Inc.* 564 S.W.2d 544, 546-49 (Mo.Ct.App.1978). But see *J.F., Inc. v. S.M. Wilson & Co.* 504 N.E.2d 1266, 1269-71 (Ill.App.Ct.1987).

the expenses of other primes resulting from its delays. Breach of such a promise by Prime 1 is best remedied by allowing a suit by Prime 2. Often, the owner will suffer no damages from such a breach. For example, Prime 2 may manage to complete its performance on time, despite Prime 1's delay, by accelerating its efforts at an increased cost to compensate for the delay. The promise by Prime 1 would lose much of its effect if Prime 2 was not allowed to bring suit in such a case.

In other cases, each co-prime promises the owner that it will cooperate or coordinate with the other primes, but does not explicitly promise to pay the expenses that its co-primes incur as the result of its breach. In such cases too, Prime 2 should be allowed to recover against Prime 1. Because breach of a promise to cooperate or coordinate may also cause damage to the co-primes even though it does not cause damage to the owner, unless Prime 2 is allowed to sue Prime 1 the objective of the cooperate-and-coordinate provision may not be fully effectuated.

If Prime 1 will be liable to Prime 2 for breach of its contract with the owner, Prime 1 will presumably include in its price to the owner a premium that reflects this extra exposure to liability. Why would a self-regarding owner pay that premium, when liability by one co-prime to another seems to benefit the co-primes rather than the owner? The answer is comparable to that found in the analysis of surety bonds. Although a prime will include in its bid a premium for becoming exposed to liability to its co-primes, in the absence of such liability a prime will include in its bid a premium for bearing the risk of uncompensated losses resulting from breaches by its co-primes. An owner may reasonably believe that the premium that a prime will charge for bearing the risk of losses resulting from breaches by its co-primes is likely to exceed the premium that a prime will charge for bearing the risk of liability to its co-primes, because a prime's own performance is largely within its control, while the performance of its co-primes is not. Furthermore, some breaches by a co-prime may subject the owner to liability for breach of an implied duty to coordinate and supervise the co-primes' activities.[43] An owner may therefore have the objective of making co-primes liable to each other for their breaches to afford an injured co-prime a more direct target than the owner himself. Indeed, if an owner owes its co-primes a duty to coordinate, and Prime 1 promises the owner that it will coordinate with its co-primes, Prime 2 could simply be treated as a creditor beneficiary of that promise.[44]

---

43 See *Shea-S & M Ball v. Massman-Kiewit-Early* 606 F.2d 1245, 1251 (D.C.Cir. 1979); *Hoffman v. United States* 340 F.2d 645, 650 (Cl.Ct.1964); *Broadway* 447 A.2d at 912.

44 See *COAC, Inc. v. Kennedy Eng'rs* 136 Cal.Rptr. 890, 893 (Ct.App.1977); *Visintine & Co. v. New York, Chi. & St. L.R.R.* 160 N.E.2d 311, 313-14 (Ohio 1959).

## Conclusion

Under the traditional rule of contract law, third-party beneficiaries could not enforce a contract. This rule was sought to be justified on purely doctrinal grounds. To a limited extent, however, the rule could be supported on normative grounds, because in many cases allowing a third-party beneficiary to sue would be inconsistent with the performance objectives of the contracting parties. Nevertheless, it is clear that there are a number of cases in which third-party beneficiaries should be allowed to enforce contracts. In some cases, allowing such enforcement furthers the performance objectives of the contracting parties. In other cases, allowing such enforcement is supported by reasons of morality or policy and does not conflict with the contracting parties' performance objectives. As a result, the rule that prohibited *any* third-party beneficiary from bringing suit was normatively unjustified. The problem, then, is to determine a principle that identifies the third-party beneficiaries who should be allowed to enforce a contract.

The third-party-beneficiary principle provides a general and principled standard, anchored in the basic aims of contract law, for determining when a third-party beneficiary should be allowed to bring suit. For some recurring classes of cases, such as those discussed in Part II, the principle can be elaborated into more specific rules. In other, non-recurring cases, the principle provides a standard for judgment and forces to the surface the considerations that should determine the result.

# 10 Is Privity Worth Defending?

JOHN GAVA

Is privity worth defending? In this paper I will answer this question, in a preliminary fashion, by placing the attack on privity within a larger attack on classical, common law contract. In other words, my defence of privity is based on the belief that the doctrinal integrity of common law contract is under threat and that the attack on privity is one front, so to speak, in a far larger battle. If this is the case, to defend contract is to defend privity. Of course, there are perfectly respectable arguments for thinking that privity is not central to contract and that, therefore, the rejection of privity does not entail an attack on contract.[1] There are also perfectly respectable arguments for thinking that, despite the aura of change surrounding contract from the days of the Mason High Court, common law contract is not under severe threat.[2] While I do not agree with these positions I do not want to enter into a debate about them. Rather, I want to consider whether, if the attack on privity is part of a larger attack on contract, contract is worth defending.

One way in which this attack manifests itself is through a belief that contract, as presently understood and conceived, is not suited to the needs of commerce. I will call this a functionalist criticism and this position will be the foil against which this paper will develop. By functionalism I mean a belief that the law of contract should clearly reflect the practices and expectations of those in business and, that if it does not, it should change so that it does. Because contract has been and still is largely judge made, functionalism in contract concentrates on judges and their development of the law. As a consequence, this essay will concentrate on judges rather than legislators.[3] But, as will be seen below, legislation cannot be ignored

---

1 See, for example, the discussion of these arguments in P. Kincaid, "The U.K. Law Commission's Privity Proposals and Contract Theory" (1994) 8 Journal of Contract Law 51.

2 See, for example, N. Seddon, "Australian Contract Law: Maelstrom or Measured Mutation?" (1994) 7 Journal of Contract Law 93 and, for a contrary view, J. Gava and P. Kincaid, "Contract and Conventionalism: Professional Attitudes to Changes in Contract Law in Australia" (1996) 10 Journal of Contract Law 141.

3 See, for example, R. Brownsword, "Static and Dynamic Market-Individualism" in *Exploring the Boundaries of Contract*, R. Halson (ed.), (Aldershot 1996), pp. 48-67 for a clear exposition of this position. For the purposes of this paper the distinction between

in a discussion of functionalism.

An essay in a book might seem an inappropriate place to mount a defence of contract. That would be true if an attempt were made to do so in any detail. However, it may be appropriate to conduct the equivalent of a thought experiment and outline how one would go about creating the structure for a defence of common law contract. This will be the approach that will be followed in this essay.

I will begin by giving academic and judicial examples of functionalist thinking in contract. The next step will involve an investigation of the historical relationship between contract and the market. In particular, I consider whether contract has changed to suit the changing needs of the market. This will be examined by discussing Alan Watson's views on the relationship between law and society and then considering the functionalist views of legal history written by Richard Danzig and Morton Horwitz and criticisms of them by A.W.B. Simpson. It will be argued that Simpson's criticisms of functionalist views of contract are convincing and that his belief that there has not been, historically, a particularly close link between contract and the perceived or real needs of the market is equally convincing. This raises doubts about the possibility of such a relationship today.

Thirdly, an overview of the literature, empirical and theoretical, on the use and non-use of contract in the market today will be given to show that the role of contract is not that which is commonly accepted. It will be argued that contract law is not a template around which contracting parties organise their bargaining but, rather, that contract is used more or less tactically, depending on the particular industry, the particular time in the economic cycle and on the particular nature of the transaction. If this is the case, it seems unwise and even pointless to argue that contract law should be developed to suit the real or perceived needs of commerce.

Fourthly, it will be argued that for reasons of institutional competence it would be wrong to reform contract along functional lines. Common law judges do not have the knowledge and common law courts do not have the staff to act as roving law reform commissioners. It will be argued also that the search for business custom is misconceived and that the flexibility supposedly associated with functionalist judging would actually

---

anti-formalism and formalism in contract law as expressed in the following articles referred to in this paper is equivalent to the difference between functionalism and classical contract. L. Bernstein, "The Questionable Empirical Basis of Article 2's Incorporation Strategy: A Preliminary Study" (1999) 66 University of Chicago Law Review 710; O. Ben-Shahar, "The Tentative Case Against Flexibility in Commercial Law" (1999) 66 University of Chicago Law Review 781 and D. Charny, "The New Formalism in Contract" (1999) 66 University of Chicago Law Review 842.

work against the needs of the market.

Finally, the values of contract and the constitutional appropriateness of a functionalist view will be considered. It will be argued that the value of keeping one's promises is a longstanding feature of the common law, one which should not be readily or easily set aside because its implicit associations about the worth of individuals and respect for their autonomy are so valuable. Since the evidence suggests that contract cannot and has not tracked the demands of the marketplace it seems perverse to ditch such a fundamental legal tool on a pointless crusade. The activism that would result from such a role would, in any event, severely challenge notions of democratic law making and governance.

This essay will then consider the implications of these arguments for an understanding of the role of classical contract today.

## Functionalism and Contract

One finds examples of a functionalist approach to privity, and contract more generally, in both academic writing and judicial decisions. First, an academic view.

Hugh Collins has called for a functional approach to the law of contract based on changes to the vision of justice underlying contract and the reality of business dealings in contemporary society. According to Collins, the underlying vision of justice of contract has changed in the following manner.

> Liberty, equality, and reciprocity: these ideals of the justice of exchange make up the conception of the market order expressed by the classical law of contract. . . [I argue], however, that this ideal has long since lost its moral force and explanatory power. The advent of the Welfare State signals a loss of faith in the justice of exchange. . . [E]ven in the sphere of social interaction left to market transactions, this disenchantment with the classical ideal pervades the detailed rules of the law of contract. We cannot pretend [10] that society's adoption of communitarian values has left untouched the fundamental rules governing ordinary market transactions. Texts which ignore this transformation of the law of contract hamper our understanding and impede the realization of the new market order of power and wealth defined by the ideals of the Welfare State.[4]

He also argues that the nature of market exchange has been transformed.

---

4 H. Collins, *The Law of Contract* (London 1986), pp. 9-10.

> As a result of the increasing division of labour, the simple model of a brief exchange transaction envisaged by the classical law rarely corresponds to modern business transactions. These days, a business deal often involves multiple parties with varying degrees of interdependence over a period of time. . . Within this complex web of economic relations, some transactions can be described as an exchange, but others only amount to more diffuse forms of reliance. . . In order to resolve disputes arising in these complex economic relations, the modern law of contract drops its premiss that all market transactions may be conceived in the shape of simple exchange transactions. It draws upon principles of fair dealing to impose a normative framework around the parties. . . Contractual obligations arise in circumstances where persons rely upon each other without the necessity for an explicit agreement or consent to the formation of the obligation and without the exchange of values envisaged by the classical law. Moreover, liability extends beyond the [11] parties to the agreement to other dependent persons within a complex business association.[5]

As the last sentence in the quote makes clear, Collins thinks that current market structures and behaviour are inconsistent with the classical rules of privity (and much else in classical contract, for that matter).

The joint judgment of Mason C.J. and Wilson J. in *Trident v. McNiece*[6] is a clear judicial example of this type of thinking. It will be recalled that McNiece, although not a party to a contract of insurance and not having provided any consideration for that contract, had sought an indemnity from an insurance company, Trident. Trident had contracted with Blue Circle and this contract included a provision that all contractors and sub-contractors associated with Blue Circle would be covered. Subsequent to this, Blue Circle engaged McNiece and a sub-contractor engaged by the latter was injured. McNiece sought the indemnity as compensation for losses associated with that injury. After discussing the problems raised by privity and the flaws of suggested "exceptions" to that rule, Mason C.J. and Wilson J. decided that it would be unjust to apply the traditional rules of privity to insurance contracts.

> The injustice which would flow from such a result arises not only from its failure to give effect to the expressed intention of the person who takes out the insurance but also from the common intention of the parties and the circumstance that others, aware of the existence of the policy, will order their affairs accordingly. . . In the nature of things the likelihood of some degree of reliance on the part of the third party in the case of a benefit to be

---

5 Ibid., at 10-11.

6 *Trident General Insurance Co. Ltd. v. McNiece Bros. Pty. Ltd.* (1988) 165 C.L.R. 10.

> provided for him under an [124] insurance policy is so tangible that the common law rule should be shaped with that likelihood in mind.
>
> This argument has even greater force when it is applied to an insurance against liabilities which is expressed to cover the insured and its sub-contractors. It stands to reason that many sub-contractors will assume that such an insurance is an effective indemnity in their favour and that they will refrain from making their own arrangements for insurance on that footing. That, it seems, is what happened in the present case.[7]

Apart from a general belief that privity caused injustice by not giving effect to the expressed wishes of the contracting parties, it is clear that Mason C.J. and Wilson J. also thought that the traditional rules should be changed if they ran counter to business expectations or practice.

Does legal history show that common law judges have displayed such functionalist attitudes in their judging in the past? The next section will consider this question.

## Functionalism and Legal History

What is the relationship between law and society? Alan Watson[8] thinks that the relationship is not as close as is commonly assumed. While he does not rule out the possibility of close links between the needs of society, or of powerful groups in society and particular rules or changes in rules, he does not think that this is generally the case. Rather, he argues that there is good reason to think that, often, the law will be dysfunctional in that it is at odds either with general notions of efficiency or with the interests and desires of ruling groups. As he says, how could one think that the arcane rules surrounding land law in England, which survived for so many centuries, served the interests of any group in England, lawyers excepted. In his eyes these rules were dysfunctional and were known to be so for a very long time. Yet they were not changed.

Watson argues that legal historians and sociologists have misread both the past and the present. He thinks that they have underestimated the cultural strength of law and the substantial distance between it and the rest of society. Legal historians have failed to recognise the importance of legal borrowing for the development of law and that this borrowing often paid no attention to the differences between borrower and borrowee. In other words, rules often would be adopted which were either dysfunctional or not

---

7 Ibid., at 123-4, per Mason C.J. and Wilson J.

8 Alan Watson has provided a neat summary of his views in "Legal Change: Sources of Law and Legal Culture" reproduced in A. Watson, *Legal Origins and Legal Change* (London 1991), pp. 69-105.

entirely appropriate to the adopting society. Partly this was due to the continuing lure of authority. Roman law was thus important to the Western legal tradition because, in large part, it was considered to be intellectually advanced in comparison with existing legal systems. Partly this was due to a natural economy of effort. Why bother to create rules to deal with complicated legal problems when others have done it for you? Watson also thinks that the development of these adopted or created rules has been misunderstood. He recognises that not all rules could be totally dysfunctional but he thinks that many can be and that many others are often less than optimal and fail to reflect societal or even elite demands.

Far from reflecting changes in society or economy, rules, according to Watson, are primarily influenced by the legal culture. This operates in two ways. First, lawyers have a vested interest, both financial and institutional in existing rules. After all, they are the ones who can guide lay people through the legal maze. Greater simplicity is not necessarily in the financial interests of lawyers. Neither will it ensure their continued employment. Second, lawyers have a craft perspective on the law. Logical consistency and the allurements of technical mastery and virtuosity in the deployment and development of rules are strong forces operating on law which do not directly reflect societal desires or interests. The empirical evidence garnered over the last 25 years about the relative unimportance of contract in business today, which will be considered in the next section, supports Watson's account.

If we consider functionalism from the narrower perspective of the relationship between contract law and the market the salience of Watson's position becomes clear. Thus, for example, Richard Danzig and Morton Horwitz have claimed that contract rules changed directly to reflect changes in the market. Danzig argued that one could only understand the rule in *Hadley v. Baxendale*[9] by understanding the context in which it was created. For Danzig the state of industrialisation, the form of transport and the nature of the legal system which characterised England in the 1850s together explained the genesis and acceptance of the rule of damages associated with that case.[10] Horwitz's argument was more ambitious. He argued that contract law changed fundamentally in the United States and England from the 18th to the 19th centuries to reflect similar, fundamental changes in the nature of the economy. For Horwitz contract changed from a relationship based on partly performed transactions over which the courts had a residual power to police fairness, to one based on expectation damages in which the parties were seen as the best judges of the fairness of

---

9 (1854) 9 Ex. 341, 156 Eng. Rep. 145.

10 R. Danzig, "Hadley *v.* Baxendale: A Study in the Industrialization of the Law" (1975) 4 Journal of Legal Studies 249.

a transaction. In other words, the basis of contractual obligation changed from the inherent fairness of an exchange to the will of the contracting parties.[11] Horwitz thought that this change reflected the emergence of a market economy in both the U.S. and England.[12]

In a series of articles A.W.B. Simpson has responded to these claims. Simpson finds Horwitz unconvincing because the evidence that he provides is ambiguous at best and inconsistent at worst. In particular, Simpson argues that the cases and textbooks used by Horwitz to support his specific and general propositions simply did not back him up. It is not appropriate here to detail the criticisms made by Simpson but they are exhaustive and convincing.[13] Simpson's criticism of Danzig's position follows the same lines. Unlike Danzig, Simpson does not think that societal changes and pressures explain the genesis of the rule in *Hadley v. Baxendale*. If Danzig is correct, he asks, how are we to explain the existence of a similar rule in non-industrialising, 18th century France?[14] *Hadley v. Baxendale*[15] is better understood, according to Simpson, as part of a more general reception of continental legal ideas into the common law caused by the growth of a previously non-existent, systematic, textbook tradition in the common law. In his words:

> At least in the Western European legal tradition of private law successful creative work consists in a combination between intelligent plagiarism and systematisation of what is lifted from others. This is so partly because of the ramifications of the concept of authority; what the writer says appears more persuasive if it is the same as what others have said. Partly the explanation lies in the close connection between private law and certain moral ideas which have remained relatively static over long periods, thus constantly generating similar principles and problems; it is I think this fact which made plausible the idea that there might exist a general jurisprudence of contract.[16]

The parallels with Watson are clear, especially in the first part of this

---

11 M. Horwitz, "The Historical Foundations of Modern Contract Law" (1974) 87 Harvard Law Review 917. This article was incorporated, with some additions in M. Horwitz, *The Transformation of American Law 1780-1860* (Harvard 1977).

12 Ibid., at 918.

13 A.W.B. Simpson, "The Horwitz Thesis and the History of Contracts" (1979) 46 University of Chicago Law Review 533.

14 Ibid., at 591. Simpson's criticism of Danzig concerns interpretation. He does not criticise Danzig's scholarship.

15 (1854) 9 Ex. 341, 155 Eng. Rep. 145.

16 A.W.B. Simpson, "Innovation in Nineteenth Century Contract Law" (1975) 91 Law Quarterly Review 247 at 254. The derivation of the rule in *Hadley v. Baxendale* from its civilian antecedents is given in some detail at 273-7.

quotation. Legal borrowing explains the genesis of the rule in question. Danzig recognised the origin of the rule. What was at issue was the cause of its reception. Was it, as Danzig thought, an opportunistic borrowing responding to needs driven directly by the industrialising market of mid-19th century England and thus a substantial change to the law? Or was Simpson right when he argued that it was the impetus of a newly emerging textbook tradition in the common law that drove the adoption of foreign rules to fill gaps? Presumably for Simpson, the new rules did not represent a changed attitude to contract or the operation of a fundamentally new understanding of contract. Rather, the "new" rule established in *Hadley v. Baxendale*[17] elaborated and presented in acceptable, intellectual fashion a damages calculus which meshed with the principles and case law of the existing common law of contract.

The second half of the quotation is consistent with such a view. If "contract" is substituted for "certain moral ideas" the image that is conveyed is rich with meaning. What it suggests is that the keeping of promises is one of those moral ideas and that the common law has treated the keeping, or more accurately, the enforcing of promises as central to contract. If this is the case and the common law has maintained this link for a number of centuries (at least from the early 17th) one can see legal development in contract as largely technical or intellectual. Since the fundamental nature of contract, the enforcement of promises, is fixed, the role of the law is constantly to elaborate and bring to a higher state of perfection the legal rules that have been developed to give effect to this central idea. Seen in this light the adoption of the rule in *Hadley v. Baxendale*[18] is an example of legal borrowing from a more sophisticated legal culture by a less sophisticated one. As Simpson suggests, rather than being an example of law being driven by changes in society, what needs to be understood here is the internal, intellectual and institutional evolution of the common law as it moved towards a previously non-existent, textbook tradition.

It may not be totally misleading to compare law in this view with mathematics. At the risk of laughter from relativist intellectual historians one could argue that mathematics has developed almost purely in intellectual terms, by polishing, improving and creating solutions in an organically linked fashion. It may appear old fashioned to say this but it seems utterly unlikely that economic or other social changes played an important role in the development of mathematics. Of course, material and ideological conditions would affect when, by whom and where

---

17 (1854) 9 Ex. 341, 155 Eng. Rep. 145.
18 Ibid.

mathematics would be investigated but the particular mathematical relationships which make up the discipline would be the same in ancient Egypt and modern India and whether the participants were 60 year old women or 20 year old men. Without doubt, the common law is dissimilar to mathematics in many ways. But the analogy may explain the spirit behind common law reasoning.

One could imagine that Watson would find this view convincing. The rules of contract, including the particular rule discussed by Danzig, have not been derived directly from the needs or expectations of the market and, as Watson argues, it may be that they are more or less dysfunctional. Instead of being an area of law that functionally satisfies the needs of commerce, contract can be better understood as a creature of a legal culture, reflective of the intellectual and institutional pressures of a small, craft profession. It is not intended here, as was explained above, to enter into a comprehensive justification of this view but a consideration of some of the possible arguments both for and against this view may clarify the argument being presented.

Those robust English historians John Baker and S.F.C. Milsom have emphasised time and again that in trying to understand English legal history one has to appreciate that for most of its history the common law was applied and developed by a very small group of men who were the sole masters of an arcane and literally unintelligible (to anyone who did not know law French) body of learning. Both emphasise the essential continuity of the common law and, in particular, contract,[19] and their views would seem to mesh easily with those of Watson.[20] Both emphasise the intellectual or, to put it another way, the technical legal development of doctrine and rules. The law of contract evolved in an organic fashion, through the elaboration of existing rules, an elaboration that was always constrained by the overall intellectual consistency or integrity of the existing body of rules. For centuries lawyers and judges argued about what we now call contract and this took the form familiar to lawyers today – arguing from existing cases (or writs – for this argument the difference is not important) and the arguments that won, in the main, changed the law

---

19 See, for example, J.H. Baker, *An Introduction to English Legal History* (London 1979); "The Law Merchant and the Common Law before 1700" (1979) 38 Cambridge Law Journal 295; *The Legal Profession and the Common Law: Historical Essays* (London 1986) and S.F.C. Milsom, *Historical Foundations of the Common Law* (London 1981); *Studies in the History of the Common Law* (London 1985).

20 Watson would probably argue that both have been too insular and have failed to recognise the pivotal, strong and long impact of Roman law in its various guises on the common law. But this would not affect in any way the general argument being presented here. I would be surprised if either of Baker or Milsom would disagree with Watson's scepticism about functionalist views of law.

incrementally, if they changed it at all. Thus, one would search in vain for any argument in these cases which is based on sources that lie outside the reports. Of course, this last point does not invalidate a functionalist argument but it does raise doubts about it.

As Baker makes quite clear, business custom is an unlikely source for the common law. Common law judges have never, for example, admitted expert evidence about the rules of the common law and they would have great difficulty in accepting that changeable custom was part of the unchanging common law. For example, it certainly would be difficult to square day to day business custom with immemorial customs, such as those of gravelkind in Kent, which have been recognised by the courts.[21] What business disputes before the courts would have provided was the factual background to which the developing common law could attach its rules. In fact, it is likely that business disputes would have made up a large proportion of the cases before the courts. Because of this the rules of contract would deal with the problems of commerce. But this does not necessarily mean that the origin and focus of those rules would be functional, in the way that I have defined the term. It is my argument that the rules were developed within an existing intellectual and institutional framework and then *applied* to whatever disputes came before the judges. Of course, if business disputes made up a large proportion of the common law's work the resulting case law would *appear* to display a concentration on business needs. This, in turn, might lead any student of contract to think that business disputes drive the development of contract doctrine. However, it is more plausible to see that these changes resulted from the intellectual development of certain basic principles within a profession and that business disputes provided the opportunity for these rules to be articulated. Contract doctrine was used to "solve" contract disputes and it would have a superficial commercial "hue" as a consequence. Appearance should not, however, be confused with origin or taken to be proof of utility.

If we consider privity a similar pattern emerges. Peter Karsten has investigated functional and doctrinal positions on the development of third-party beneficiaries in the law of contract in England and the United States.[22] His examination of 19th century cases leads him to the following conclusion.

---

21 J.H. Baker, "The Law Merchant and the Common Law before 1700" (1979) 38 Cambridge Law Journal 295 at 298.

22 P. Karsten, "The 'Discovery' of Law by English and American Jurists of the Seventeenth, Eighteenth, and Nineteenth Centuries: Third-Party Beneficiary Contracts as a Test Case" (1991) Law and History Review 327.

> This paucity of utilitarian or instrumentalist opinions is due to the fact that America's nineteenth-century appellate courts, both after and before the Civil War, approached the claims of third-party beneficiary [sic] to actions of assumpsit with a deep respect for doctrine, precedent, and legal principles, a respect flowing from "taught legal traditions".[23]

In a speculative essay one should be wary of adopting dogmatic positions. Nevertheless, it does seem appropriate at this stage to suggest that functionalism does not seem to offer a persuasive interpretation of the history of contract or the common law more generally.

If we move from history to the present and consider empirical and theoretical work on the use and non-use of contract in the marketplace, other problems arise for a functionalist understanding of contract. Contract law, it seems, is not used a great deal in commerce and it does not appear that the market is greatly influenced by it. A functionalist view of contract seems unpersuasive if this is the case.

## Contract in the Marketplace

Stewart Macaulay's "Non-contractual relations in the marketplace: A preliminary study", after something of a delay, ignited an explosion in the study of the use of law, particularly contract, in commerce. Macaulay found that contract had a limited role in the everyday transacting of the business people whom he had interviewed. Many transactions took place even though they were legally unenforceable. He also found that contract was rarely used to settle disputes. Instead, a variety of non-legal sanctions and enforcement mechanisms were used in place of law. Reputation, pride in proper dealing and internal governance mechanisms in large organisations were, it appeared, sufficient to ensure the relatively smooth working of transactions and, as a consequence, contract was little used.[24]

Subsequent studies by other scholars have not fundamentally challenged his findings,[25] although Macaulay did suggest in the mid-1980s that the then decline in the U.S. economy and the resultant harsher trading

---

23 Ibid., at 359.

24 S. Macaulay, "Non-Contractual Relations in Business: A Preliminary Study" (1963) 28 American Sociological Review 55.

25 The literature in this area is simply enormous. The following can be used as a source for further reading. D. Charny, "Non-legal Sanctions in Commercial Relationships" (1990) 104 Harvard Law Review 373; Symposium, "The Informal Economy" (1994) Yale Law Journal 2119; Symposium, "Law, Economics, Norms" (1996) 144 University of Pennsylvania Law Review 1643; Symposium, "Formalism Revisited (Formalism in Commercial Law)" (1999) 66 University of Chicago Law Review 710-857.

conditions may have led to a decrease in the effectiveness of non-legal sanctions and, presumably, an increased recourse to the law.[26] These later studies have, however, suggested that matters are more complicated than he originally thought. This work, in a variety of countries and industries and conducted at different times, suggests that the use of contract, especially in settling disputes and governing relationships arising from a transaction, does vary but not in a way which challenges Macaulay's original findings. These studies have added further dimensions in explaining why and how other, non-legal devices operate and what is their relationship to the law. At the risk of oversimplification, one can divide the literature in this area into two schools.

The first is derived from the Law and Economics movement. Thomas Palay's investigation of contracting between railway companies and shippers is a fine illustration of this type of work. There Palay tested a hypothesis that the "most significant factor affecting the governance choice [between transacting parties] is the extent to which the parties have made idiosyncratic investments in support of their transaction".[27] The transactions investigated were interesting because the contracts used were designed to avoid regulatory restraints and were legally unenforceable.[28] Palay found that the governance options varied according to the type of transaction. Thus, in a simple shipping contract for the delivery of general goods that did not require special equipment, the availability of alternatives plus the threat of limiting future dealings kept people in line. However, as the transactions began to involve more idiosyncratic investment, either by the shipper or the railway company, the governance structure moved to reputation (the potential to trade with this party or other people again) to trust based relationships built up over time and at some cost in resources and effort, and finally to vertical integration where the capital invested was so idiosyncratic that the best way of protecting it was to become one company. Crucially, the law did not have a significant role in the creation of these governance structures.

The second position one might label as sociological and is concerned with the nature of relationships in particular industries or geographical areas and how these work to replace contract, or other forms of law, as the means of governing transactional relationships. Campbell and Harris have

---

26 S. Macaulay, "An Empirical View of Contract" [1985] Wisconsin Law Review 465. See also, P. Vincent-Jones, "Contract Litigation in England and Wales 1975-1991: A Transformation in Business Disputing?" (1993) 12 Civil Justice Quarterly 337 where the author argued that contract disputes before the courts were increasing as a proportion of all disputes.

27 T. Palay, "Comparative Institutional Economics: The Governance of Rail Freight Contracting" (1984) 13 Journal of Legal Studies 265 at 265-6.

28 Ibid., at 266.

argued that the empirical findings show that long-term transactors typically eschew narrowly legal options in the regulation of their relationship. This is because these parties are not driven by short term, opportunistic behaviour.

> Efficient long-term contractual behaviour must be understood as consciously co-operative. We see long-term contract as an analogy to a partnership. The parties are not aiming at utility-maximisation directly through performance of specified obligations; rather, they are aiming at utility-maximisation indirectly through long-term co-operative behaviour manifested in trust and not in reliance on obligations specified in advance. The co-operative mechanism by which utility is achieved in a long-term relationship is radically different from that in the paradigmatic, short-term, specified contract.[29]

In other words, Campbell and Harris argue that the rules of classical contract, apart from not being used, are poorly designed to regulate long-term contracting. They cite a study by Daintith of long-term contracts in the iron ore business where he showed that even in time of economic distress the parties avoided use of law and preferred to renegotiate to overcome the problems caused by an economic recession.[30]

These studies show that there is a rich array of reasons why commercial actors would avoid using contract to settle disputes or to govern transactions. Just as importantly, however, they also help predict when the law will be used or, at least, where it will be a genuine alternative to non-legal sanctions or governance structures. Rubin's study of the vicissitudes of tallymen (the 19$^{th}$ century version of door-to-door salesmen) in the county courts shows clearly how some areas of commerce are dependent on the courts. The tallymen were not involved in long-term, repeat trade and the courts were the only mechanism that could ensure that they received payment. As Rubin shows, unfortunately for the tallymen (and fortunately for the purchasers) the county courts were extraordinarily hostile to this form of sale and used all forms of legitimate and not so legitimate devices to avoid giving judgment in the tallymen's favour.[31] The tallymen might have preferred not to use the courts but the nature of their trade meant that this was impossible.

---

29 D. Campbell and D. Harris, "Flexibility in Long-Term Contractual Relationships: The Role of Co-operation" (1993) 20 Journal of Law and Society 166 at 167.

30 T. Daintith, "The Design and Performance of Long-Term Contracts" in T. Daintith and G. Teubner (eds), *Contract and Organisation* (Berlin 1984), pp. 164-89.

31 G. Rubin, "The County Courts and the Tally Trade, 1846-1914" in G. Rubin and D. Sugarman (eds), *Law, Economy and Society, 1750-1914: Essays in the History of English Law* (Abingdon 1984), pp. 321-48.

Other writers have probed further into the role of contract. Deakin, et al., think that law's most important role is not as an alternative, if little used, mechanism for solving disputes or governing long-term relationships. Rather, they think that law plays a pivotal role in establishing trust between transacting partners and that it is trust, not law, which is the process which solves disputes and helps generate governance structures. Understood in this fashion, the particular rules of contract are not of prime importance. Instead, it is the expected enforcement, via the state, which assures parties that there is a safety net. This safety net in turn allows parties to build a trust relationship, which in turn allows for the creation of far richer dispute settlement and governance mechanisms than offered by the law.[32] Indeed, one might say that it is the guaranteed enforcement of the law which is sought after by the parties and that certainty is intimately tied to this form of legal enforcement. Judicial activism, by attempting to anticipate market needs would threaten certainty and, thus, trust.

Steve Hedley's application of this work to 19th and 20th century relationships between law and commerce presents a persuasive conclusion. In his view business has selectively used the law for its own purposes, with a preference for informal mechanisms in solving disputes. He thinks that business people have viewed the law with suspicion because of lawyers' lack of knowledge of trading conditions and practices and that business people have been loath to get involved in what are often lengthy and expensive legal suits.[33] Campbell and Harris's discussion of the litigation surrounding the *Westinghouse* and *Alcoa*[34] cases provides a fine example of this tactical use of law by business in negotiations and disputes, and shows how a concentration on the legal aspects of a dispute distorts understanding about the total relationship between commercial parties.[35] Mnookin and Wilson's detailed study of the litigation in the Texaco takeover battle again shows quite clearly the tactical use to which the law was put in this hugely expensive and potentially fatal, to one or more of the participants, corporate stoush.[36] In all these cases the parties used the law for their purposes; it was *not* the framework around which the disputes were settled.

---

32 S. Deakin, et al., "'Trust' or Law? Towards an Integrated Theory of Contractual Relations between Firms" (1994) 21 Journal of Law and Society 329. See also C. Rose, "Trust in the Mirror of Betrayal" (1995) 75 Boston University Law Review 531.

33 S. Hedley, "The 'Needs of Commercial Litigants' in Nineteenth and Twentieth Century Contract Law" (1997) 18 Journal of Legal History 85.

34 *In re Westinghouse Electricity Corporation Uranium Litigation* (1975) 405 F. Supp. 316; *Aluminum Company of America v. Essex Group Incorporated* (1980) 499 F. Supp. 53.

35 See Campbell and Harris (1993) 20 Journal of Law and Society 166 at 167.

36 R. Mnookin and R. Wilson, "Rational Bargaining and Market Efficiency: Understanding *Pennzoil v. Texaco*" (1989) 75 Virginia Law Review 295.

If the above suggestions are correct, then functionalism seems to miss the point. Law is relatively important to those in business because it can help generate trust and because it offers recourse to the enforcement power of the courts. Occasionally, especially in areas where trust is lacking or the economics of the transactions render trust irrelevant or unimportant, law will be used. But the overwhelming preponderance of evidence suggests that law plays a minor role in market transactions. If this is the case the certainty created by even inconvenient rules would seem to be more likely to meet the needs of business than ham-fisted attempts by judges to anticipate its needs. Certainty also allows trust to develop because both parties know where they stand. Judicial activism, in contrast, would only add more uncertainty to an already sometimes-unpredictable legal system.

A study of a related area of commercial law may illustrate the point being argued. Sarah Derrington has shown that certainty, even if based on what might appear to be inconvenient rules, is the preferred position of the commercial community in marine insurance. She cites a Memorandum presented to the House of Lords by Lord Herschell about what was to become the Marine Insurance Act 1906 (U.K.).

> In dealing with the rules of law, which may be modified by the stipulations of the parties, it is to be born in mind that the certainty of the rule laid down is more important than its theoretical perfection.[37]

When the Law Commission in England examined the law of insurance in 1980 it expressly declined to make changes to marine, aviation and transport (M.A.T.). It said, inter alia, that

> contracts falling with M.A.T. are generally effected by 'professionals' - that is to say, persons whose everyday business dealings involve the making and carrying out of insurance contracts. Thus, in the vast majority of cases it is merchants, ship owners, aircraft operators etc. and not private individuals who seek insurance in the field of M.A.T. They operate in a market governed by longstanding and well-known rules of law and practice and can reasonably be expected to aware of the niceties of insurance law.[38]

Although not all industries will operate with such a presumed, exact knowledge of law the general point may be of broader application. To the

---

[37] S. Derrington, "Does the Marine Insurance Act 1909 (Cth) Still Serve the Needs of the Business Community?" (1995) 7 Insurance Law Journal 31 at 33; originally cited in Hardy Ivamy, *Chalmers' Marine Insurance Act 1906, Introduction to First Edition of Digest* (1901), 9th ed., p.vii.

[38] Quoted in Derrington, op. cit., at 34.

extent that knowledge of legal rules is important to market participants it seems unlikely that naïve attempts to anticipate business needs by lawyers will be anything other than counterproductive.

Adams and Brownsword's proposal to change privity rules based on notions of commercial convenience[39] can be considered in light of the above discussion. They think that what amounts to judicial lip service to the privity principle and the widespread evasion of it by "result-oriented judges"[40] demand an open acknowledgment that the privity rules should be swept aside in appropriate commercial situations. They argue

> that, as between network contractors, the privity principle should have no application. In other words, whereas, at present, the privity doctrine operates in relation to strangers to *particular* contracts (irrespective of whether such contracts comprise a network), we propose that privity should operate in relation only to strangers to a particular *network* of contracts (but not as between the network contractors themselves).[41] (Emphasis in original.)

Whilst one can have sympathy for an approach that recognises the contortions which result-oriented judges have resorted to in their endeavours to avoid privity, the real problem is that the Adams and Brownsword approach displays the same flaw which underlies the reasoning of the judges they criticise. Neither group points to any empirical evidence to support their theoretical position that the rules of privity should be set aside to aid commerce, either generally or for the parties in dispute. Unless this is provided it is not clear that the network contract exemption proposed by Adams and Brownsword will benefit either justice or commercial efficiency. As with all theoretical improvements suggested by lawyers which are not based on empirical evidence, it is just as likely that these moves will either be of no use, because they are not required by commerce, or, that these moves may prove to be detrimental to commercial actors because they work against their practices and requirements.[42]

In summary, it appears that functionalism runs counter to the needs of commerce. However, the problems of functionalism do not end with its historical implausibility or its inappropriateness for commerce. It seems

---

39 J. Adams and R. Brownsword, "Privity and the Concept of a Network Contract" (1990) 10 Legal Studies 12.

40 Ibid., at 26.

41 Ibid., at 13.

42 Much the same criticisms can be made of another jointly authored paper by Adams and Brownsword; J. Adams and R. Brownsword, "Privity of Contract - That Pestilential Nuisance" (1993) 56 Modern Law Review 722.

that judges lack the capacity to be functionalists, that functionalism is based on a faulty understanding of business custom, and that functionalism misconceives the relationship between that custom and the courts.

## Can Judges be Good Functionalists?

I think not. Judges just do not have the expertise and knowledge required for such a role. Traditionally they have been drawn from the ranks of the bar, usually at the highest levels, and their experience and expertise consist of knowing, shaping and arguing about cases and statutes. Of course, barristers and judges may specialise in commercial areas, but as that respected judge, Donaldson M.R. has noted, this still does not make them market players.[43] A spectator of cricket, however devoted, does not have the same knowledge and skill as a Test player. Judges and barristers are observers, not participants and, in any event, any knowledge of the market that they may have is likely to be partial, and probably out of date as well. One learns to be a market player by being one, not by watching. If this were not the case, newspaper reporters specialising in crime could claim expertise in practising criminal law. Or, for that matter, a nurse working in operating theatres could claim expertise in brain surgery. Even if this were wrong and judges could acquire expertise by being involved in the legal affairs of business people it would require a heroic (and impossible) amount of experience to have expertise which ranged across the whole spectrum of business dealings. In fact, the only way that judges could acquire a real knowledge of what is happening in the market would be for them to participate in it. And even then, their knowledge would necessarily be limited to the areas of participation. Leaving aside questions of competence, would this be considered appropriate activity for a judge who might then be asked to judge in these matters? This has never been considered a problem for commercial arbitrators but they have never been considered to be judges, dispensing justice (blindly) on behalf of the crown (the people).

Courts are poorly designed for a functionalist role. As Lawrence Friedman and Stewart Macaulay showed some years ago, judges favour clear rules because of the institutional limitations of the courts. They are not fact-finding bodies and, even if they were, they lack the experience, power and resources to perform such a role in any convincing way.[44]

43 *Pando Compania Naviera S.A. v. Filmo S.A.S.* [1975] 1 Q.B. 742 at 746.

44 L. Friedman, "Law, Rules, and the Interpretation of Written Documents" (1964-65) 59 Northwestern University Law Review 751 and S. Macaulay, "Private Legislation and

Friedman and Macaulay give plausible explanations for the law's preference for binding, even if inflexible, rules over a judicial discretion which would be based on an unavoidable ignorance about the operation of the market. Just as importantly, their role as dispute-settling bodies does not really allow courts to act as fact-finding bodies. Parties to a dispute want their dispute settled according to the law. They do not want their dispute to be primarily a means to consider a wider social, economic, or even legal problem. In fact, if the arguments made in the preceding section are valid, this is the very last thing market players would want. When law is used tactically or as a last resort it would seem inconceivable that such parties would want to be involved in a long term, potentially open-ended search for the business expectations and practices of their area of business. The profit imperative of business rests very uneasily with a court acting as a roving law reform commission.

It is these qualifications which raise doubts about the persuasiveness of calls for the judicial reformation of privity. For example, in an article published in 1995 in a context where legislative reform of privity was in the air, but not certain, Hugh Beale considered the merits of judicial reform of privity as an alternative to legislation.[45] While he seemed to think that judicial action had intrinsic merits, Beale indicated that his call for judges to reform privity was based on a belief that legislative reform, even if intrinsically superior, was unlikely.[46] Beale's support for a judge-based reform is well encapsulated in the comments of Steyn L.J. in *Darlington Borough Council v. Wiltshier Northern Ltd.*[47]

> No doubt there will be a report by the Law Commission in the not too distant future recommending the abolition of the privity of contract rule by statute. What will then happen in regard to the proposal for legislation? The answer is really quite simple: probably nothing will happen.
>
> But on this occasion I can understand the inaction of Parliament. There is a respectable argument that it is the type of reform which is best achieved by the courts working out sensible solutions on a case by case basis, e.g. in regard to the exact point of time when the third party is vested with enforceable contractual rights . . . But that requires the door to be opened by the House of Lords reviewing the major cases which are thought to have entrenched the rule of privity of contract. Unfortunately, there will be few opportunities for the House to do so. After all, by and large, courts

---

the Duty to Read - Business run by I.B.M. Machine, the Law of Contracts and Credit Cards" (1965-66) 19 Vanderbilt Law Review 1051 at 1066-7.

45 H. Beale, "Privity of Contract: Judicial and Legislative Reform" (1995) 9 Journal of Contract Law 103.

46 Ibid., at 124.

47 [1995] 1 Q.B. 65.

> of law in our system are the hostages of the arguments deployed by counsel. And . . . [counsel for Darlington], the third party, made it clear that he will not directly challenge the privity rule if the matter should go to the House of Lords.[48]

Although Steyn L.J. was to be proved wrong about the inactivity of the legislature (the Contracts (Rights of Third Parties) Act 1999 is now in force), his underlying argument is what is significant here. Was privity (or any other area of contract, for that matter) an area where the case by case approach could have achieved the sort of the wide-ranging and fundamental law reform that the judge and Beale wanted? Of course, neither Beale nor Steyn L.J. has provided any empirical evidence to support their obvious beliefs that privity is dysfunctional for commerce. On this ground alone, one can wonder why they believe so strongly that reform of privity is necessary. Without knowing what commerce wants, how commercial actors feel about privity or how their activities are affected by these rules, it seems unwise, to say the least, to be calling so strongly for the transformation, if not outright abolition, of privity. Neither Beale nor Steyn L.J. explains how judges would discover such information. Even if one limited oneself to what might be called lawyers' law, it is not at all clear that speedy change to give effect to changing commercial practice and expectations could be achieved without detrimentally affecting the rest of the common law. Brennan J. devoted some pages to a discussion of this very problem in *Trident v. McNiece*[49] in response to claims that an exception to privity ought to created or recognised in that case.

> To admit a third party's right to sue into the common law, it would be necessary to postulate a new source of legal rights and obligations arising independently of contract and equity and to create a new set of rules prescribing the availability of the rights and the limits of the obligations to which the third-party promise gives rise. And if such a new source of legal rights were postulated, our laws with respect to agency, trusts, estoppel and damages which have been constructed around the doctrine of privity of contract would have to be reworked. . .
>
> [135] If an exception [to the doctrine of privity] were now introduced and a jus quaesitum tertio were recognized in respect of some contracts, the exception would raise at least as many [136] problems as it might solve.[50]

---

48 *Darlington Borough Council v. Wiltshier Northern Ltd.* [1995] 3 All E.R. 895 at 905 per Steyn L.J., quoted in Beale (1995) 9 J.C.L. 103 at 104.

49 (1987-1988) 165 C.L.R. 107.

50 Ibid., at 134-7 per Brennan J.

Putting these criticisms aside for the moment, there is something else that is decidedly unconvincing about Steyn L.J.'s argument. As he acknowledges, there are few cases dealing with privity which are reaching the highest appellate courts. Does this not tell its own story? Is it possible that the existing privity rules comport with market expectations and behaviour, in which case "reform" would be misguided? Or is it that privity is just unimportant to those in commerce? It may be that here we have another example of what Hedley describes as a lawyerly belief that suitably reformed laws will meet the needs of commerce when, in reality, it appears that those in commerce see law as either the problem or put little faith or importance in law reform.[51] What seems to be driving change in the law here are lawyerly conceptions of what is good for commerce, conceptions that are not based on empirical evidence.

Ironically, even if all these concerns were to be ignored, it is not clear that the courts would find anything if they did go looking for business custom upon which to base changes to contract. As Lisa Bernstein and others have shown, the notion of business customs waiting "out there" to be discovered and applied is, at best, misleading. In a recent article Bernstein argues that the "incorporation strategy" of the U.S. Uniform Commercial Code is misplaced. The incorporation strategy is based on a belief that unwritten customs and usages of trade exist and that courts should apply them in resolving commercial disputes. Bernstein examined several merchant industries and discovered that industry wide customs and usage did not exist in a form that would allow the incorporation strategy to work. Instead, she noted that customs were important in ways unrelated to the incorporation strategy.

> ...[W]hile the types of generally agreed-upon practices that [Karl] Llewellyn thought merchants viewed as supplying implicit contract provisions do not consistently exist, merchants do consider it valuable to have an understanding of the ways transactions are usually done, an understanding gleaned from a rough aggregation of practices in the market as a whole.[52]

Bernstein calls the latter "weak-form" customs. They are invaluable in the early stages of a contractual relationship because they allow the parties to assess whether the other party is, in her terms, a "cooperator" or a "defector", "thereby facilitating the emergence and maintenance of repeat-

---

[51] See Hedley, note 37 above, (1997) 18 Journal of Legal History 85 at 89-91.

[52] See Bernstein, note 3 above, (1999) 66 University of Chicago Law Review 710, at 716-7.

dealing, cooperative contracting relationships".[53] This type of custom is too idiosyncratic and evanescent to be used in settling disputes. In any event, would it not be inappropriate for a court to apply to such pre-contractual customs to disputes arising *after* the creation of a contract?

Obviously business operates in ways that are familiar to its participants but it is not at all clear that these amount to more than ever changing practice. Fluid, changing activities will not always coalesce into discrete, relatively long lasting customs and, surely, it is only the latter which can applied by courts. To attempt to apply fluid, ever-changing practice would be like harvesting a cloud – it would disappear before one's very eyes.

Ben-Shahar offers a different criticism of judges applying unwritten commercial practices in commercial disputes. Unlike the criticisms made above, which refer to judicial ignorance and the doubtful existence of industry wide, relatively stable norms, Ben-Shahar's belief is that the incorporation strategy is self-defeating. He argues, in short,

> that practices of mutual flexibility and leniency [amongst commercial actors] might be deterred if courts treat these practices as amendments to, or variations of, the parties' explicit contract. Parties will require strict adherence to the formal provisions of the contract if they expect that their leniency today will bind them in the future, potentially eroding their express rights. . . Like a scientist who by mere examination of her subjects interferes with and biases their behavioral patterns, the law's attempt to mimic the life conditions of the commercial relationship influences the formation of that reality.[54] (Citation omitted)

In other words, attempts by the courts to incorporate the customs and behaviour of business will detrimentally affect the very flexibility that the courts are trying to incorporate into the law.

An example from another area of commercial law may help illustrate the point that has been made in this section. Retention of title (R.T.) clauses are devices used by suppliers of goods on credit to protect themselves if the buyer is placed in receivership. By maintaining property in these goods even after they have been sold to the buyers, the sellers are able to remove the goods from the pool established by a receiver to pay debts in accordance with the rules and procedures of bankruptcy law. In a series of cases starting with *Aluminium Industrie Vaasen B.V. v. Romalpa Aluminium Ltd.*[55] common law courts have dealt with increasingly

---

53 Ibid., at 717.

54 See Ben-Shahar, note 3 above, (1999) 66 University of Chicago Law Review 781, at 784.

55 [1976] 2 All E.R. 552.

complicated clauses trying to give effect to ever wider attempts to attach security to the goods being sold.[56] Early on the courts, especially the English courts, were sympathetic towards these devices.[57] The judges recognised from the very first that the effect of R.T. clauses was to prefer the suppliers of goods to other creditors, especially debenture holders.[58] And, from very early on, the judges paid much attention to notions of business efficacy in their responses to R.T. clauses.[59] A voluminous literature has developed around this area of law; much of it critical, and much of it from what might be called orthodox, doctrinal scholarship. However, if the early judicial acceptance and development of R.T. clauses is seen as a functionalist response to commercial needs and practice the failings of this approach become starkly evident. Wheeler's study of the operation of R.T. clauses outside of the courts shows how law in action is, indeed, different from law in the books.[60]

Wheeler noted that the formal legal requirements for a valid claim under an R.T. clause were that, first, the clause must be part of the contract of sale between the supplier and buyer; second, it must reserve legal title to the goods to the supplier and, third, the goods must be identified as unpaid. But, as Wheeler shows, this is only the beginning of the story.

> No guidance is given as to what must be shown in order to satisfy these elements; this is a matter for the parties and if they disagree, then they can resort to litigation to solve their differences. In practice, the administrative structure is designed and imposed by the dominant actors – in the case of R.T. clauses, this is the insolvency practitioner and his lawyer – and the administrative structure designed reflects the gap between the requirements of the formal law and what is required at the practical level to fulfill these requirements. . .
>
> This insolvency practitioner is the dominant actor for a variety of reasons; first, he is in possession of the goods; secondly, he knows whether he wishes to use the goods in future production or whether he needs to order [90] more from the supplier; and, thirdly, there is a significant power

---

56 "Sold" here is used neutrally. What it means in the context of an R.T. clause is the essence of the dispute over its meaning and operation.

57 See the recent decision of the High Court in *Associated Alloys Pty. Limited v. CAN 001 452 106 Pty. Limited* [2000] HCA 25, especially at [60-69] per Kirby J. This decision shows that the High Court has taken on board the criticisms of Everett and other critics of the judicial treatment of Romalpa clauses.

58 See for example, the judgment of Roskill L.J. in *Aluminium Industrie Vaasen v. Romalpa Aluminium Ltd.* [1976] 2 All E.R. 552 at 558.

59 Ibid., at 562, 563 per Roskill L.J.; at 565-6 per Goff L.J.

60 S. Wheeler, "Capital Fractionalized: The Role of Insolvency Practitioners in Asset Distribution" in M. Cain and C. Harrington (eds), *Lawyers in a Postmodern World* (New York, 1994), pp. 85-104.

> imbalance between the two parties in terms of their financial capacity, legal competence and familiarity with the problem. In short, insolvency practitioners display all the classic characteristics of repeat players in relation to this particular type of highly specialised work.[61] (Citation omitted)

When it is remembered that debenture holders appoint the insolvency practitioners to whom Wheeler ascribes such a powerful position, the full import of her study becomes clear. As she has shown, there has been a tremendous growth in the use of R.T. clauses but very, very few are argued before the courts. At the time of writing her article in the early 1990s Wheeler could only identify nine reported cases in the United Kingdom. In the real world of the market the specialised insolvency practitioners run rings around the sellers holding R.T. clauses and their unspecialised lawyers. The creditors who seem to lose out in the courts win where it matters, in the commercial world. The judges may have believed that they were recognising commercial practice by accepting the ever-wider use of R.T. clauses. They may even have thought that they were being commercially savvy in moving the law in a direction that they thought commerce would appreciate. But the reality was the exact opposite of what appeared from the pages of the law reports.

But the matter does not end here. It is not just that the real world's response to case law was the opposite of what the judges might have supposed. The judicial embrace of R.T. clauses in their widest manifestation has actually had detrimental effects. First, as Everett shows, the development of R.T. clauses has damaged the law by introducing confusion in what had earlier been a relatively coherent and certain set of rules and principles. Additionally, the underlying operation of the Sale of Goods legislation has been undermined by a wholesale evasion of one of its central principles, i.e., that the parties cannot change the nature of a transaction by the insertion of contrary words. By failing to recognise that in most transactions the parties do intend to pass title when they are supplied and that R.T. clauses are in reality security devices and should be treated as such, the courts threatened to unravel longstanding commercial law principles.[62]

Reservation of Title clauses also may present problems for the market. Bradgate has shown that the enthusiastic judicial embrace of R.T.

---

61 Ibid., at 89-90.

62 D. Everett, "Romalpa Clauses: The Fundamental Flaw" (1995) 68 Australian Law Journal 404. Of course, the Australian High Court has recently moved a long way from the earlier, sympathetic treatment of Reservation of Title clauses.

clauses is not necessarily in the best interests of those in commerce.[63] For example, in comparison with floating charges, a reservation of title is a hidden security. Floating charges need to be registered and potential creditors can, if they wish, search and then make a calculated risk assessment in deciding whether to advance money or not. This cannot be done with R.T. clauses. It is likely that lenders have treated the search for R.T. clauses as an additional cost to be passed on to borrowers. In addition, Bradgate thinks that the increasing use of R.T. clauses would make banks more reluctant to lend, likely to charge more if they do, and to bring in receivers earlier on default than they would do otherwise, thus hindering commerce by making credit more difficult to obtain.[64]

In other words, the original judicial sympathy to the development of R.T. clauses did not reflect the operation of those clauses in the market; this development detrimentally affected the integrity of an important area of law and, it seems that R.T. clauses may not have been and may not be a good thing for the market. There are lessons here for aspiring judicial functionalists.

To sum up the argument so far. I have argued that functionalism has several problems. First, the history of the common law suggests that the courts have not adopted this approach. Secondly, scholarly study of the law in action suggests that market players do not want an activist judiciary. Third, judges and the courts are not equipped to be functionalists and even if they were it is not clear that business practice can be neatly and tidily found and applied. In any case it is not clear that the adoption of such customs would aid flexibility in the market place. But, even if these arguments are misplaced it will be argued below that functionalism raises profound constitutional concerns.

## Contract as Part of the Common Law Constitutional Heritage

Quite simply to be a functionalist judge, constantly to update the law to suit the ever changing needs, expectations and experiences of the market, would involve a judge in judicial activism of the most pronounced kind. Judicial activism is a denial of the constraints which have been traditionally accepted by judges when faced by uncertainty in the interpretation of legislation or the presence of alternative lines of authority. Rather than limiting oneself to incremental changes, trying to remain faithful to earlier decisions and having an appreciation of caution and restraint as appropriate

---

63 J. Bradgate, "Reservation of Title Ten Years On" (1987) The Conveyancer and Property Lawyer 434.

64 Ibid., at 443-7.

judicial attitudes, activism leads to the adoption of a legislative or executive role. It is the replacement of a belief in law as authority by one that sees law as a matter of will.

Lest one be misunderstood here I want to make it clear that there is more involved here than a simple difference between "timorous souls" and "bold spirits" as defined by Denning L.J.[65] For Denning L.J. these differences of attitude were the type of law making open to judges from *within* the common law tradition. He recognised that the common law allowed for development and that the range of development and the speed of change gave individual judges room to move. But Denning L.J. would have been surprised to see this transformed into a belief that change was no longer limited by constraints imposed by the tradition – both in materials and method. Functionalism replaces that tradition and has as its standard for development the needs, expectations and practices of the market.

The extent of judicial activism that would flow from a consistently functionalist judiciary would a fundamental challenge to commonly accepted notions of judging. Of course, suggestions that judicial activism in commercial cases can be quarantined cannot be convincing. Once let free, judicial activism will assume a life of its own. One cannot expect that judges will adopt a free wheeling activist role in one aspect of judging and eschew it for others. Proponents of functionalist judging need to explain how they would justify such a fundamental change to our constitutional and legal conceptions of judging.

If this were not enough judicial activism on this scale also raises constitutional questions about the role of judges and contract. Put simply, the common law of contract has been a constituent part of the common law for many hundreds of years. In my own country, for example, it was incorporated into our constitutional structure when British rule was established in Australia and with the adoption of the Australian constitution. If judges adopt a functionalist approach this would transfer their allegiance to the market. It would be a matter of some moment for our constitutional structure if judges divested themselves of their allegiance to the common law. Can common law judges, who have sworn to uphold the law, simply give up their fidelity to the law and swear new allegiance to the marketplace?

Advocates of judicial activism based on a functionalist understanding of commercial law have to explain and justify the constitutional change inherent in such a change. Express trusts aside, contract is the only part of the common law which allows citizens to assume legally binding obligations of their own choosing. It would be surprising if the keeping of

---

65 *Candler v. Crane, Christmas & Co* [1951] 2 K.B. 164 at 178 per Denning L.J.

promises (at least in the areas in which the law feels are appropriate for enforcement) is not considered by the majority of people in Australia (and other common law countries, for that matter) to be important and worth preserving. Contract provides an arena for citizens to act and not just respond to law. It also recognises and treats people as equals in their dealings with others who may be socially and economically more powerful. This in turn contributes to the development of equality in the political and legal arenas. A wholesale reformation of contract which removes its private aspect and treats it as another area of law where duties are imposed on parties will be, in effect, to treat all of us as not being responsible enough to make considered judgments about what obligations we want to assume. While contract is not the same as politics it might be illustrative to consider how a proposal to deny the vote to certain classes of people would be treated by those who argue for the destruction of classical contract.

When one considers that contract and the common law are constituent elements of our constitution, it may be relevant to consider what role they may play in animating the constitutional spirits of the people. Andrew Fraser has argued that

> [c]itizens of the common law countries have not always looked to an universal code of human rights to safeguard their liberties. Rights of resistance to tyranny were once the entailed inheritance of every free-born British subject. The spirit of liberty was long seen as the distinguishing feature of the ancient British constitution. Those liberties were. . . the hard-won achievement of ancestors, whose memory could best be honoured by passing on the free constitution of the British peoples to their own heirs and successors. Down through the ages, stories of resistance by sturdy Anglo-Saxon yeomen to the Norman yoke imposed by William the Bastard and other tyrants endowed the myth of the ancient constitution with meaning and mystery, drama and romance. Stripped of that ancestral authority, the law becomes little more than an instrument of social control.[66]

Is it drawing too long a bow to suggest that the freedom given to adults of sound mind by contract is part of that ancient constitution? If this is the case the destruction of contract amounts to thoughtless damage of our constitutional heritage by judges who should know better.

Contract is a form of law that is bounded and its extent may vary according to legislative changes from time to time. However, changing its boundaries is one thing; transforming it out of recognition is another. One cannot expect a fundamental aspect of the constitution to be ditched

---

[66] A. Fraser, "Marx of the Managerial Revolution: Habermas on Law and Democracy", unpublished manuscript on file with author.

without at least some questions being raised. And one can ask whether judges have the right to destroy a part of the constitution that belongs to all of us. Just as many in England asked who had stolen their eleven days when the Gregorian calendar was adopted, if contract were to be destroyed, many people might ask why their constitution was changed without their permission.

Kincaid's study of the impact of changes to privity advocated by the English Law Commission and now given effect by the Contract (Rights of Third Parties) Act 1999 illustrates the constitutional problems raised by ill-considered "reform". He argues that these reforms reflect and effect fundamental changes to the nature of contract, of private law in the courts and the place and importance of coherent legal reasoning in the common law system.

First, as he shows, the Law Commission's proposals amount to changing the focus of contract away from being a private affair of its originators to being a matter of public concern. Duties in contract will not only be those agreed to by the parties but will also include those "imposed by the state where a mixture of private interests and public interests. . . warrant doing so". Second,

> [t]he goal of the law in an area of private law like contract ceases to be doing justice between the parties according to a coherent scheme for balancing their private interests. Private law becomes instead an area where public and private interests compete. . .

Third, the "requirement of coherent logical reasoning in terms of values, principles, and rules as they rationalise balancing the interests of the plaintiff and the defendant with reference to the relationship between them" is dropped in favour of functional goals. As Kincaid emphasises, the former kind of reasoning is not just a matter of technique; it is tied intimately to the rule of law and in the British constitution.[67]

Kincaid argues that the proponents of change to privity fail to realise the immensity of the threat that they are posing to contract. These concerns are magnified if what is being transformed is contract in its entirety.

Kincaid's warnings also bring to light the fact that legislation is as much a threat to contract as judicial activism. As he shows, apart from abstract concerns about justice and the rights of third parties, commercial efficiency and expediency (or lawyers' beliefs about them) lie at the heart of this attempt to change the law through legislation.

Legislation does not, of course, raise questions of legitimacy in the

---

[67] P. Kincaid, "Privity and Private Justice in Contract" (1997) 12 Journal of Contract Law 47 at 63-4. The article is reproduced in this book.

same way as judicially effected functional changes do. It does, however, raise questions of wisdom, prudence and appropriateness. One way of elaborating this claim is to consider Lawrence Friedman's description of the relationship between contract and legislation in 19th and 20th century America. Friedman argued that change in contract had much, much more to do with the expansion and contraction of its field of operation than to changes to its rules and principles. During the latter half of the 19th and the first third of the 20th centuries contract covered vast areas of American life. (Its effect, of course, is another matter.) Contract's field of operation shrank, however, as more and more areas such as family law, trade practices law, consumer law, employment law, etc., were hived off and dealt with by special regulatory regimes created by statute. Whilst the details may have varied amongst various countries one could imagine that a similar position applied generally across the common law world.

Of course, different values are held by people at different times and the legislative implementation of these differences will, in turn, affect the areas over which contract will operate. But, if the particular virtues of contract are to be maintained, contract must have some area to operate. In other words, there must be a genuine space for people to transact using contract. Ensuring this requires wisdom from politicians and people more generally. Both must make sure that the pressing claims of the moment, however worthy, do not threaten the existence of a realm of private contract. For example, one can question, as does Kincaid, whether the good to be gained from changing the operation of privity in contract is so great as to outweigh the damage done to contract. But to do so one has to appreciate that contract is important and that its demise should not be lightly contemplated. It is not obvious that such an understanding is commonplace amongst lawyers today.

## Does it Matter that Contract does not Matter?

The conclusions arrived at in each section suggest strongly that utility to the market is not why contract matters. I have argued that contract has not developed with utility in mind, that its contemporary utility for the market is inconsistent with a direct relationship with the market, that the courts could not be functionalists even if they wanted to and, finally, that there are very good reasons why judges should not aspire to the activism demanded by such a belief.

Once contract is understood in this fashion critiques of its failure to deal with real world contracting seem to miss the point. Certainly, *if* the sole or predominant purpose of contract law was to further economic growth by making exchange more efficient (however one defines efficiency), one would be perfectly entitled to evaluate how well, or badly, classical contract achieves this goal. David Campbell, for example, has written persuasively to this effect.[68] And, of course, it is perfectly open to argue that formalist adjudication (which rests comfortably with classical contract) is actually the best way of achieving economic efficiency through contract.[69] As is apparent from the arguments made above, I do not believe that a functionalist view of contract would aid economic efficiency because the market does not want functionalist judges and, in any event, the judges could not operate satisfactorily in this fashion even if they wanted to. But even if I am wrong, a belief that the sole or primary purpose of contract law is to aid economic efficiency deflects attention away from contract's potential institutional role in otherwise institutionally impoverished societies.

In fact, a functionalist view of contract seems curiously naïve. Despite Marxist and other instrumentalist views which see contract as an intrinsic part of free market capitalism, it is probably more accurate to view contract, and the common law more generally, as parasitic on capitalism rather than its tool. This is the conclusion that one can draw from Kostal's study of the relationship between law and English railway capitalism in the 19th century and Luttwak's understanding of law's impact on contemporary U.S. business. Kostal saw the relationship between law and English railway capitalism as one where "lawyers and their institutions remained overwhelmingly a world apart from railway capitalism".[70] Viewed from the perspective of the railway industry the relationship was little short of a disaster. From the incorporation of the first railway companies, to the hugely damaging speculative bubble organised by lawyers, to the monopoly position of parliamentary lawyers and the often antagonistic attitude of the courts to the railway industry, lawyers and the common law presented a perplexing, alien and expensive challenge to the railway capitalists. So damaging were the efforts of the lawyers on the industry that

---

68 See, for example, D. Campbell, "The Undeath of Contract: A Study in the Degeneration of a Research Programme" (1992) 22 Hong Kong Law Review 38; D. Campbell and D. Harris, "Flexibility in Long-Term Contractual Relationships: The Role of Co-operation" (1993) 20 Journal of Law and Society 166 and D. Campbell, "Classification and the Crisis of the Common Law" a review of P. Birks (ed), *The Classification of Obligations* (Oxford, 1997) in (1999) 26 Journal of Law and Society 369. Of course, given Campbell's acknowledgment of the lack of use of contract in transacting, especially long-term contracting, one would have to ask whether remodelling contract to reflect the norms of long-term contracting would render it any more useful or attractive to business.

69 This is the argument of O. Ben-Shahar, "The Tentative Case Against Flexibility in Commercial Law" (1999) 66 University of Chicago Law Review 781.

70 R. Kostal, *Law and English Railway Capitalism 1825-1875* (Oxford, 1994), p. 359.

by the 1870s some railway spokesmen were calling for state regulation to remove the industry from the clutches of law and lawyers.[71]

Luttwak sees law today as one of the major institutional constraints on an otherwise uncontrollable market system.[72] He argues that the American legal system, in both public and private guises, acts to limit, deter and even damage business, small and large. He sees U.S. anti-trust legislation and enforcement as a very effective check on corporate monopolistic tendencies. Had Microsoft, to use a topical example, arisen in the United Kingdom or France or Japan he argues that that company would have been treated as a national treasure and governments would have seen it as their duty to support and encourage its endeavours.

> In the United States, by contrast, Microsoft has become the chief target of the anti-trust division of the Department of Justice, energized by the best and brightest young lawyers. . .[73]

Luttwak also thinks that two procedural features of the private law system in the United States, contingency fees and the reluctance of courts to award costs against losing litigants, has led to a legal environment where suing corporations of all sizes is a relatively easy exercise.

> The unsurprising result is that big corporations, so greatly empowered by deregulation as well as by sheer magnitude and wealth, are constantly besieged by private lawsuits of every kind, energetically pressed by lawyers eager for their contingency fees…[14]
>
> Almost *two million* lawsuits against corporations are started each year in Federal and State courts, and business big and small must also contend with the suits pressed by local, State and Federal authorities, charging environmental, occupational safety, consumer protection, financial and, of course, anti-trust violations… Total damage awards throughout the United States were last estimated at $150,000 million per year, of which at least one-quarter went to lawyers rather than their clients.[74] (Emphasis in original)

For Luttwak this amounts to an unplanned but thoroughly successful "taming of big business in all sorts of ways".[75]

[71] Ibid, pp. 358-72.
[72] E. Luttwak, *Turbo-Capitalism: Winners and Losers in the Global Economy* (New York, 1999).
[73] Ibid., p. 8.
[74] Ibid., pp. 13-14.
[75] Ibid., p. 14.

> Famously greedy American lawyers, ruthless in manipulating juries, for whom plaintiffs are often mere puppets rather than respected clients, thus serve a higher purpose after all, by intimidating structurally greedy corporations.[76]

Undoubtedly the common law has been closely associated with commerce and the rise of capitalism. It is not surprising that lawyers saw and see capitalism as a means of making money. More generally, it is not surprising that lawyers gravitate to the sources of power and wealth in a society. What has to be determined and not just *assumed* is the nature of the relationship. Too often the law is seen as an instrument, either designed or well adapted to the needs of the market. Kostal and Luttwak provide strong evidence for suggesting that the common law uses capitalism as much as it is used by capitalism. As has been argued above, market players use law tactically and for their own purposes and it seems that the reverse also happens. Rather than being a tool of capitalist development the history of the common law suggests that contract is an independent institution not necessarily in thrall to the demands of the market.

If this is the case an exciting possibility becomes evident. In a world where there are fewer and fewer constraints on what Luttwak has called "turbo-capitalism", contract, and the common law generally, may have roles as institutional bulwarks against free market capitalism.

## Contract and Turbo-Capitalism

Writers as diverse in their viewpoints as John Gray[77] and Karl Marx have noted that capitalism is by its very nature restless and destructive. Left to its own devices it is an uncontrollable beast and may devour the very conditions that have spawned it and allowed it to prosper. A totally unbridled capitalism has probably never existed but it is probably uncontroversial to think that the last few decades have seen a gradual but significant loosening of the shackles which limited its freedom of operation. Gray, for one, argues that governments have to create legislative and regulatory frameworks around the capitalist free market if its corrosive nature is to be controlled. However, governmental controls have not always been the only, or indeed, the primary, means of shackling capitalism. Institutions, I think, have been at least as important in setting barriers against the encroachment of capitalist values and behaviour across

---

76 Ibid., p. 15.

77 See, for example, J. Gray, *False Dawn: The delusions of global capitalism* (London 1998).

the whole of society. Professions, sport, organised religion, law and universities are some of the institutions that have defended and maintained values and practices that are not derived from the market. These institutions may not have been designed or created to act as counterweights or barriers to capitalism but they seem to have achieved this purpose. It seems to me that the gradual destruction of these institutions by their incorporation into the market system has left a dangerous hole in our safeguard against the commodification of all aspects of life.

Institutions may act in different ways in this regard. For example, religion in its various manifestations may outlaw some types of behaviour which, in turn, restricts the operation or reach of the market. The medieval ban on usury in Christian Europe and present day Islam is a good example of this. Or it may demand from its believers that a certain percentage of income be given away as charity. Certainly, most religions expect that time and effort be devoted to worship and other mandated tasks. Whilst none of this behaviour is necessarily designed to control the reach and operation of the market it certainly has this effect.

Organised sport has until recently demanded time and energy from participants and fans. As with religion, organised sport was once a depository of values that were either divorced from the market or antagonistic towards it. Thus, for example, until recently the Olympic ideal was that unpaid athletes challenged each other for honours. Whilst this may have been often observed in the breach, it must have acted as a stimulus to many people for the emergence of values and behaviour other than those derived from the market. Cricket is another example where a large part of Australia's male population saw it not as a form of entertainment but as something approaching a secular religion. How else would we explain the phenomenon of the current Australian Prime Minister intimating that his first preference would have been the captaincy of the national cricket team? It is not just a matter of "old fashioned values" and suggestions that certain forms of behaviour "were just not cricket", although this was significant. It is also the fact that for many people a significant part of their lives was devoted to non-market activities (or activities where the market influence was small and incidental). In John Carroll's words, sport

> is thick with that rare blend of experience and memory, of smells and sounds that make people feel that they belong, that this is home and I like it.[78]

---

78 J. Carroll, "Let's reclaim the game", *The Age* 1 May 2000. Carroll is concerned here with the increasing commercialisation of Australian Rules football but the description seems to fit other forms of sport.

The professions, universities and schools are other sites of social engagement where, to a significant if varying degree, modes of behaviour, sources of value and sheer quantities of time and effort were regulated either entirely or significantly outside of the market. Lawyers, for example, have always made their living from the market but the professional ethos and the structure of their profession acted as a countervailing force against a total integration into the market. The recent push in Australia to the incorporation of law firms is more than symbolic. Many lawyers now find that professionalism, with its attendant limits on acceptable behaviour and defined and restricting organisational structure, limits their ability to deal as profit-making market players. Universities were once seen, to a large degree at least, as places of higher education. Undoubtedly in Australia and elsewhere they were bastions of privilege. Nevertheless, they were engaged in non-market activities and were run in non-market ways. In Australia today they may have been "opened up" to more general participation but at the cost of being seen as training institutes and research factories for the national economy. They are now far along the track of being seen and run as corporate entities with corporate goals and corporate ideals.

Despite the beliefs of some on the left, institutions cannot be created overnight. They need time to grow and develop and they need the reinforcing power of tradition to develop strength to survive. The common law, for all its many faults, has shown that it can survive. And, with all its faults, it also has a lot of virtues. In its law of contract it has a body of law which gives legal effect to a moral standard of long heritage – that one should keep one's promises when they are have been made in exchange for another promise or for an act. Yet this institution is being threatened by misguided attempts to render it more suitable to perceived needs and practices in the market.

Contract has a heritage and a force of tradition which, until now at least, has channelled the thinking of lawyers. As seen above, while law might not be of direct importance to the market, it remains a powerful force. After all, it has the backing of the force of the state. If the common law understanding of contract were vigorously defended and applied by the courts this would be a countervailing force to the working of the market. In other words, if commerce wanted to avail itself of contract it would have to be on terms which give effect to the rules and ethos of common law contract. It is this potential for contract to act independently of the market which would be given up if judges were to become functionalists. Law also has a potential educative role. It is likely that it matters to ordinary people that promises are kept, that all, weak or strong, rich or poor, can be made to go through with agreements. If, on the other hand, these values of contract are sacrificed on the altar of the market a message of sorts is being sent that the values of the marketplace trump all other values.[79]

The survival of common law contract, on its own terms, may also act as a stimulus for other, perhaps more powerful institutions to resist the corrosive effects of the market. As I have argued above, universities, professions, organised religion, and sport are all areas that are being transformed to meet the dictates of the market. A successful defiance of the market demands by the law might act to encourage people in these institutions to do the same.[80] The survival of contract and the common law may help create the "Machiavellian moment"[81] necessary for such an important challenge to existing power structures in our society.

## Conclusion

One can write in defence of the common law of contract and not be blind to its flaws. One could accept, for example, that contract has never been an effective protector of the weak and still lament its passing. Irrespective of such flaws, be they real or perceived, it could be argued that, in an "age of statutes", common law contract is an anachronism or doomed to irrelevance. Certainly, any defence of contract needs to do more than praise its heritage or unthinkingly support it merely because it is there. I wish to support contract for positive reasons and with an open acknowledgment of its strengths and weaknessness.

Contract deserves to survive because of the service it may offer to a world where an unholy alliance between the market and bureaucratic government has unleashed the destructive forces of turbo-capitalism; an unholy alliance which worships at the altars of perpetual economic growth and relentless social change. Those who argue for a more utilitarian, functional law of contract should realise that this will inevitably destroy a potential institutional counterweight to the menace of an out-of-control market. Indeed, their actions can only accelerate the transformation of society into one huge market. Is this what they really want?

---

[79] See, for example, J. Whitman, "The Moral Menace of Roman Law and the Making of Commerce: Some Dutch Evidence" (1996) 105 Yale Law Journal 1841 where the author argues that the prestige of the Roman law was used to legitimate and make more acceptable modern, market-oriented forms of bankruptcy.

[80] One could add corporations to the list. See A. Fraser, *Reinventing Aristocracy: The Constitutional Reformation of Corporate Governance* (Aldershot, 1998).

[81] See J.G.A. Pocock, *The Machiavellian Moment: Florentine Political Thought and the Atlantic Republican Tradition* (Princeton 1975).

# 11 The Rights of Third Parties to Contracts: A Suggested Basis for Recognition

JOHN SWAN

## 1. Introduction

The law regarding the enforcement and recognition of rights of third parties to contracts is in considerable confusion. In this paper I cannot hope to deal comprehensively with anything but a small aspect of it. The confusion arises from several factors. One of the most important factors is that identified by Peter Kincaid, *viz.*, that arguments for the enforcement of third-party rights have not dealt well, if at all, with the fundamentalbasis or justification for giving third parties rights to sue under a contract.[1] Another factor is the existence of closely related but doctrinally distinct "pockets" of law where the results of cases differ, even though the basis for the original distinctions between the pockets is not obvious.[2] From the point of view of the practising lawyer, one of the most important sources of confusion is the fact that courts are often moved to give third parties rights under a contract by finding (though "creating" might often be the more appropriate word) an

1 Kincaid, "Privity Reform in England" (2000) 116 L.Q.R. 43 ("Reform"); Kincaid, "Privity and Private Justice in Contract" (1997) 12 J.C.L. 47 ("Private Justice"); Kincaid, "The U.K. Law Commission's Privity Proposals and Contract Theory" (1994) 8 J.C.L. 51 ("Law Commission"); Kincaid, "The *Trident Insurance* Case: Death of Contract?" (1989) 2 J.C.L. 160 ("*Trident*"); Kincaid, "Third Parties: Rationalising a Right to Sue" [1989] C.L.J. 243 ("Rationalising"). I shall not discuss the contribution that the recent United Kingdom legislation, Contracts (Rights of Third Parties) Act 1999, has made to the resolution of the issues that concern Kincaid or to the development of the law.

2 Several of these problems are identified and usefully analysed in two articles by Graham Battersby, "Exemption Clauses and Third Parties" (1975) 25 U.T. Law J. 371, and "Exemption Clauses and Third Parties: Recent Decisions" (1978) 28 U.T. Law J. 75. The "bailment on terms" basis for enforcement adopted in *Elder Dempster & Co. Ltd. v. Paterson Zochonis & Co. Ltd.* [1924] A.C. 522, [1924] All E.R. Rep 135, is an example of such a pocket. The "bailment on terms" exception to the third-party beneficiary rule is analysed in *The "Pioneer Container"* [1994] 2 A.C. 324, [1994] 2 All E.R. 250, and *The "Mahkutai"* [1996] A.C. 650, [1996] 3 All E.R. 502.

agency or trust relation on which the decision to enforce can be based.[3] The law of third-party beneficiary contracts is also characterised by many legislative interventions made necessary by the courts' refusal to recognise that such contracts had sometimes to be enforceable if serious injustice were not to be done[4] and this extensive legislative reversal of the common law rule has sometimes caused courts to wonder if the traditional common law rule should be strictly applied in all cases.

Kincaid's argument is that the enforcement of rights of third parties does not acknowledge the fact that the doctrines of privity and consideration reflect the idea that a contract is a bargain, the elements of which are promise and exchange.[5] Kincaid asks how it can be unjust to deny a third party a right of action "when the promise was not made to it and it had not paid for it".[6] More dramatically, he has asked, "has the English law of contract, based as I think it is on bargain, been abolished in [Australia]"?[7] This question was prompted by a decision of the Australian High Court in *Trident General Insurance Co. Ltd. v. McNiece Bros. Pty. Ltd.*[8] In that case a contractor on a construction site was held to be entitled to the protection of an insurance policy taken out by the owner of the site even though the contractor was not a party to the contract represented by the policy and had not given consideration for the insurer's promise.

Now that the English legislation, the Contracts (Rights of Third Parties) Act 1999, is a *fait accompli*, Kincaid has seen it as exemplifying another approach to the enforcement of promises, *viz.*, that, as a matter of public, not private law, Parliament has chosen to justify protecting the parties' intentions,[9] whether or not the traditional tort (fault) or contract (bargain) requirements are met.

I would like to take up the challenge offered by Kincaid and suggest that there are good reasons why a third party should be able to claim the protection of a contract and that giving such rights does not justify the fear that contract is dead, that the values of the common law have been

---

3 Perhaps the most famous demonstration of this source of confusion in provided by Corbin in an article, (1930) 46 L.Q.R. 12, and in his treatise, *Corbin on Contracts*, Vol. 4, §§ 836-854, pp. 353-400. More recent examples are the decision of the House of Lords in *Beswick v. Beswick* [1968] A.C.58, [1967] 2 All E.R. 1197, and by the Canadian cases that I shall discuss, including principally *London Drugs Ltd. v. Kuehne & Nagel International Ltd.* [1992] 3 S.C.R. 299, [1993] 1 W.W.R. 1, 97 D.L.R. (4th) 261, ("*London Drugs*").

4 See, e.g., below at note 11.

5 Kincaid, Private Justice, at p. 47.

6 Kincaid, Private Justice, at p. 47.

7 Kincaid, *Trident*, at p. 160.

8 (1988) 165 C.L.R. 107, 80 A.L.R. 574, ("*Trident Insurance*").

9 Kincaid, Reform, above 1, at p. 46.

subverted or that the matter must be left to some expression of public law values. In fact, I am prepared to go further and to suggest that there is a way in which the cases that I shall discuss can be seen as neither exceptions to the traditional rule nor examples of unprincipled analysis. Instead they can be seen as examples of what is the correct approach to the problems of at least some common third-party beneficiary contracts and of the proper response to the arrangements that the parties made. I acknowledge that my analysis does not find explicit support in the cases and that for some of the cases that I shall discuss, I shall be offering more of a rationalisation than an application of generally accepted rules.

I do not want to re-work several of the various topics that come with the ambit of a discussion of the third-party rule. I accept as the background to my analysis the general statement that third parties cannot enforce a contract to which they are not a party. Some situations in which the rule was used to expose third parties to risks have now been generally dealt with either by the common law or by statute so that, for many practical problems, the issue will no longer arise. For example, it is probable that, with a properly drafted contract, stevedores or sub-carriers will be protected under a bill of lading.[10] Other problems, like the need to permit the beneficiary of a life insurance policy or the driver of a car to sue the insurer under the liability insurance policy issued to the owner, have been dealt with by legislation.[11]

## 2. The Practical Pattern

There are, as a practical matter, a number of common business relations where the recognition of third-party rights is required if the enterprise with which the relation is concerned is not to be seriously hampered. One of the most obvious of these is the relation that exists among all the parties to a large construction project. The other, more general relation, is that where, again for good business reasons, waivers of rights of subrogation have been

---

[10] The limits on, for example, the effect of a Himalaya clause are illustrated by the judgment of the Privy Council in *The Mahkutai* [1996] A.C. 650, [1996] 3 All E.R. 502. The judgment of Lord Goff in that case does not affect the validity of what I have said. The judgment is less an analysis of the problem of third parties than it is an interpretation of a contractual term. If the parties to a bill of lading want to bring a choice of jurisdiction clause within the scope of a Himalaya clause, it would not be hard to re-draft the language, as indeed *The Pioneer Container* [1994] 2 A.C. 324, [1994] 2 All E.R. 250 illustrates.

[11] See, e.g., *Insurance Act*, R.S.O. 1990, c. I.8, s. 195 (beneficiary of a life insurance policy) and s. 244 (driver). These provisions are standard in the *Insurance Acts* of the common law provinces of Canada.

given. I shall briefly discuss the Canadian and Australian law on these points. I shall then turn to two decisions of the Supreme Court of Canada which attempt to deal with what is becoming a serious problem in the broad category of third-party beneficiary contracts, *viz.*, the extent to which employees can shelter behind their employers when the latter are protected from those with whom they deal. In the course of this analysis I shall also deal with *Trident Insurance*, the Australian case that caused Kincaid such distress.

I shall deal first with the cases and then turn to the challenge that I have accepted.

### *(a) General Contractors and Subcontractors*

It is standard for the owner or the general contractor of a construction project to take out insurance to cover the risks of fire and other perils on a construction site. This insurance will be extended to cover subcontractors because it is cheaper for the parties to have one policy of insurance and because the owner and general contractor will want to make sure that there is insurance in place to cover any risk of loss. Neither the owner nor the general contractor want to have to rely on each subcontractor's having its own liability insurance or to face the problems that enforcement of any claim against the subcontractor might involve.

In *Commonwealth Construction Co. v. Imperial Oil Ltd.*,[12] the owner of a construction site, the plaintiff, respondent, took out insurance, described as "course of construction insurance",[13] to cover the risk of fire at a site on which a fertiliser plant was being constructed. Through the negligence of a subcontractor, the defendant, appellant, the works were seriously damaged by fire. The insurer paid under the policy and then commenced a subrogated action against the subcontractor.

The policy defined the "Insured" as "Imperial Oil Limited and its Subsidiary Companies and any Subsidiaries thereof and any of their Contractors and Subcontractors" and described the coverage under the policy in the following way:[14]

> This Policy covers all materials, machinery, equipment including labour charges, and all other property of any nature whatsoever owned by Insured or in which the Insured may have an interest or responsibility or for which the Insured may be liable or assume liability prior to loss or damage to be used or incidental to the [construction of the plant].

---

12 [1978] 1 S.C.R. 317, 69 D.L.R. (3d) 558, [1976] 6 W.W.R. 219, ("*Commonwealth Construction*"). All references will be to D.L.R.

13 The coverage is also described as "Builder's Risk" insurance.

14 *Commonwealth Construction*, p. 561.

In addition, the policy contained a clause, called the "Trustee Clause", which provided:[15]

> (a) It is hereby declared and agreed that the insurance provided by this Policy is obtained by the Owner on his own behalf and as trustee for the benefit of any and all Contractors who heretofore or hereafter enter into a contract with the Owner, or other insured contractor relating to the construction of the project described in Clause 1 of the wording.
>
> (b) In consideration of the premium charged, the Insurers hereby waive any right they have or may have to contest the inclusion as an insured under this Policy of any person, firm or corporation qualifying as an insured by virtue of [the trustee] clause … above, …

The Supreme Court, in a judgment by de Grandpré J., gave two reasons for its conclusion that the appeal should be allowed and the subrogated action dismissed. The court held that the negligent subcontractor had an insurable interest in the whole project such that rights of subrogation could not be asserted against it or against (or between) any of the parties covered by the policy. The second ground was that the insurer had released its rights of subrogation against the subcontractor. In support of this conclusion de Grandpré J. said:[16]

> [The] function [of the policy] is to provide to the owner the promise that the contractors will have the funds to rebuild in case of loss and to the contractors the protection against the crippling cost of starting afresh in such an event, the whole without resort to litigation in case of negligence by anyone connected with the construction, a risk accepted by the insurers at the outset. This purpose recognizes the importance of keeping to a minimum the difficulties that are bound to be created by the large number of participants in a major construction project, the complexity of which needs no demonstration. It also recognizes the realities of industrial life.

The court made reference to the potential third-party beneficiary problem created by the decision in *Vandepitte v. Preferred Accident*

---

15 *Commonwealth Construction*, p. 563.
16 *Commonwealth Construction*, p. 566.

*Insurance Corporation of New York*[17] and noted that, by including the "trustee clause" in the policy, the parties might have avoided any difficulty in holding that the subcontractor was entitled, as the beneficiary of a trust, to enforce the contract against the insurer.[18] The precaution was, however, said to be unnecessary. What this decision means is that in the construction industry, at least as regards insurance of the type described by the Supreme Court, the third-party beneficiary problem simply does not arise.[19]

In *Trident Insurance*[20] the Australian High Court had to deal with the right of a contractor under a builder's risk insurance policy taken out by the owner of a construction site. The policy defined the term "Assured" to include the owner and "all its subsidiary, associated and related Companies, all Contractors and Sub-Contractors and/or Suppliers". It also provided:

> The insurance … indemnifies the Assured against all sums which the Assured shall become legally liable to pay in respect of
>
> 1. Death of or bodily injury to or illness of any person not being a person who at the time of the occurrence is engaged in and upon the service of the Assured under a Contract of service or apprenticeship …

A person working for the principal contractor was injured and brought an action against the contractor. The contractor sought an indemnity from the insurer. The High Court, by a majority, upheld the right of the contractor to sue the insurer under the policy. As Kincaid has pointed out, the judgments are not easy to understand and the majority in favour of the plaintiff's position reflected very different approaches to the problem of the third-party beneficiary rule and, indeed, to contractual liability.[21] I shall not deal with the judgments in detail because Kincaid has already analysed them[22] and because it is more important for my purposes to consider whether the result can be justified than the reasons for the

17 [1933] A.C. 70, ("*Vandepitte*").

18 The drafter of the policy had obviously taken to heart the problem of enforcing third-party beneficiary rights when there is no express "trustee clause" and the court is asked to infer a trust. See, e.g., Corbin, above note 3, *Re Schebsman* [1944] Ch. 83, and *Greenwood* [1980] 2 S.C.R. 228, 111 D.L.R. (3d) 257, below note 38.

19 Which is, of course, not quite the same thing as saying that some insurer will not try to avoid the allocation of risk intended by the policy by seeking to make a negligent subcontractor or its employees liable. See, e.g., *Madison Developments Ltd. v. Plan Electric Co. Ltd.* (1997) 36 O.R. (3d) 80, 152 D.L.R. (4th) 653, (Ont. C.A.). In this case, too, the attempt to make a subcontractor (and its employees) liable was unsuccessful. The case is dealt with in more detail below following note 61.

20 (1988) 165 C.L.R. 107.

21 Kincaid, *Trident*, above note 1.

22 Kincaid, *Trident* and Rationalising, above note 1.

decision. It is sufficient for my purposes to note that Mason C.J. and Wilson J. regarded the existing law as unsatisfactory. They said, "we consider that it is the responsibility of this Court to reconsider in appropriate cases common law rules which operate unsatisfactorily and unjustly".[23] Toohey J. took much the same position. The majority in favour of the contractor was supplied by Gaudron J. but she took, as Kincaid has pointed out, a radically different approach, one that does not really touch on the issue of third-party beneficiary contracts.[24] Brennan and Dawson JJ. dissented on the ground that established doctrine should not be overturned. The seventh judge, Deane J., is also described as dissenting because he would have allowed the appeal, but he indicated that he would have found for the contractor on the basis that its claim could be based on a trust that was created by the policy. The basis for Deane J.'s decision to allow the appeal was that the insurer should be permitted to show, however difficult that might be, that a trust should not be found in the circumstances.

*(b) Waiver of Subrogation Rights*

A result similar to that in *Commonwealth Construction*[25] was reached in the more recent decision of the Supreme Court in *Fraser River Pile & Dredge Ltd. v. Can-Dive Services Ltd.*[26] The facts were that the plaintiff owned a barge and had taken out insurance on it. The barge was chartered to the defendant and was lost by the defendant's negligence. The insurance policy issued to the owner provided in its "General Conditions" for "additional assureds" and provided:[27]

> It is agreed that this policy also covers the Insured, associated and affiliated companies of the Insured, be they owners, subsidiaries or interrelated companies and as bareboat charterers and/or charterers and/or sub-charterers and/or operators and/or in whatever capacity ...

The policy contained a clause, referred to as a "Trustee Clause", in the General Conditions which provided:[28]

---

23 (1988) 165 C.L.R. 107 at p. 123.

24 Kincaid, *Trident*, above note 1, at pp. 164-168.

25 (1978) 69 D.L.R. (3d) 558.

26 [1999] 3 S.C.R. 108, 176 D.L.R. (4th) 257, [1999] 9 W.W.R. 380 ("*Fraser River*"). All references will be to D.L.R.

27 *Fraser River*, p. 260.

28 *Fraser River*, p. 260.

> It is understood and agreed that the Named Insured who obtained this Policy did so on his own behalf and as agent for the others insured hereby including those referred to by general description.

The policy also contained a "subrogation and waiver of subrogation clause" which provided:

> In the event of any payment under this Policy, the Insurers shall be subrogated to all of the Insured's rights of recovery therefor, and the Insured shall execute all papers required and shall do everything that may be necessary to secure such rights, but it is agreed that the Insurers waive any right of subrogation against:
>
> ...
>
> (b) any charterer(s) and/or operator(s) and/or lessee(s) and/or mortgagee(s).

After the insurer had paid the owner, the insurer and the owner made an agreement in which the owner agreed to permit the insurer, notwithstanding the express waiver of subrogation in the policy, to sue the defendant.

The defendant argued that it was protected by the fact that it was an "additional insured" under the policy and by the waiver of the insurer's rights of subrogation. The trial judge allowed the plaintiff's claim. He relied on the decision of the Privy Council in *Vandepitte*[29] as governing in the circumstances. In his view, certain recent cases in the Supreme Court of Canada, particularly, *London Drugs*[30] (to be dealt with more fully in the next section of this paper) did not change the law in regard to waiver of subrogation rights and to apply it in the circumstances would be more than an incremental change in the law. In the trial judge's view, the defendant was unable to rely on the waiver of subrogation because, though the policy described the plaintiff as acting as "agent" for the defendant, the fundamental problem was that the defendant, as principal, had to have ratified the contract made on its behalf and it had not done so. The British Columbia Court of Appeal allowed the defendant's appeal. The court refused to treat *Vandepitte* as an authority. Esson J.A. referred to the legislative abrogation of the result on the particular facts of that case[31] and

---

29 [1933] A.C. 70.

30 (1992) 97 D.L.R. (4th) 261.

31 The result in *Vandepitte* had been legislatively reversed even before the decision of the Privy Council upholding the rule had been given: S.B.C., 1932, c. 20, s. 5 (adding s. 159F(2) to the *Insurance Act*). The amendment provided that,

> [a]ny person insured by but not named in a policy may recover indemnity in the same manner and to the same extent as if named therein as the insured, and for that

to the fact that the case had not been applied when it might have been.[32] He concluded that *Commonwealth Construction*[33] made the waiver of subrogation clause effective.

In the Supreme Court, Iacobucci J. gave the judgment of the Court. He declined to deal with the defendant's argument that the doctrine of agency provided a defence to the action. Instead, he approached the case on the basis that the question to be dealt with was whether an exception to the doctrine of privity should be made in the circumstances. He described his approach in the following way:[34]

> In terms of extending the principled approach to establishing a new exception to the doctrine of privity of contract relevant to the circumstances of the appeal, regard must be had to the emphasis in *London Drugs* that a new exception first and foremost must be dependent upon the intention of the contracting parties. Accordingly, extrapolating from the specific requirements as set out in *London Drugs*, the determination in general terms is made on the basis of two critical and cumulative factors: (a) did the parties to the contract intend to extend the benefit in question to the third party seeking to rely on the contractual provision; and (b) are the activities performed by the third party seeking to rely on the contractual provision the very activities contemplated as coming within the scope of the contract in general, or the provision in particular, again as determined by reference to the intentions of the parties?

Iacobucci J. had no difficulty in holding that the plaintiff had intended that the waiver of subrogation would extent to the defendant. The

---

purpose shall be deemed to be a party to the contract and to have given consideration therefor.

This provision is now found in the uniform *Insurance Acts* of the common law provinces. See above note 11.

32 The case referred to by Esson J.A. in this context was *Scott v. Wawanesa Mutual Insurance Company* [1989] 1 S.C.R. 1445, 59 D.L.R. (4th) 660. In that case the insureds under a policy of fire insurance claimed an indemnity when their house burnt down. The fire was caused by arson committed by the son of the insureds. A majority of the Supreme Court had held that because the policy provided that the son was also an "insured", his arson prevented them from recovering on the policy since the loss was caused by an excluded peril, *viz.*, the deliberate act of an "insured". The irony in the argument of Esson J.A. lies in the fact that the inclusion of family members in the class of insureds under a fire insurance policy was to overcome the problem that the "true" insureds, *i.e.*, the homeowners, had no insurable interest in their children's property. The "not following" referred to by Esson J.A. lay in the fact that in *Scott* the Supreme Court did not make the argument that, as a third-party beneficiary under the policy, the son, even if he were defined as an insured, would have had no claim to an indemnity.

33 (1978) 69 D.L.R. (3d) 558.

34 *Fraser River*, p. 270.

issue that made this point more difficult – and which is a general problem of the enforcement of third-party contracts – was the existence of the agreement between the owner and its insurer waiving the waiver of subrogation. Iacobucci J. held that, once the right of the defendant to be protected by the waiver had "crystallised" by the occurrence of the loss, the subsequent agreement by the owner and its insurer could not affect the defendant. He also held that the second requirement had been met and that the defendant had been engaged in the activity, i.e., the chartering of the barge, explicitly provided for in the policy.

Finally, Iacobucci J. took the same position as Esson J. on the decision in *Vandepitte*. He noted that it had been legislatively reversed and that it was inconsistent with cases like *Commonwealth Construction*.[35] He concluded by saying "that relaxing the doctrine of privity in these circumstances establishes a default rule that most closely corresponds to commercial reality".[36]

### *(c) The Employee Cases*

The third practical problem is one that has divided the Supreme Court and created considerable practical and theoretical problems. The background to the problem is a common arrangement between two parties, a landlord and a tenant or a general contractor and a subcontractor, under which one of them is to insure property against loss by fire. A consequence of this arrangement is that, if a loss occurs through the negligence of the party who had not taken out the insurance, the one that has taken out the policy cannot sue the other for damages for its negligence.[37] No third-party issue arises in such a situation for the parties are free between themselves to agree that one will insure against loss by fire and that rights of subrogation will be waived. The twist to *Commonwealth Construction* was, of course, that the protection of the insuring agreement was claimed by and given to a subcontractor who was not a party to the agreement between the owner (who had taken out the insurance) and the contractor with whom the agreement regarding the insurance had been made. The additional twist that causes the problem in the cases that I now want to examine is the fact that the employees of the party protected by the agreement are sued by the

---

35 (1978) 69 D.L.R. (3d) 558.

36 *Fraser River*, p. 274.

37 The cases reaching this conclusion in the context of a landlord and a tenant include *Agnew-Surpass Shoe Stores Limited v. Cummer-Yonge Investments Limited* [1976] 2 S.C.R. 221, *Ross Southward Tire Limited et al. v. Pyrotech Products Limited et al.* [1976] 2 S.C.R. 35 and *T. Eaton Company Limited et al. v. Smith et al.* [1978] 2 S.C.R. 749. *Commonwealth Construction* (1978) 69 D.L.R. (3d) 558 is authority for the result in the case of the general contractor and the subcontractor.

other's insurer under its rights of subrogation. The argument of the insurer is that the employees are third parties to the contract and that, even though their employer is protected, they have no claim to be similarly protected.

In *Greenwood Shopping Plaza Ltd. v. Beattie*[38] the Supreme Court held two employees of a tenant of a shopping centre personally liable to the landlord of the centre for their negligence even though their employer was protected from liability to the landlord's insurer by a waiver of subrogation rights.[39] The Supreme Court held that the terms of the lease which protected the tenant did not as a matter of fact provide that the tenant was acting as agent for its employees or that they would be protected as beneficiaries of a trust. McIntyre J. justified the court's conclusion by saying:[40]

> The rule of privity has not always been applied with the rigour which has developed during modern times. It has been clear, however, since *Tweddle v. Atkinson*[41] that the rule has had decisive effect in this branch of the law. There are many cases which have applied this principle but those most commonly referred to in England in recent times are *Dunlop Pneumatic Tyre Co. Ltd. v. Selfridge & Company*[42] decided in 1915, and *Scruttons Ltd. v. Midland Silicones Ltd.*,[43] decided in 1962, both in the House of Lords. The law on this point has been settled in England. In Canada, the same rule has generally been followed. In this Court, in *Canadian General Electric Co. Ltd. v. Pickford & Black Ltd.*,[44] the case of *Scruttons Ltd. v. Midland Silicones Ltd.* was adopted and approved as correctly stating the law but on facts which involved an independent contractor rather than an employee. There have been many attempts to break out of the rigid mould imposed by the concept of privity and some statutory relief has been provided in special cases but the concept remains one of general application. If the case at bar cannot be brought into one or other of the exceptions which have become known in the law, or if it cannot be distinguished on its facts from the various cases which would otherwise bind us, this appeal would have to succeed.

The Supreme Court returned to the issue of third-party beneficiary contracts in *London Drugs*.[45] The facts of *London Drugs* are standard: the

---

38 [1980] 2 S.C.R. 228, 111 D.L.R. (3d) 257, ("*Greenwood*"). All references will be to D.L.R.

39 See the cases cited above note 37.

40 *Greenwood*, p. 263.

41 (1861) 1 B. & S. 393, 121 E.R. 762.

42 [1915] A.C. 847 (H.L.).

43 [1962] A.C. 446, [1962] 1 All E.R. 1.

44 [1971] S.C.R. 41, 14 D.L.R. (3d) 372.

45 [1992] 3 S.C.R. 299, [1993] 1 W.W.R. 1, 97 D.L.R. (4th) 261. All references will be to D.L.R.

plaintiff, appellant, stored an electrical transformer with the defendant, respondent. The plaintiff accepted a contract that limited the defendant's liability to $40 in the event that the transformer was damaged. The transformer was damaged by the negligence of the defendant's employees as they were carrying out their duties. The plaintiff sued the defendant and the individual employees involved. I shall not review the decision of the British Columbia Supreme Court or those in the Court of Appeal as they have already been described by Grant Huscroft.[46] It is sufficient to note that the trial judge[47] made the employees personally liable to the plaintiff and that the Court of Appeal, by a majority, reversed that decision.[48]

The plaintiff appealed to the Supreme Court seeking judgment against the employees personally for the full amount of its loss. The employees cross-appealed, arguing that they should not be liable for any amount of the loss. The plaintiff argued that the employees were not protected by the contract; the employees that they owed no duty of care to the plaintiff. Three judgments were given in the Supreme Court. The majority of that Court[49] in a judgment given by Iacobucci J. held, dismissing the cross-appeal, that the employees owed a duty of care to the plaintiff and had breached that duty. Iacobucci J. also held, dismissing the appeal, that in the circumstances it was intended by both the plaintiff and corporate defendant that the contractual allocation of risk should extend to the defendant's employees. La Forest J., in a separate judgment dissenting on this point, would have allowed the cross-appeal and held that the employees owed no duty to the plaintiff. McLachlin J., in a separate judgment, noted that tort and contract were separate regimes, that the employees would be liable in tort and that they could not take advantage of a contract to which they were not parties. She held, however, that the plaintiff must be taken to have accepted the risk that, if the defendant's employees were negligent, it would not be able to claim against them.

The principal case standing in the way of protecting the employees was, of course, *Greenwood*. Iacobucci J. distinguished *Greenwood* on four grounds: (i) the contract in *Greenwood* was a lease of premises rather than a contract for services and, as such, "the intervention of the lessee's employees was not at all necessary for the execution of this agreement";[50] (ii) the relevant provision of the contract in *Greenwood* dealt with the mutual undertakings by the lessor and the lessee with respect to insurance of the premises and the granting of subrogation rights and was not a general

---

46 Huscroft, "Bad Doctrine and Incremental Reform" (1994) 7 J.C.L. 181.
47 [1986] 4 W.W.R. 183, 2 B.C.L.R. (2d) 181.
48 [1990] 4 W.W.R. 289, 45 B.C.L.R. (2d) 1, 70 D.L.R. (4th) 51.
49 L'Heureux-Dubé, Sopinka, Cory and Iacobucci J.
50 *London Drugs*, p. 354.

limitation of liability clause; (iii) there was little, if any, evidence to support a finding that the parties to the contract intended to confer a benefit on the employees by the provisions of the lease; and (iv) the parties seeking to obtain benefits from the contract in *Greenwood* were "viewed as complete strangers and not third-party beneficiaries".[51]

Iacobucci J.'s judgment is a curious mix of extreme caution[52] in dealing with *Greenwood* and a willingness to face the fact that making employees personally liable in the circumstances of *London Drugs* was unpalatable. The point that I want to emphasise is the focus on the characterisation of the employees as "complete strangers" as the touchstone of the two decisions: in *Greenwood* the employees were held to be "complete strangers" and in *London Drugs* they were not. As Iacobucci J. pointed out, this distinction had been made in two other Canadian cases, *Canadian General Electric Co. Ltd. v. Pickford & Black Ltd.*,[53] the Canadian parallel to *Scruttons Ltd. v. Midland Silicones Ltd.*,[54] and *ITO – International Terminal Operators Ltd. v. Miida Electronics Inc.*[55] the Canadian equivalent of *New Zealand Shipping Co. Ltd. v. A.M. Satterthwaite & Co. Ltd. (The "Eurymedon")*.[56] In each situation the distinction between giving protection to the third party and denying protection was said to be based on the intention of the parties[57] and the wording of the contracts in the circumstances of each case.[58]

In justifying the need for a new rule Iacobucci J. gave several reasons: He pointed to the fact that "there is clearly an identity of interest between the employer and his or her employees as far as the performance of the employer's contractual obligations is concerned"[59] and that the "doctrine of privity fails to appreciate the special considerations which arise from the relationships of employer-employee and employer-customer".[60]

Iacobucci J.'s delicate treatment of *Greenwood* and the thoroughly unsatisfactory basis on which the distinction between that case and *London Drugs* was based has led to inevitable and only-to-be-expected confusion.

---

51 *London Drugs*, p. 355.

52 Grant Huscroft takes the view that there was no justification for the Court's caution and that the judgment of the majority, in contrast to that of La Forest J., was disappointing. (1994) 7 J.C.L. 181.

53 [1971] S.C.R. 41, 14 D.L.R. (3d) 372.

54 [1962] A.C. 446, [1962] 1 All E.R. 1.

55 [1986] 1 S.C.R. 752, 28 D.L.R. (4th) 641.

56 [1975] A.C. 154, [1974] 1 All E.R. 1015 (Privy Council).

57 *London Drugs*, p. 367.

58 *London Drugs*, p. 369.

59 *London Drugs*, p. 361.

60 *London Drugs* at p. 361.

In *Madison Developments Ltd. v. Plan Electric Co. Ltd.*[61] the Ontario Court of Appeal held that employees of a subcontractor on a construction site were protected by the fire insurance policy taken out by the general contractor. The court applied *Commonwealth Construction*[62] not only to protect the subcontractor from liability for its employees negligence, but, following *London Drugs*, to protect the employees too. In giving the judgment of the Court of Appeal, Carthy J.A. said:[63]

> As I read these lengthy excerpts from *London Drugs Ltd.*, the Supreme Court has not just distinguished the facts in *Greenwood*; it has applied new reasoning to create an incremental change in the law of privity, and has set forth a test for the application of that change which is not restricted to cases involving limited liability. In my view, it is now unnecessary to compare the facts of this case to those in *Greenwood*. It is rather a matter of applying the general principles enunciated in *London Drugs Ltd.* to a case involving an obligation to obtain fire insurance, as opposed to one imposing a limitation of liability. Looked at in that fashion there is no doubt in my mind that the parties to this subcontract implicitly intended the benefit of the fire insurance to extend to the employees.

In spite of the language in *London Drugs* and the judgment of the Ontario Court of Appeal in *Madison Developments*, the British Columbia Supreme Court in *Laing Property Corp. v. All Seasons Display Inc.*[64] held that the employees of the landlord of a shopping centre *were* exposed to the risk of liability in an action brought by tenants whose premises had been damaged in a fire. Lowry J. held that *Greenwood* was to be applied and that the factors that Iacobucci J. had relied on to distinguish it from *London Drugs* all pointed to the conclusion that the employees were not intended to be protected by the insuring obligations in the leases.[65]

## 3. A Principle for Recognition?

I have an initial difficulty with Kincaid's argument for the overriding supremacy of the bargain principle: I think that he invests the principle with far too much significance. I agree that there are many cases in which the principle has been stated in the terms that Kincaid describes; cases like

---

61 (1997) 36 O.R. (3d) 80, 152 D.L.R. (4th) 653.
62 (1978) 69 D.L.R. (3d) 558.
63 *Madison Developments*, p. 665 (D.L.R.).
64 (1998) 53 B.C.L.R. (3d) 142.
65 The fact that, under the leases in *Laing Property*, the obligation to insure was on the tenants and not the landlord, was not seen as relevant.

*Eastwood v. Kenyon*,[66] *Tweddle v. Atkinson*,[67] *Dunlop v. Selfridge*[68] *Vandepitte*[69] and *Scruttons Ltd. v. Midland Silicones Ltd.*[70] What is not so obvious is the fact that courts have in as many if not more cases strained to find consideration so that the promise can be enforced even as the bargain principle is upheld. What distinguishes the cases is not disagreement over the application of the principle, but the attitude of the court to the problem that it has to deal with. If the court wants to enforce the defendant's promise, it will, like the court in *Thomas v. Thomas*,[71] find consideration and it will be a curiously unimaginative court that will be unable to find it if it looks hard enough. In other words, the bargain principle does not, *as a matter of fact*, have the effect that Kincaid claims for it: in practice, it is far more flexible than it is taken to be.[72]

Kincaid argues[73] that some principled justifications for permitting a third party to sue on a contract would necessarily entail the enforcement of gratuitous promises. While the rights of some third parties may well be similar to those of intended donees, the facts of the cases where third parties have sued typically bear no resemblance to promises to make gifts. The Canadian cases that I have referred to, the principal English cases that I have just mentioned and *Trident Insurance* bear no relation to cases on the enforcement of gift promises. They all arise in a commercial context. It is important to remember that there are often very good reasons that justify a refusal to enforce a gratuitous or gift promise. The pattern of litigation over wholly gratuitous promises discloses that an action will often be brought only when the donor is dead. In such a situation, the promise to make the gift not being performed or the donee having been left out of the will, the donee's sole chance of obtaining anything depends on the chance that a court will treat the promise as enforceable. If the promise is

66 (1840) 11 Ad. & El. 438, 113 E.R. 482.

67 (1861) 1 B. & S. 393, 121 E.R. 762.

68 [1915] A.C. 847 (H.L.).

69 [1933] A.C. 70.

70 [1962] A.C. 446, [1962] 1 All E.R. 1.

71 (1842) 2 Q.B. 851, 144 E.R. 330.

72 Corbin's analysis (above note 3) makes this point. It is not an answer to Corbin's conclusion that English courts have *as a matter of fact* frequently enforced third-party beneficiary contracts to characterise it, as Kincaid does (Rationalising [1989] C.L.J. 243 at p. 249), as a "campaign" (presumably to change the English law of third-party beneficiary contracts). The only question is whether Corbin accurately showed what the courts had done. His analysis (Vol. 4, § 848, at pp. 378-381) of cases like *Les Affréteurs Réunis Société Anonyme v. Leopold Walford (London) Ltd.*, [1919] A.C. 801, is convincing proof of the fact that English courts did not for all that they said, take the bargain principle and its logical offspring, the traditional third-party beneficiary rule, seriously or as seriously as Kincaid has claimed they did.

73 Kincaid, Rationalising [1989] C.L.J. 243 at p. 245.

enforced, the donee is now able to claim as a creditor against the deceased's estate. The real creditors of the deceased's estate have enriched it; they have either lent the deceased money or supplied goods or services for which they have not been paid. The donee who has given nothing should not be allowed to make a claim that will reduce the amount available to true creditors. Nor should the donee be able as a creditor to claim from the estate in priority to those who are recognised as dependants of the deceased and be given rights in the estate even against the deceased's will. In short there are many reasons to separate cases of claims by third parties from those of donees. If the bargain principle is so crude as to be unable to distinguish main-stream commercial cases from cases of pure gratuitous promises, it is another indication that the principle is neither useful nor one that is likely to be assiduously or willingly followed.

There is a further point to be made: it is necessary to note that there are degrees of enforceability. In the commercial exchange, where the defendant's promise is bought by payment of the price or, to put it another way, where there is an exchange of commercial equivalents, damages are calculated by reference to the compensation principle of *Robinson v. Harman*[74] or *Sally Wertheim v. Chicoutimi Pulp Co.*,[75] what Fuller & Perdue[76] call the expectation measure or expectation damages, i.e., the measure that gives the plaintiff what it would have had had the contract been performed. When some other principle is adopted for enforcement, promissory estoppel or reliance for example, the measure of protection - to use the broadest term - can be limited to what is necessary to protect the plaintiff's reliance.[77] All that had to be done to protect the tenant in *Central London Property Trust Ltd. v. High Trees House Ltd.*[78] was to prevent the landlord from suing for the full amount of the original rent. Throughout the law, a party can be prevented from going back on its word when the other has (reasonably) relied on that word.[79] The importance and ubiquity of this principle can be seen in its development not only in promissory estoppel but also in the tort of negligent misrepresentation. The

74 (1848) 1 Exch. 850, 154 E.R. 363, [1843-60] All E.R. Rep. 383.

75 [1911] A.C. 301.

76 "The Reliance Interest in Contract Damages" (1936) 46 *Yale L. Rev.* 52, 373.

77 This principle is, for example, expressly adopted in Restatement Second, Contracts, § 90 which states:

> A promise which the promisor should reasonably expect to induce action or forbearance on the part of the promisee or a third person and which does induce such action or forbearance is binding if injustice can be avoided only by enforcement of the promise. The remedy granted for breach may be limited as justice requires.

78 [1947] 1 K.B. 130.

79 See, e.g., all the cases based on *Hughes v. Metropolitan Railway Company* (1877) 2 App. Cas. 439, 46 L.J.Q.B. 583.

recognition of reliance as a basis for enforcement of a promise or duty of care does not necessarily entail giving the promisee a right to sue for expectation damages.[80]

Kincaid has generally discussed the problem of the justification for giving third parties rights under a contract to which they are not parties in terms of giving the third party a right to sue under the contract. He has used the word "enforcement" or has talked of the third party "suing" on the contract.[81] He has stated that the approach of the law is to "ask the plaintiff to show why justice demands that he have a cause of action against the defendant. In contract, the plaintiff can do this by showing that he has paid a requested price for the promise made to him".[82]

One distinction that I would like to make is that I would prefer not to talk only of "enforcement" but also of "recognition" so that the question is not only whether a third party can sue on the contract, but also whether the third party can use a contractual provision as a defence to a claim or in some other similar way. In other words, I would like to have the opportunity to give the third party only as much protection as is necessary to protect its interest. Whether one adopts the vivid (but not very helpful) notion that recognition only involves a "shield" while enforcement requires a "sword" or the demonstration of Graham Battersby that third parties, as a matter of fact, have frequently been protected by the terms of contracts to which they are not parties,[83] it seems easier to argue that recognition, as opposed to enforcement, should be given to the claims of the third parties.[84]

The obvious parallel, if one is going to talk of swords and shields, is, of course, the law of promissory estoppel where courts are in general more willing to protect a party by preventing the other from going back on its

---

80 See, e.g., *Esso Petroleum Co. Ltd. v. Mardon* [1976] Q.B. 801, [1976] 2 All E.R. 5. That the problem is more complicated than Lord Denning M.R. saw is demonstrated in *V.K. Mason Construction Ltd. v. Bank of Nova Scotia* [1985] 1 S.C.R. 271, 16 D.L.R. (4th) 598, where the plaintiff's reliance interest, protected by an action for negligent misrepresentation, was held to include its opportunity costs. In terms of the size of the cheque that the defendant had to write, this case illustrates that the distinction between reliance and expectation damages largely if not completely disappears.

81 See, e.g., Kincaid, Private Justice (1997) 12 J.C.L. 47 at p. 47, and Rationalising [1989] C.L.J. 243 at p. 243. A similar focus is found in Stephen Smith, "Contracts for the Benefit of Third Parties: in Defence of the Third-Party Rule" (1997) 17 Oxford J.L.S. 643.

82 Kincaid, *Trident* (1989) 2 J.C.L. 160 at p. 167.

83 Battersby, above note 2.

84 This point is also made by Iacobucci J. in *London Drugs*, p. 361:

> Moreover, recognising a right for a third-party beneficiary to rely on a limitation of liability clause should have relatively little impact on the rights of contracting parties to rescind or vary their contracts, in comparison with the recognition of a third-party right to sue on a contract.

word than by granting a judgment for damages. It will appear that, just as in the case of promissory estoppel where shields can become long and pointed and quite as efficient as swords as offensive weapons,[85] the distinction between recognition and enforcement is hard to maintain on principle and I shall explore the extent to which the method that I shall suggest for dealing with the "recognition" cases can deal effectively with the "enforcement" cases.

If the cases that I have analysed are considered in the light of the fundamental issue raised by Kincaid and the points that I have just made, what answers can be found? To the extent that all the cases, except *Greenwood*, recognise a third party claim in some way, they reach a result that Kincaid would, as I understand his argument, consider a violation of the rule that a third party cannot have rights under a contract to which it is not a party.

It is important to be clear what Kincaid's argument entails. He appears[86] to argue in *Trident Insurance* (and I assume would do so in *Commonwealth Construction* and *Fraser River* as well) that even though the insurer agreed to assume the risk of loss and, moreover, had explicitly agreed to include the contractor, subcontractor or charterer in the coverage provided by the policy and was fully paid for assuming that risk, a fundamental principle of the law of contracts, the bargain principle, requires the court to permit the insurer to deny coverage to the contractor, subcontractor or charterer and, in the latter two situations, recover the loss that it had paid to the owners. And this result should follow even though the insurers who were denied their rights of subrogation can hardly be heard to argue that they secretly intended, in spite of the terms of the policies that they issued, to undo the allocation of the risk of loss that the insureds, their customers, had achieved. It is important to note that Kincaid does not suggest that there is anything wrong with the kind of agreement that the owner and the insurer made; they could easily have made it enforceable by adding, as did the policy in *Commonwealth Construction*, a

85 See, e.g., *Waltons Stores (Interstate) Ltd. v. Maher* (1988) 164 C.L.R. 387, (H.C.A.).

86 I say, "appears", because Kincaid's discussion of the judgments in *Trident Insurance* focuses principally on the validity of the arguments of the members of the High Court who found for the plaintiff and he does not deal with my argument that denying enforcement appears to condone conduct that cannot (apart from the doctrine of privity) be defended or justified. In his most recent paper, Reform, Kincaid acknowledges that denying enforcement of promises made to third parties may "frustrate the intentions of the contracting parties [and disappoint] the legitimate expectations of the third party", but he still regards the traditional bargain principle as being justifiably indifferent to these consequences. If the expectations of the third party are, as Kincaid says, "legitimate", where does this legitimacy come from, if not from the law? I wonder how much is conceded by Kincaid's use of the word "legitimate".

"trustee clause". The only reason for denying enforcement is that the enforcement by the contractor would violate the bargain principle.

Kincaid now admits that enforcement can now, after the Contracts (Rights of Third Parties) Act 1999, be justified on "a broader more public-spirited concern with the good of the community at large".[87] But this conclusion is a very sad commentary on the common law: it is an admission that the bargain principle, blindly applied by generations of judges and defended by academics, simply could not deal fairly or justly with the simple problems that the cases I have discussed illustrate. As I have said, I do not want to deal with the new legislation; I want to deal with the common law and with its ability to do exactly what has to be done, *viz*., to consider the intentions of the parties and the expectations of the third party. Since the common law provinces of Canada have nothing like the United Kingdom legislation, it remains necessary here to deal with the implications of the bargain principle.

The application of the bargain principle to deny protection to the third parties in *Commonwealth Construction* and *Trident Insurance* would appear to achieve a result that can only be described as bizarre. The result would seem to say to the parties that, regardless of the efforts that they made to plan the allocation of the risks of loss by fire or marine misfortune and the willing and bargained for acceptance of that allocation by the party now asked to bear the risk, nevertheless the law requires that these arrangements be ignored and the risk allocated to a party who had not expected to bear it.[88] It seems to me that, put this way, the onus is on the person who would argue for the application of the bargain principle, not the other way round.

At this point I would be prepared to say that recognition or enforcement of third-party rights can be justified on the basis that not to do so ignores the purpose that the law of contracts exists to forward and that if recognition or enforcement is inconsistent with the bargain principle, so much the worse for that principle. Another way of justifying the results that I believe have to be reached is to shift our focus and to consider the bargain principle and contractual relations in a different context.

I shall deal with what I think are the easier cases first. Both *Commonwealth Construction* and *Fraser River* are cases where all that had

---

87 Kincaid, "Reform" (2000) 116 L.Q.R. 43 at p. 47.

88 It is, of course, possible that the subcontractor and the charterer might have had their own liability insurance so that they do not themselves bear the actual loss, but it is also possible that their policies excluded coverage for the loss that occurred precisely because coverage was expected to be provided by the owners' insurance. In any case, whether or not the subcontractor or charterer had insurance is irrelevant to the argument: the point of the parties' arrangement was to avoid any calls on this insurance.

to be done to protect the third parties was to deny the insurer its claim. That denial neatly and completely protects the third parties and what I can call the integrity of the relations represented by the parties' arrangements. This argument also makes the result in *London Drugs* easy to justify and shows why *Greenwood* is so wrong. As I have argued, it is unnecessary to treat those cases as if the issue were the one that Kincaid sees, *viz.*, whether the third party can sue to enforce a promise by obtaining damages: all the third party needs is to have the other party prevented from suing. I shall argue that a simple "adjustment" to the bargain principle could provide a justification for the recognition of the rights of the third parties, but the basic principle of reliance which, as promissory estoppel, co-exists with the bargain principle can equally do the job. It is not necessary, in applying that doctrine, to conclude that it has to lead to an award of expectation damages, all that is needed is to have the plaintiff's claim dismissed, just as the landlord's claim was dismissed by Lord Denning in *High Trees*.

It is, however, possible to go further and *Trident Insurance* presents the opportunity to do so. The important fact in the cases where the Supreme Court protected the third party, *i.e.*, *Commonwealth Construction*, *London Drugs* and *Fraser River*, is that the parties were engaged in a common enterprise. The insurers who initially bore the risk of loss – and all the cases involved insurers – were paid by one of the parties who, at least with regard to that coverage, had undertaken and was expected by the others to provide for the coverage.

It is at this point that the attitude that one has to the bargain principle becomes important. It is true that in each case the claim is made by a person other than the one who wrote the cheque that represents payment to the insurer, the promisor. But this fact is not fatal to a claim to enforce the promise. A case that illustrates exactly this point is *Coulls v. Bagot's Executor and Trustee Co. Ltd.*[89] In that case the question was whether the widow of a man could claim to be entitled to the benefit of an contract that had been made by her and her husband with a construction company to exploit a quarry on land that he owned. In holding that the widow had a right to the payments due from the company, Windeyer J. said:[90]

> The transaction can then be analysed, in terms of contract, in either of two ways. One is that the company … promised Coulls and his wife, for valuable consideration (actually provided by him but on behalf of both of them), that it would pay the royalties to them for their joint lives and afterwards to the survivor.

---

89 (1967) 119 C.L.R. 460 ("*Coulls*").
90 (1967) 119 C.L.R. 460 at p. 493.

This way of analysing the transaction is the one that Windeyer J. considers correct. Kincaid agrees with Windeyer J.'s analysis and says:[91]

> It is irrelevant that A actually produces the price as long as he does so on behalf of the *entity*, in which case the consideration is seen as emerging from the promisee, the *entity*, and the rule is complied with, not just in form but in spirit. (Emphasis added.)

It is clear that the parties, the owner, contractor and subcontractors, engaged on a construction project are perhaps not joint promisees in the sense that Mr. and Mrs. Coulls were joint promisees, but it is not a large stretch of the imagination – and none at all of the facts – to regard them as having an interest in the common enterprise that closely resembles that of Mr. and Mrs. Coulls in the transaction with the construction company. One party provides the price, the premium paid to the insurer, on behalf of all the parties involved and each party is entitled to the protection provided by that payment. Kincaid refers to the payment by Mr. Coulls as being made on behalf of the "entity", *i.e.*, Mr. and Mrs. Coulls together or jointly. It is clear that Mr. and Mrs. Coulls did not constitute a legal entity or a firm; they were two individuals doing something together. If Mr. and Mrs. Coulls constituted an entity, why can't the owner, contractor and subcontractors on a construction site similarly constitute an "entity"?

It may be slightly harder to regard the parties in *Fraser River* as an entity, but it is possible to regard them as having a relation to the enterprise, *i.e.*, the profitable exploitation of the barge, that can justify their both being regarded as parties to the transaction in issue. What is important is not the careful analysis of the terms of the insurance policy that Kincaid's approach would require, but the recognition that what matters is that the insurer was paid to accept the risk and that this payment, while coming from the owner, was certainly at least partly paid by the charterer and was made on its behalf.[92]

Having gone this far, it is not hard to bring in the employee cases. It is bizarre to impose personal liability on the only people involved in the enterprise who do not have and who would not be expected to have insurance. What is important is again the realisation that an employer and its employees are engaged in a common enterprise; the employer cannot operate without employees and if the employer cannot operate, it cannot pay rent or provide services to its customers.

---

91 Kincaid, Rationalising, [1989] C.L.J. 243 at p. 261.

92 An example of the courts trouble with (and attitude to) the problem of consideration is provided by the judgment of the Privy Council in *The "Eurymedon"*, above note 56, where the device of a unilateral contract was used to avoid it.

It is, of course, these concerns that underlie the judgments of La Forest J. and McLachlin J. in *London Drugs*. In effect, they assimilate the employees into the employer: La Forest J., does so by denying that in the circumstances the employees owed the customer a duty; McLachlin J., does so by holding that the customer took the risk that, by using the services of the employer, it might suffer loss caused by its employees' negligence. These judges approach what I can call the "enterprise argument" from a point of view that, by dealing with the customer's claims as tort claims requiring a tort answer, they entirely avoid the third-party beneficiary rule. Though Battersby does not make the point in the terms that I have, the examples that he offers are consistent with the assimilation of several parties into one for the purpose of determining the extent to which one party, the defendant, is to be exposed to the risk of liability to the plaintiff. In other words, the fact that the performance of a contract of, for example, through carriage by rail required more than one carrier did not take the second carrier out of the protection of the contract made with the first carrier.[93]

Even if the solutions suggested by La Forest J. and McLachlin J. are much neater than that of Iacobucci J., it is possible to give a more secure basis to the latter's judgment by developing Kincaid's idea of the promise of the customer as having been made to an entity: the employer and its employees are engaged in an enterprise and together they constitute an entity. In recognising that the employees in *London Drugs* were not "complete strangers" to the contract, Iacobucci J. is, I think, expressing an idea that bears a close resemblance to the idea of the enterprise that I am exploring. In *London Drugs*, the protection of the employees comes, not from the provision of an insurance policy obtained by the employer for their protection (though I am certain that there was such a policy in the background, even though Iacobucci J. suggests that if they actually needed it they could not claim its protection because to do that they would have had to use a "sword"[94]) but from an allocation of the risk of loss to the customer. Of course, the employees are not parties to that contract in the sense that traditional contract doctrine would regard the relation, but they are part, even the *sine qua non*, of the employer's enterprise. Just as the third parties in the construction and waiver cases had the insurance

93 Above note 2 at pp. 383-390, referring to *Hall v. North Eastern Railway Co.* (1875) L.R. 10 Q.B. 437, 44 L.J.Q.B. 164, as the leading case. It is odd that although Iacobucci J. refers to Battersby's articles, McLachlin J. does not.

94 *London Drugs*, p. 361. Iacobucci J. states:

> Of course, I am in no way suggesting that employees are a party to their employer's contracts in the traditional sense so that they can bring an action on the contract or be sued for breach of contract.

premium paid on their behalf, so too the employer in *London Drugs* has allocated the risk of loss to its customer for the protection of itself and on behalf of its employees and has, on their behalf as well as its own, bought the limitation of liability by its agreement to store the plaintiff's goods for an amount that was less than it would have charged had the loss been allocated to it.

Apart from the fact that *Greenwood* is a nasty, vicious decision on, as it were, its own merits, it can now be seen to have ignored the nature of the relation between the tenant and its employees. While Iacobucci J. was anxious not to say that *Greenwood* was a dreadful decision which should be overruled and, instead, danced around it by characterising the employees in that case as "complete strangers" to the contract, there is no more basis for saying so in *Greenwood* than there was in *London Drugs*.[95] It is not the words of the contract or the lease that are important; it is the nature of the relation between the employer and its employees on the one hand and the landlord or customer on the other. It is the focus on the relation between Mr. and Mrs. Coulls, the entity that they constitute, that makes the approach of the High Court (and Kincaid) in that case so attractive and powerful; it is the failure to recognise the relations that make decisions like *Greenwood* so bad.[96]

One further point needs to be dealt with. In *Fraser River* the owner and its insurer had agreed that the waiver of subrogation in the policy was itself to be waived. Neither the British Columbia Court of Appeal nor the Supreme Court had any difficulty in holding that the right of the charterer to the protection of the policy could not be affected by something done after that right to protection had "crystallised" on the occurrence of the loss. The right of the parties to an agreement to change it to the possible detriment of a third party is one of the perennial issues of the third-party beneficiary rule. Where the rule has been changed by statute, it has been necessary to provide especially for changes.[97]

*Fraser River* was an easy case because an event which could easily be identified as crystallising the right of the charterer to the protection of the policy had occurred. In the broader class of contracts that I have been dealing with, problems of change to the detriment of the third party are unlikely to occur. The factors that would force the owner and the contractor on a construction project to maintain insurance for the benefit of

---

95 The decision in *Laing Property* (1998) 53 B.C.L.R. (3d) 142 is, of course, as bad as that in *Greenwood*. It will be interesting to see what the British Columbia Court of Appeal will do with the case when it hears the appeal.

96 See *London Drugs* (1992) 97 D.L.R. (4th) 261 at p. 354.

97 See, *e.g.*, *Insurance Act*, R.S.O. 1990, c. I.8, s. 197, and the U.K. Contracts (Rights of Third Parties) Act 1999, s. 2.

subcontractors would persist to the end of the project. Similarly, it is unreasonable to think that an employer who allocates the risks of loss to its customers would decide to expose its employees to the risk of liability to its customers. A solution to the general problem of amendment of the contract could take the same form that the protection of reliance takes. Where reliance is reasonable and expected, the person who induced that reliance has to give notice that any continued reliance is misplaced. This principle is applicable widely in the law, in cases of promissory estoppel and in situations like, for example, waiver of "time of the essence" clauses or any other contractual requirement. Of course, there may be difficult cases that will not offer a simple solution but, as a matter of fact, it is unlikely that there will be many cases where in the kind of relations that I have examined the contract will be amended. The clue to this observation lies in the comparison of the relation in *Fraser River* and *London Drugs*. The relation in the former case was limited to the particular charterparty and neither the owner nor the charterer saw the relation as existing beyond that. In contrast and as I have mentioned, the relations of those engaged on a construction project will exist for as long as the project continues (and the subcontractor needs protection). Similarly, an employer is not going to change the ordinary terms of the standard shopping centre lease or contract of storage (or anything else) and expose its employees to the risk of liability, whether to the employer's landlord or its customers.

There are other situations where potential third-party beneficiary problems lurk. It is, for example, standard in a business acquisition agreement for the parties to provide cross-indemnities. In each case the indemnity will usually be expressed to include the parties' directors, officers and employees. Careful solicitors will frequently include a clause dealing specifically with the possibility that a defendant may argue that the other party's directors are third-party beneficiaries.[98] But even if such a clause were not present (and ignoring the risk that its absence may be taken to indicate an intention to limit the indemnity to the parties alone) the enterprise approach offers a simple solution; the seller and buyer can only act or operate with officers and employees and it distorts the nature of the transaction to regard either party for this purpose as an entity separate from those who make its decisions and operate it. Many other commercial agreements have the same structure and, while many will be very carefully drafted to avoid any third-party problems, it should not be necessary to take such care. If a general solution is not found, the result will be, as has too often been the case, that only those without legal advice will be exposed to

---

[98] The standard clause used by major Canadian law firms uses a belt-and-suspenders approach, making each party both the agent for and trustee of its directors, etc., for the purposes of making the indemnity enforceable.

the risk that their arrangements will be upset.

The treatment of a corporation and its directors and employees as an entity for purposes of the third-party beneficiary rule does not entail the rejection of *Saloman v. Saloman & Co. Ltd.*[99] The only purpose of the enterprise argument is to make enforceable a promise, as in *Trident Insurance*, that could have been enforceable, had the parties chosen to use the correct language to make it so. The standard Himalaya clause, by making the sub-carrier or stevedore the principal of the carrier that issued the bill of lading, avoids the problems of the third-party beneficiary rule but does not otherwise distort the relation between the parties: no one argues that the carrier as the agent or even trustee of any sub-carriers or the stevedores now owes general fiduciary duties to them.

## 4. Conclusion

My initial approach to Kincaid's arguments was that they had to be wrong if their effect was to turn reasonable and common commercial arrangements on their heads or to visit on individuals consequences of their actions that would be regarded by anyone who thought about them for a moment as pointless, cruel and harsh. The repeated invocations by Canadian courts of "commercial reality" or "business reality" to justify what they did, indicates that the judges were struggling to find solutions that would work, that would permit people to plan their affairs in reliance on the belief that, if necessary, the arrangements they made would be respected and recognised by the courts.

I do not suggest that the bargain principle should be abandoned or that the doctrine of consideration should be replaced by something else. We have to have some method for determining what contracts should be enforced by a court and which should not be. I can agree with Kincaid that there are problems with the idea that all contracts for the benefit of third parties should be enforced. I part company with him when he argues that none can justifiably be enforced. The problems of the bargain principle and the doctrine arise when they are pushed too far. The common law has generally developed by incremental stages and is bothered by principles when they are taken too literally. A principle that says that the result in *Greenwood* is justifiable and proper or that the result in *Trident Insurance* is wrong has departed so far from what the law of contracts exists to do that it has to be limited so that such results will not occur. I believe that, by taking a small step in how we regard the relations where the problems arise,

---

99 [1897] A.C. 22, [1895-99] All E.R. Rep. 33.

the bargain principle can easily be applied so that common and reasonable commercial arrangements will be protected.

The cases that I have examined and the solutions that I have offered probably will not deal with all the problems of third-party beneficiary contracts because those problems will arise in situations that are not characterised by the existence of extensive relations between all the parties involved. It is, however, interesting to note that the principal cases in England, Canada and Australia have almost all arisen in the context of the kind of relations that I have argued can provide a basis for the application of the bargain principle to justify giving protection to the third party. By focusing on the parties' relations and on what those relations entail, it is possible to show that there are principled solutions for giving protection to those who reasonably expect it.

Kincaid quotes from the speech of the Lord Chancellor, Lord Irvine of Lairg, on second reading on the United Kingdom legislation in the House of Lords, "The one question … about the Bill is not why it has been introduced, but why it has not been introduced before".[100] That question is exactly the tragedy of the common law and its long struggle to hold fast to a principle, the bargain principle, that far too often existed or was applied only to frustrate the efforts of people to enforce sensible and common commercial arrangements. Legislation should never have been necessary; I hope that I have shown that the common law could have done the job quite well, had it not been for the refusal of courts to acknowledge what had to be done.

---

[100] Kincaid, "Reform" (2000) 116 L.Q.R. 43 at pp. 43, 44.

# 12 Reciprocity Beyond Privity

SIMON WHITTAKER

> It would be a monstrous proposition to say that a person was a party to the contract for the purpose of suing upon it for his own advantage, and not a party to it for the purpose of being sued.[1]

Reciprocity has been significant in English contract law for a very long time, a *quid pro quo* being gradually seen as necessary for informal contracts in the course of the fourteenth and fifteenth centuries.[2] With the rise of *assumpsit* this requirement of reciprocity was not marginised, but instead was channelled into the developing doctrine of consideration needed to support a promise not under seal.[3] Most writers would agree that this remains the case in the modern law, consideration giving effect in general to a requirement of reciprocity, even if it plays other roles at times and in particular contexts.[4]

The common law has also long recognised the dual principle of privity of contract, that is, that in general only the parties may bear the burdens and enjoy the rights arising from the contract.[5] The reason for these general rules differ, one being negative and one positive. In the case of conferring rights on a third party, in my view the most convincing argument is a negative one: the mere fact that the parties have concluded a contract does not justify the recognition of a legal right in a third party.[6] In the case of imposing obligations, as a matter of principle it is contrary to personal liberty to allow two persons to impose burdens on a third party in

---

1 *Tweddle v. Atkinson* (1861) 1 B. & S. 393, 398 *per* Crompton J.

2 D. Ibbetson, *A Historical Introduction to the Law of Obligations* (1999), pp. 80 *et seq.*

3 Ibid. pp. 141 *et seq.*

4 G. Treitel, *The Law of Contract* (10th ed., 1999), p. 63 who describes reciprocity as "the basic feature" of the doctrine of consideration.

5 Ibbetson, ibid., pp. 76 *et seq.*, pp. 140-141.

6 This justification also suggests its major exception, for where the parties to a contract have intended to create a right in a third party, then giving effect to this intention may be thought to be a good reason for the creation of such a right. Giving effect to the intention of the parties was the main justification advanced by the English Law Commission for reform which resulted in the Contracts (Rights of Third Parties) Act 1999: Law Commission, *Privity of Contract: Contracts for the Benefit of Third Parties* Law Com. No. 242 (1996), para. 3.1.

the absence of the latter's consent. However, these rules, while sufficiently important and wide-ranging to deserve the status of principle, should in my view be thought of as no more than general rules, susceptible to exception where this can be justified. The common law itself has recognised some true exceptions to the principles of privity (where the law recognises directly that a third party may be burdened by or enjoy rights under a contract)[7] and even more circumventions, where the law reaches this effect but in another guise or by another route.[8] I have argued elsewhere that the law should feel able to recognise true exceptions to privity of contract where these are justifiable on particular grounds of policy, though whether this should be done by the courts or legislation will depend on the particular situation in question.[9] For me, this sort of development is not inconsistent with the nature of contracts in the modern law. For, I do not see contracts as promises or sets of promises backed by consideration (or clothed in a deed), but rather as agreements triggering a set of legal consequences, some of which arise directly from that agreement (the terms of the contract) and some of which arise from its regulation by law.[10] Of course, this sort of approach downgrades the significance of reciprocity between parties to a contract from being their defining element (contracts as bargains), reducing it to a mere threshold condition for recognising that any particular agreement is capable of having this triggering effect. Indeed, I would argue that one should go further and see the requirement of consideration not as giving rise to a positive requirement for the creation of a contract, but rather as negative, used to exclude a fairly narrow range of agreements ("gratuitous agreements") from the domain of legal contract.[11] As a result, in my view there is nothing in the *conception* of contracts in modern English law which prevents the recognition of true exceptions to privity of contract where these can be justified.

However, given the continuing significance of the idea of reciprocity in English contract law, the question arises whether a right in a third party

---

7 See, notably, the law on negotiable instruments (on which see W. S. Holdsworth, *A History of English Law*, Vol. VIII, p. 162, 167-168) and the position of undisclosed principals, on which see below, text following n. 55.

8 These are collected conveniently in the Law Commission's Report, No. 242, para. 2.8 *et seq*.

9 S. Whittaker, "Privity of Contract and the Tort of Negligence: Future Directions" (1996) 16 O.J.L.S. 191.

10 Ibid., at pp. 193, 215-216.

11 A comparison may be made here the with so-called doctrine of intention to create legal relations. While this doctrine is expressed as a positive requirement for the creation of a contract, the courts do not in general investigate whether the parties to an agreement *do* possess such an intention: this is generally assumed. Rather, in certain classes of case they ask whether they *do not* possess such an intention, with the view to excluding the agreement from contract if this question is answered in the affirmative.

beyond privity should be balanced by a corresponding burden or burdens in that third party. In this way, the rhetorical argument from fairness implicit in the *dictum* of Crompton J. in *Tweddle v. Atkinson* quoted at the beginning of this article could be turned on its head and used to argue for the recognition of a certain reciprocity *beyond* privity.[12] As the traditional adage puts it, *qui sentit commodum sentire debet et onus*, "a person who enjoys the benefit must also bear the burden".[13]

In modern English law, there are a number of situations in which a person can come not merely to enjoy a right under a contract to which he is not party, but also come to bear a burden arising from it. These cases form exceptions not merely to both aspects of privity of contract, but to two related general rules: that a party to a contract may assign a right under it (its benefit) but not an obligation (its burden)[14] and that a person may not be substituted in a contract for one of the parties so as to enjoy its benefits and bear its burdens by way of contractual novation without the consent of all three parties to the transaction.[15] In this article, I shall explore the extent to which English law already does recognise the existence of reciprocity beyond privity of contract (whether overtly or covertly) and also ask whether these apparently disparate instances have any common elements or themes. To do so, I shall look at one situation governed entirely by common law (the position of the undisclosed principal);[16] one partly by common law and partly by statute (leasehold covenants);[17] and two cases governed entirely by legislation implementing European directives (rights of employees on the transfer of undertakings and transfer of a package holiday).[18] In looking at the significance of an idea such as reciprocity beyond privity we should not look only at the common law, but at English law as a whole. I shall also ask whether the law does or should recognise any more general *principle* as regards reciprocity beyond privity.

Before doing so, I wish though to draw attention to three particular aspects of what we mean by reciprocity in the creation of a contract as expressed through the doctrine of consideration.[19] As I have noted, the

12 Whittaker, op. cit. pp. 193, 222-223 (applied to the context of sub-agency).

13 See Coke, 1 Inst. 230b ("He who derives the advantage ought to sustain the burden").

14 *Chitty on Contracts* (gen. ed. H. Beale, 28th edn., 1999), § 20-075 (A. Burrows).

15 Ibid, § 20-84.

16 Below, text following footnote no. 55.

17 Below, text following footnote no. 22.

18 Below, texts following footnotes no. 35 & 67 respectively.

19 Reciprocity between parties to a contract may be significant at later stages. So, for example, in bilateral contracts the issue of the interdependence of obligations in cases of non-performance may be seen to reflect an idea of reciprocity in performance. Thus, where A's non-performance justifies B's refusal to perform (or even B's repudiation or rescission of the contract), we may think of the *performances* of the parties' obligations as being reciprocal, one *in return for* the other. Reciprocity may also be seen to lie

requirement of consideration for the existence of a contract not contained in a deed may clearly be seen in the case of a contract under which A promises B to do something if B promises to do something for A from which A benefits: here, the benefit to the promisor and the detriment to the promisee form the mirror image of each other and are directly reciprocal. But reciprocity can also be seen in those contracts termed unilateral by English lawyers, where A promises B to do something if B *does something* for A from which B benefits (such as where A promises a reward to B if B finds her lost pet). The "one-sideness" of unilateral contracts refers only to the existence of an *obligation* in one party, but not in the other: both parties have to furnish "something of value in the eyes of the law" for there to be a contract and in the above example A benefits from B's doing of an act. Here, the reciprocal "something" from B is not obligational, but rather a prestation which forms a condition for A's obligation.

However, in some examples of either bilateral or unilateral contracts, there is a lack of reciprocity in either of these direct senses. Let us take the case where A agrees to pay B a sum of money in return for B's performance of a service for C.[20] Here, while B's undertaking to perform or actual performance of a service satisfies the requirement of consideration (being detrimental to the promisee), B's undertaking does not stand to benefit A, nor does B's performance actually benefit A. But as the famous definition of consideration in *Currie v. Misa* makes clear, benefit to promisor and detriment to promisee are alternative requirements.[21] While it may be argued that in circumstances such as this in a general way B's undertaking or prestation is "in return" or "in exchange" for A's promise, any benefit from B is at most an indirect one and in this sort of tri-partite case, the idea that the doctrine of consideration does indeed give effect to a requirement of reciprocity is rather less convincing.

Let us now turn to the particular exceptions to or qualifications on privity which may be thought to contain an element of reciprocity.

---

behind the availability of some restitutionary remedies recognised in a contractual context: so, notably, a claim for the restitution of money paid under a failed contract on the ground of total failure of consideration may be thought to rest on the need to reverse an enrichment where the expected reciprocal advantage for the payment has not materialised.

20 Unlike Roman law, English common law has not denied the validity of a contract for the benefit of a third party as between the parties, but simply as regards the creation of a right in a third party: see notably, *Beswick v. Beswick* [1968] A.C. 58. On the Roman rule and its qualification, see R. Zimmermann, *The Law of Obligations, Roman Foundations of the Civilian Tradition* (1990), pp. 34 *et seq.*

21 (1875) L.R. 10 Ex. 153, 162.

## 1. Leasehold Covenants

Leases were originally thought of as a matter of contract rather than of feudal tenure[22] and this contractual nature has been more or less prominent in the course of their subsequent development. In the modern context, leases are considered to be contracts but of a special kind, this reflecting the proprietary nature of both their subject matter and the nature of the tenant's interest. For present purposes, of particular significance is the way in which the law has responded to the transmissibility of the benefit and burden of leasehold covenants, that is, of express or implied promises in the original contract of lease.

Interestingly, as regards assignments by landlords, the matter was first dealt with by statute and with a very particular motive. When Henry VIII dissolved the English monasteries and wished to dispose of monastic land profitably, he found that much of it was leased. It therefore became important to provide that the grantees of the lands should be able to benefit from their tenants' covenants (notably, to pay rent), it being also thought that the grantees should be liable to the burdens arising from the original lessors' covenants.[23] This was the reason for the passing of the Grantees of Reversions Act in 1540,[24] and the key substance of this provision, which subjects the assignee of a reversion to the burden of covenants, though revised and extended in the course of the centuries, remains in force.[25] Moreover, in 1583 the judges accepted the effectiveness of leasehold covenants against *both* parties' assignees, although they restricted this to those covenants which "touch and concern" the land itself, rather than being merely personal to the parties to the original agreement.[26]

How was the effect of these developments viewed? Generally it came to be expressed in terms of saying that while there was privity of contract between the original parties to the lease, there was privity of estate

---

22 See F. Pollock, *The Land Laws* (1883) p. 137; A. W. Brian Simpson, *A History of the Land Law* (2nd ed., 1986), p. 74.

23 Simpson, op. cit., pp. 255-256. pp. 255-256.

24 32 Hen. VIII, c. 34.

25 Law of Property Act 1925, ss. 141, 142 as regards "old tenancies". "New tenancies" are not governed by these provisions, but by the Landlord and Tenant (Covenants) Act 1995, s. 3 (this Act drawing the distinction between "old" and "new" tenancies for this purpose).

26 *Spencer's Case* (1583) 5 Co. Rep. 16a. Simpson, op. cit., p. 255 notes that it also had to be expressed to be made with the assigns of the lessee. On the interpretation of the idea of "touching and concerning" the land in the modern law, see K. Gray, *Elements of Land Law.* (2nd edn., 1993), pp. 855 et seq.

between a party and the other's assignees or between both their assignees.[27] Indeed, it was in the context of distinguishing privity of estate, that the phrase "privity of contract" can first be seen in the reports in the later sixteenth century, though here "privity" itself is used simply to denote a relationship of a particular type (contract or tenure under a lease).[28] In this way, the original contract of lease was made both to benefit and burden certain classes of third parties (the original parties' assignees) during the term of the lease, while making no formal qualification on the personal nature of contracts.

On the other hand, one consequence of relying on the relationship of tenure and inventing the distinct category of "privity of estate" to effect the purpose of extending the rights and duties created by the contract to non-parties, was that it left intact the duties of the *original* parties to the lease arising by way of "privity of contract". For while, for example, a tenant's assignee becomes liable to pay rent to the lessor (or his assignee), this did not extinguish the liability of the original tenant, either to hisown lessor or the latter's assignee. This had the practical effect of making the original parties to the lease the "guarantors" of the performance of the obligations of their successors in title.[29]

In this situation, in 1995 Parliament intervened with a radical solution:[30] privity of contract was to be "cut" on assignment by either party. As a result, as regards new tenancies, after assignment, neither the original tenant nor, subject to certain further conditions, the original landlord would be liable on their covenants,[31] although provision was made so as to continue to allow a tenant on assignment to guarantee future performance of tenancy obligations by his assignees.[32] However, the significance of "privity of estate" was extended by abolishing the requirement that

---

27 Gray, op. cit., pp. 846 *et seq.*

28 See the important discussion in *Walker v. Harris* (1587) 3 Co. Rep. 22a at 23a. Cf. *Thursby v. Plant* (1669) 1 W. Saund. 237, 241 where the court referred to the Grantees of Reversions Act "transferring" privity of contract. See also *Lord Ward v. Lumley* (1680) 5 H. and N. 87, 90 where it was held that the cancellation of a lease by mutual consent terminated the privity of contract between the parties, but left the privity of estate: "actions founded on the privity of contract are gone, but actions founded on the privity of estate remain so long as the term lasts."

29 For an early example, see *Brett v. Cumberland* (1619) Cro. Jac. 521, 523 ("[t]his covenant may charge the assignee who hath the estate, and the lessee and his executors who made the covenants all at one and the self-same time; but execution shall only be against one of them ..."). The original parties are not, however, guarantors in the technical sense, as they are primarily liable: *Baynton v. Morgan* (1888) 22 Q.B.D. 74.

30 This reform had been recommended by the Law Commission: *Landlord and Tenant: Privity of Contract and Estate*' Law Com. No. 174 (1988).

31 Landlord and Tenant (Covenants) Act 1995, ss. 5-8.

32 Landlord and Tenant (Covenants) Act 1995, s. 16.

leasehold covenants need "touch and concern the land" to run with it.[33] In the result, while this is disguised behind the terminology of privity of estate, what has been created by a combination of common law and statutory developments has been a system of genuine contractual substitution of parties to one, original and continuing contract of lease.

What is the justification for these developments, given that they do not conform to the general rules of privity of contract, assignment or novation? It seems to me that there are three driving forces at work. The first lies in the potentially long-term nature of leases of land: these may be very long-term contracts indeed, requiring continuing performances long beyond the lives of the original natural parties to the contract. Secondly, and clearly related to this, leases may be seen as an important way in which very considerable wealth may be divided as well as managed. This means that any refusal by the law to recognise the bilateral nature of the continuing relations of those "sharing" land would cause greater (financial) injustice. Thirdly, some of the developments which I have just described, including the "cutting of privity of contract",[34] can be thought of as based on a concern to protect the reasonable and typical expectations of the parties to the contract or series of contracts in question. Where all parties contract on the understanding that transferees will take both the benefit and burden of their new positions, it would defeat the collective intentions of all parties that they should not in law do so. In this sense, the law of leasehold covenants represents a triumph of party intention over privity of contract. privity of contract. Here, then, reciprocity remains beyond privity of contract because the contract creates a relationship (of landlord and tenant) of a particular type which is held to remain reciprocal even beyond the contract's original parties.

## 2. Transferring Contracts of Employment

At common law, employers may not without the consent of their employee assign their rights against that employee,[35] nor may employees assign their

---

33 Ibid., s. 3.

34 See Law Commission, *Privity of Contract and Estate, Duration of Liability of Parties to Leases,* Working Paper No. 95 (1986) para. 3.1 (quoted in Law Commission, report no. 174, cit. n. 23, (1988)). "[Original parties] regard the contractual obligations undertaken in a lease as only properly regulating the terms on which the owner for the time being of a property permits the tenant for the time being to occupy and use it, or as the case may be, to sublet and profit from it. They see no reason why responsibility should last longer than ownership of the particular interest in the property."

35 *Nokes v. Doncaster Amalgamated Collieries Ltd.* [1940] A.C. 1014, 1018, 1026.

rights against their employer without the latter's consent.[36] Moreover, in keeping with the general rule, the burden of such a contract may not be "assigned" without the consent of all the relevant parties (assignor, assignor's contractual partner, and assignee), when in law the contract of employment is novated.[37] However, this position has been significantly changed as a result of the implementation and re-implementation of the Acquired Rights Directive[38] into English law. The purpose of this directive is to protect the rights of employees in the event of a change of their employer[39] and its controls are centred on the "transfer of an undertaking".[40] When such a transfer is effected, the directive provides in principle that "the transferor's rights and obligations arising from a contract of employment or from an employment relationship existing on the date of a transfer within the meaning of Article 1(1) shall, by reason of such transfer, be transferred to the transferee".[41] The directive further provides that a Member State may (but need not) provide that the transferor shall continue to be liable in respect of obligations which arose from a contract of employment or an employment relationship.[42] Thus, the Directive effects a transfer of rights in a former employer to the new employer, but while it requires that the new employer be subject to the former employer's obligations arising out of the employment, it does not require that they be *transferred*, for it allows Member States to retain the burden of the employment contract on the former employer. In all this, under the Directive there is no explicit requirement of any consent to the transfer of the rights and obligations in any of the parties. Clearly, the former and new employer may consent to the transfer of the undertaking,[43] but neither of them nor the employees need consent to the transfer of the benefit and burden of the employees' rights. On the other hand, the Directive does provide that either the employees' representatives or, in their absence, the employees themselves be informed in advance of the circumstances relating to the transfer and consulted as to the effect of the transfer on their

36 However, the wages or salary due to an employee are generally assignable: *Russell & Co. Ltd. v. Austin Fryers* (1909) 25 T.L.R. 414.

37 Above, footnote no. 15 and accompanying text.

38 Directive 77/187/EEC.

39 Directive 77/187/EEC preamble.

40 The notion of a "transfer" is by no means unproblematic: see the discussion in *Harvey on Industrial Relations and Employment Law*, Vol. I, F. Transfer of Undertakings by C. Osman (updated to 1999), § 70 *et seq.* The protection for employees' rights is by no means complete, transfers of corporate businesses by means of the sale of their shares being excluded since here the employer (the company itself) formally remains the same: *Brookes v. Borough Care Services* [1998] I.R.L.R. 636.

41 Art. 3(1) §1.

42 Art. 3(1)§ 2.

43 The Regulations apply also to involuntary transfers by operation of law: Reg. 3(2).

conditions of work and employment.[44]

When implementation of this directive into English law was first undertaken by the Transfer of Undertakings (Protection of Employment) Regulations 1981,[45] it was provided that "the transfer shall not operate so as to terminate the contract of employment of any person employed by the transferor . . . but any such contract which would otherwise have been terminated by the transfer shall have effect after the transfer as if originally made between the person employed and the transferee".[46] It therefore provided for the "automatic continuation between different parties but without their consent of an essentially consensual agreement".[47] However, in 1993 the European Court of Justice held that nothing in the Directive precluded a Member State from providing that an employee may object to the transfer of his or her rights from the transferor to the transferee business.[48] In response to this, the U.K. Parliament amended the directive's implementing regulations so as to provide for a right of objection in the employee to the transfer of his rights from the transferor to the transferee business,[49] though in so doing it failed to provide that the employee be informed by the transferor or transferee of the consequences of his objecting to the transfer of his rights.[50] The 1981 Regulations also reflect the U.K.'s choice allowed by the Directive[51] not to retain obligations or liabilities arising from the employment contract in the transferor employer.[52]

It has been said that the effect of the 1981 Regulations is to effect a form of "statutory novation".[53] This is true to the extent that its effect can be to substitute the new employer for the old one. However, even after the creation of a right to object in employees, the effect of these Regulations differs from novation as it is normally understood in that there is no requirement of consent in the transferor and transferee *to the transfer of*

---

44 Art. 6.

45 S.I. 1981/1794.

46 Reg. 5.

47 *Premier Motors (Medway) Ltd. v. Total Oil Great Britain Ltd.* [1983] I.R.L.R. 471, 473 *per* Browne-Wilkinson J.

48 *Katsikas v. Konstantinidis* Joined Cases Nos. C-132/91, C-138/91, C-139/91 [1993] I.R.L.R. 179.

49 Trade Union Reform and Employment Rights Act 1993 s. 33 (1)(4), inserting new (4A) and (4B) into Regulation 5 of the Transfer of Undertakings (Protection of Employment) Regulations 1981.

50 *Hay v. George Hanson (Building Contractors) Ltd.* [1996] I.R.L.R. 427, 428 *per* Lord Johnston (Scottish E.A.T.).

51 Art. 3(2).

52 Reg. 5 (2); *Wilson v. St. Helen's B.C.* [1998] 3 W.L.R. 1070, 1080, 1087.

53 Treitel, p. 650; *Wilson v. St. Helen's B.C.* [1998] 3 W.L.R. 1070, 1080 "'novation' takes place by operation of the regulations".

*rights and obligations arising under the contract of employment*: this transfer occurs by operation of law irrespective of their consent. Moreover, there is no positive requirement of consent to the transfer in the employee, but only an opportunity in the employee to oppose the transfer. To distinguish it from novation proper, perhaps the expression "contractual substitution" is more appropriate.

Whatever the terminology employed, it is clear that in principle the "transfer of a business" transfers the burden as well as the benefit of the employees' employment contracts. This has a double significance. First, the new employer must respect the "acquired rights" of the employees of the business, acquired, that is, during the period of employment of its predecessor: it reflects a view, therefore, that it should not be able to take the benefit of the *business* without also taking (at least) this aspect of its burden. Secondly, though, it makes clear that for the future the employees' work for the new employer must be reciprocated by performance of an employer's obligations. Even if at a formal level the former employer merely assigns its rights under the contracts of employment to the new employer, the employees' work for the new employer will be reciprocated with obligations in that "employer" relating to that work.

The effect of this legislation is not dissimilar to the position already described governing leasehold covenants. Both effect a form of contractual substitution, the current parties to a particular legal relation (the holding of land, employment) being substituted for the original parties who created the relation. The law's approach to leasehold covenants reflects a recognition that the economic relationship of the lease continues beyond the practical involvement of the parties who created them. There, the modern law both gives legal effect to the relations of the current parties to the tenure of the land (even if these parties have in no sense agreed with each other that they should) and in principle frees earlier parties to the tenure of the land, even if it was by their contract that the lease itself arose. By contrast with the position in English law under the 1981 Regulations where the transferor employer ceases to be liable under the contract of employment on transfer of the business, in the case of leases, the tenant may on assignment of his interest preserve his liabilities by guaranteeing performance of covenants by his assignee;[54] in the case of transfer of the landlord's, the landlord's will be released only with the consent of the tenant or the court.

What can be said is that as regards both leases and employment, the law recognises and regulates a continuing legal relation which may originally have arisen by contract but whose significance transcends the

---

54 Landlord and Tenant (Covenant) Act 1995 s. 16, which restricts this possibility in a number of ways.

particular original parties. In the case of leases, the continuity beyond the original parties is clearly seen in the legal recognition of the interests of both landlord and tenant which form the proprietary aspect of the lease relationship, proprietary both in the sense that the relationship concerns a particular item of property and that it creates rights in rem in relation to that property. In the case of employment, the Acquired Rights Directive may be seen as reflecting a vision of employment as a legal relation rather than merely a contractual relationship, the continuity beyond the original parties being found in the continuing work done by the employee for the "business" which has been transfered. In both these situations, though, where the original relationship created by contract is a reciprocal one, its "continuance" for those not party to that contract is also held to be reciprocal. It is not that the justification for extending these rights and obligations beyond privity is that they continue to be reciprocal: the justification for and purposes of these extensions are primarily ones of policy relating to the particular context (so, for example, the protection of employees' interests on the transfer of undertakings). It is rather that the proper putting into effect of these purposes requires the recognition of the same type of legal relation between those *not* party to the original contract as obtained between those original parties. And in both the cases of leases and employment, reciprocity of right and duty forms a key element in that original relationship; it should therefore form part of the relationship recognised by law as existing between the (special category) of non-parties.

## 3. Undisclosed Principals

English law has long recognised that a person, A, who has given his actual authority to an agent, B, to enter contracts with another person or persons, C, may sue and be sued on the contract made by B with C, even though B purported to contract with C on his own behalf, rather than on behalf of A.[55] This special position of A is refered to as the doctrine of the undisclosed principal. As Bowstead and Reynolds roundly state, "[i]t is difficult to deny that the undisclosed principal is really a third party intervening on a contract which he did not make".[56] The doctrine forms a clear exception at common law to both aspects of privity of contract, the undisclosed principal being subjected to burdens as a result of the contract

---

55 F.M.B. Reynolds, *Bowstead and Reynolds on Agency* (16th ed., 1996) § 8-069 ("*Bowstead and Reynolds*").

56 *Bowstead and Reynolds* §8-070; A.L Goodhart and C.J. Hamson, "Undisclosed principals in contract" [1932] C.L.J. 320, 346; *Welsh Development Agency v. Export Finance Co. Ltd.* [1992] B.C.L.C. 148, 173.

made by his agent as well as being given rights. Moreover, it is to be noted that an undisclosed principal's rights arise from the contract made by his agent in the absence of any mention of his position, let alone any intention in the parties to that contract to this effect.[57] It does not form, therefore, a common law example of a contract for the benefit of a third party before these became recognised by statute in English law in 1999.[58] In the result, the undisclosed principal may in principle sue C on the basis of and subject to the terms of the contract made by his agent with C.[59] On the other hand, C may elect to sue either the agent or the undisclosed principal.[60]

The legal position of the undisclosed principal is clearly a very different type of exception to privity of contract from the ones which we have just examined in the context of leases and employment. First, while it may arise only as a result of a particular type of legal agreement (agency),[61] it is not restricted as to the types of agreement to which it may relate: the only restrictions on the contracts which an undisclosed agent may make are those which result from the limits of his own authority and any express or implied terms of the contracts which he makes which exclude undisclosed principals. To this extent, then, the law governing undisclosed principals belongs to the general law of contract. It is for this reason also that (unlike the position as regards leases and employment) this exception to privity of contract may not be justified by the existence of any continuing legal relation beyond privity. Secondly, there is a limited reciprocity between the undisclosed principal and the person with whom the agent makes a contract, a reciprocity which has tempted judges at times to treat the contract made by the agent as being that of the principal, a position which must be rejected given the continuing rights and liabilities of the agent.[62] Thirdly, these continuing rights and liabilities in the agent also show that an undisclosed principal is not *substituted* to the position of his contracting agent. To this extent, the position of the undisclosed principal and his agent resembles that of a current tenant and former tenant at common law

57 *Bowstead and Reynolds*, §8-070.

58 Contracts (Rights of Third Parties) Act 1999.

59 There are qualifications on this general right in the principal to sue, notably where the contract expressly or impliedly excludes undisclosed principals. C's liability to the principal is also subject to any set-off which he enjoys against the agent. On both points, see *Siu Yin Kwan v. Eastern Insurance Co. Ltd.* [1994] 2 A.C. 199, 207.

60 *Bowstead and Reynolds*, § 9-012.

61 In keeping with general principle, there is no need for the agency to be contractual, as long as it arises from agreement, but the undisclosed principal's actual authority is required, thereby excluding authority by ratification: *Keighley, Maxted & Co. v. Durant* [1901] A.C. 240, though see the discussion in *Bowstead and Reynolds*, § 8-071.

62 *Bowstead and Reynolds*, §8-070.

before the cutting of privity of contract by statute in 1995.[63]

While a number of justifications for the doctrine of the undisclosed principal have been advanced, the generally accepted one is that it is justified only on the ground of commercial convenience.[64] However, its historical explanation has been found in the principal's right to sue on the basis of property in goods sold by his factor. So, Goodhart and Hamson conclude:

> The undisclosed principal seller was first allowed to receive money direct from the third-party buyer, so as to avoid the injustice of having to claim in the bankruptcy of the agent-factor acting in his own name. Because he could receive direct, it was decided he could sue. Because he could sue, it was considered just that he should be liable to be sued. Because he could sue and be sued, it was said, in a phrase convenient if not taken as a statement more exact than it purports to be, that he had privity of contract.[65]

We have already seen that use of the language of privity of contract is inappropriate to describe the relations between the undisclosed principal and the person with whom his agent makes a contract, given the remaining rights and liabilities of the agent,[66] but what this passage brings out is the significance of the idea of reciprocity in the development of the position of the undisclosed principal and not merely in its present form.

## 4. Package Holidays

A more recent example of reciprocity beyond privity may be found in the Package Travel, Package Holidays and Package Tours Regulations 1992.[67] The main purpose of these Regulations is to introduce a number of requirements as to the information to be furnished to the purchaser of a package holiday, also providing such a person with rights of cancellation and compensation. However, Regulation 10(1) provides that

> In every contract there is an implied term that where the consumer is prevented from proceeding with the package, he may transfer his booking to a person who satisfies all the conditions applicable to the package, provided that the consumer gives reasonable notice to the other party to the contract

---

63 Above, text following footnote no. 30.

64 *Sin Yin Kwan v. Eastern Insurance Co. Ltd.* [1994] 2 A.C. 199, 207.

65 Op. cit., p. 352.

66 Above, text accompanying footnote no. 52.

67 S.I. 1992 No. 3288, implementing an E.C. Council Directive 90/314/EEC of 13 June 1990 on package travel, package holidays and package tours.

of his intention to transfer before the date when departure is due to take place.

The Regulations also provide that the protections which it creates for the benefit of "consumers" also apply for the benefit of "transferees".[68] Thus, where the conditions of regulation 10(1) are satisfied, it effects a legislative *transfer* of rights from the original party to the contract to the "transferee". The Regulations assume that on transfer the original party to the package holiday contract loses his rights under the contract; on the other hand, they provide that on transfer the transferee becomes subject to its burdens of the contract even though the transferor is *not* relieved of them: "the transferor and the transferee shall be jointly and severally liable to the other party to the contract for payment of the price for the package ... and for any additional costs arising from such transfer."[69]

This legislation therefore forms an example of a power (in certain circumstances) for the consumer party to a contract to substitute another person to his own rights and obligations. There is an implicit requirement of consent in the transferee consumer (in particular, before becoming liable under the contract made by the transferor consumer). However, there is no requirement, explicit or otherwise, that the supplier of the package tour needs to consent to the transfer and while the U.K. Regulations use the language of implied term to give effect to the original consumer's power of transfer, this is merely resort to an English legislative technique to implement what in the Directive appears as an independent right in the consumer.[70] Instead, the legislation protects the legitimate interests of the supplier by subjecting the consumer's right to transfer to the double condition that the transferee satisfies all the conditions applicable to the package and of reasonable notice, and by preserving the supplier's right in respect of payment against the original contractor.

Why was this right to transfer a booking created? The thinking behind it may be seen in the other condition of its existence: a consumer may transfer the booking "where [he] is prevented from proceeding with the package". The typical situation would be where a person books a holiday in advance and then finds that he or she is subsequently unable to take advantage of it, for example, because of illness or even, perhaps, commitments at work. Where circumstances have changed between making the contract and performance, and where transfer does not stand to prejudice the package travel supplier, the original party should be able to

---

68 Regulation 2(2).

69 Reg. 10(2).

70 Art. 4.3 of the Directive: "Where the consumer is prevented from proceeding with the package, he may transfer his booking . . ."

find a substitute: this means that the holiday is not wasted and the original consumer does not stand to lose his money paid or payable on the holiday (as long as he chooses his substitute wisely). However, I would not wish to overemphasise the temporal aspect of these circumstances, for Regulation 10(1) seems to me rather to reflect a view that the original party to a contract has bought a package and that this package should be transferable, as to burdens as well as its benefits, leaving the original contractor as "guarantor" of the payment by his transferee.[71] It therefore forms a legislative example of the recognition of reciprocity of rights and obligations beyond the privity created by the original contracting parties.

## 5. The Death of the Parties: Privity and Personal Representatives

English law long encountered difficulties in dealing with the continuity of the legal position of a person after death, even where a testament provided an executor. As regards a testator's contractual rights and liabilities, an executor's position was sometimes expressed in the language of privity of contract, it being argued that the executor was a third party to the contract made by his testator.[72] However, in 1609 in *Pinchon's Case*[73] it was established that assumpsit would lie against an executor, although only up to the value of the estate (*de bonis testatoris*).[74] As Willes J. stated in 1869 "[g]enerally speaking, contracts bind the executor or administrator though not named".[75]

In the modern law statute expressly provides that in principle rights and liabilities existing in the deceased on death accrue to the benefit or burden of the estate.[76] It is clear under this law that neither an executor nor an administrator himself enjoys rights or bears obligations personally under the deceased's contracts: both rights and obligations affect the estate which these personal representatives manage for the benefit of legatees or next of kin.[77] Thus, the contractual position of the deceased may by law be continued after his death for a time, but not by substituting a personal representative for the deceased, but rather by attaching the rights and

---

71 Technically, of course, the transferor is not "guarantor" as he is primarily liable.

72 See, for example, *Overton v. Sydal* (1597) Cro. Eliz. 555.

73 (1607) 9 Co. Rep. 86b.

74 S. J. Stoljar, *A History of Contract at Common Law* (1975) pp. 92-104, notes that an executor could also be liable personally (*de bonis propriis*) after *Slade's Case* (1602) 4 Co. Rep. 92 on the basis of any promise to a creditor of the testator, this promise being supported by the creditor's forbearance to sue.

75 *Farrow v. Wilson* (1869) L.R. 4 C.P. 744, 746.

76 Law Reform (Miscellaneous Provisions) Act 1934, s. 1(1).

77 Treitel, p. 649.

liabilities created by the deceased's contract to a non-personal legal entity, the deceased's estate.[78] This is not a true example of the recognition of reciprocity beyond privity; instead, the transmissibility of claims for and against the deceased to his estate may be seen as the legal continuation of the position of one of the parties *within* privity.

## 6. Freehold Covenants

Since the fourteenth century the benefit but not the burden of a covenant, (whether positive or negative) could run with the land at common law as long as it "touched and concerned" the land,[79] but until 1848, the courts refused to allow the burden of a covenant in relation to freehold land to run with that land.[80] However, in that year in *Tulk v. Moxhay*[81] a vendor of land brought an action for an injunction ordering its sub-purchaser not to build on the land and to keep it as a pleasure garden, thereby keeping to a covenant made by the intervening purchaser of which the sub-purchaser had express notice. In holding for the plaintiff, Lord Cottenham L.C. dodged around the earlier authority,[82] and instead declared that the law was settled in the way which he then expounded. For Lord Cottenham, the question was not whether or not the covenant runs with the land (according to the established rules on that subject) but rather

> whether a party taking property with a stipulation to use it in a particular manner – that stipulation being imposed on him by the vendor in such a manner as to be binding by the law and principles of this Court – will be permitted by this Court to use it in a way diametrically opposite to that which the party has stipulated for.[83]

Lord Cottenham noted that the original purchaser would have given less money for it than if it had been unencumbered and continued:

> Can there, then, be anything much more inequitable or contrary to good conscience, than that a party who takes property at a less price because it is subject to a restriction, should receive the full value from a third party, and

[78] A similar approach is taken to the position of personal insolvency: "again there is no true transfer of liability as the trustee [in bankruptcy] is not personally liable": Treitel, p. 650.

[79] Simpson, op. cit., pp. 117-118.

[80] See *Keppell v. Bailey* (1834) 2 My. & K. 517 at 540 *et seq.*

[81] (1848) 2 Ph. 774; 1 Ha. and Tw. 105.

[82] See (1848) 1 Ha. & Tw. 105, 116.

[83] (1848) 1 Ha. and Tw. 105, 113.

> that such third party should then hold it unfettered by the restriction under which it was granted? That would be most inequitable, most unjust, and most unconscientious.[84]

We can see how very widely this doctrine is stated: the buyer of any property who takes it knowing of a previous stipulation regarding the property cannot be allowed to act inequitably by taking free of the stipulation. There is no restriction as to the nature of the stipulation (restrictive rather than positive), to the nature of the property sold (land rather than movables) or in relation to the position of the vendor of the property (whether or not himself the owner of "dominant" property to which the burdened property may be "servient").

For a while the courts took the principle at its face value, but subsequent developments soon cut it down considerably, some restrictions being taken by analogy from the law of easements, some from the law of leasehold covenants. First, the covenant must originally have been intended to run with the covenantor's land, though this is rebuttably presumed by statute.[85] Secondly, in the modern law, the burden of covenants runs with freehold land only if they are restrictive or negative in their content[86] and this means that they cannot be unrelated to the use of the land itself.[87] Thirdly, by analogy with easements, the covenant must not merely burden one piece of land (the "servient tenement"), it must benefit another (the "dominant tenement").[88] Fourthly, the dominant modern view is that the doctrine of restrictive covenants does not apply to chattels, except, perhaps, ships.[89]

---

84 Ibid. at 114.

85 Law of Property Act 1925, s. 79(1).

86 This was first held in *Haywood v. Brunswick Permanent Benefit Building Society* (1881) 8 Q.B.D. 403 by the Court of Appeal.

87 Gray, op. cit., p. 1140.

88 Simpson, op. cit., p. 259; *London County Council v. Allen* [1914] 3 K.B. 642.

89 The nineteenth century authority which appeared to support the application of *Tulk v. Moxhay* to all types of property was a dictum of Knight Bruce L.J. in *De Mattos v. Gibson* (1858) 4 De G. & J. 276 at 282 in interlocutory proceedings. However, while this dictum appeared to relate to what Lord Cottenham had decided 10 years earlier, it did not expressly do so; moreover, the decision of Lord Chelmsford L.C. at trial in *De Mattos* (which on the facts rejected an injunction) was based rather on the (also recent) judgment of the court in *Lumley v. Gye* (1853) 2 E. & B. 216, i.e. the tort of inducing breach of contract. The leading authority in favour of the application of allowing restrictive covenants to run with chattels is the Privy Council's decision in *Lord Strathcona Steamship Co. Ltd. v. Dominion Coal Co. Ltd.* [1920] A.C. 108, which concerned a ship and where "the principle in *De Mattos v. Gibson*" (i.e. in Knight Bruce L.J.'s judgment) was cited. However, in *Port Line Ltd. v. Ben Line Steamers Ltd.* [1958] Ch. 146 Diplock J. did not follow the approach of the Privy Council and in *Swiss Bank Corpn. v. Lloyds Bank Ltd.* [1979] Ch. 548 Browne-Wilkinson J. expressed the

So, how does this development relate to our present concern with reciprocity beyond privity? Clearly, one could express the doctrine of restrictive covenants as allowing the burden of a contractual obligation (arising under the original contract of sale) to apply to a third party, the sub-purchaser. This can find a parallel with the position long existing at common law, by which the benefit of a covenant may be transmitted to sub-purchasers of the benefited property: there *may* be therefore a reciprocity of benefit and burden between original vendor and sub-purchaser depending on the the content of the original contract. On the other hand, while the origin of the covenantee's rights under a restrictive covenant clearly originated in a contract, English lawyers soon saw them as proprietary in their nature, properly to be characterised as an "equitable proprietary interest" in the burdened property,[90] thereby reconciling the effect of the original contract beyond privity by reclassification of the original party's right as proprietary rather than personal. However the result of the doctrine is expressed, one can indeed see the law of restrictive covenants as recognising that the original contract may initiate a legal relationship between the "dominant" and "servient tenements", but that this relationship may (subject to certain conditions) continue through successor owners of these two "tenements".

However, the reaction of the courts to the very wide doctrine as it is stated in *Tulk v. Moxhay* itself illustrates again that the courts are not willing to allow the logic of a particular technique to run away to the detriment of privity of contract. Clearly, the restriction of the doctrine to land is a recognition of the importance of the use of covenants to control the use of this most enduring of assets. Its restriction to *negative* obligations may be seen simply as a way of cutting the doctrine down, but as we shall see, it has recently been held to reflect the basis of the doctrine in the idea of a conditional transfer by the original vendor to the original purchaser, thereby restricting the range of rights which that purchaser has to pass on to his successors.[91] If this analysis is sound, then it strikes at the independent nature of the obligation imposed on the third party, sub-purchaser, denying the sub-purchaser the right to do certain things not because he is affected by his predecessor's contractual obligation not to do so, but because his predecessor was not granted the right to do so. Here, then, analysis in terms of proprietary right (or rather the lack of it) takes over entirely from analysis in terms of contract beyond privity.

---

opinion that Knight Bruce L.J.'s principle was "merely the equitable counterpart" of the tort of interference with contract.

90 Gray, op. cit. n. , p. 1148.

91 Below, text following footnote no. 106.

## 7. A General Principle of Benefit and Burden Beyond Privity?

So far in this paper, I have looked at particular examples of exceptions to the principle of privity of contract from the point of view of reciprocity. However, the question has been raised as to whether there is a principle which may lead in the same direction, a principle sometimes called the "pure principle of benefit and burden". In *Tito v. Waddell (No. 2)*[92] Megarry V.-C. noted two historical and very particular applications of the principle that he who takes the benefit of a transaction must bear the burden in relation to deeds, and then addressed the question of the existence of a broader principle. For, in his view,

> Side by side with these technical instances, and probably underlying them, was the simple principle of ordinary fairness and consistency that from the earliest days most of us heard in the form "You can't have it both ways", or "You can't eat your cake and have it too," or "You can't blow hot and cold".[93]

He then distinguished cases in which a person receives a conditional benefit and ones in which a person receives a benefit but is also (and, possibly,) thereby subjected to an independent obligation. In the former case, "you take the right as it stands, and you cannot pick out the good and reject the bad. In such cases it is not only the original grantee who is bound by the burden; his successors in title are unable to take the right without also assuming the burden".[94] In the latter case, "X grants a right to Y, and by the same instrument Y independently covenants with X to do some act".[95] Here, while Y is bound by his covenant, it will be a question whether or not the successors of title to his right will take free from the obligations or instead "they are bound by them under what for want of a better name I shall call the pure principle of benefit and burden".[96]

The transfer of a conditional right by a party to a contract to a person (and to that person's successors in title) does not give rise to any truly obligational relationship between the holder of that right and the original contracting party, even though it may still give effect to reciprocity.[97] On the other hand, Sir Robert Megarry V.-C.'s second class

---

92 [1977] 1 Ch. 106.
93 [1977] 1 Ch. 106, 289.
94 Ibid. at p. 290.
95 Ibid. at p. 290.
96 Ibid.
97 Cf. the position as regards reciprocity between parties to a unilateral contract, above, text following footnote no. 19.

of case may be thought of as illustrative of the sort of reciprocity of obligation which we find between the parties to bilateral contracts.[98] The learned Vice-Chancellor of course accepted the general principles that the benefit of positive burdens would not run with land and that contractual burdens are not assignable, but nevertheless considered that there was "ample authority" for the existence of the "pure principle of benefit and burden".[99]

However, more recently this view of the "principle of benefit and burden" has met with a distinctly cold reception. Thus, in 1993 Hoffmann J. noticed (in refusing to apply the "pure principle" to very different facts from those to which it apparently applied)[100] that Sir Robert Megarry V.-C. had himself recognised that "without some limits, the "pure principle" could completely subvert the doctrine of privity of contract and the principle that a purchaser of goods or the assignee of a contract or other chose in action is not bound to perform the obligations undertaken by the seller or assignor".[101] The potential conflict between the "pure principle" of benefit and burden and privity of contract and the limits of its established exceptions came to a head in *Rhone v. Stephens* in 1994.[102] This case concerned a conveyance by which an owner of two adjoining properties sold one of the properties to a purchaser, the vendor covenanting that he and his successors in title would maintain the roof of the retained property. The House of Lords had to decide whether the burden of this positive covenant ran with the land either at common law or in equity so as to bind the vendor's successors in title. Lord Templeman, with whom the other members of the House agreed started by declaring the principle that "[a]t common law a person cannot be made liable upon a contract unless he was a party to it".[103] He noted the qualifications on this principle as regards

98 Sir Robert Megarry V.-C. accepted a third class of case concerning assignments, where in his view the cases distinguished between the situation where the assignor intended to retain the burden of the contract (where the assignee would take free) and the situation where there was a purported assignment of the whole contract to the assignee. Here, "unless the benefit and burden principle is to be rejected in its entirety" then placing the assignee under the burden would accord with the intentions of the parties: [1977] 1 Ch. 106, 302-303.

99 [1977] 1 Ch. 106, 302. The authorities on which he relied were a dictum of Sir Herbert Cozens-Hardy M.R. in *Ellison v. Reacher* [1908] 2 Ch. 665, 669; *Halsall v. Brizell* [1957] Ch. 169 (though he recognised that this was based on a concession by counsel); *E.R. Ives Investment Ltd. v. High* [1967] 2 Q.B. 379.

100 In particular, "[t]he right and burden do not arise under the same instrument": *Law Debenture Corpn. Plc v. Ural Caspian Ltd.* [1993] 2 All E.R. 355 at p. 364.

101 Ibid. at p. 365.

102 [1994] 2 A.C. 310.

103 Ibid. at p. 67.

leasehold covenants, both at common law and by statute[104] and as regards the benefit but not the burden of freehold covenants at common law.[105] As regards the further exception relating to freehold *restrictive* covenants in equity which was first recognised in *Tulk v. Moxhay*,[106] Lord Templeman took the view that

> Equity does not contradict the common law by enforcing a restrictive covenant against a successor in title of the covenantor but prevents the successor from exercising a right which he never acquired.[107]

For Lord Templeman, "[r]estrictive covenants deprive an owner of a right which he could otherwise exercise".[108] Put in the language adopted by Sir Robert Megarry V.-C. in *Tito v. Waddell (No. 2)*, the person "burdened" by a freehold covenant is not subject to an independent obligation, but merely enjoys restricted or conditional rights of ownership received from his own seller. While there is, as Lord Templeman indicated, support for this view in the judgment of Lord Cottenham L.C. in *Tulk v. Moxhay* itself,[109] as Simpson has observed this type of "argument ... begs the whole question, for it assumes that the equity *is* attached to the property".[110] Be this as it may, Lord Templeman's interpretation of the law founded in *Tulk v. Moxhay* allowed him to justify the law of restrictive covenants relating to freehold land without threatening privity of contract, but would not allow its extension to positive covenants. For,

> To enforce a positive covenant would be to enforce a personal obligation against a person who has not covenanted. To enforce negative covenants is only to treat the land as subject to a restriction.[111]

In this context, at the very end of his speech, Lord Templeman recorded counsel's argument that the rule against the running of the burden of positive covenants had been blunted by the "pure principle of benefit and burden" distilled by Sir Robert Megarry V.-C. in *Tito v. Waddell (No. 2)*. However, Lord Templeman stated that "I am not prepared to recognise the 'pure principle' that any party deriving any benefit from a conveyance must

---

104 Above, text following footnote no. 22.
105 *Austerberry v. Oldham Corpn.* (1885) 29 Ch. D. 750.
106 (1848) 2 Ph. 774.
107 [1994] 2 A.C. 310, 317.
108 Ibid. at p. 318.
109 2 Ph. 774, 777-778.
110 A.W. Brian Simpson, *A History of the Land Law* (2nd. ed., 1986), p. 259.
111 At p. 71.

accept any burden in the same conveyance"[112] and he treated *Halsall v. Brizell*,[113] the main authority on which Sir Robert Megarry V.-C. had relied in support of the principle, as a case of the granting of a right subject to a condition. Lord Templeman continued

> It does not follow that any condition can be rendered enforceable by attaching it to a right nor does it follow that every burden imposed by a convenant may be enforced by depriving the covenantor's successor in title of every benefit which he enjoyed thereunder. The condition must be relevant to the exercise of the right. In *Halsall v. Brizell* there were reciprocal benefits and burdens enjoyed by the users of the roads and sewers.[114]

On the facts before him, Lord Templeman could see that the rights of support of the adjoining properties contained in the relevant conveyance imposed reciprocal benefits and burdens, but the duty to repair the roof in the vendor (which was in issue before the House of Lords) was "an independent provision".[115] He also noted that in *Halsall v. Brizell* the covenantor's successor had "at least in theory" a choice whether or not to enjoy the right and pay for its cost or instead give up the right and save his money, whereas on the facts before him the vendor's successors in title could not be deprived of the benefit of mutual rights of support even if they failed to repair the roof. In the result, the positive covenant was not enforceable against the covenantor's successor in title.

Given the approach of the House of Lords in *Rhone v. Stephens* the existence as a matter of law of a "pure principle" of benefit and burden must be more than open to doubt. Certainly, the House recognised the validity of the subjection of rights to conditions, conditions which would therefore govern any right to be transferred to a successor in title, as long as, first, the burden arising from the condition and the right are "reciprocal" (which here means related) and as long as, secondly, the right-holder is in a position to choose whether or not to enjoy the right and, consequently, bear its accompanying burden. However, as Harpum has observed, Lord Templeman's speech gives little guidance as to when a party will be regarded as having a genuine choice.[116]

In my view the coldness of the reception given to the "pure principle" of benefit and burden by the House of Lords in *Rhone v. Stephens* is entirely justified. It is not that the law should not recognise

---

112 At p. 73.
113 *Halsall v. Brizell* [1957] Ch. 169.
114 Ibid. at p. 322.
115 Ibid.
116 C. Harpum in *Megarry and Wade's Law of Real Property* (6th ed., 2000), p. 1009.

circumstances in which a third party to a contract should not bear a burden arising from it (possibly reciprocally to its benefit). I have already set out a number of situations where the law does indeed do this, for justifiable reasons. However, the "pure principle" is misconceived by its very expression as a principle: principles of this type are propositions of law which should (either owing to their generality or their importance) apply to facts within their scope in the absence of a justifying reason. The qualification of the principle as "pure" serves only to emphasise that its application is not restricted to any particular context or sets of circumstances. But the idea that a third party to a contract may bear a burden (even where this is reciprocally related to a right also arising from the contract) squarely contradicts the principle of privity of contract. While privity is accepted as a general principle (as it is in English law even after the Contracts (Rights of Third Parties) Act 1999), there is no room for a *principle* of benefit and burden, even if does accord with some vague sense of fairness. It should therefore be rejected as tending towards legal incoherence and transactional uncertainty.

This is not to say, of course, that the cases in which the "pure principle" has been applied cannot be justified on their facts or by reference to more narrow doctrines: this was indeed the approach of the House of Lords in *Rhone v. Stephens.* But these cases must be thought of as exceptions and must be justified by reference to particular considerations.

## Conclusion

There are three main observations which I would wish to draw from the forgoing discussion by way of conclusion.

First, we can see that the idea of reciprocity beyond the parties to a contract may mean one of two things. It may mean that A bears an independent obligation to do something for the benefit of B, who owes him (A) an obligation (as is the case in leasehold covenants, transfer of business, and undisclosed principals); sometimes, though, it means instead that A's obligation to B is *conditional* on B doing something for the benefit of A, even though B owes no *obligation* to do A. This is the way in which Lord Templeman sought to explain the law of restrictive covenants in freehold land.[117] These two meanings are reminiscent of the different significances given to the requirement of reciprocity as between the original parties to a bilateral and a unilateral contract.[118] However,

---

[117] Above, text following footnote no. 106.
[118] Above, text following footnote no. 19.

reciprocity by performance of a condition is much more significant beyond the original parties to a contract; for where a party acquires rights under a third party by transfer either of the rights themselves or the subject matter of the contract to which they relate (for example, freehold land), this transfer affords an opportunity for these rights to be made subject to conditions.

Secondly, each of the examples of reciprocity beyond privity of contract discussed in this article has its own particular attributes and reasons, this perhaps reflecting the typically heterogeneous character of exceptions. Even so, the rules governing the transfer of business and leasehold covenants have in common that the exceptions to privity of contract which they create give legal recognition to a continuing legal relation (employment or tenure) initiated by contract but transcending changes in the contract's original parties. As has been suggested, the law governing freehold covenants may be seen in the same light, the relation being that between the owners of the dominant and servient tenement.

Thirdly, while the legal recognition of reciprocity beyond privity may be justified in certain particular types of situation, it must be recalled that the recognition of *any* rights or obligations in third parties to a contract should remain exceptional: the dual principle of privity of contract should remain the general rule. In particular, no "pure principle" of benefit and burden should be used to undermine the impact of that aspect of privity of contract which prevents the imposition of burdens beyond the parties without special justification. Recognition by the law of the need for reciprocity beyond privity does not mean that whenever it recognises a right under a contract in a third party then that third party should also shoulder some burden. So while Crompton J.'s dictum in *Tweddle v. Atkinson*[119] allows us to consider the possibility of reciprocity beyond privity, its argument from the "monstrous proposition" is in itself unconvincing, a conclusion which has been finally recognised by the English legislature by the enactment of the Contracts (Rights of Third Parties) Act 1999. It may sometimes indeed be right to recognise one-sided (unreciprocated) rights beyond the parties to contracts.

Thus, while in my view there is no logical or conceptual reason why the law should not recognise exceptions to the principle of privity of contract where these can be justified, these justifications may be quite different in their nature or range of application. Thus, without entering on the desirability of this change nor the validity of its justification, those who support the change made by the Contracts ( Rights of Third Parties ) Act 1999 in the main do so simply on the basis of the desirability of giving

---

[119] Quoted, above, text accompanying footnote no. 1.

effect to the intention of the contracting parties. By contrast, the exceptions to privity described in this paper often relate to much more specific concerns arising from the nature of the transactions involved. For this purpose, I do not argue that the need to give effect to reciprocity is *in itself* a justification for an exception to privity of contract nor that it is a *necessary* part of any justification for such an exception. However, it may figure as an element in the shaping of some of the exceptions which are indeed created, whether or not it does so depending on the particular context of the exception. Thus, the law should inquire whether any right or duty imposed on a third party should find some reciprocal right or duty in the person to whom it is owed.

# 13 Privity and Exclusion Clauses

J. L. R. DAVIS

## Introduction

This Chapter is concerned with the effect to be given to a clause, in a contract between two parties, which seeks to affect the liability of a third party. A consideration of that topic must necessarily distinguish between those contractual clauses which seek to grant the benefit of the exclusion or limitation to the third party, and those which seek to impose the burden of the clause on the third party. It is to be regretted that the Law Commission, in its Report on *Privity of Contract: Contracts for the Benefit of Third Parties*,[1] did not refer to the possibility of a contract between A and B imposing the burden of an exclusion clause therein on a third party. It will, however, be argued below that such is at least possible, and that the Law Commission Report, and the Contracts (Rights of Third Parties) Act 1999 passed as a result of that Report, is to that extent defective. Furthermore, in considering the circumstances in which a contract between A and B might confer the benefit of an exclusion clause on a third party, the Law Commission was of the view[2] that a statutory abrogation of the doctrine of privity of contract was necessary in order to ensure that a third party might enjoy that benefit. This approach has obviously been accepted by the United Kingdom Parliament, as the Contracts (Rights of Third Parties) Act 1999 includes, in subsection 1(5), the provision recommended by the Law Commission to achieve that end. It is the further purpose of this Chapter to demonstrate that the views of the Law Commission are based on a misunderstanding of the nature and effect of exclusion clauses, and that the existence of the doctrine of privity of contract is irrelevant to the issue of whether a person may take the benefit of an exclusion clause contained in a contract to which that person is not a party.

In view of the fact that different principles of law apply, depending on whether one is considering the application of the benefit or the burden of an exclusion clause, the two issues need to be dealt with separately.

---

1 Law Com. No. 242, Cm. 3329, 1996.

2 Ibid., para. 2.35.

## The Benefit of an Exclusion Clause

The effect to be given to an exclusion clause in a contract to which the person whose liability is sought to be excluded is not a party is an issue that has been given a varied response during the course of the twentieth century. While at one stage it was assumed that the doctrine of privity was not relevant, to some of the Judges of a later generation privity was self-evidently relevant. More recently still, the Courts have taken a variety of approaches, all of which allow effect to be given to the clause of exemption or limitation, but the legal principles permitting that result have differed markedly.

### *1. A Principle of Vicarious Immunity*

The first discussion by a court of final appeal of the question of whether an exclusion clause in a contract between A and B could be relied on by one who was not a party thereto was in the House of Lords decision in *Elder Dempster & Co. Ltd. v. Paterson Zochonis & Co. Ltd.*[3] The appellant shipping line had chartered a vessel, which they used to carry a cargo to England for the respondents. A clause in the bill of lading, which was entered into by the appellants and respondents only, provided exemption from liability for any loss or damage arising from bad stowage. The respondents' cargo was damaged through bad stowage and they sued both the appellants and the owners of the chartered vessel for the loss. The House of Lords held that the shipowners, although not a party to the bill of lading, could take the benefit of the exclusion clause therein. Regrettably, it is difficult, if not impossible, to discern the ratio of the decision, as the members of the House who delivered opinions took such widely divergent views of the basis for that immunity. The most that can be said about the decision is that it may well have supported – as Scrutton L.J., in the following year,[4] suggested it did – a principle of vicarious immunity, whereby any person who performs any part of the obligations contained in a contract is entitled to the benefit of any exclusion or limitation of liability contained therein.

However, it is not necessary to attempt to discern the ratio of the *Elder Dempster* case, as both the High Court of Australia, in *Wilson v.*

---

3 [1924] A.C. 522.

4 *Mersey Shipping & Transport Co. Ltd. v. Rea Ltd.* (1925) 21 Ll.L.R. 375.

*Darling Island Stevedoring & Lighterage Co. Ltd.*,[5] and the House of Lords in *Midland Silicones Ltd. v. Scruttons Ltd.*[6] have robbed the case of whatever authority it had.

*2. Privity to the Fore*

In rejecting a principle of vicarious immunity, both the High Court and the House of Lords were required to consider afresh the issue of whether it were possible for a non-party to take the benefit of an exclusion clause. Both Fullagar J. in the *Darling Island* case, and a majority of the House of Lords in the *Midland Silicones* case, were of the view that such was not possible.

In the *Darling Island* case, the appellant consignee of goods sued the respondent stevedore for damage to the goods caused by the respondent's negligence in unloading them. To the respondent's argument that it was protected by a clause in the appellant's bill of lading, Fullagar J. considered the "obvious answer" to be that "[the respondent] is not a party to the contract evidenced by the bill of lading, that it can neither sue nor be sued on that contract, and that nothing in a contract between two other persons can relieve it from the consequences of a tortious act committed by it against [the appellant]".[7] This view was adopted and applied, to facts not materially different, by a majority of the House of Lords in *Midland Silicones Ltd. v. Scruttons Ltd.*,[8] Viscount Simonds going so far as to say[9] that he agreed with every line and every word of the judgment of Fullagar J. And the decision of the House of Lords was, in turn, accepted as correct, and applied to a similar combination of facts, by the Supreme Court of Canada in *Canadian General Electric Co. Ltd. v. Pickford & Black Ltd.*[10] As a result of these decisions, it is now often assumed by text writers that the doctrine of privity prevents a third party from obtaining the benefit of an exclusion clause contained in a contract to which that person is not a party. Thus, *Chitty on Contracts*[11] states as a general rule that "[t]wo persons cannot by contract confer the benefit of an exemption clause on one who is not a party to that contract", and the Law Commission, in its

5 (1956) 95 C.L.R. 43 at 74-5 per Fullagar J. (with whom Dixon C.J. agreed), at 80-1 per Kitto J.
6 [1962] A.C. 445.
7 (1956) 95 C.L.R. 43 at 67.
8 [1962] A.C. 442.
9 Ibid. at 472.
10 [1971] S.C.R 41 at 43-44 per Ritchie J.
11 27th ed., 1994, Vol. 1, para. 14-033; see also, to the same effect, Seddon and Ellinghaus, *Cheshire and Fifoot's Law of Contract* (7th Aus. ed., 1997), para. 7.37.

Report on the matter,[12] referred to "the privity doctrine, which ...prevent[s] third parties taking the benefit of exclusion clauses".

While it is true that in each of the above cases the respective Judges asserted that an exclusion clause could not be relied on by a person not a party to the contract containing that clause, it must also be borne in mind that in each case a stevedore was seeking the benefit of a clause which was expressed to protect only the carrier of the goods and its servants or agents. The relevant clause in each case did not in terms extend to an independent person engaged by the carrier for the purpose of loading or unloading the goods. The decisions are therefore consistent with the much more limited proposition – indeed, one might even say the self-evident proposition – that an exclusion clause will not protect a person who is not referred to therein, whether expressly or by necessary implication. This point is on occasion overlooked. Thus, *Chitty on Contracts*[13] cites not only the above three decisions in support of the general principle which has already been quoted, but also the decision of the United States Supreme Court in *Robert C. Herd & Co. Inc. v. Krawill Machinery Corp.*[14] But reference to that judgment makes it clear that the decision holding a stevedore not to be protected by an exclusion clause in a bill of lading was based solely on the fact that the bill of lading was expressed to protect the carrier only. The Supreme Court said merely that "contracts purporting to grant immunity from, or limitation of, liability must be strictly construed and limited to intended beneficiaries".[15] Indeed, in light of the fact that the United States has generally abandoned the doctrine of privity,[16] it would have been surprising if the Supreme Court had sought to re-introduce that doctrine in relation to exclusion clauses designed to benefit a non-party. At least with respect to clauses in bills of lading which expressly seek to protect third parties such as stevedores, there is now no question in that country as to the effectiveness of such clauses.[17]

---

12 Law Commission, *Privity of Contract: Contracts for the Benefit of Third Parties* (Law Com. No. 242, 1996), para. 2.19.

13 27th ed., 1994, Vol. 1, para. 14-033, n. 15.

14 359 U.S. 297 (1959).

15 Ibid. at 305.

16 See, e.g., *Restatement, Second, Contracts*, § 302(1).

17 Some examples of the application of such clauses to protect third-party stevedores and others, in cases before the United States Court of Appeals, are: *Tessler Bros (B. C.) Ltd. v. Italpacific Line* 494 F. 2d 438 (1974); *Institute of London Underwriters v. Sea-Land Service Inc.* 881 F. 2d 761 (1989) and *Barretto Peat Inc. v. Luis Ayala Colon Sucres Inc.* 896 F. 2d 656 (1990).

*3. A More Rational Approach?*

Neither Fullagar J. in the *Darling Island* case, nor any member of the majority of the House of Lords in the *Midland Silicones* case, explained why they regarded the doctrine of privity as a necessary bar to the third party's right to claim the benefit of the exclusion clause. That reason has, however, been supplied by Professor Coote in his book on *Exception Clauses*, published in 1964. As he points out – and as is now well accepted[18] – clauses which exclude or limit the liability which one party may otherwise be under are of two types. On the one hand, such a clause may limit, or provide a defence to, a liability which has already accrued, but on the other hand the clause may be read as preventing any liability from arising in the first place.

If a particular clause is interpreted as being in the former of these categories, then one may readily accept that the doctrine of privity is relevant to its field of application. If it is assumed that one party is already under a liability – whether in contract or tort – then that liability cannot be diminished or removed by anything other than a contract between the party who is under the liability and the one who has acquired the right to sue for that wrong. It must therefore be assumed that both Fullagar J. and the majority in the *Midland Silicones* case took it for granted, and as not requiring any overt recognition, that the clause with which each of them respectively was concerned was of the former type, and did no more than provide a defence to an accrued cause of action.

But a different view is open as to the interpretation of the clauses subject to consideration in both of those cases. It is at least equally probable (and, indeed it will be argued shortly that it is highly likely) that the clauses fell into the second of the above categories. That is, the clauses operated to qualify or limit the obligation which the parties named therein were undertaking. In such a case, the doctrine of privity is irrelevant. Liability – and especially liability in negligence – may generally be excluded or limited by means of a notice given to the person whose rights may be infringed, and, so long as there is some evidence of assent to the limitation or exclusion thus asserted, a contract is not necessary. As Kitto J. explained in *Wilson v. Darling Island Stevedoring & Lighterage Co. Ltd.*,[19]

---

18 See, e.g., Treitel, *The Law of Contract* (9th ed., 1995), pp. 218-9; Greig and Davis, *Law of Contract* (1987), p. 597.

19 (1956) 95 C.L.R. 43 at 81.

> a provision found in a document to which A and B are the only parties may well, either alone or with other circumstances, provide a stranger, C, with a defence to [an action brought against C].

Having explained that the document may provide the basis for a defence of leave and licence to an action in trespass brought by A against C, his Honour went on to say:[20]

> So too where the cause of action is not trespass but negligence. A defence of volenti non fit injuria may be perfectly good, it seems to me, notwithstanding that the plaintiff's consent to accept the risk of the injury for which he sues is expressed in a contract to which the defendant is not a party. ... It is not necessary to the defence that the consent should have been given by a *contract* between the plaintiff and the defendant... Hence, if A in his contract with B agrees expressly or impliedly that C need take no care to avoid injuring A in carrying out particular work which (as he knows) involves danger to A and that B may so inform C who then proceeds with the work and in the course of it injures A, the defence of volenti is as clearly made out as it would have been if A had himself told C that he accepted, in exoneration of C, the whole risk of injury from C's activities. The absence of privity of contract between A and C would be irrelevant. It is all a question of consent or no consent.

Although the Judge spoke in terms of the defence of voluntary assumption of risk, it can be seen from the tenor of his judgment that he was not concerned with the defence of that particular name, but rather was using it as a short-hand expression to describe a circumstance where one person has consented to accept the risk of another's carelessness. Viewed in that light, the judgment of Kitto J. is completely in accord with that of Lord Denning, the dissentient in the House of Lords in the *Midland Silicones* case. In words which are reminiscent of those of the Australian Judge, although without direct reference thereto, Lord Denning said:[21]

> it is an accepted principle of the law of tort that no man can complain of an injury if he has voluntarily consented to take the risk of it on himself. This consent need not be embodied in a contract. Nor does it need consideration to support it. Suffice it that he consented to take the risk of injury on himself.

However, on the facts before him, Lord Denning, like Kitto J, held that the stevedores could not gain the protection of the clause in the bill of lading, since it was not expressed widely enough to include them within its ambit.

---

20 Ibid. at 82.

21 *Midland Silicones Ltd. v. Scruttons Ltd.* [1962] A.C. 446 at 488.

## *4. Exclusion Clauses as Notice of Assent to the Risk*

On the unspoken assumption that the exclusion clause in question operates substantively, to prevent a cause of action arising, such a clause serves as a notice that one of the contracting parties is prepared to assume the risk of damage caused by the person for whose benefit it has been drafted. To substantiate that view, it is necessary to consider in general terms the circumstances in which a non-contractual notice may negative or limit liability, and in particular when such a notice will be found in the terms of an exclusion clause. It is also necessary to rebut the judicial attack that was launched on this approach by Lord Simon in *New Zealand Shipping Co. Ltd. v. A. M. Satterthwaite & Co. Ltd. (The Eurymedon).*[22]

*(a) In general* It is now well accepted that a person who might otherwise come under a liability in negligence is entitled to limit or exclude that liability by a notice which is brought to the attention of the person who suffers loss or damage. The very fact that one undertakes, or continues, some activity in the face of the notice of disclaimer is regarded as sufficient evidence of assent to the possibility of harm.

Thus, one who enters another's land is presumed to consent to the risk of physical harm about which the occupier has provided information by a notice placed at the entrance to the property.[23] And a person who accepts a lift in a car is presumed to consent to any limitation or exclusion of liability for injury or compensation therefor contained in a notice displayed sufficiently prominently.[24] And one who receives financial advice – whether it concerns a customer's capacity to pay[25] or the value of property about to be mortgaged[26] – is regarded as having assented to the risk of carelessness by the adviser if the latter has disclaimed responsibility to anyone other than adviser's client, even though that disclaimer is contained

22 [1975] A.C. 154.

23 *Ashdown v. Samuel Williams & Son Ltd.* [1957] 1 Q.B. 409; *White v. Blackmore* [1972] 2 Q.B. 651. The Unfair Contract Terms Act 1977 (U.K.), s. 2(1), now renders void such notices, but there is no similar legislation in Australia.

24 *Buckpitt v. Oates* [1968] 1 All E.R. 1145; *Bennett v. Tugwell* [1971] 2 Q.B. 267; *Birch v. Thomas* [1972] 1 All E.R. 905 . Those decisions have been abrogated by statute in England (see Road Traffic Act 1988 (U.K.), s. 149), but are apparently still good law in Australia.

25 *Hedley Byrne & Co. Ltd. v. Heller & Partners Ltd.* [1964] A.C. 465.

26 *Omega Trust Co. Ltd. v. Wrightson & Pepper* (1996) 75 P. & C.R. 57. The Unfair Contract Terms Act 1977 (U.K.), s. 2(2), requires such notices to satisfy a statutory test of reasonableness: *Smith v. Eric S. Bush* [1990] 1 A.C. 831.

in a contract between the adviser and the client, to which the recipient of the advice is not a party. Of course, such a disclaimer will be construed strictly against the person seeking to rely on it,[27] but since its only purpose is to limit or exclude liability in negligence, there is less cause for courts to adopt a strained construction than in relation to contractual provisions which seek to limit or exclude the liability otherwise flowing from entry into that contract.[28]

*(b) Notice of assent contained in an exclusion clause* The earliest examples of judicial acceptance of the proposition that an exclusion clause in a contract between A and B may constitute assent to the risk of injury or damage by a third party are in a series of cases decided in England in the late nineteenth and early twentieth centuries, concerned with the carriage of passengers and goods by rail. At that time, there were a number of railway companies. Each owned its own lines and was responsible for their management, but it was the regular practice for one company to enter into a contract for the carriage of passengers and goods both by it and another company. If the first company had, by the terms of its ticket, excluded liability for injury or damage, and such injury or damage occurred in the course of carriage by the second company, the latter was held to be protected by the terms of the ticket.[29] The basis of that protection of the second company was put very firmly on the basis of the passenger's assent to the risk of that injury. As Blackburn remarked, in the first such case:[30]

> I think it must be taken that the plaintiff intended the terms on which he travelled to be communicated to [the second company] and that he must be taken to have assented that the ticket should protect [the second company] just as much as [the first company], and that the terms of this ticket extended to all risks connected with the journey which the plaintiff might meet with as a passenger.

More than a hundred years later, similar conclusions have been reached in England in a series of cases relating to building work. In *Norwich City*

---

27 *BT Australia Ltd. v. Raine & Horne Pty. Ltd.* (1983) 3 N.S.W.L.R. 221 at 236 per Wootten J; *Mackman v. Stengold Pty. Ltd.* (1991) A.T.P.R. ¶41-105 at 52,632-3 per Spender J.

28 *Hedley Byrne & Co. Ltd. v. Heller & Partners Ltd.* [1964] A.C. 465 at 492 per Lord Reid.

29 *Hall v. North Eastern Rly Co.* (1875) L.R. 10 Q.B. 437; *Barratt v. Great Northern Rly Co.* (1904) 20 T.L.R. 175; *Reader v. South Eastern & Chatham Rly Co.* (1921) 38 T.L.R. 14.

30 *Hall v. North Eastern Rly Co.* (1875) L.R. 10 Q.B. 437 at 442.

*Council v. Harvey*[31] the plaintiff owner had agreed with the head contractor that it would accept the risk of loss or damage by fire to both the building works and to existing structures. The premises were damaged by fire caused by the negligence of an employee of a subcontractor, but the English Court of Appeal accepted that both defendants were protected by the clause in the head contract. Although May L.J., speaking for the Court, was apparently concerned by the fact that there was no privity of contract between the parties,[32] the conclusion, that the contractual provisions prevented a duty of care from arising on the part of the subcontractor or its employee, can be seen as another instance of assent to a particular risk being demonstrated by means other than a contract between the relevant parties. To the same effect is the decision of Judge Smout, the Official Referee, in *Southern Water Authority v. Carey*,[33] and the comments of the English Court of Appeal in *Pacific Associates Inc. v. Baxter*.[34] In the last-named case, the defendant engineer was held to be protected by a clause in the head contract between the employer and the contractor, Russell L.J. remarking[35] that the provision "destroys the duty of the engineer, if duty there ever was".

Naturally, protection can be granted only by a provision which purports to bring a third party within its ambit. If, as in *Edgeworth Construction Ltd. v. N.D. Lea & Associates Ltd.*,[36] the clause seeks to protect the employer only, it is simply a matter of construction of the clause to arrive at the conclusion that a third party (in that case, engineers engaged by the employer) will remain liable for any negligence that it may have committed.

The cases discussed in the preceding paragraphs might be regarded as special examples, limited to particular types of contracts. An approach which is applicable to any type of contract is that taken by McLachlin J. in *London Drugs Ltd. v. Kuehne & Nagle International Ltd.*[37] The appellants had stored a transformer with the respondent warehousing company pursuant to a contract under which the respondent's liability on any one package was limited to $40. Employees of the respondent carelessly

---

31 [1989] 1 W.L.R. 828.

32 See esp. at 837. His Lordship laid stress on the fact that the two contracts – with the head contractor and the subcontractor – were in similar if not identical terms, but the conclusion that the defendant employee of the subcontractor was also protected can only be based on notions of the plaintiff having assented to risk of damage by any person connected with the works.

33 [1985] 2 All E.R. 1077, esp. at 1086.

34 [1990] 1 Q.B. 993.

35 At 1038.

36 [1993] 3 S.C.R. 206.

37 [1992] 3 S.C.R. 299.

damaged the goods. The appellant sued both the respondent company and the employees in an attempt to recover the full extent of the loss, but the Supreme Court of Canada held that neither defendant was liable to any greater extent than $40. The majority of the Court arrived at that conclusion by creating yet another exception to the doctrine of privity, as will be considered below. Of greater relevance to the present discussion is the judgment of McLachlin J. Her Ladyship observed[38] that the appellant's action against the employees was in tort, and hence it was the principles of the law of tort, rather than those of the law of contract, which were relevant to the disposition of the appeal. She went on to say that the question of whether the employees owed a duty of care to the appellants, or the extent of any such duty, was only to be resolved by reference to all the circumstances of the case. She then said:[39]

> The existence of a limitation on liability, whether contractual or otherwise, may affect the ambit of that duty of care. In this case, the majority of the [British Columbia] Court of Appeal, applying these principles, concluded that the duty of care of the defendants was limited to damage under $40, the plaintiff having accepted the risk of damage over that amount. I would affirm that conclusion.

*(c) Judicial attack and its rebuttal* In only one case has a Judge taken it upon himself to launch a sustained attack on the theory that an exclusion clause in a contract may act as a notice to a non-party of assent to the risk of the matters specified in that clause. That attack is to be found in the opinions of the Privy Council in *New Zealand Shipping Co. Ltd. v. A.M. Satterthwaite & Co. Ltd. (The Eurymedon)*,[40] voiced by Lord Simon (with whom Viscount Dilhorne agreed on this point).

The respondents were the consignees under a bill of lading of machinery which had been shipped from England to New Zealand. The bill of lading contained a clause which sought to protect not only the shipper but also any independent contractors employed by it from liability for loss or damage to the goods. The appellant stevedores damaged the goods in the course of unloading them in New Zealand, and the respondents sued to recover the loss they had suffered. One of the contentions put forward by the appellants was that, irrespective of any principles of contract law, the cargo owners' acceptance of the bill of lading acted as evidence of their assent to the risk of damage by the stevedores. A majority of the Privy Council upheld the stevedores' claim to immunity on the basis of there

38 Ibid. at 454.
39 Ibid. at 460.
40 [1975] A.C. 154.

being an additional contract between the parties to the litigation, a proposition which will be considered shortly. That conclusion rendered it unnecessary to consider the argument currently under consideration. Lord Simon, however, not only disagreed with the majority on the contractual aspects of the case, but put forward three reasons for rejecting the argument based on assent to the risk. It is submitted that each of those reasons is flawed.

First, his Lordship said that if the stevedores' arguments were correct, the *Midland Silicones* case "should have been decided the other way".[41] But it has been pointed out above[42] that in the *Midland Silicones* case, the relevant clause was not expressed sufficiently widely to include independent contractors such as stevedores; it has also been observed[43] that Lord Denning, who considered that an exclusion clause might, in principle, act as notification of assent to a risk, would not have allowed the stevedores to succeed in that case, because of the drafting of the clause.

Lord Simon's second assertion[44] was that the stevedores' argument was "inconsistent with both the reasoning and the actual decision in *Cosgrove v. Horsfall*".[45] In that case the plaintiff, while travelling on a bus by virtue of a free pass, was injured by the negligence of the driver of the bus. The free pass had been issued on condition that neither the operator of the bus nor its employees would be liable for injuries sustained by the holder, but the English Court of Appeal nevertheless allowed the plaintiff to sue the driver in negligence. The Court insisted that the pass could protect the driver only if he were a party to the contract evidenced by it. But such a conclusion is not inconsistent with the stevedores' contention in *The Eurymedon*. The point has been made above[46] that the question of whether privity is relevant to the applicability of an exclusion clause depends upon the interpretation and effect of that clause. If it is treated as no more than a defence to an accrued cause of action, it can protect only those who are parties to the contract in which it was inserted. The conclusion in *Cosgrove v. Horsfall*, in other words, depended on the Court's view that the exclusion clause operated as a defence only, and is of no relevance if the clause is construed as one which denies a cause of action in the first place.

Lord Simon's third reason for rejecting the stevedores' arguments in

---

41 Ibid. at 182.
42 See text before note 13.
43 See text to note 21.
44 *The Eurymedon* [1975] A.C. 154 at 182.
45 (1945) 175 L.T. 334.
46 See text to note 18.

*The Eurymedon*[47] was that their reliance on *Hedley Byrne & Co. Ltd. v. Heller & Partners Ltd.*,[48] and cases in which a licence is coupled with a disclaimer of liability, was misplaced. His Lordship considered it relevant that in those cases the right or service had been granted or provided gratuitously, because "obviously any person making a gift can delimit its extent". It is far from easy to follow the logic of this remark. On the one hand, the stevedores had, in his Lordship's view, provided their services to the cargo owners gratuitously, he having refused to countenance a contractual nexus between those parties. And on the other hand, his Lordship gave no reason for confining to gifts the right to delimit their extent; there is no juridical reason for asserting that a person who enters into a contract cannot delimit the extent of the obligations thereunder.

Lord Simon's attack on the notion of exclusion clauses operating as notice of assent to a risk of damage having been shown to be difficult to sustain, it is suggested that there is nothing standing in the way of the general acceptance of that notion.

### 5. *Privity By-passed*

While some courts have given full effect to an exclusion clause, as discussed in the preceding section, by regarding it as providing notice of assent to a risk of injury or damage, other courts have arrived at the same conclusion, but by by-passing the doctrine of privity. Acting on the assumption (the reasons for which are never articulated) that a contractual nexus is essential to allow an exclusion clause to provide the promised protection, the courts have been able to fashion a new and separate contract between A and C out of the bargain between A and B.

This step was first taken in *The Eurymedon*,[49] the facts of which have been given above.[50] The majority of the Privy Council were able to discern, in the contract between the cargo owner and the shipping company, an offer of a further contract between the cargo owner and the stevedores, limited to providing immunity to the latter, which was accepted upon the stevedores commencing unloading operations on the arrival of the ship in New Zealand. The decision was initially treated with caution, both by academics and the courts. A number of academic writers[51] took the view

47 [1975] A.C. 154 at 182.

48 [1964] A.C. 465.

49 [1975] A.C. 154.

50 See text after note 40.

51 See, e.g., Reynolds, "Himalaya Clauses Resurgent" (1974) 90 L.Q.R. 301; Coote, "Vicarious Immunity by an Alternative Route – II" (1974) 37 M.L.R. 453; Palmer, "The Stevedore's Dilemma: Exemption Clauses and Third Parties – I" [1974] J.B.L. 101.

that the reasoning was artificial, and the decision was distinguished or limited in its operation by some courts.[52] However, in *Port Jackson Stevedoring Pty. Ltd. v. Salmond & Spraggon (Australia) Pty. Ltd. (The New York Star),*[53] the Privy Council, on appeal from the High Court of Australia, re-affirmed its earlier decision, and declared[54] that the decision in *The Eurymedon*

> does not support, and their Lordships would not encourage, a search for fine distinctions which would diminish the general applicability, in light of established commercial practice, of the principle

that a suitably worded clause in a bill of lading is capable of conferring on third parties such as stevedores the defences and immunities conferred thereby on the carrier, as if such persons were parties to the contract evidenced by the bill of lading.[55]

Subsequent to the decision in *The New York Star*, the principles stated therein have been accepted and applied by the Supreme Court of Canada to, once again, protect stevedores with the clauses of exemption contained in the bill of lading.[56] And, although the decisions of the Privy Council are expressed in terms which would appear to confine the principles applied there to the sea-carriage of goods, at least the Supreme Court of New South Wales has applied those same canons of construction to contracts concerned solely with the carriage of goods on land.[57] The only critical comment that has been made about *The Eurymedon* and *The New York Star* was voiced by Lord Goff, delivering the opinion of the Privy Council in *The Mahkutai*.[58] His Lordship stressed the highly technical nature of the solutions provided by those decisions, but it must be

---

52 See *The Suleyman Stalskiy* [1976] 2 Lloyd's Rep. 609 (B.C. S.C.); *Herrick v. Leonard & Dingley Ltd.* [1975] 2 N.Z.L.R. 566; and especially *Port Jackson Stevedoring Pty. Ltd. v. Salmond & Spraggon (Australia) Pty. Ltd. (The New York Star)* (1978) 139 C.L.R. 231, in which the High Court of Australia held a stevedore not to be within the protection of the clause in the bill of lading once the goods had been discharged from the ship. That decision was reversed by the Privy Council [1981] 1 W.L.R. 138.

53 [1981] 1 W.L.R. 138.

54 Ibid. at 144.

55 Although appeals can no longer be taken from the High Court of Australia to the Privy Council, the decision in *The New York Star* is regarded as binding by Australian courts: *Rockwell Graphic Systems Ltd. v. Fremantle Terminals Ltd.* (1991) 106 F.L.R. 294 (W.A. F.C.).

56 *ITO – International Terminal Operators Ltd. v. Miida Electronics Inc.* [1986] 1 S.C.R. 752.

57 *Celthene Pty. Ltd. v. W.K.J. Hauliers Pty. Ltd.* [1981] 1 N.S.W.L.R. 606; *Life Savers (A'asia) Pty. Ltd. v. Frigmobile Pty. Ltd.* [1983] 1 N.S.W.L.R. 431.

58 [1986] A.C. 650 at 664-5.

observed that his remarks were a prelude to his raising the possibility that the cases should be recognised as "a fully-fledged exception to the doctrine of privity of contract", a step which the Privy Council regarded, in the circumstances, as one which it was inappropriate to take.

### *6. Judicial Limitation of the Privity Doctrine*

While the decision in *The Eurymedon* provided a means of allowing an exclusion clause to protect a person who was not a party to the contract containing that clause, it has been limited in its application to contracts relating to the carriage of goods. An attempt, in *Southern Water Authority v. Carey*,[59] to apply the same principles of construction to a building contract, in order to provide protection to a subcontractor, was rejected by Judge Smout, the Official Referee.[60] A more direct approach, which is capable of applying to any type of contract, was taken by a majority of the Supreme Court of Canada in *London Drugs Ltd. v. Kuehne & Nagle International Ltd.*[61]

The appellants, it will be recalled, had sued the employees of the respondents for the damage they had caused to goods stored in the respondents' warehouse. The employees sought to rely on a clause in the contract between the appellants and the respondents under which the liability of the warehouseman was limited to $40 per package. The majority opinion was delivered by Iacobucci J, who assumed that the doctrine of privity was the only stumbling block to the employees being granted the benefit of the limitation clause. As his Lordship said:[62]

> Except for a rigid adherence to the doctrine of privity of contract, I do not see any compelling reason based on principle, authority or policy demonstrating that this Court, or any other, must embark upon a complex and somewhat uncertain 'tort analysis' in order to allow third parties such as the respondents to obtain the benefit of a contractual limitation of liability clause, once it has been established that they breached a recognised duty of care. In my view, apart from privity of contract, it is contrary to neither principle nor authority to allow such a party, in appropriate circumstances, to obtain the benefit *directly* from the contract (i.e. in the same manner as would the contracting party) by resorting to what may be referred to as a 'contract analysis'. The main obstacle to such an approach resides in the

---

59 [1985] 2 All E.R. 1077.

60 It has been explained above (see text to note 33) that the subcontractor was able to gain the protection of the clause by relying on the argument that it provided notice of assent to the relevant risk.

61 [1992] 3 S.C.R. 299.

62 Ibid., at 413-4.

> fact that the party relying on the limitation of liability clause is not a party to the contract, not in the alleged principle that if one starts in tort, one must end in tort.

The Judge, it will be noted, put forward this proposition on the basis that the relevant third parties had "breached a recognised duty of care". It must be assumed from that expression that he considered that *any* contractual limitation or exclusion of liability operates only as a defence to an accrued cause of action, and is incapable of modifying or excluding the duty in the first place. It will be argued below that such a view of the operation of exclusion clauses suffers from some logical difficulties.

Having accepted that a "contract analysis" was the only path to resolution of the case before him, the Judge then undertook a wide-ranging review both of the doctrine of privity in general and of the various criticisms that have been levelled at it. He concluded that the facts before him presented an opportunity to create a further exception to the doctrine – or, in his words, to "relax" the doctrine by another incremental step. The extent of the exception to, or departure from, the doctrine of privity he expressed in a relatively limited compass. He said:[63]

> In the end, the narrow question before this Court is: in what circumstances should employees be entitled to benefit from a limitation of liability clause found in a contract between their employer and the plaintiff (customer)? Keeping in mind … the circumstances of this appeal, I am of the view that employees may obtain such a benefit if the following requirements are satisfied:
>
> 1. The limitation of liability clause must, either expressly or impliedly, extend its benefit to the employees (or employee) seeking to rely on it; and
> 2. the employees (or employee) seeking the benefit of the limitation of liability clause must have been acting in the course of their employment *and* must have been performing the very services provided for in the contract between their employer and the plaintiff (customer) when the loss occurred.

The decision has been the subject of a considerable degree of academic comment, much of it supporting this relaxation of the privity doctrine. However, a view expressed by many is that the majority judgment will give rise to uncertainty. The employees of Kuehne & Nagle Ltd. were included within the protection of the exclusion clause by implication only, and academic concern has been expressed that it will not

---

63 Ibid., at 448.

be easy to determine in future cases whether a particular person can be regarded as impliedly within the ambit of an exculpatory provision.[64] It is well known that the question of whether a term may be implied into a contract is one fraught with difficulty and uncertainty, and one more likely than not to be answered in the negative.[65] This concern is not relevant to the judgment of McLachlin J. The "tort analysis" which she used looks to all the relevant circumstances to determine whether the contracting party has done whatever is necessary to notify the defendant of the former's assent to the specified risk, without becoming embroiled with issues of contractual intention.

A further point may be made about the judgment of the majority in the *London Drugs* case. While it may give rise to uncertainty, no academic commentator has suggested that the conclusion was not the correct one in terms of justice and the proper allocation of resources and risk. However, it is far from clear whether employees in the same position as those of Kuehne & Nagle Ltd. would be able to rely on the Contracts (Rights of Third Parties) Act 1999 to gain the protection of an exclusion clause such as the one used in that case. The reason for this doubt is that the Act does not require merely the implication of a term in order to include persons not expressly referred to, but demands proof of a dual intention by the contracting parties – that the third party is an intended beneficiary of the contractual promise, and that the contracting parties intended that the third party have an enforceable right to rely on the promise. While such a dual intention test is no doubt necessary in the creation of positive contractual benefits, it is less obviously necessary for the purpose of extending the benefit of defences to a third party.[66] But it must also be acknowledged that any difference between the Act of 1999 and the views of the Supreme Court of Canada may be more apparent than real. As that Court has recently explained the *London Drugs* case,[67] the exception to privity is based on a dual intention test relating, on the one hand, to the range of

---

64 Waddams, "Privity of Contract in the Supreme Court of Canada" (1993) 109 L.Q.R. 349 at 351; Fleming, "Employee's Tort in a Contractual Matrix: New Approaches in Canada" (1993) 13 O.J.L.S. 430 at 437; MacMillan, "Privity and the Third Party Beneficiary: The 'Monstrous Proposition'" [1994] L.M.C.L.Q. 22 at 28; Huscroft, "Bad Doctrine and Incremental Reform" (1994) 7 J.C.L. 181 at 188.

65 See. e.g., Treitel, *The Law of Contract* (9th ed., 1995), at 187; Seddon and Ellinghaus, *Cheshire & Fifoot's Law of Contract* (7th Aus. ed., 1997), para. 10.47.

66 See Reynolds "Contract and Tort: The View from the Contract Side of the Fence" (1993) 5 Canta. L. R. 280 at 292; Adams and Brownsword, "Privity of Contract – That Pestilential Nuisance" (1993) 56 M.L.R. 722 at 729-30.

67 *Fraser River Pile & Dredge Ltd. v. Can-Dive Services Ltd.* (1999) 176 D.L.R. (4th) 257 at 269-70. The Supreme Court extended the *London Drugs* exception to apply also to an insurer's waiver of its right of subrogation.

possible beneficiaries and, on the other, to the activities which come within the terms of the contract.

### *7. Policy Considerations*

The above survey has shown that, at least since the decision of the Privy Council in *The Eurymedon*, the courts in every common law jurisdiction are fully prepared to give effect to an exclusion clause in favour of one who is not a party to the contract containing that clause.

This unanimity of result is far from surprising, since in all the cases the loss of which the plaintiff was complaining related either to its property interests or its financial well-being. The relevant exclusion clause was part of an overall transaction which was commercial in nature, and in which there was little doubt that each of the contracting parties was well able to protect its own commercial interests. As the High Court of Australia has pointed out, in both *Darlington Futures Ltd. v. Delco (Australia) Pty. Ltd.*[68] and *Nissho Iwai (Australia) Ltd. v. Malaysian International Shipping Corp. Berhad*,[69] in such circumstances it would serve no useful purpose to give an exclusion clause a strained interpretation, as that would be likely to frustrate the parties' true intentions. If the parties have allocated various risks between themselves, the court's only role is to give effect to the intentions thereby expressed.

While the courts are willing to include third parties within the ambit of exclusion clauses, they continue to differ on the means by which this is to done. It has been shown in the preceding pages that the reason for that difference lies in the interpretation of the clause. When a majority of courts act on the assumption that privity must be by-passed, or an exception created to its application, they must be taken to interpret the clause as being no more than a defence to an accrued right of action against the tortfeasor. But such an interpretation flies in the face of reality. When the contracting parties included the relevant clause in their contract, they must surely have intended that it would be effective to protect the third party. But no contracting party could have *intended* either that a court would create an elaborate and artificial structure for the purpose of by-passing the doctrine of privity, or that a court would create an exception to that doctrine. It is surely more rational to suggest that the intention of the contracting parties was to give notice to any affected third party that one of those contracting parties accepted the risk of damage or injury to its interests. If the courts are now prepared to give full effect to the terms of an exclusion clause,

---

68 (1986) 161 C.L.R. 500.
69 (1989) 167 C.L.R. 219.

when the issue arises as between the parties to that contract, then surely they should be prepared to do the same when the issue is the protection of a third party.

It has been argued[70] that, while a clause which completely excludes liability may readily enough be interpreted as one which is effective by preventing a duty of care from arising in the first place, a clause which merely provides a limit on the amount recoverable can only act as a defence, as it assumes that a duty exists and has been breached. To the same effect is the comment of Lambert J.A. in the British Columbia Court of Appeal in *London Drugs Ltd. v. Kuehne & Nagle International Ltd.*[71]

> I do not believe that the law knows anything of a $40 duty of care, limited in scope, embodying an obligation to be careful but only until $40 worth of care has been expended and after that the duty ceases. Nor do I think that the law recognises a duty of care which imposes such a minimum or selective standard of care that any breach of duty could not give rise to more than $40 worth of damages.

It is submitted, with respect, that these views are misconceived. Although some of the decisions discussed above are couched in terms of the exclusion clause denying the existence of a duty of care, it has been argued in these pages that the better analysis of the situation is that the clause operates as a notice of the risk to which one of the contracting parties has assented. That party may just as readily assent to the risk of damage being caused to its goods that is greater in extent than $40 as it may assent to the risk of all the damage that may befall the goods, including their total loss.

Were the courts to give effect to the only rational interpretation which can be placed on the intentions of the contracting parties, the doctrine of privity would cease to be relevant. The pity is that, simply because of the passage of the Contracts (Rights of Third Parties) Act 1999, the courts, in England at least, will assume that its abrogation of the privity doctrine is somehow relevant, and continue to apply what Iacobucci J. describes as a "contract analysis". Had the legislation not been passed, the courts would have retained the opportunity to develop the law, based on sound principles of the interpretation of contracts and the means by which tortious liability may be modified, limited or excluded.

---

70 Beale, "Privity of Contract: Judicial and Legislative Reform" (1995) 9 J.C.L. 103 at 112; Treitel, *The Law of Contract* (9th ed., 1995), at 573. Compare Coote, *Exception Clauses* (1964), at 128-9, who suggests that even in the case of limitation clauses, no contractual nexus is required to enable a third party to obtain the benefit of the clause.

71 (1990) 45 B.C.L.R. 1 at 43.

## The Burden of an Exclusion Clause

The circumstances under consideration in this Part are that a contract between A and B limits or excludes the liability of one of those parties, and that party wishes to invoke the terms of that clause against one who is not a party to the contract. This was a situation which was not addressed by the Law Commission in its Report on *Privity of contract: Contracts for the Benefit of Third Parties*,[72] and consequently not dealt with by the Contracts (Rights of Third Parties) Act 1999 (U.K.). It is suggested that this omission is to be welcomed because, for one thing, the matter is not one in relation to which the doctrine of privity is relevant, and for another thing, it is one in respect of which the common law is at least in the process of developing an adequate response.

There are two types of contractual arrangement in which it is now accepted that the terms of exclusion or limitation of liability contained in A's contract with B will also apply to C, a non-party. These are the transfer of ownership by the consignor to the consignee in goods which are in the course of sea-carriage, and a sub-bailment of goods. There is some authority suggesting that similar principles apply in relation to a sub-contractor of building works. Each of these classes of arrangement will be considered in turn. This Part will conclude by considering whether there is any general principle, applicable to all types of contract, to be drawn from these specific instances.

### *1. Consignee of Goods Covered by a Bill of Lading*

*The Eurymedon*[73] and *The New York Star*[74] gave rise to two issues of the relationship between privity and exclusion clauses. It has already been explained[75] that the stevedores were held to be able to take the benefit of the exclusion clause in the bill of lading by virtue of the additional contract, between them and the goods owner, which was implied from the terms of that clause. But although the burden of that clause had initially been accepted by the consignor of the goods, it was the consignee who brought the proceedings for the damages caused to them. The Privy Council, in *The Eurymedon*, disposed of this point very briefly, saying that the consignee "is bound by the stipulations in the bill of lading by his acceptance of it and

---

72 Law Com. No. 242, 1996.

73 [1975] A.C. 154.

74 [1981] 1 W.L.R. 138.

75 See above, text to note 49.

request for the delivery of the goods thereunder".[76] It appears, from the authority relied on by their Lordships,[77] that they assumed an implied assignment of those contractual liabilities from consignor to consignee. The important point for present circumstances is that the consignee, by its possession of the bill of lading, must be taken to have known of the liabilities thereunder, and accepted their imposition. The decision can thus be distinguished from *Midland Silicones Ltd. v. Scruttons Ltd.*,[78] in which the stevedores sought, inter alia, to rely on the exclusion clause in their contract with the shipowner, but failed in that attempt, as there was nothing to indicate that the consignee was aware, or ought to have been aware, of the terms of that contract.

*2. Sub-bailment on Terms*

It is now well established that if the owner of goods gives possession of them to a bailee, who in turn sub-bails them with the consent of the owner, the latter is bound by any exclusion or limitation of liability in the contract between bailee and sub-bailee.

This principle was put forward by Lord Denning M.R. in *Morris v. C. W. Martin & Sons Ltd.*[79] The plaintiff had taken her fur to a furrier to be cleaned. The latter, with the plaintiff's consent, sent it to the defendants, but it was stolen by one of their employees while it was in their custody. The English Court of Appeal held that a clause in the furrier's contract with the defendants was not expressed in sufficiently wide terms to cover the events which had happened. It therefore did not have to determine whether the clause might have bound the plaintiff. However, Lord Denning M.R. expressed the view[80] that as a matter of principle the plaintiff would have been bound by the clause. Because she had agreed that the goods should be sent to the defendants, she had impliedly consented to the furrier contracting with the defendants "on the terms usually current in the trade",[81] which included the clause in question.

Although initially stated as no more than a dictum, Lord Denning's

---

76 [1975] A.C. 154 at 168.

77 *Brandt v. Liverpool, Brazil & River Plate Steam Navigation Co. Ltd.* [1924] 1 K.B. 575 and s. 1 of the Bills of Lading Act 1855 (U.K.), or its equivalent in New Zealand or New South Wales.

78 [1962] A.C. 445.

79 [1966] 1 Q.B. 716.

80 Ibid., at 729-30, relying both on his own judgment in *Midland Silicones Ltd. v. Scruttons Ltd.* [1962] A.C. 446 at 489-90 and on *Tappenden v. Artus* [1964] 2 Q.B. 185.

81 [1966] 1 Q.B. at 730.

views have been accepted as correct,[82] most notably by the Privy Council in *The Pioneer Container*.[83] In that case, the plaintiffs had shipped their goods on board one vessel, with the understanding that that shipper would subsequently transfer them to another ship for further onward carriage. The plaintiffs were held bound by an exclusive jurisdiction clause in the bill of lading issued by the second shipper to the first. In coming to that conclusion, their Lordships held that the sub-bailee could rely on the terms of the sub-bailment, so long as it could be shown that the owner had expressly or impliedly consented those terms.

In some respects, the decision in *The Pioneer Container* is not relevant to the arguments propounded in this chapter, since it was concerned with the enforcement of a positive obligation – the promise to sue only in a specified jurisdiction – against a third party to the contract, rather than simply permitting a person in whose favour an exclusion clause has been drawn to rely on that clause as a defence to an action brought by the third party. It is nevertheless important for present purposes, in that the Privy Council rejected the reasoning of Donaldson J. in *Johnson Matthey & Co. Ltd. v. Constantine Terminals Ltd.*,[84] and stressed that the consent of the goods owner to the sub-bailment is an essential aspect of the sub-bailee's right to rely on the exculpatory terms of its sub-bailment.

It is thus suggested that, although the Privy Council based it decision on nothing but the law of bailment,[85] the conclusion and the reasoning are entirely consistent with the approach of the Privy Council in *The Eurymedon* and in *The New York Star*, as discussed in the preceding section. In both situations, where the issue is the imposition of the burden of an exclusion clause, the solution depends, and depends solely, upon whether the plaintiff had sufficient notice of the clause and may thereby be taken to have assented to it. Any difference in result in either of the two situations lies in the fact that implied consent is much more difficult to prove in the case of a bailment on terms. The consignee of goods under a bill of lading must necessarily receive that document, and thus may readily be taken to know of the clause protecting the stevedore. But if a sub-bailee seeks to rely on the terms of the sub-bailment, to provide protection against

---

82 See, e.g., *Singer Co. (U.K.) Ltd. v. Tees and Hartlepool Port Authority* [1988] 2 Lloyd's Rep. 164; *Compania Portorafti Commerciale S.A. v. Ultramar Panama Inc. (The Captain Gregos (No. 2))* [1990] 2 Lloyd's Rep. 395 at 405 per Bingham L.J.

83 [1994] 2 A.C. 324.

84 [1976] 2 Lloyd's Rep. 215. Donaldson J. had considered that the owner's right of action depended on proof of the sub-bailment, and was therefore limited by the terms of that contract; the Privy Council ([1994] 2 A.C. 324 at 340-341) observed that it was no more than the sub-bailee's taking of possession which imposed on it the duties of a bailee, for breach of which the owner might sue.

85 [1994] 2 A.C. 324 at 339.

a claim by the owner, the terms of exclusion or limitation must be those normally used in the relevant trade or business before it can be said that the owner must be taken as having assented to them.[86]

### *3. Sub-contractors of Building Works*

There is some – admittedly slight – authority to support the proposition that a sub-contractor to a building contractor may rely on an exclusion clause in its sub-contract as against the building owner, subject, once again, to the requirement that the owner be taken to have knowledge of the clause and to have assented to it. In *Rumblelows Ltd. v. A.M.K. (A Firm)*,[87] the plaintiffs had engaged the defendant firm to carry out renovations to their warehouse. The second defendants, Firesnow Sprinkler Installations Ltd., were nominated sub-contractors for part of that work. Due to their lack of care, damage was caused to the plaintiffs' warehouse. In the ensuing action against both A.M.K. and Firesnow, the latter pleaded a limitation of their liability in their contract with A.M.K. The Official Referee said[88] that the views of Lord Denning in *Morris v. Martin* were as applicable in the case of a building contract as they were in the case of a bailment and sub-bailment. He therefore considered that if "the plaintiffs had not only known of but also consented to the second defendants' conditions", they would have been binding on the former, but that the evidence did not establish such a state of affairs.[89] And in *Norwich City Council v. Harvey*,[90] which has already been discussed,[91] the English Court of Appeal, in holding the sub-contractor immune from liability, appeared to rely as much on the terms of the sub-contract as on those of the head contract.[92]

### *4. A General Principle?*

It might be thought, from the above illustrations, that there is in the course of development a general principle that one who suffers loss or damage

---

86 Compare *Spectra International p.l.c. v. Hayesoak Ltd.* [1997] 1 Lloyd's Rep. 153 at 156, where such consent was implied, with *Westpac Banking Corp. v. Royal Tongan Airlines* (1996) Aust. Torts Reports ¶81-403 at 63,665-6, in which the owner was found not to have assented to the terms of a sub-bailment.

87 (1980) 19 B.L.R. 25.

88 Ibid., at 48.

89 Ibid., at 49. Similarly, in *Twins Transport Ltd. v. Patrick* (1983) 25 B.L.R. 65 at 86-7, Judge Hawser held that the plaintiff developers did not know of the limitation contained in the defendant's sub-contract, and hence was not bound by it.

90 [1989] 1 W.L.R. 828.

91 See above, note 31.

92 [1989] 1 WLR at 836-7.

from the negligence of another is unable to seek compensation if the conduct of the alleged tortfeasor came within the terms of an exclusion clause contained in a contract with another, provided that, prior to suffering the loss or damage, the plaintiff knew of, or must be taken to have known of, and assented to, the terms of that exclusion clause. Such a principle would, of course, be a mirror image of the principle the existence of which has been argued for in the preceding Part of this chapter. Although, in each case, the relevant exculpatory clause is contained in a contract, that fact is of no moment. The only point of importance is that the injured party must have had sufficient notice of, and may be regarded as having assented to, the clause of exclusion or limitation before it can be of any effect.

There is, however, a number of comments from members both of the House of Lords and the High Court of Australia which appear to suggest that notice of, and assent to, such a limitation or exclusion is not necessary. In *White v. Jones*,[93] the plaintiff, who had been intended by the testator to benefit under the latter's will, was prevented from receiving that benefit because of the negligence of the defendant solicitor. The House of Lords held that the plaintiff was entitled to recover the amount of that intended benefit in an action in negligence against the solicitor. The concern that arises from that decision is the remark of Lord Goff, that the solicitor's liability "will of course be subject to any term of the contract between the solicitor and the testator which may exclude or restrict the solicitor's liability".[94] A similar approach was taken by the High Court of Australia in *Bryan v. Maloney*.[95] The builder of a house was held liable for negligence in its construction to the plaintiff, who had purchased the dwelling some time after it had been built, and with neither knowledge, nor the means of knowledge, of the defect. Although the issue did not arise on the facts, the majority of the High Court[96] appeared to take the same view as that expressed by Lord Goff in *White v. Jones*.

The reason for this attitude is that liability in negligence, at least for the purely economic loss suffered in the above two cases, depends upon the defendant's assumption of responsibility, and if he or she has, by the terms of a contract, assumed only a limited responsibility, that liability cannot be expanded merely because action is brought by one who is not a party to that contract. To that argument it may be retorted that assumption of

---

93 [1995] 2 A.C. 207.

94 Ibid., at 268. Lord Nolan, at 294, left the point open, but in *Hill v. Van Erp* (1997) 188 C.L.R. 159 at 196, Gaudron J. expressed views similar to those of Lord Goff.

95 (1995) 182 C.L.R. 609.

96 Ibid., at 624-5; see also Brennan J. at 641, Toohey J. at 662.. To the same effect, in not dissimilar circumstances, are the remarks of Windeyer J. in *Voli v. Inglewood Shire Council* (1963) 110 C.L.R. 74 at 85 and of Richmond P. in *Bowen v. Paramount Builders Ltd.* [1977] 1 N.Z.L.R. 394 at 407.

responsibility is a relative matter, and must depend upon the relationship between the defendant and others. In the course of one transaction, a person may surely assume a different degree of responsibility towards different people, depending on the extent to which the latter are aware of that person's commitment to the transaction. There appears to be nothing wrong in principle with the solicitor in *White v. Jones* assuming a greater degree of responsibility towards the disappointed beneficiaries, who had no knowledge of, control over, or ability to consent to, a term of limitation in the contract of retainer, than he assumed towards the testator, with whom he might have bargained for a reduction in the standard of care.

At the very least, it is to be hoped that if the relevant circumstances were to arise, the comments referred to above would be rejected in favour of the countervailing principle that limitations or exclusions of liability can only affect those who have actual or constructive knowledge of them, and the freedom to give or withhold consent thereto.

## Conclusion

The limitation or exclusion of liability, whether contained in a contract or in a non-contractual notice, serves a useful commercial purpose. It makes clear where the risk of certain eventualities will lie, and who, therefore, should insure against that occurrence. It follows that such a limitation or exclusion should only be given effect to if those on whom the risk is thus intended to be cast are aware of that intention. Such knowledge may often come, at least constructively, from entering into a contract which contains the exculpatory provision. However, it has been the purpose of this chapter to demonstrate that entering into a contract is by no means the only way in which notice may be given.

And there is a complete theoretical justification for insisting that the shifting of that risk by a limitation or exclusion of liability should be upheld by the law. If the notice of limitation or exclusion is contained in a contract, the very fact of entry into that bargain, with those terms, is the justification for maintaining the effectiveness of the clause. If, on the other hand, the limitation or exclusion is contained in a non-contractual notice, of which the affected party is, or should be, aware, the justification is the simple moral precept that everyone should abide by the decisions which they have made, and should not be permitted to disavow the responsibility which they have undertaken. Such notices are invariably provided at the outset of a transaction of some sort. On receiving notice of the limitation or exclusion, the person on whom the risk will thereby be placed has the choice of continuing with the transaction and accepting that risk, or of withdrawing forthwith. Having made the choice to continue, it would offend good conscience for the law to allow the affected party subsequently to disavow that choice.

It is to be hoped that the courts in all common law countries will come to recognise that terms of exclusion or limitation affect all those who have adequate notice of them. If that were to occur, the persistent myth of the relationship between exclusion clauses and the doctrine of privity of contract may finally be exploded.

# 14 Privity, Property, and Pragmatism

*Can American Law Answer Kincaid's Questions?*

ANTHONY JON WATERS

> [W]hat "privity" is or why the lack of it should be fatal is never inquired into. We may take the word "privity" as a sort of mystical absolute. To lack privity is to have failed to achieve the requisite state of contractual grace.[1]

In this essay, I propose to address four questions raised by Peter Kincaid, by reference to the American[2] experience with the third-party beneficiary rule, which is a common law rule permitting enforcement of a contract by an "intended beneficiary".[3] The questions are these:

1. Why is there need for a general rule favouring third-party enforcement, given the existence of numerous specific exceptions, or devices, by which the same outcome is achieved in most if not all of the situations that matter?
2. Given the absence of any "private justification"[4] for permitting a non-party plaintiff to enforce a contract, is it necessary for us to engage in less coherent reasoning than traditional contract law demands, to resort to "a fuzzy mixture of reasons"[5] in

---

[1] Kessler, Gilmore & Kronman, *Contracts: Cases & Materials* (2d. ed. 1985), 1330.

[2] Much as I dislike this usage, for convenience I use the term "American" to mean of or pertaining to the United States of America.

[3] *Restatement (Second) of Contracts (1979),* §302
Intended and Incidental Beneficiaries
(1) Unless otherwise agreed between promisor and promisee, a beneficiary of a promise is an intended beneficiary if recognition of a right to performance in the beneficiary is appropriate to effectuate the intention of the parties and either
(a) the performance of the promise will satisfy an obligation of the promisee to pay money to the beneficiary;
or
(b) the circumstances indicate that the promisee intends to give the beneficiary the benefit of the promised performance.
(2) An incidental beneficiary is a beneficiary who is not an intended beneficiary.

[4] Kincaid, "Privity and Private Justice in Contract" (1997) 12 J. of Contract Law 47, 64.

[5] Id. at 64.

order to accommodate third-party enforcement? If so, what are the consequences?

3. Does embracing third-party contract rights (i) necessarily; or (ii) in fact shift the focus of Contract[6] from strictly private grievances to some unarticulated, generalised "public interest"? Specifically, is Kincaid right in saying that if the proposed new rule does not conform to the bargain theory of contract, it must reflect a public, rather than a private, interest?[7]
4. Taking all the above into account, how would the inclusion of third-party beneficiary rights change the nature of Contract?

In the conclusion, I will suggest what we can and cannot usefully learn from the U.S. experience in connection with the contemplated introduction of a similar rule by statute, always bearing in mind that enacting a rule is very different from growing it.

## 1. The History of the American Rule

The history of the American third-party beneficiary rule is nothing less than bizarre. The unexpurgated facts of the seminal case[8] (which was decided

6 I use the capital C here for the same reason that Grant Gilmore used it throughout Gilmore, *The Death of Contract* (1974). It denotes bargain-based contract law, the same meaning that Kincaid attaches to the word without the capital letter. In the United States, it is generally accepted that bargain-based contract law is but a small part of a much larger idea of contract.

7 Kincaid, (1997) 12 J.C.L. 47, 57.

8 *Lawrence v. Fox* 20 N.Y. 268 (New York Court of Appeals 1859). Professor Eisenberg has argued that the conventional view that Lawrence is the seminal case is unfounded. He says that it "was not very remarkable for its time" and "broke little or no new ground". Eisenberg, "Third-Party Beneficiaries" 92 Colum. L. Rev. 1358 (1992), 1362. My response to him is published in Linzer, *A Contracts Anthology* (2d. Ed. 1995), 197-98. Eisenberg's conclusions were based in large part on Karsten, "The 'Discovery' of Law by English and American Jurists of the Seventeenth, Eighteenth and Nineteenth Centuries: Third Party Beneficiary Contracts as a Test Case" 9 Law & Hist. Rev 327 (1991). For a devastating analysis of Professor Karsten's mode of historical research, see Friedman, "Losing One's Head: Judges and the Law in Nineteenth Century American Legal History" 24 Law & Soc. Inquiry 253 (1999).

on expurgated facts) were these. The promisee (Hawley[9]) (A),[10] who was not a party to the lawsuit, incurred a debt of exactly three hundred 1854 dollars[11] to the plaintiff, Lawrence (C), on Day One. On Day Two, A lent exactly three hundred dollars to the defendant/promisor, Fox (B) in return for B's promise to pay that amount to C. When Fox refused to pay, Lawrence chose to sue not his debtor, Hawley, but his debtor's debtor, Fox. Why? Was Hawley dead? Bankrupt? Outside the jurisdiction? Not exactly. He was President of the Buffalo Board of Trade in the year of the trial.[12] But there is every indication that his debt to Lawrence was a gambling debt and thus unenforceable.[13] Hawley's loan to Fox, the next day, was allegedly made to enable Fox to gamble, which tainted that transaction indirectly, if at all.

If the seminal case was decided in response to a felt need, was it the need to permit creditors of gambling debts to circumvent the problem of direct enforcement by suing their debtors' debtors, thereby sanitising their claims? This new rule would be useful only if the debtor made a subsequent bargain with someone else to pay his creditor. And it would seem to work best where the two transactions involve the same amount of money, to the penny. All in all, not a particularly useful rule, and not a rule worth turning Contract on its head for.

But the sanitised story presented to, and passed on by the highest

---

9 "Hawley" in the Complaint became "Holley" in the Bill of Exceptions and "Holly" in the Court of Appeals. As to how this may have occurred, see Waters, "The Property in the Promise: A Study of the Third Party Beneficiary Rule" 98 Harv L. Rev. 1109 (1985), 1123 note 40, hereinafter "Waters".

10 The accepted use of A, B and C in this context in the United States is that C is the beneficiary/plaintiff, B the promisor/defendant, and A the promisee. See, e.g., Illustrations of §§ 302, 313 in Restatement (Second) Contracts (1979).

11 Grover Cleveland, later President of the United States, wrote to his sister that he was to be paid $500 per annum in 1858, his third year with a Buffalo, New York, law firm. See A. Nevins, *Grover Cleveland* 40, 43 (1932).

12 See L. Graham & F. Severance, *The First Hundred Years of the Buffalo Chamber of Commerce* 259 (1945).

13 Both Fox and Hawley were affluent businessmen. The transaction took place in a horse trader's premises in a notorious part of town where gambling was commonplace. "Canal Street was more than a street. It was the name of a district, a small and sinful neighborhood...[it was a]...nineteenth century example of Sodom and Gomorrah...." (L. Graham, *Niagara Country* (1949) 205-06). The only witness in the case was William Riley, another horse trader. He was prepared to testify that Hawley lent the money to Fox for Fox to gamble with it. The trial judge ruled that evidence inadmissible. And there is one more clue that the debt owed to Lawrence may well have been unenforceable The fact that he chose not to sue his debtor, who was both affluent and available. See: The Bill of Exceptions, *Lawrence v. Fox*, reprinted in Waters, 98 Harv. L. Rev. 1109 (1985) at 1132-33.

court, left out the dirty parts, as though the Lord Chamberlain had been lurking in the law libraries of New York.[14] Thus A, being indebted to C (although that debt was never proved[15]), "loaned" that amount to B in return for B's promise, made when C was not present, that he, B, would pay that amount to C.

The original American third-party beneficiary rule, "the rule of *Lawrence v. Fox*" as it came to be called,[16] permitted only a "creditor beneficiary" to enforce a beneficial contract. No restrictions were placed on what kind of creditor of the promisee the third party could be. She could, for example, have supplied A with goods or services, and there could be a warranty in effect, of which a breach might still be possible. The subsequent contract between A and B might be an executory contract, so that B might at some time have a defence against A's claim for payment, just as A may yet have a legally cognizable grievance against C. In such a situation, we need to know what this third party's right is *made of*, because if questions arise about requiring B to argue A's defence against C, for example, good old-fashioned contract law has not a single tool in its toolbox that is of any help at all.

Because we, too, have no tools, we must revert to basic principles. Does C's right to enforce the A-B contract against B *derive from* A's debt to C? If so, we have a principle to work with: C's right against B can be no greater than her right against A, presumably. If not, if the creditor beneficiary's right derives entirely from the A-B contract, then we must look for a different principle, and it may not prevent C from circumventing A's defences against her by suing B. Which is it? Let us return to the seminal case.

Was Lawrence (C), the first creditor beneficiary, in fact a creditor?[17] What, precisely, did the Court of Appeals hold with respect to proof of Hawley's (A's) debt to him? Fox's (B's) attorney, Jared Torrance, had from the outset objected that the only evidence of a pre-existing debt from A to C was the testimony of the sole witness in the case, William Riley,

---

14 In the final year of the life of the office of Lord Chamberlain (1967), a group of drama students at the University of Keele penned a word which His Lordship saw fit to delete from their play, to be performed at the Edinburgh Festival. The word in question was schizoknickerbockers. We made exceptionally good use of it, in Edinburgh, the following year.

15 See text accompanying note 17, infra.

16 See e.g., *Security Pacific Business Credit, Inc. v. Peat Marwick Main & Co.* 79 N.Y.2d 695, 718; 597 N.E.2d 1080, 1093 (Court of Appeal, New York, 1992).

17 Just as Sir Alec Douglas Home found it useful to have a box of matches handy when he thought about economic problems, I find a triangle very useful when thinking about third-party beneficiary rights. A triangle already adapted to this purpose may be found in Waters, 98 Harv. L. Rev. 1109 (1985), 1123, but any triangle will do.

who said that he heard A tell B when handing him the money, that he, A, owed that amount to C. And that evidence, Torrance argued, was hearsay if introduced to prove the debt. Edward Chapin, representing C, had pleaded that A was indebted to C in the amount of three hundred dollars, but at no time did he attempt to prove that debt. Riley's evidence was of course hearsay if used to prove the debt, and there was no other evidence of A's debt to C.

Remember that we are asking about the repercussions of having a three dimensional contractual relationship, specifically with regard to defences, modification, and rescision. I suggested that the seminal case might offer some guidance, specifically as to whether the creditor beneficiary's right *derives from* the promisee's indebtedness to him or her. When we look closely at the case, however, we find that the first ever creditor beneficiary was not in fact a creditor.[18] How come? And what did the appellate courts in *Lawrence* have to say about that?

The intermediate appellate court, presided over by the trial judge,[19] had only the hearsay argument to deal with. That court said this of Riley's testimony about what Hawley said to Fox: "It was a part of the Res Gestae. The Defendant, by receiving money under it, admitted the truth of the declaration."[20] This sounds like a cross between an admission against interest (evidence) and the terms of a constructive trust (equity), but it certainly does not sound like contract. In the Court of Appeals, Judge Gray addressed the hearsay argument differently.

> All the defendant had the right to demand in this case was evidence which, as between [the promisee] and the plaintiff, was competent to establish the relation between them of debtor and creditor. For that purpose, the evidence was clearly competent....[21]

---

18 The *Restatement of Contracts* (1932), §133(1)(b), defined a "creditor beneficiary" in terms of "an actual or supposed or asserted" duty of the promisor to the beneficiary. There is no accompanying explanation of how a "supposed" duty could be the basis of any legal right.

19 At this time, the Superior Court of Buffalo had only three judges. Therefore, the trial judge was certain to be on the three-judge appellate panel. Judge Masten, however, presided over the appeal and wrote the opinion of the court. What is more, he may have had a reputation for unusual partiality to his own previously articulated views. "[T]he spirit of severe judicial inquiry which he exercised upon appeals undoubtedly gave him confidence in his rulings below." Charles B. Guthrie's "remarks" made to a meeting of the Erie County Bar held to mark Judge Masten's death in 1871. At the same meeting, another Buffalo attorney said: "Conscious of his attainments and the rectitude of his intentions, he adhered with becoming tenacity to his own judgment...." *Buffalo Com. Advertiser*, April 18, 1871 at 3, col. 2.

20 Per Masten J. The General Term opinion of Judge Masten is reprinted in the Record of *Lawrence v. Fox* at page 10 (copy on file at the Harvard Law Library).

21 *Lawrence* 20 N.Y. 268 (1859), at 269-70.

Of that, I wrote:

> If our earlier reconstruction of events is essentially accurate – specifically, if Hawley's debt to Lawrence was unenforceable because it was a gambling debt – then the Delphic distinction between proving the debt and proving the debtor-creditor relationship may represent the ultimate expression of Chapin's triumph, for it enabled Judge Gray to walk the very tightrope that Chapin walked when he drafted the complaint and when he proved his case.[22]

Instead of dealing with the hearsay question, which was the vehicle for determining whether or not Lawrence's right derived from Hawley's debt to him, "Judge Gray fashioned a middle road, and so left a central uncertainty that remained with the creditor beneficiary rule until the American Law Institute abandoned that classification in 1967".[23]

As for the only other kind of third-party beneficiary who had rights under the Restatement (First),[24] the "donee beneficiary" (introduced by the court which had decided *Lawrence* sixty years earlier[25]), one would have guessed that the creditor class would have better rights than donees. After all, donees could not enforce a gift promise *directly*, whereas creditors could enforce their debts. And yet not so. According to the First Restatement, the donee beneficiary acquired an immediate, vested interest.[26] The creditor beneficiary did not.[27] How come?

In the process of generalising from the peculiar, old cases were placed in the new categories. The daughter in the "family tie" cases, for example,[28] became a donee beneficiary and the family tie exception disappeared. Among other cases thrown into this mix were those in which courts permitted beneficiaries of insurance policies to enforce the beneficial terms against the insurer, even though they were not party to the insurance contract. The insurers decided that the beneficiary was not in privity and therefore had no rights under the policy (one of many ways in which

---

22 Waters 98 Harv. L. Rev. 1109 (1985) at 1142.
23 Id. at 1141.
24 Supra. n.18.
25 *Seaver v. Ransom* 224 N.Y. 233; 120 N.E. 639 (1918).
26 See *Restatement (First) of Contracts* §142 (1932).
27 See §143 id. The creditor beneficiary's right vested only when she had "in reliance...placed herself in a position from which she could not retreat from loss", *Morstain v. Kircher*, 250 Minn. 737 (1933), 738.
28 See text accompanying note 54, infra.

insurers have enriched our jurisprudence[29]). Because of the injustice that would have resulted otherwise, the courts held that the beneficiary could enforce the contract of insurance. These plaintiffs, too, became "donee beneficiaries", and the specific sub-rule that the beneficiary of a life insurance policy acquired an immediate vested right (because the courts applied a property/trust theory) became the general rule for donee beneficiaries.[30]

To summarise, the third-party beneficiary rule enshrined in the Restatement in 1928[31] was first and foremost the product of the mutation which took place in the New York Court of Appeals in 1859, Judge Gray concluding his plurality opinion with the observation that if "a more strict and technically accurate application of the rules ... would lead to a different result ... the effort should not be made in the face of manifest justice".[32] Six decades later, in 1918, the same court saluted "the great case of *Lawrence v. Fox*"[33] and added the donee beneficiary category, also cut from whole cloth, to prevent a particular injustice from taking place.[34] In neither case were the repercussions considered[35] so that later on, there was simply no law to apply in situations involving defences, modification and rescision. The creditor beneficiary did not actually have to be a creditor, which makes the rule more bizarre yet, and the donee beneficiary's right was superior to that of the creditor beneficiary. All in all, not a rite of

29 *Trident General Insurance Co. Ltd. v. McNiece Bros. Pty. Ltd.* (1988) 165 C.L.R. 107; 80 A.L.R. 574 is another example of this phenomenon.

30 Professor Page, who was a member of the Committee on Contracts, which drafted the Restatement, objected to the generalisation of this sub-rule on the grounds that "the rights which arise should be determined by the principles of contract law; and not by the principles of gift, trust, and subrogation". Page, "The Power of the Contracting Parties to Alter a Contract for Rendering Performance to a Third Person" 12 Wis. L. Rev. 141 (1937), 184. Another member, George Rose, objected that the proposed Restatement formulation converted "an iniquitous rule peculiar to life insurance...into a uniform rule applicable to every form of donee beneficiary" 5 A.L.I. Proc. 383 (1927).

31 *Restatement (First) of Contracts*, Ch. 6, §§133-147 (Official Draft 1928).

32 *Lawrence*, 20 N.Y. 268 (1859), at 275.

33 *Seaver v. Ransom* 224 N.Y. 233, 236, 120 N.E. 639, 640 (1918).

34 In *Seaver*, the promisee was the wife of Judge Beman, who promised his dying wife that if she would sign the will he had drafted, which did not bequeath the house to her niece (the plaintiff), as Mrs. Beman had wished, he would leave the niece enough money in his will to make up the difference. Had the court not upheld the niece's right to sue as a third-party (donee) beneficiary, Judge Beman's estate would have retained the money unjustly.

35 For example, Judge Gray refused to consider these ramifications in *Lawrence*: "It was also insisted that Holly could have discharged the defendant from his promise ... and therefore the plaintiff was not entitled to maintain this suit for the recovery of a demand over which he had no control. It is enough that the [promisee] did not release the defendant from his promise, and whether he could or not is a question not now necessarily involved...." 20 N.Y. 268 (1859), 274.

passage one would recommend to an up-and-coming common law rule.

When the American Law Institute abolished the creditor and donee beneficiary categories in favour of the broader *intended beneficiary* of the Restatement (Second) of Contracts in 1967,[36] one important, if unintended consequence was that the tie to money was cut. Creditor beneficiaries were almost always claiming money; donees, money or tangible property. The seed had been planted in *Lawrence*, when the promise to pay was substituted for the proprietary interest in the money itself.[37] But the seed did not bear fruit until the intended beneficiary was enshrined in the First Tentative Draft of the Restatement (Second) of Contracts in 1967.[38] Only then was a whole range of possible benefits of contractual promises substituted for the bag of coins, or the bundle of bills, involved in the seminal case and its direct descendants.

Even that might not have mattered, had some apparently unrelated developments not taken place elsewhere in the law, at about the same time. For reasons I shall describe presently, thousands of intended beneficiaries (as they were called, independently of any contract law rule) of a variety of federal programmes, many suing as part of a class,[39] found that the usual legal routes to securing their intended benefits had been closed.[40] Almost all these programmes use funding contracts as a means of both distributing federal funds, and controlling how they are used. Typically, the recipient is to build low income housing,[41] care for Medicaid recipients,[42] or run the

---

36 *Restatement (Second) of Contracts* (Tent. Draft No. 3, 1967). Although the Second Restatement was not published in final form until 1981, the intended beneficiary formulation remained essentially unchanged from the 1967 draft.

37 Lawrence's claim was drafted as an action "for money had and received for and to the use of the plaintiff", as it had been called until the Field Code did away with the common counts in New York in 1848 in favour of the sole form of action permitted under the new Code: "a civil cause". That particular common count was a claim to property, and the property happened to be money. (Other common counts dealt with other kinds of property.) Because Fox was a borrower, and therefore could not be a trustee of the money, no such action would lie, and because Lawrence was not in privity with Fox, no contract claim would lie either. By cutting and splicing, and using a blender marked "The Field Code", the highest court in New York performed a kind of judicial sleight of hand by which the benefit of a promise to pay money was substituted for the right to the money itself.

38 Note 36, supra.

39 In these cases, the class is invariably created and defined by statute: the class of intended beneficiaries of the statute is the same as the class of intended beneficiaries of the funding contract.

40 See text accompanying notes 85-87, infra.

41 See, e.g., *Holbrook v. Pitt* 643 F.2d 1261 (7th Cir. 1980), discussed in Waters 98 Harv. L. Rev. 1109 (1985), at 1188-89, and *Zigas v. Superior Court* 120 Cal. App. 3d 827; 174 Cal. Rptr. 806 (1981), cert. denied 455 U.S. 943 (1982) discussed id. at 1109-92.

42 See, e.g., *Fuzie v. Manor Care, Inc.* 461 F. Supp. 689 (N. D. Ohio 1977) discussed in Waters 98 Harv. L. Rev. 1109 (1985), at 1186-1188.

local public schools.[43] In return, the entity being funded agrees to abide by federal rent tariffs,[44] Medicaid regulations,[45] or to comply with anti-discrimination provisions of a federal Civil Rights Act.[46]

Notice three salient features of these cases and others like them.[47] First, none of the plaintiffs could be described as a creditor or donee beneficiary without some violence being done to those words. Second, the intended benefit being claimed is rarely money or its equivalent, such as food stamps.[48] More typically, the remedy sought is injunctive relief, as in all but one of the cases referred to above. The one exception, *Zigas*,[49] is that rare case in which the plaintiffs (tenants) were claiming money. Because the money claimed came from excessive rents, paid by the tenants to the defendant landlord in the first place, a simple tool from yester-year, our old friend the common count for money had and received (*Lawrence*'s daddy,[50] not coincidentally) would have been the perfect choice.[51] Instead, plaintiffs sued, and won, as intended beneficiaries of the funding contract, but the court recognised that it was not so much a contract right as a right to the money itself: "The money sought is not a *consequence* of breach, it is

43 See, e.g., *Bossier Parish School Board v. Lemon* 370 F.2d 847 (5th Cir.), cert. denied 388 U.S. 911 (1967), discussed in Waters 98 Harv. L. Rev. 1109 (1985), at 1184-86.

44 In *Zigas* 174 Cal. Rptr. 806 (1981), the defendant landlords had charged tenants more than the permitted maximum rents.

45 In *Fuzie* 461 F. Supp. 689 (1977), defendant nursing home operators were allegedly planning to remove Stella Fuzie from one of their homes for non-medical reasons, a breach of Medicaid regulations promulgated under statutory authority.

46 In the *Lemon* case 370 F.2d 847 (1967), the federal Civil Rights Act placed no obligation on the parish with respect to children who were neither residents nor citizens of the State of Louisiana. The federal funding contract, however, extended the recipient school board's obligation not to discriminate on the grounds of race, to all children living within the geographic boundaries of Bossier Parish. Plaintiff children lived on a federal Air Force base. The third-party beneficiary rule both created their right and gave them standing to sue.

47 For example, Medicaid recipients have recently claimed that they are third-party beneficiaries of the large settlements recently made between various tobacco companies and the states. *Gomer ex rel. Gomer v. Philip Morris Inc.* 2000 WL 1071825 (July 31, 2000) and in another recent case, Medicaid patients were held to be third-party beneficiaries of the "balance billing provisions" in the county's agreement with the state, which in turn were required by statute. *Mallo v. Public Health Trust of Dade County* Florida, 88 F.Supp. 2d 1376 (March 31, 2000).

48 Food stamps may be used to buy food; they are issued under various federal programmes.

49 174 Cal. Rptr. 806 (1981).

50 See supra. n. 37.

51 "Had and received" cases, unlike *Lawrence*, often involved just two people, as did the seminal case, *Moses v. Macferlan* (1760) 2 Burr. 1005; 96 Eng. Rep. 120 (K.B.). At least as often, as in *Lawrence*-like situations, they involved three.

the breach".[52]

For our purposes, one lesson to be learned from this history is that in the United States, the third-party beneficiary rule finds itself on the fringes of public law only by virtue of an almost freakish combination of legal and non-legal events. In that respect, and others, it is true to its heritage. This history will serve as a reference point for much of the remainder of this essay.

## 2. Why the Need for a General Rule?

Kincaid asks why there is need for a general rule favouring third-party enforcement, given the existence of numerous specific exceptions by which the same outcome is achieved in most if not all of the situations that matter. What is more, says he, these "limited instances of public interests exceptionally outweighing private interests" do not impinge on "the idea that private law is about private interests".[53]

To elaborate on Kincaid's point, it is important to note at the outset that none of these specific devices takes the giant step involved in the general recognition of a third party's right to enforce a contract. The most specific of them was the so-called family tie exception to the privity requirement. The need for this exception arose from the fact that women could not own real property. When Father wished to leave as much wealth to his daughter as to his son, he sometimes left his land to the son (rather than sell it, or cut timber, to raise cash for his daughter) in return for the son's promise to share the wealth, in due course, with the daughter, his sister. When the wicked son inherited the land and kept everything for himself, his sister sued him. When the defendant objected that the plaintiff was not a party to the contract, the courts responded by saying that she was. Her close "blood tie" to the promisee, her father, made her "a party to the consideration" and thus entitled her to enforce the contract.[54]

The function of this fiction was to deem the plaintiff a party to the contract. Everything else followed from that, and it followed the rules of traditional contract law. If we were to ask: Did the family tie exception to the privity requirement change the nature of contract?, we would have to answer in the negative. No because any impact was *de minimis*, and no because the family tie exception co-opted the rules of contract law rather than confronting them. The broader exceptions made use of the ideas of

---

52 *Zigas* 120 Cal. App. 3d 827, at 836-838; 174 Cal. Rptr. 806, at 810-12, 836-38 (1981), per Feinberg, J.

53 Kincaid, (1997) 12 J. of Contract Law 47, at 60.

54 See, e.g., *Dutton v. Poole* (1677) 83 Eng. Rep. 523.

agency and trust but these, too, plugged right into contract law. If the promisee was the plaintiff's agent, then the plaintiff was a party to the contract, and the law of agency said that a principal could ratify the act of his agent even if he did not know about it at the time.[55] If the promisor was trustee of certain property, in trust for the plaintiff, then of course the plaintiff could enforce the beneficial terms of the trust.

The problem with these trust and agency ideas is that the cases employing them range from those in which "a constructive trust" or "an implied agency" is a perfectly reasonable description of the relationship, to those in which the trust or agency is entirely fictitious, and the court is abusing that central idea.[56] But the strength of these devices is precisely that they exploit established legal principles. The "family tie" was cut from whole cloth, it is true, but that device, and even the most imaginative uses of trust and agency, all served the same limited purpose. Each of them gave the plaintiff standing to enforce the contract. And each of them did it by making the plaintiff a party. They did not create a rule by which non-parties could enforce; indeed the whole point of these devices, in this context, was to avoid that.

What the third-party beneficiary rule did, first in New York and later nationwide, involved another dimension altogether. We know that it failed the "acid test" for contractual liability which was generally applied in American law at around that time (privity), and that it failed another such test, developed later.[57] There was no privity between plaintiff and promisor; and there was no "mutuality of obligation", because the plaintiff had none. (The requirement that consideration move from the plaintiff to the promisor had previously been abandoned in New York.[58]) In contrast

---

55 "[T]he promise was to be regarded as made to the plaintiff through the medium of his agent, whose actions he could ratify when it came to his knowledge, though taken without his being privy thereto." *Lawrence v. Fox* 20 N.Y. 268 (1859), 275, Johnson, C.J. and Denio J. concurring on separate grounds.

56 "The life of the common law has been in the unceasing abuse of its elementary ideas. If the rules of property give what now seems an unjust answer, try obligation; and equity has proved that from the materials of obligation you can counterfeit almost all the phenomena of property." S. Milsom, *Historical Foundations of The Common Law* (1969) at ix.

57 The other such test was called "mutuality of obligation", meaning exactly that. Given the existing tests of privity and consideration, the mutuality requirement was superfluous, but it did appeal to many courts and commentators. The mutuality test originated in *Baily v. Austrian* 19 Minn. 535 (Gil. 465) (1873). See also: E. Farnsworth, *Contracts* (1999) §3.2.

58 *Farley v. Cleveland* 4 Cow. 432 (N.Y. Sup. Ct.), unanimously aff'd, 9 Cow. 639 (N.Y. 1827). This is still good law in the United States today: "The consideration may 'move' from the promisee to someone other than the promisor, or it may 'move' to the promisor from someone other than the promisee". Farnsworth, *Contracts*, §2.3. (Emphasis original.)

to the specific devices discussed above, this development threatened the very idea of bargain-based contract law. First, it contradicted fundamental contract doctrine. Second, it appeared to have no doctrinal moorings of its own and so threatened to become a loose canon in the common law.

What is less obvious perhaps is that the American third-party beneficiary rule really did take contract law into the third dimension. The family tie device might have done the same, had Father been alive. But he wasn't. The agency idea has the same potential, in the context of a real agency relationship because that, too, is contractual. We might be asking whether the agency agreement between the plaintiff and the promisee gave the latter actual, or merely apparent authority to do what he did. Or whether the agent is personally liable and, if so, whether the principal's recovery from the promisor extinguishes the agent's liability. We would be asking, in short, how three "live" sides of the triangle, possibly three executory contracts, interact with one another. Instead, the courts used the family tie, implied agency and constructive trust ideas to permit the plaintiff to enforce a good old fashioned, two-dimensional contract. The device employed was no more than an access ramp; it did not introduce another "live" contractual relationship into the picture, as the third-party beneficiary rule was to do.

How does the American story help us to decide whether those common law jurisdictions which do not have a general rule favouring third-party enforcement really need one? It helps if it tells us whether those who do have it, need it. If we conclude that in the United States, the rule is more trouble than it is worth, that would be of value. Likewise, if its true value lies in some sorts of cases, but not in others that, too, would be useful. I have tried to set the stage for our taking a quick look at all U.S. cases, state and federal, decided between January 1st and June 30th of this year, in which a third-party claim was made. It is those cases, along with this background, which more directly answer the question whether such a rule is necessary. I consider those in Part V below, and I will answer Kincaid's second question more directly thereafter.

## 3. Can a Fuzzy Set of Reasons Constitute a Coherent Concoction? And Does It Matter?

Kincaid raises the following question about the kind of reasoning which he believes inherent in a general recognition of third-party contract rights: Will it do? He contrasts what he calls the "fuzzy set of reasons" given in justification of such a rule, with the "coherent" reasoning which he says is characteristic of bargain based contract law. Because Stephen Smith's positions[59] strike me as very similar to Kincaid's, I shall address those here as well.

Kincaid's first and clearest premise is that traditional contract law rests on coherent reasoning or, if you will, logic. If we mean bargain-based Contract, I agree entirely. And I would observe that the simpler the model, the more coherent (or logical) the reasoning. The more courts refuse to consider any factors that fall outside the narrow confines created by this set of rules, the more coherent (or logical) their stated reasons will be. In this scheme of things, even reasonableness is a "fuzzy" idea.[60] And equity becomes a big ball of fluff.[61]

Bargain based contract law is perfectly suited to just one, increasingly rare type of transaction: the true bargain. Were we to search the American cases, state and federal, and identify those involving no law at all other than bargain based contract law, my guess is that apart from employment contract litigation, they would fall mainly into two groups. In one we would find the Exxons of the world suing the Unilevers; in the other, we would find Mr. Jones selling his old lawn mower to Mr. Smith. In both situations, the law of the nineteenth century face-to-face marketplace is entirely suited to the task at hand. Yet even the Exxons and the Unilevers are subject to the Statute of Frauds, and to restrictions on liquidated damages, whether they like it or not, and even Mr. Jones has to be careful about non-disclosure of material facts.

When we venture into the modern retail marketplace, however, we are at once bombarded and hemmed in by expressions of concern about the public interest, in the form of warranties implied by law ("merchantable quality" being a suitably fuzzy idea), limits placed on exclusion and limitation clauses, judicial suspicion of form contracts in general and "contracts of adhesion" in particular,[62] and so on. Our freedom to bargain has been all but extinguished by courts and legislatures acting, time and again, to curtail or prevent the myriad abuses being visited on the weaker contracting parties, notably consumers. Because the instrument of these abuses was Contract, Contract was changed. The general recognition of third-party contract rights was one part of that change.

We will consider the general nature of that change presently. It is the fuzziness of reasoning allegedly inherent in it with which we are concerned

---

59 Smith, "Contracts for the Benefit of Third Parties: in Defence of the Third-Party Rule" (1997) 17 Oxford J. Leg. Stud. 643.

60 Some years ago, a student asked a colleague of mine, during class, how courts decide what is reasonable. My colleague replied: "The same way you and I do."

61 Ermine with purple highlights, I assume.

62 See: Kessler, "Contracts of Adhesion - Some Thoughts about Freedom of Contract" 43 Colum. L. Rev. 629 (1943).

at the moment. What, precisely, do Peter Kincaid and Stephen Smith contend is missing? What exactly do they mean by "rigorous defensible reasoning from principles to rules"[63] or "a third party's right is some sort of *sui generis* right" unsupportable by any principle "otherwise recognised in the law"?[64]

While neither attempting nor pretending to do justice to either author's argument, my singularly simplified synopsis is this. The bedrock of Smith's analysis, with which he touches base in several places in his article,[65] is expressed in several ways. The rule barring third-party enforcement "is a fundamental feature of contract law".[66] The reason why "the communication must be addressed to (and received by) the person to whom the obligation is undertaken" is that this "is a general feature of voluntary obligations".[67] "[T]he reason that C ... should not be able to enforce [the promisor's] promise is the simple but profound fact that [the promisor] did not make a promise to C."[68] Simple, yes. Fact, yes. Reason?? The reason why "the promisee alone is the person to whom the promissory duty is owed" is that: "This is what it means to be a promisee...".[69]

This is the law on which I was raised, at the dinner table[70] and as an undergraduate,[71] and it is the law which I later dispensed to students in a form amenable to their writing it down, memorising it, and at exam time writing it down again, without looking at their notes.[72] The object was for them to tell me what I had told them. In class, questions were neither encouraged nor often asked. If anyone dared ask "Why?" the answer was always a variation of "it is so because it is so". Only the promisee can enforce because "this is what it means to be a promisee". I am not holding Smith responsible for the state of English legal education. I am simply saying that I find no reasons in his reasoning, save one or two perfectly round ones.

Kincaid demands that the plaintiff be able to demonstrate "according to a defined criterion of justice", how "a principle of law establishes a relationship between the [plaintiff and defendant]" such as to justify the

63 Kincaid, (1997) 12 J. of Contract Law 47, at 61.
64 Smith, (1997) 17 Oxford J. Leg. Stud. 643, at 660.
65 Smith, (1997) 17 Oxford J. Leg. Stud. 643.
66 Id. at 643.
67 Id. at 645.
68 Id. at 645.
69 Id. at 646.
70 My father, Montague Waters Q.C., was a practising barrister in London for forty years.
71 B.A. (Hons) Keele, 1972.
72 I taught as a Visiting Lecturer at the University of Bristol, Faculty of Law, 1990-91.

promisor's responsibility to the defendant.[73] "According to the bargain theory, privity and consideration provide the reasons",[74] whereas a rule permitting third-party enforcement "does not fit the pattern of justification".[75] Which is to say, *that* pattern of justification. No, says, Kincaid, there is *no* pattern of justification. There is instead "a mixture of pragmatism and justice" and "justice becomes an impressionistic thing".[76] By contrast, "the coherent view of classical law is that contract is bargain".[77] Well, yes. Which is only to say that the so-called classical theory of contract is the bargain theory.

Kincaid's first requirement is "a defined criterion of justice". Where do we find this defined criterion in bargain based contract law? "Privity" and "consideration" are not self evidently criteria of justice, though they may provide justification, in Kincaid's sense, which is also perfectly round. (The bargain theory requires privity and consideration; therefore, the presence of privity and consideration justifies placing responsibility on the promisor under the bargain theory.) But what of the "defined criterion of justice"? Are we searching for something like "fair" or "reasonable" or even "just"? Or is the problem that these are criteria which dictionaries can define, but lawyers cannot?

Here is where Kincaid finds the requisite criteria in contract: The defendant's conduct has affected the plaintiff *and* the "defendant promisor in a bargain has induced the plaintiff promisee to trust him and raised the promisee's expectations" by his promise *and* "the plaintiff promisee has given something up" in exchange for that promise.[78] This is what he distils into "privity and consideration provide the reasons".

Let us change one or two of Kincaid's words, and see what happens. Defendant's conduct has affected the plaintiff (for example, he failed to pay the plaintiff $300, which he had promised to do) *and* "defendant promisor has induced the plaintiff to trust him and has raised [his] expectations as well as those of the promisee" *and* "the promisee has given something up" in exchange for that promise. Do these three factors, taken together, constitute any less "a defined criterion of justice" than Kincaid's? I think the answer is only if conforming to the traditional idea of bargain based contract is somehow more just, or better defined, than law which breaks free of those anachronistic bonds while retaining the same basic notions of justice.

---

73 Kincaid, (1997) 12 J. of Contract Law 47, at 58.
74 Id.
75 Id.
76 Id. at 62
77 Id. at 56.
78 Id. at 58.

There is nothing "fuzzier" about the reasoning in favour of third-party contract rights than the reasoning we find all over the legal map, and always have. If we employ a formulation such as "if the term purports to confer a benefit on him",[79] it will likely function like an electrostatic air cleaner, collecting fluff from all directions and becoming, in time, covered in the stuff.[80] To get to the statutory language, you will have no choice but to wade through numerous layers of fluff. If instead, the statute requires an express term in the contract,[81] that particular source of fuzziness – not only with respect to the statutory language but, more important to Kincaid, with respect to a justifying relationship – is eliminated, or strictly limited.

For example, I have no difficulty explaining why it would have been unfair, or unjust, to let Fox keep the three hundred dollars, and perfectly just to permit Lawrence (in whose favour there was an express term in the oral contract) to make Fox pay him. If we look at the seminal American case, we need not look at it only from the perspective of bargain based contract. If we do that, as Kincaid has shown, it is impossible to justify the result. Although it was assumed for years that the third-party beneficiary rule in the States was either the offspring of a single mother, or an immaculate misconception, we now know who the father was. Why not ask the same questions from *his* side of the family instead? That side of the family, the quasi-contractual forms of *indebitatus assumpsit*, were all founded on a "promise implied by law for the sake of the remedy". After *Slade's Case*,[82] the assumpsit had to be pleaded, but not proved. "The law" would take care of that. The action for money had and received was a specific form of quasi-contractual recovery. Whatever else it was, it was not an action on the promise.

We know what happened after that. The benefit of the promise to pay money, rather than the money itself, was what Lawrence was entitled to claim. Much later, this rule was generalised to embrace all "intended beneficiaries" of other parties' contracts. Only if we proceed from the non-contractual side of the family does this all make coherent, principled, sense. But not if we persist in calling it a contract right.[83]

---

79 Contracts (Rights of Third Parties) Act 1999, Section 1(1)(b).

80 See generally Gilmore, "On Statutory Obsolescence" 39 U. Colo. L. Rev. 461 (1967).

81 California's statute, for example, applies only to contracts "made expressly for the benefit of a third person". Cal. Civil Code §1559. The same limitations pertains in Florida and Illinois, among other jurisdictions.

82 (1595) 4 Co. Rep. 91a, 76 Eng. Rep. 1072; (1601) 4 Co. Rep. 92b, 76 Eng. Rep. 1074.

83 "[F]rom *Slade's Case* until this good day there has been more or less confusion in the minds of legal thinkers between the conceptions of contractual duty imposed by law [quasi-contract] and the conception of the obligation of promise. ... Men have talked about the implied promise, which is nominally the foundation of the action of indebitatus assumpsit, until they have actually come to think that the same conception of

Looked at that way – and there are other reasons to look at it that way – we may conclude that these third-party rights, created by beneficial contracts, are no more puzzling, fuzzy, or incoherent, no more devoid of justificatory nexuses, or rational explanation, than any other form of restitution. And if we then take note of happenings elsewhere in the law, we see at once that the idea of intangible property rights, once unheard of, is all the rage. The law dealing with information technology is only the most visible manifestation of this. In American law, for example, intangible rights of precisely the kind later claimed as third-party beneficiary rights, have long been protected as property.[84]

The mechanism is that of an action for money had and received for and to the use of the plaintiff, *which in justice and equity* (indefinable criteria of justice?) defendant ought to hand over. What has changed is the nature of the right being secured, not the mechanism employed. The plaintiff in an action for money hand and received, like the plaintiff claiming corn, using another common count, was laying claim to property which belonged to him. So long as the defendant was in effect a trustee, that was that.

If we agree, then, that the third-party beneficiary's right is not in any useful sense a contract right, we can also agree, I think, that the fuzziness of which Kincaid and Smith complain is a product of that erroneous classification. Whether it makes good sense to classify this as a property right in common law countries other than the United States, countries where neither the history of the rule nor its established use, serves to reinforce that idea, is a question I address in the conclusion of this essay.

## 4. Public and Private

Unlike, say, "contract" and "tort," which may be thought of as boxes, "private" and "public", are more usefully thought about as ends of a

---

liability is here presented to view as in the ordinary engagement by actual promise. ... [T]he obligation on which [a] stranger is permitted to sue is not an assumptual obligation created by contract, but is an obligation in the nature of an assumpsit created by law on the facts of the case." T. Street, *Foundations of Legal Liability* (1906 & photo. reprint 1980), 65, 161. Street also traces the privity requirement in contract not to bargain, but to the need, originally, to prove a deceitful promise. See id. at 152-56. Other historians agree. See, e.g., A. Simpson, *A History of the Common Law of Contract* (1975), 475-85.

84 After the publication of Charles Reich's celebrated article "The New Property" 73 Yale L. J. 733 (1964), the idea of constitutionally protected intangible property rights, created by government programmes, has become woven into the fabric of American constitutional law, "the new property" being now a term of art.

continuum. Some transactions, such as a contract made without any constraint imposed by the legislature or the courts, are for present purposes private. Others, like the dozens of cases in which third-party beneficiaries, often suing in class actions, seek their intended benefits under a statutory scheme, are for our purposes at the "public" end of the continuum. And it hardly needs saying that there are untold numbers of cases which lie somewhere in between.

Kincaid's question, as I understand it, focuses on the intrinsic altruism of a rule permitting a non-party to enforce a contract, compared with the more nearly atomistic nature of bargain based contract law. I have taken the liberty of reformulating his question thus: To what extent does a third-party beneficiary rule's intrinsic altruism create the potential for use in more or less public situations, where public policy, or public laws, outweigh the private nature of contract? I will also address the narrower theoretical question of the less-than-private nature of this private law rule.

The American experience was that this potential was not realised (arguably, could not have been realised) until the "intended beneficiary" displaced the "creditor" and "donee" beneficiaries.[85] Even then, the defining forces were more political than legal. Soon after Ronald Reagan became President in 1981, he appointed a number of people unsympathetic to a whole range of welfare and civil rights programmes to head the very agencies charged with administering them.[86] In the years that followed, agencies which were generally unsupportive of their own stated missions, specifically failed to enforce the terms of various funding contracts by which the recipients of federal funds had agreed to abide by limits and prohibitions laid down by the enabling statute, or by regulations promulgated thereunder. Those contracts were intended to benefit the "intended beneficiaries" of the statutory scheme, as they were called long before the third-party beneficiary appeared on this particular scene. Although there was sometimes room for argument about whether the parties to the funding contract intended to create an enforceable right in the intended beneficiaries of the public programme, there was no room for arguing that the pertinent terms of the contract, or even the contract itself, were not intended to benefit the plaintiffs. They had no other purpose. These contracts were simply conduits by which the benefits of the public programme were distributed.

For some years before the Reagan administration took office, the

[85] See text accompanying n.31, supra.

[86] One of many examples was Ronald Reagan's appointment of Clarence Thomas to head of the Office of Equal Opportunity. Many of Justice Thomas's subsequent judicial opinions, from the bench of the Supreme Court, have made plain his abiding hostility to precisely the kinds of programmes which that office is charged with administering.

Supreme Court of the United States had been closing the door on so-called implied private rights of action.[87] This, together with the inertia afflicting various federal agencies, created pressure to find another legal route by which intended beneficiaries could secure their intended benefits.

To describe these cases as "private law" or "contract" is to let the tail wag the dog. In most instances, the statute both mandates and informs the funding contract. The contract is a conduit in the statutory scheme. Yet it is precisely the private-ness of the action brought "on the contract" by the third-party beneficiary which gives him standing to sue, there being no separate question about "a private right of action" when the action is, at least formally, a contract action.

## 5. The Nature of Contract

### *Does the Recognition of Third-Party Beneficiary Rights Change "The Nature of Contract"?*

If we insist on squeezing third-party rights into the rather battered old box labelled "Contract", the box will bulge where it didn't bulge before, and more than a few splits will appear in the cardboard. Triangles, after all, have sharp corners. But if we find a better box, ideally one made to fit, and we put third-party rights there, then the box marked "Contract" need not be distended. That much is easy because it leaves out of account the rather crucial question of *why* we classify. To what end do we put these things in boxes?

Suppose that in a world of gloves, someone suddenly invents the mitten. Whether that development changes the nature of gloves depends first on what we call this invention.[88] If we decide that the mitten really is a glove, that fitting up to the wrist and protecting the hand are elements of *gantitude* which together outweigh the fact that the fingers are missing,

---

87 In the years immediately preceding this change of heart on the Court, "implied private rights of action" were commonly upheld. The idea was that the relationship between the presumed legislative intent behind the statute, and the plaintiff's claim, was enough for the court to find an implied private right of action. (This resembles the English idea of a breach of statutory duty.) Once the Supreme Court had changed its view, nothing less than an express private right of action in the statute itself would do. It was this change, together with the studied indifference of the federal government, which created the pressure to find an alternative legal avenue. The funding contracts combined with the third-party beneficiary rule provide just that.

88 Chaucer called it a *mytayne*. In Old French, as in modern, a mitten is *une mitaine*. The etymology of those words suggests a glove cut short, a fingerless glove rather than a closed mitten. So much for etymology. See: *The Oxford Dictionary of English Etymology* (1976) at 582.

then we may need sub-categories, such as Digital Gloves and Non-Digital Gloves. But we need to think about *why* we are classifying. Why exactly is a mitten not a glove at all, but "a glove-like covering for the hand with a separate division for the thumb only"?[89] Is it so that retailers can put them on separately marked shelves? Or the manufacturers in different boxes? Or is it so that we can make distinctions and, thus, know what we are talking about?

We lawyers need to know what we are talking about, particularly when there is "no there there", when the "what" is a figment of the legal imagination, such as "a promise implied by law". We need to make distinctions. Glove merchants have gloves to sell. We have nothing but words. But perhaps we do not have enough words, or the right ones. "Contract" is one word we have,[90] but the box so labelled now houses all sorts of bits and pieces. Those bits and pieces have no names, so that they not only become part of contract, ineluctably they change its nature. It is as though mittens were gloves.

So what does it mean, in American law, to speak of a "third-party beneficiary's right" to enforce a contract? Is it now, or was it ever, something obviously different from a traditional contract right? The American Law Institute put it the "Contracts" box, as had Williston and Corbin, the two dominant American contract scholars of their times. So a contract right it is. But what is it *really*? Was it born in a box? If so, which one? Or was it found on the floor, like a single mitten, picked up by someone who knew not what it was, who then tossed it in with the gloves?

It *was* found on the floor. Really. And it was found between the contract box and a stack of thin files labelled "Common Counts".[91] It did have its own label, but the man who picked it up didn't recognise "a civil cause"[92] as belonging in one box or another. None of the thin files would accommodate it, so the contract box is where it went. And stayed.

But what is it *really*? This is law, common law, and *"What is it really?"* can in a limited sense be determined by reference to its history, exactly as the meaning of a word can be determined, in a limited sense, by reference to its etymology. The history of a common law rule tells us what

89 Id.

90 CON- + trahere, to draw, either on paper, or as in drawing a plough. The root L. tractus (f) is also the root of traction. Thus, a tract is created by traction, pulling or drawing, and a tract of land can mean an "area contained by lines drawn" or by lines on the land itself, made by pulling a plough. Thus a contract is made together, that is, by more than one person, typically by two. Thus, the contract rights belong to the parties to it, and we need a different work for an outsider laying claim to the benefits of it. If we call them adtract rights, would that solve the problem?

91 See note 37, supra.

92 Id.

the rule is made of, whence it came; but just as a word can acquire a meaning at odds with its dictionary definition,[93] so too can legal rules.

The more direct value of the American story comes from looking at the third-party beneficiary rule today. How is it used in fact? Is it mainly a private law rule, used in commerce, like contract? Or is it more important for some unrelated application altogether, in a context we would not think of as "commercial"? The American third-party beneficiary rule does now embrace a vast range of causes, some private, some public, some hybrid, some contract, some not. If we now ask how the inclusion of third-party rights affected the nature of contract, the answer will depend not only on whether we push third-party rights into the box marked "contract," but also on how seriously we take them. One way to get some sense of how seriously the courts take the third-party beneficiary rule in the United States, is to look at the cases.

A "Lexis" search for all appellate cases, state and federal, decided between January 1 and June 30, 2000 which include the term "third-party beneficiary" or "third-party beneficiaries" found two hundred and thirty-seven cases. Because I did not read the full reports, but relied instead on "KWIC", I eliminated every case in which the fate of the third-party claim was unclear, and I excluded all cases in which the term was used in *dicta* or was otherwise not germane to the issue before the court. I erred heavily on the side of exclusion. This very rough cut brought the number of cases down to one hundred and thirty-one.

Of these 131 cases, 84 were hard-core commercial, 19 were claims against insurers, 9 involved arbitration clauses, and 4 alleged medical or legal malpractice. I classified the remaining 15 cases as miscellaneous non-commercial.[94] I confess surprise. My prejudice was that the third-

---

93 According to *The New York Times* (the "newspaper of record" in the U.S.) for example, "$3-a-car valet parking" at the movies is a nicety, as are "more horsepower, a better suspension [and] a glass rear window", and of course "fireplaces and two-car...garages". *The New York Times* 29/12/97 D1 col 3; 27/12/98 Section 12 , p.1 col 1; 3/5/98 Section 11, p.1 col 4. Has the meaning of nicety now changed? Or are three different writers for *The New York Times* not entirely literate? The same question may be asked about usage. My phone bill tells me my long-distance usage in minutes, my gas bill in BTUs, and my electricity bill in kilowatt hours. And Microsoft is currently offering "3 months free usage" of something they sell. Has the meaning of usage now changed, or are all these folk simply wrong? More important, what do I say if I really mean nicety? Or has misusage or even misutilisation done it in? Likewise usage. Or should I give up, grab a felt-tip pen and change the name of my Fowler to *Fowler on the Use of English*?

94 These include a claim by a sperm donor that he was a third-party beneficiary of the term of the contract between Cryobank and the recipient binding them not to disclose his identity: *Johnson v. Superior Court of Los Angeles* 80 Cal. App. 4th 1050, 95 Cal. Rptr. 2d 864 (May 18, 2000); a claim by an optician that he was a third-party beneficiary of a large employer's insurance contract, and that therefore his having been excluded from

party beneficiary rule makes no more commercial sense today than it did in 1859, and that therefore most of the cases would involve welfare programs, family arrangements, and other non commercial activities. In the event, of one hundred and thirty-one cases, more than 64% are commercial, and if we treat the insurance and arbitration cases as commercial as well, more than 85% of the cases fit that description.

Why was my guess about the cases so far off the mark? Have commercial entities taken to suing their debtors' debtors as never before? Has the third-party beneficiary rule in fact become commercially useful? Let us take a closer look. Of the 84 cases I classified as hard-core commercial, the third-party beneficiary claim succeeded as a matter of law in 6 of them (7%), and failed in 78 (93%). Of the 19 insurance cases, the numbers are 4 (21%) and 15 (79%) respectively. The 9 arbitration cases include 2 in which the claim failed and 7 in which it succeeded because the express language of the contract made the plaintiff a third-party beneficiary.

My guess was that the third-party rule would be seen to be useless in strictly commercial settings. I was wrong. It has proved worse than useless. Lawyers frequently add a third-party beneficiary claim, or base their cases on that rule, but hardly ever does it succeed. The true beneficiaries may be the lawyers. Although the rule fared better in the insurance cases, we should bear in mind that insurance contracts are very often for the benefit of a non-party. To anyone familiar with American law, the truly surprising thing about the *Trident* case is that it was decided as late as 1988. As for the arbitration cases, it appears well settled that a third-party beneficiary of a contract containing an arbitration clause is bound by that clause.[95] The nine cases I found each involved such a scheme.

What do we gain, then, by looking at these cases, even superficially? Bearing in mind, as always, that this is common law in the United States, and that we are seeking guidance in shaping a statutory rule, we can at least say that nature works in wondrous ways. In its "natural" form, contract law appears to have its own defences, its own immune system if you will, and has effectively expelled this foreign body from that part of its domain which deals with strictly private grievances: bargain-based contract.[96] This

---

the insurer's "preferred provider" network was an actionable breach: *Yuchnitz v. PCA Health Plan of Texas, Inc.* 2000 Tex. App. LEXIS 65 (January 1, 2000); and several legal and medical malpractice claims.

95 See, e.g., *Dietz v. Northeast Illinois Regional Commuter R.R. Corp.* 2000 U.S. Dist. LEXIS 6933 (May 12, 2000).

96 I realise of course that these conclusions are based on an extremely impressionistic, superficial review of more than two hundred cases. Even so, the numbers are impressive.

is not to understate its value elsewhere. And we ought not to overlook the possibility that many commercial lawyers in the United States have made good use of the rule in drafting contracts which never see the light of litigation. Their use in connection with arbitration clauses[97] appears to have become standard, although that use binds the beneficiary to the arbitration requirement which is, to say the least, a little off centre.[98]

The problem is that statutes are different. It is much more difficult for courts to expel a foreign body from the law when it is encased in a statute. What is more, once such a rule – or any other – is enacted, it really is so because it is so, and the search for justifying relationships, acceptable nexuses and coherent criteria becomes meaningless outside of the academy, and of limited meaning within. That said, we can do better. There is no cause to dismiss such a rule as "some sort of *sui generis* right".[99] There is cause to conclude, however, that it cannot be a contract right according to traditional contract theory, and that only by distending the category "contract" can it be accommodated by any contract theory.

It makes sense, then, to consider the matter from another perspective. Although the detailed history of the American rule enables us to understand *how* it came to be what it is, the real value of that story for our purposes lies in appreciating *what* it has become. What the third-party beneficiary rule has become in American law strongly suggests another, non-contractual explanation of the rule and, hence, a very different perspective on the matter.

We live in an age of intangibles. Money becomes "funds" when transferred electronically; music becomes "files", this essay "an attachment" which is not physically attached. I assume that the rudimentary legal idea of a trust satisfies the Kincaid-Smith criteria, so that if A gives money to B to be held in trust for C, and C is able to enforce the terms of the trust against B, neither Kincaid not Smith would complain of fuzzy thinking or inadequate justification. If we think trust thoughts, and use trust language, there is no problem. But the moment we think contract and say, accordingly, that C is enforcing the promise B made to A, all those problems arise.

## Conclusion

In the essay, I have attempted to address, albeit impressionistically, four

97 See note 51, supra.

98 I use that phrase because it binds the beneficiary rather than creating a right in him or her, which is highly unusual.

99 Smith, (1997) 17 Oxford J. Leg. Stud. 643, at 660.

questions raised by Peter Kincaid, in the light of the U.S. experience with a general rule permitting third-party enforcement of beneficial contracts. The first of these asks whether there is need for a general rule, given the existence of exceptions which cover most of the situations that matter.

My first answer, based on the American story, is that the exceptions, the cases based on "other rules",[100] do not cover all the cases that matter. Agency and trust would have had some stretching to do before they could swallow the benefits of public programmes. If, as I suspect, this use of a general third-party rule has no potential application in Australia for example, then at least we can conclude that Kincaid's instinct is right. Given its head, taken to its logical conclusion (fuzzy or not) a generalised third-party contract right can come to be more concerned with public than with private justice.[101] Although Kincaid's third question addresses that aspect of the problem directly, it is not to be ignored here, when we ask about the need for such a rule. But the more direct answer comes from the current cases, which suggest rather strongly that as a commercial law rule it is at least as much trouble as it is worth. So whence cometh the demand in Australia? Academics? Judges? Merchants? The English influence? Where, if at all, is there clamouring for a general rule? If there is a need for such a rule, follow the sound of the clamouring, and ask when you get there.

My first response to Kincaid's second question is that I do not share his premise that contract law is more coherent, more principled, less dependent on "a fuzzy mixture of reasons" than any general third-party rule could ever be. Only if we use a lens whose focus is fixed on bargain, with minimal depth of field, does all else seem fuzzy. If a catch-phrase like "the avoidance of unjust enrichment" can pass muster as a justification for making B pay money to C, why is it not enough to say that permitting C to enforce beneficial terms of the A-B contract is the fairest of the options available? Or, stated from the perspective of the other side of the American family, why is it not enough to say that C is entitled to claim the intended

---

[100] The argument in favour of using "other principles" instead of adopting a general rule was made by Professor Samuel Williston of Harvard Law School in Williston, "Contracts for the Benefit of a Third Person" 15 Harv. L. Rev. 767 (1902).

[101] We need not go as far afield as the cases involving public programmes to see this phenomenon. One of the earliest problems involving the third-party beneficiary rule arose out of a homeowner's claim against a water company, for allegedly breaching its contract with the township, by failing to keep adequate water pressure at a hydrant close to the homeowner's home. See: *H.R. Moch Co., Inc. v. Rensselaer Water Co.* 247 N.Y. 160, 159 N.E. 896 (1928). Section 313, Government Contracts, of the Restatement (Second) of Contracts reverses the usual rule by providing that members of the public have no rights as third-party beneficiaries in the absence of an express term saying otherwise.

intangible benefit of the promised performance? Why are these not justification enough?

Kincaid's third question involves the shift in focus from purely private interests to partly public concerns which is, I agree, part and parcel of a general third-party right. The modern American story depicts a very "public law" application of the general rule, Kincaid's fears writ large, perhaps. But writ small, as an abstract concern about the theoretically private nature of contract, it interests me only insofar as it suggests that bargain based contract, which had been largely dead in the U.S. for some time before Gilmore wrote his celebrated chronicle of its demise, is still alive and well in other parts of the common law world.[102]

My answer to the fourth and final question largely overlaps with my response to the third. If we are asking about the impact of a general third-party rule upon bargain based contract law, which was its impact on American contract law *circa* 1920, Grant Gilmore has answered thus:

> The eventual triumph of the third-party beneficiary idea may be looked on as still another instance of the progressive liberalisation or erosion of the rigid rules of the late nineteenth century theory of contractual obligation....In our own century we have witnessed what it does not seem too fanciful to describe as a socialisation of our theory of contract. The progressive expansion of the range of non-parties allowed to sue as contract beneficiaries as well as of the situations in which they have been allowed to sue is one of the entries to be made in this ledger.[103]

But what if, as I have suggested, we look at the beneficiary's right as other than a contract right. When I suggest that we think about the third-party beneficiary's right as more property than promise – that is, more akin to a claim to property than to an action on the promise – I am neither playing with words, nor straining to come up with a new and catchy way of looking at the problem.

We lawyers work with but a few, crude categories. Once we accept that a particular right does exist, or should be made to exist by statute, it is simply a question of which box we put it in. The American story is very helpful to anyone pondering that question anew, because it demonstrates two important, and separate, characteristics of the third-party beneficiary's right, at least as it has developed in the U.S. First, it shows that this is not a contract right in any meaningful sense of that term. Second, it suggests, at least, that there may be better ways of understanding the phenomenon than

---

[102] See: Waters, Book Review, 36 Md. L. Rev. 270, 280-84 (1976) comparing the law of promissory estoppel in England and the U.S., and suggesting that bargain based contract was alive and well in English law.

[103] Kessler, Gilmore & Kronman, *Contracts: Cases & Materials* (2d. ed. 1985), at 1332.

as part of contract law. Although the idea of the beneficiary's right as a kind of property right is powerfully reinforced in American law both by the history of the rule itself, and by its recent role in securing "new property" rights, the idea merits consideration by itself.

Let us agree to begin with that the contract in these cases is at least a "but for" cause, a necessary element of the plaintiff's case, just as it is in malpractice cases. In those cases, but for the contract between doctor and patient, for example, the doctor would owe her no duty of care. But it is the breach of that duty of care which is the gravamen of the plaintiff's cause, and the remedy sought is rarely the expectation interest, the benefit of the bargain, as in contract damages. It would be both inadequate and inaccurate to call the patient's right a contract right. Similarly, in many of the most important American cases, the intangible benefit being claimed by the third-party beneficiary is not a contract right, and the remedy sought is rarely a contract remedy. But the contract provides the legal link; it makes the defendant liable directly to the beneficiary. Whether it is useful to think about the beneficiary's right as a property right in other common law countries may be best assessed by trying it on, if you will.

The scene in the fitting room might be this: "Well, of course it feels uncomfortable at first, sir. But not only is it the latest fashion, it seems to be the way of the future. We are not used to wrapping our minds around any single, definite idea of intangible property, sir, and it takes a little while for those muscles to get used to it. At the same time, other muscles are trained to think of this as an action on the promise, sir, and many customers find that their initial discomfort decreases as those muscles are used less. There's no gain without pain, sir, but I think you will enjoy the greater freedom of movement, and your posture will improve."

The case for viewing the contract beneficiary's right as a species of intangible property may be made without reference to the American saga. The nature of property has in fact changed, perhaps more drastically and without doubt more rapidly, than ever before. Less than twenty years ago, the term "intangible property" had a very limited, specific legal meaning. Copyright, patents, licences, easements, and rights of way just about covered it. The term "intellectual property" would have drawn blank stares. Today, if you don't know what "I.P." means, you are dangerously out of touch. Knowledge or information as property is only one part of the picture. The computer age has given us the ability to move things, and thereby to acquire them, without any physical taking, or indeed any physical thing.[104] Almost every day, there is a news story, or a court case,

---

104 In the early days of computers, my father defended a man who had made himself a small present when leaving the employ of a certain bank in one of the oil-producing gulf states by transferring, electronically, a rather handsome sum of money to his own account in

dealing with allegedly unauthorised downloading of music on the internet,[105] or the "stealing" of e-mail,[106] and myriad other forms of intangible things of value on which the law is having difficulty keeping tabs.

It would be a mistake to think that this incorporealisation of property is limited to areas of the law directly affected by technological advance. In the U.S., as we have seen, the development of the intangible property idea in the constitutional context owes nothing to technology. And in England, it is more than thirty years since Parliament first recognised that the tangibility requirement in the law of stealing was anachronistic, by making the obtaining of "a pecuniary advantage" a species of theft and defining "property" capable of being stolen to include "intangible property" for the first time.[107] In federal criminal law in the U.S. the range of property which may properly be the object of a "scheme or artifice to defraud" under the mail fraud statute came to include "the right to honest government", since replaced, by statute, by the broader, undefined "right to honest services".[108]

In short, the idea that property is almost always tangible is as limited and as anachronistic as the idea that without asportation – the picking up and carrying away of the property – there can be no stealing. Of course we can still steal the old fashioned way, and of course tangible property even yet abounds. But intangible property is becoming increasingly familiar, if not visible, increasingly important, if not tangible.

Now let us return, for the last time, to the matter of the third-party

---

London. Once in London, he withdrew the money and was promptly arrested. The threshold question was jurisdictional: Where did the unlawful taking occur?

105 For example, under the heading "Web Music Battle Heats Up", *The New York Times* reported on August 22, 2000 at page C6: "MP3Board.com, a Web site that provides links to and searching of music sites, asked a federal court in New York to declare that Gnutella, a software used to exchange music files via the Web, does not violate copyright law. The request escalates the legal battle between the site and the recording industry."

106 A related non-crime was the focus of an announcement by prosecutors in the Philippines, on August 21, 2000, that they were unable to bring charges against the man accused of letting loose the "I love you" e-mail virus in May, 2000, causing millions of dollars in losses, because they had no law that would fit. *New York Times* 22/8/2000 C6, col. 4.

107 Theft Act 1968, Section 16(2)(a): "Obtaining a Pecuniary Advantage by Deception". *See*: Waters, "The Deception of Section 16" (1972) Crim. L. Rev 400.

108 The idea that the "right to honest government" could be the object of "a scheme or artifice to defraud" under the federal mail and wire fraud statutes was judge-made law endorsed by all seven federal appellate courts which addressed the question. The Supreme Court threw it out in *United States v. McNally* 483 U.S. 350 (1987), and Congress responded by substituting the "right to honest services" by adding §1346 to the mail fraud statute.

beneficiary. Assume that the right of a third-party beneficiary to enforce the beneficial terms of a contract is to be created by statute. Assume also that no one thinks it appropriate, or helpful, to categorise this as a contract right, but that everyone agrees that the baby must be given a name. There is a limited range of names available, and we know what they are. So what shall we call it?

I suggested earlier that it might prove useful to think trust rather than thinking contract. If we are now better able to wrap our minds around the idea of intangible property than we were, and if we can think trust rather than contract, we may sensibly speak of the beneficiary's right, although created by contract, as a right to the benefit so created rather than as a right to enforce the contract. A little awkward perhaps, but less so than calling it a contract right. Not a perfect fit, but arguably the best available, if the object of the exercise is to determine the nature of this legal right and to classify it accordingly. By so doing, I believe we can both assuage the Kincaid-Smith concerns, and demonstrate that they stem not from the fact of the third-party beneficiary's proposed right but, rather, from its having been classified as a contract right.

In this essay, I have not attempted to answer the ultimate question, which is whether it would be a good thing, or a bad thing, for Australia, New Zealand and other common law countries to adopt a rule in favour of third-party beneficiary rights. My claim for this essay is more modest by far. It is that the American experience with its own third-party beneficiary rule offers many valuable insights, much food for thought, which may prove helpful with that ultimate question.

A more general lesson to be learned from observing American common law "up close" is that we must always take care when comparing it with, say, English law. There are many small, and often hidden differences between the systems, spawning a host of unarticulated assumptions. Indeed, in many ways, we may be two people divided by a common law.[109*]

---

109 For a different perspective, see: Mooney, "Hands Across the Water: The Continuing Convergence of American and Australian Contract Law" (2000) 23 UNSW Law Journal 1.

* I thank the University of Oregon School of Law for its generous support in connection with this essay.

# Appendix: Contracts (Rights of Third Parties) Act 1999

[11th November 1999]

## Section 1. Right of Third Party to Enforce Contractual Term

(1) Subject to the provisions of this Act, a person who is not a party to a contract (a "third party") may in his own right enforce a term of the contract if-

(a) the contract expressly provides that he may, or

(b) subject to subsection (2), the term purports to confer a benefit on him.

(2) Subsection (1)(b) does not apply if on a proper construction of the contract it appears that the parties did not intend the term to be enforceable by the third party.

(3) The third party must be expressly identified in the contract by name, as a member of a class or as answering a particular description but need not be in existence when the contract is entered into.

(4) This section does not confer a right on a third party to enforce a term of a contract otherwise than subject to and in accordance with any other relevant terms of the contract.

(5) For the purpose of exercising his right to enforce a term of the contract, there shall be available to the third party any remedy that would have been available to him in an action for breach of contract if he had been a party to the contract (and the rules relating to damages, injunctions, specific performance and other relief shall apply accordingly).

(6) Where a term of a contract excludes or limits liability in relation to any matter references in this Act to the third party enforcing the term shall be construed as references to his availing himself of the exclusion or limitation.

(7) In this Act, in relation to a term of a contract which is enforceable by a third party-

"the promisor" means the party to the contract against whom the term is enforceable by the third party, and

"the promisee" means the party to the contract by whom the term is enforceable against the promisor.

## Section 2. Variation and Rescission of Contract

(1) Subject to the provisions of this section, where a third party has a right under section 1 to enforce a term of the contract, the parties to the contract may not, by agreement, rescind the contract, or vary it in such a way as to extinguish or alter his entitlement under that right, without his consent if-
(a) the third party has communicated his assent to the term to the promisor,
(b) the promisor is aware that the third party has relied on the term, or
(c) the promisor can reasonably be expected to have foreseen that the third party would rely on the term and the third party has in fact relied on it.

(2) The assent referred to in subsection (1)(a)-
(a) may be by words or conduct, and
(b) if sent to the promisor by post or other means, shall not be regarded as communicated to the promisor until received by him.

(3) Subsection (1) is subject to any express term of the contract under which-
(a) the parties to the contract may by agreement rescind or vary the contract without the consent of the third party, or
(b) the consent of the third party is required in circumstances specified in the contract instead of those set out in subsection (1)(a) to (c).

(4) Where the consent of a third party is required under subsection (1) or (3), the court or arbitral tribunal may, on the application of the parties to the contract, dispense with his consent if satisfied-
(a) that his consent cannot be obtained because his whereabouts cannot reasonably be ascertained, or
(b) that he is mentally incapable of giving his consent.

(5) The court or arbitral tribunal may, on the application of the parties to a contract, dispense with any consent that may be required under subsection (1)(c) if satisfied that it cannot reasonably be ascertained whether or not the third party has in fact relied on the term.

(6) If the court or arbitral tribunal dispenses with a third party's consent, it may impose such conditions as it thinks fit, including a condition requiring the payment of compensation to the third party.

(7) The jurisdiction conferred on the court by subsections (4) to (6) is exercisable by both the High Court and a county court.

## Section 3. Defences etc. Available to Promisor

(1) Subsections (2) to (5) apply where, in reliance on section 1, proceedings for the enforcement of a term of a contract are brought by a third party.

(2) The promisor shall have available to him by way of defence or set-off any matter that-
(a) arises from or in connection with the contract and is relevant to the term, and
(b) would have been available to him by way of defence or set-off if the proceedings had been brought by the promisee.

(3) The promisor shall also have available to him by way of defence or set-off any matter if-
  (a) an express term of the contract provides for it to be available to him in proceedings brought by the third party, and
  (b) it would have been available to him by way of defence or set-off if the proceedings had been brought by the promisee.

(4) The promisor shall also have available to him-
  (a) by way of defence or set-off any matter, and
  (b) by way of counterclaim any matter not arising from the contract, that would have been available to him by way of defence or set-off or, as the case may be, by way of counterclaim against the third party if the third party had been a party to the contract.

(5) Subsections (2) and (4) are subject to any express term of the contract as to the matters that are not to be available to the promisor by way of defence, set-off or counterclaim.

(6) Where in any proceedings brought against him a third party seeks in reliance on section 1 to enforce a term of a contract (including, in particular, a term purporting to exclude or limit liability), he may not do so if he could not have done so (whether by reason of any particular circumstances relating to him or otherwise) had he been a party to the contract.

## Section 4. Enforcement of Contract by Promisee

Section 1 does not affect any right of the promisee to enforce any term of the contract.

## Section 5. Protection of Promisor from Double Liability

Where under section 1 a term of a contract is enforceable by a third party, and the promisee has recovered from the promisor a sum in respect of-
  (a) the third party's loss in respect of the term, or
  (b) the expense to the promisee of making good to the third party the default of the promisor,

then, in any proceedings brought in reliance on that section by the third party, the court or arbitral tribunal shall reduce any award to the third party to such extent as it thinks appropriate to take account of the sum recovered by the promisee.

## Section 6. Exceptions

(1) Section 1 confers no rights on a third party in the case of a contract on a bill of exchange, promissory note or other negotiable instrument.

(2) Section 1 confers no rights on a third party in the case of any contract binding on a company and its members under section 14 of the Companies Act 1985.

(3) Section 1 confers no right on a third party to enforce-
- (a) any term of a contract of employment against an employee,
- (b) any term of a worker's contract against a worker (including a home worker), or
- (c) any term of a relevant contract against an agency worker.

(4) In subsection (3)-
- (a) "contract of employment", "employee", "worker's contract", and "worker" have the meaning given by section 54 of the NationalMinimum Wage Act 1998,
- (b) "home worker" has the meaning given by section 35(2) of that Act,
- (c) "agency worker" has the same meaning as in section 34(1) of that Act, and
- (d) "relevant contract" means a contract entered into, in a case where section 34 of that Act applies, by the agency worker as respects work falling within subsection (1)(a) of that section.

(5) Section 1 confers no rights on a third party in the case of-
- (a) a contract for the carriage of goods by sea, or
- (b) a contract for the carriage of goods by rail or road, or for the carriage of cargo by air, which is subject to the rules of the appropriate international transport convention, except that a third party may in reliance on that section avail himself of an exclusion or limitation of liability in such a contract.

(6) In subsection (5) "contract for the carriage of goods by sea" means a contract of carriage-
- (a) contained in or evidenced by a bill of lading, sea waybill or a corresponding electronic transaction, or
- (b) under or for the purposes of which there is given an undertaking which is contained in a ship's delivery order or a corresponding electronic transaction.

(7) For the purposes of subsection (6)-
- (a) "bill of lading", "sea waybill" and "ship's delivery order" have the same meaning as in the Carriage of Goods by Sea Act 1992, and
- (b) a corresponding electronic transaction is a transaction within section 1(5) of that Act which corresponds to the issue, indorsement, delivery or transfer of a bill of lading, sea waybill or ship's delivery order.

(8) In subsection (5) "the appropriate international transport convention" means-
- (a) in relation to a contract for the carriage of goods by rail, the Convention which has the force of law in the United Kingdom under section 1 of the International Transport Conventions Act 1983,
- (b) in relation to a contract for the carriage of goods by road, the Convention which has the force of law in the United Kingdom under section 1 of the Carriage of Goods by Road Act 1965, and

(c) in relation to a contract for the carriage of cargo by air-
   (i) the Convention which has the force of law in the United Kingdom under section 1 of the Carriage by Air Act 1961, or
   (ii) the Convention which has the force of law under section 1 of the Carriage by Air (Supplementary Provisions) Act 1962, or
   (iii) either of the amended Conventions set out in Part B of Schedule 2 or 3 to the Carriage by Air Acts (Application of Provisions) Order 1967.

## Section 7. Supplementary Provisions Relating to Third Party

(1) Section 1 does not affect any right or remedy of a third party that exists or is available apart from this Act.
(2) Section 2(2) of the Unfair Contract Terms Act 1977 (restriction on exclusion etc. of liability for negligence) shall not apply where the negligence consists of the breach of an obligation arising from a term of a contract and the person seeking to enforce it is a third party acting in reliance on section 1.
(3) In sections 5 and 8 of the Limitation Act 1980 the references to an action founded on a simple contract and an action upon a specialty shall respectively include references to an action brought in reliance on section 1 relating to a simple contract and an action brought in reliance on that section relating to a specialty.
(4) A third party shall not, by virtue of section 1(5) or 3(4) or (6), be treated as a party to the contract for the purposes of any other Act (or any instrument made under any other Act).

## Section 8. Arbitration Provisions

(1) Where-
   (a) a right under section 1 to enforce a term ("the substantive term") is subject to a term providing for the submission of disputes to arbitration ("the arbitration agreement"), and
   (b) the arbitration agreement is an agreement in writing for the purposes of Part I of the Arbitration Act 1996, the third party shall be treated for the purposes of that Act as a party to the arbitration agreement as regards disputes between himself and the promisor relating to the enforcement of the substantive term by the third party.
(2) Where-
   (a) a third party has a right under section 1 to enforce a term providing for one or more descriptions of dispute between the third party and the promisor to be submitted to arbitration ("the arbitration agreement"),
   (b) the arbitration agreement is an agreement in writing for the purposes of Part I of the Arbitration Act 1996, and

(c) the third party does not fall to be treated under subsection (1) as a party to the arbitration agreement,

the third party shall, if he exercises the right, be treated for the purposes of that Act as a party to the arbitration agreement in relation to the matter with respect to which the right is exercised, and be treated as having been so immediately before the exercise of the right.

## Section 9. Northern Ireland

(1) In its application to Northern Ireland, this Act has effect with the modifications specified in subsections (2) and (3).

(2) In section 6(2), for "section 14 of the Companies Act 1985" there is substituted "Article 25 of the Companies (Northern Ireland) Order 1986".

(3) In section 7, for subsection (3) there is substituted-

"(3) In Articles 4(a) and 15 of the Limitation (Northern Ireland) Order 1989, the references to an action founded on a simple contract and an action upon an instrument under seal shall respectively include references to an action brought in reliance on section 1 relating to a simple contract and an action brought in reliance on that section relating to a contract under seal."

(4) In the Law Reform (Husband and Wife) (Northern Ireland) Act 1964, the following provisions are hereby repealed-

(a) section 5, and

(b) in section 6, in subsection (1)(a), the words "in the case of section 4" and "and in the case of section 5 the contracting party" and, in subsection (3), the words "or section 5".

## Section 10. Short Title, Commencement and Extent

(1) This Act may be cited as the Contracts (Rights of Third Parties) Act 1999.

(2) This Act comes into force on the day on which it is passed but, subject to subsection (3), does not apply in relation to a contract entered into before the end of the period of six months beginning with that day.

(3) The restriction in subsection (2) does not apply in relation to a contract which-

(a) is entered into on or after the day on which this Act is passed, and

(b) expressly provides for the application of this Act.

(4) This Act extends as follows-

(a) section 9 extends to Northern Ireland only;

(b) the remaining provisions extend to England and Wales and Northern Ireland only.

# Bibliography


Adams, J., and R. Brownsword, "Contract, Consideration and the Critical Path" (1990) 53 M.L.R. 536: 123

Adams, J., and R. Brownsword, "Privity and the Concept of a Network Contract" (1990) 10 Legal Studies 12: 127, 214

Adams, J., and R. Brownsword "More in Expectation than Hope: The Blackpool Airport Case" (1991) 54 M.L.R. 281: 123

Adams, J., and R. Brownsword, "Privity of Contract – That Pestilential Nuisance" (1993) 56 M.L.R. 722: 214, 299

Adams, J., and R. Brownsword, *Understanding Contract Law* 2nd edn. (London: Fontana Press, 1994): 109

Adams, J., and R. Brownsword, *Key Issues in Contract* (London: Butterworths, 1995): 109, 127

Adams, J., D. Beyleveld and R. Brownsword, "Privity of Contracts – The Benefits and Burdens of Law Reform" (1997) 60 M.L.R. 238: 111, 126

Andrews, N.H., "Reform of the Privity Rule in English Contract Law: The Law Commission's Report No. 242" [1997] C.L.J. 25: 61

Arymowicz, C. M., (Case Comment) (1982) 60 Can. Bar Rev. 467: 44

Atiyah, P.S., *Consideration in Contracts: A Fundamental Restatement*, Aust. Nat. Univ. Press, Canberra, 1971: 33

Atiyah, P.S., "Contracts, Promises and the Law of Obligations" (1978) 94 L.Q.R. 193: 49, 99

Atiyah, P.S., *The Rise and Fall of Freedom of Contract*, Clarendon Press, Oxford, 1979: 35, 92, 109, 152

Atiyah, P.S., *An Introduction to the Law of Contract* (3rd ed.), Oxford University Press, 1981: 45

Atiyah, P.S., *Promises, Morals, and the Law* (Oxford: Clarendon Press, 1981): 129

Atiyah, P.S., "Consideration: A Restatement" in *Essays on Contract* (Oxford: O.U.P. 1986): 118

Atiyah, P.S., *Essays on Contract* (Oxford: Clarendon Press, 1986): 67

Atiyah, P.S., "Contracts Promises and the Law of Obligations" in *Essays on Contract* (Oxford: O.U.P. 1986): 109

Atiyah, P.S., *Pragmatism and Theory in English Law* (London: Stevens, 1987): 105

Atiyah, P.S., *An Introduction to the Law of Contract*, 5th ed. (Oxford: O.U.P. 1995): 69, 109

Baker, J.H., "From Sanctity of Contract to Reasonable Expectation?" [1979] C.L.P. 17: 65, 101

Baker, J.H., "The Law Merchant and the Common Law before 1700" (1979) 38 Cambridge Law Journal 295: 207, 208

Baker, J.H., *An Introduction to English Legal History* (London 1979): 207

Baker, J.H., *The Legal Profession and the Common Law: Historical Essays* (London 1986): 207

Barker, K., "Are We Up To Expectations? Solicitors, Beneficiaries and the Tort-Contract Divide" (1994) 14 O.J.L.S. 137: 114

Battersby, Graham, "Exemption Clauses and Third Parties" (1975) 25 U.T. Law J. 371: 233

Battersby, Graham, "Exemption Clauses and Third Parties: Recent Decisions" (1978) 28 U.T. Law J. 75: 233

Beale, H., "Privity of Contract: Judicial and Legislative Reform" (1995) 9 J.C.L. 103: 61, 70, 74, 216, 301

Beatson, J., "Reforming the Law of Contracts for the Benefit of Third Parties: A Second Bite at the Cherry" (1992) 45 C.L.P. 1: 71, 104, 127, 147

Bennett, E. H., "Considerations Moving From Third Persons" (1895) 9 Harv. Law Rev. 31 41

Ben-Shahar, O., "The Tentative Case Against Flexibility in Commercial Law" (1999) 66 University of Chicago Law Review 781: 200, 227

Bernstein, L., "The Questionable Empirical Basis of Article 2's Incorporation Strategy: A Preliminary Study" (1999) 66 University of Chicago Law Review 710: 200

Beyleveld, D., and R. Brownsword, "Privity, Transitivity, and Rationality" (1991) 54 M.L.R. 48: 127

Birmingham, R. L., "Holmes on '*Peerless*': *Raffles v. Wichelhaus* and the Objective Theory of Contract" (1985) 47 U. Pitt. L. R. 183: 38

Bradgate, J., "Reservation of Title Ten Years On" (1987) The Conveyancer and Property Lawyer 434: 222

Brownsword, R., "Static and Dynamic Market-Individualism" in *Exploring the Boundaries of Contract*, R. Halson (ed.) (Aldershot: Dartmouth, 1996): 199

Brownsword, Roger, Norma J. Hird, and Geraint Howells (eds), *Good Faith in Contract: Concept and Context* (Aldershot: Dartmouth, 1999): 145

Burrows, Andrew, "Reforming Privity of Contract: Law Commission Report No. 242" [1996] L.M.C.L.Q. 467: 61, 98, 106

Campbell, D., "The Undeath of Contract: A Study in the Degeneration of a Research Programme" (1992) 22 Hong Kong Law Review 38: 227

Campbell, D., "Classification and the Crisis of the Common Law" a review of P. Birks (ed), *The Classification of Obligations* (Oxford, 1997) in (1999) 26 Journal of Law and Society 369: 227

Campbell, D., and D. Harris, "Flexibility in Long-Term Contractual Relationships: The Role of Co-operation" (1993) 20 Journal of Law and Society 166: 211, 227

Catzman, M. A., "Recent Developments in the Law of Third Party Contracts" [1975] L.S.U.C. Spec. Lec. 305: 47

Charny, D., "Non-legal Sanctions in Commercial Relationships" (1990) 104 Harvard Law Review 373: 209

Charny, D., "The New Formalism in Contract" (1999) 66 University of Chicago Law Review 842: 200

Chloros, A. G., "The Doctrine of Consideration and the Reform of the Law of Contract" (1968) 17 I.C.L.Q. 137: 51

Collins, H., "Contract and Legal Theory," in *Legal Theory and Common Law* (*ed.* W. Twining) (Oxford: Basil Blackwell Ltd. 1986): 56

Collins, H., *The Law of Contract* (London:Weidenfeld & Nicolson 1986): 201

Collins, H., *The Law of Contract*, 3rd edn. (London: Butterworths 1997): 107

Coote, B., *Exception Clauses* (1964): 301

Coote, B., "Vicarious Immunity by an Alternative Route – II" (1974) 37 M.L.R. 453: 295

Coote. B., "Consideration and the Joint Promisee" [1978] C.L.J. 301: 46, 149

Coote, B., "Contract Damages, *Ruxley*, and the Performance Interest" [1997] C.L.J. 537: 116

Corbin, "Contracts for the Benefit of Third Parties" (1930) 46 L.Q.R. 12: 45, 97, 147, 234

Daintith, T., "The Design and Performance of Long-Term Contracts" in T. Daintith and G. Teubner (eds), *Contract and Organisation* (Berlin 1984): 211

Danzig, R., "Hadley *v.* Baxendale: A Study in the Industrialization of the Law" (1975) 4 Journal of Legal Studies 249: 196

de Cruz, S.P., "Privity in America: A Study in Judicial and Statutory Innovation" (1985) 14 Anglo-Amer. L.R. 265: 46

de Wet, J.C., *Die Ontwikkeling van die Ooreenkoms ten behoewe van 'n Derde* (Leiden: Sijthoff's, 1940): 132

de Wet, J.C., & A.H. van Wyk, *Die Suid-Afrikaanse Kontraktereg en Handelsreg* (Durban: Butterworths, 5th ed 1992): 141

Deakin, S., et al., "'Trust' or Law? Towards an Integrated Theory of Contractual Relations between Firms" (1994) 21 Journal of Law and Society 329: 212

Derrington, S., "Does the Marine Insurance Act 1909 (Cth) Still Serve the Needs of the Business Community?" (1995) 7 Insurance Law Journal 31: 213

Dowrick, F.E., "A Jus Quaesitum Tertio By Way of Contract in English Common Law" (1956) 19 M.L.R. 374: 39

Dyer, D., "Pulling the privity thread: will contract law unravel?" [1999] I.T.L.Q. 105: 103

Eisenberg, M.A., "The Bargain Principle and Its Limits" (1982) 95 Harv. Law Rev. 741: 58

Eisenberg, M.A., "The Responsive Model of Contract Law" (1984) 36 Stan. L.R. 1107: 52

Eisenberg, M.A., "Third-Party Beneficiaries" 92 Colum.L.Rev. 1358 (1992): 172, 310

Everett, D., "Romalpa Clauses: The Fundamental Flaw" (1995) 68 Australian Law Journal 404: 221

Feinman, J.M., "Critical Approaches to Contract Law" (1983) 30 U.C.L.A, Law Rev. 829: 56

Flannigan, "Privity – The End of an Era (Error)" (1987) 103 L.Q.R. 564: 64, 89, 92, 99, 104
Fleming, "Employee's Tort in a Contractual Matrix: New Approaches in Canada" (1993) 13 O.J.L.S. 430: 299
Fraser, A., *Reinventing Aristocracy: The Constitutional Reformation of Corporate Governance* (Aldershot: Dartmouth 1998): 232
Fried, C., *Contract as Promise* (Harvard U.P., Cambridge, Mass., 1981): 5, 52, 67, 99, 161
Friedman, "Losing One's Head: Judges and the Law in Nineteenth Century American Legal History" 24 Law & Soc. Inquiry 253 (1999) 311
Friedman, L., "Law, Rules, and the Interpretation of Written Documents" (1964-65) 59 Northwestern University Law Review 751: 215
Friedmann, D., "The Performance Interest in Contract Damages" (1995) 111 L.Q.R. 628: 119, 148
Fuller, L., "Consideration as Form" (1941) 41 Col. Law Rev. 799: 51
Fuller, L., and Purdue, "The Reliance Interest in Contract Damages" (1936) 46 Yale L.J. 52: 148, 248
Furmston, M.P., "Return to *Dunlop v. Selfridge*?" (1960) 23 M.L.R. 373: 31, 40, 87, 140
Gava, J., and P. Kincaid, "Contract and Conventionalism: Professional Attitudes to Changes in Contract Law in Australia" (1996) 10 Journal of Contract Law 141: 199
Getz, L., "Contracts for the Benefit of Third Parties" (1962) *Acta Juridica* 38: 132
Gilmore, "On Statutory Obsolescence" 39 U. Colo. L. Rev. 461 (1967) 324
Gilmore, G., *The Death of Contract*, Ohio State University Press, Columbus, 1974: 40, 122, 152, 310
Goodhart, A.L, and C.J. Hamson, "Undisclosed principals in contract" [1932] C.L.J. 320: 269
Graham, L., *Niagara Country* (1949): 311
Graham, L., and F. Severance, *The First Hundred Years of the Buffalo Chamber of Commerce* (1945): 311
Gray, J., *False Dawn: The delusions of global capitalism* (London,1998): 229
Hamson, C.J., "The Reform of Consideration" (1938) 54 L.Q.R. 233: 47
Hedley, S., "The 'Needs of Commercial Litigants' in Nineteenth and Twentieth-Century Contract Law" (1997) 18 Journal of Legal History 85: 212
Horwitz, M., "The Historical Foundations of Modern Contract Law" (1974) 87 Harvard Law Review 917: 205
Horwitz, M., *The Transformation of American Law 1780-1860* (Cambridge, Mass: Harvard U.P., 1977): 205
Huscroft, "Bad Doctrine and Incremental Reform" (1994) 7 J.C.L. 181: 244, 299
Hutchison, D.B., "Unravelling the *Stipulatio Alteri*" (1974) 3 *Responsa Meridiana* 1: 132
Ibbetson, D., *A Historical Introduction to the Law of Obligations* (1999): 259
Kahn-Freund, O., "Reflections on Public Policy in the English Conflict of Laws" (1953) 39 Trans. Grot. Soc. 39: 76

Karsten, P., "The 'Discovery' of Law by English and American Jurists of the Seventeenth, Eighteenth, and Nineteenth Centuries: Third-Party Beneficiary Contracts as a Test Case" (1991) Law and History Review 327: 208, 310

Kerr Wylie, J., "Contracts in Favour of Third Parties" (1943) 7 *Tydskrif vir Hedendaagse Romeins-Hollandse Reg* 94: 132

Kessler, "Contracts of Adhesion - Some Thoughts about Freedom of Contract" 43 Colum. L. Rev. 629 (1943): 321

Kincaid, Peter, "Privity and the Essence of Contract" (1989) 12 U.N.S.W.L.J. 59: 60

Kincaid, Peter, "The *Trident Insurance* Case: Death of Contract?" (1989) 2 J.C.L. 160: 60, 233

Kincaid, Peter, "Third Parties: Rationalising a Right to Sue" [1989] C.L.J. 243: 60, 128, 147, 233, 243

Kincaid, Peter, "The U.K. Law Commission's Privity Proposals and Contract Theory" (1994) 8 J.C.L. 51: 60, 129, 147, 199, 233

Kincaid, Peter, "Justice in Tort Choice of Law" (1997) 18 Adelaide L. Rev. 191: 81

Kincaid, Peter, "Privity and Private Justice in Contract" (1997) 12 J.C.L. 47: 98, 101, 105, 129, 144, 225, 233, 310

Kincaid, Peter, "Privity Reform in England" (2000) 116 L.Q.R. 43: 100, 233

Kostal, R, *Law and English Railway Capitalism 1825-1875* (Oxford, 1994): 227

Kronman, A. T. and R.A. Posner, *The Economics of Contract Law*, Little, Brown and Company, Boston, 1979: 56

Langdell, C. C., *A Summary of the Law of Contracts* (2nd ed.), Little, Brown and Company, Boston, 1880: 40

Leake, S.M., *Law of Contracts* (6th ed.), Stevens & Sons Limited, London, 1912: 34

Levin, J. and McDowell, B., "The Balance Theory of Contracts: Seeking Justice in Voluntary Obligations" (1983) 29 McGill Law J. 24: 52

Linzer, *A Contracts Anthology*: 310

Lorenz and Danneman, *The German Law of Contract* (Oxford: 1997): 152

Lucke, H.K., "Striking a Bargain" (1962) 1 Adelaide L. Rev. 293: 64

Luttwak, E., *Turbo-Capitalism: Winners and Losers in the Global Economy* (New York, 1999): 228

Macaulay, S., "Non-Contractual Relations in Business: A Preliminary Study" (1963) 28 American Sociological Review 55: 209

Macaulay, S., "Private Legislation and the Duty to Read - Business run by I.B.M. Machine, the Law of Contracts and Credit Cards" (1965-66) 19 Vanderbilt Law Review 1051: 216

Macaulay, S., "An Empirical View of Contract" [1985] Wisconsin Law Review 465: 210

MacCormick, N., *Legal Reasoning and Legal Theory* (Oxford: O.U.P. 1978): 106

MacMillan, "Privity and the Third Party Beneficiary: The 'Monstrous Proposition'" [1994] L.M.C.L.Q. 22: 299

MacNeil, I. R., *Contracts: Exchange Transactions and Relations* (2nd ed.), Foundation Press, Mineola, N.Y., 1978: 55

MacNeil, I. R., *The New Social Contract, An Inquiry into Modern Contractual Relations*, Yale University Press, New Haven, 1980: 53
Markesinis, B., "An Expanding Tort Law - The Price of a Rigid Contract Law" (1987) 103 L.Q.R. 354: 4, 73, 147
McBride, "A Fifth Common Law Obligation" (1994) 14 Legal Studies 35: 161
McKerron, R.G., "The Juristic Nature of Contracts for the Benefit of Third Persons" (1929) 46 *South African Law Journal* 387: 132
Milsom, S.F.C., *Historical Foundations of the Common Law* (London, 1981): 207, 319
Milsom, S.F.C., *Studies in the History of the Common Law* (London, 1985): 207
Mnookin, R., and R. Wilson, "Rational Bargaining and Market Efficiency: Understanding *Pennzoil v. Texaco*" (1989) 75 Virginia Law Review 295: 204
Nevins, A., *Grover Cleveland* (1932): 311
Note, "The Third Party Beneficiary Concept: A Proposal" 57 Colum.L.Rev. 406: 177
Note, "Third Party Beneficiaries and the Intention Standard: A Search for Rational Contract Decision-Making" 54 Va.L.Rev. 1166 (1968): 181
Page, "The Power of the Contracting Parties to Alter a Contract for Rendering Peformance to a Third Person" 12 Wis. L. Rev. 141 (1937): 315
Palay, T., "Comparative Institutional Economics: The Governance of Rail Freight Contracting" (1984) 13 Journal of Legal Studies 265: 210
Palmer, "The Stevedore's Dilemma: Exemption Clauses and Third Parties – I" [1974] J.B.L. 101: 295
Parfit, *Reasons and Persons* (Oxford, 1984): 158
Pocock, J.G.A., *The Machiavellian Moment: Florentine Political Thought and the Atlantic Republican Tradition* (Princeton, 1975): 232
Polinsky, A. M., *An Introduction to Law and Economics*, Little, Brown and Company, Boston, 1983: 56
Pollock, F., *The Land Laws* (1883): 263
Pollock, F., *Principles of Contract* (4th ed.), Stevens and Sons Limited, London, 1888: 34
Presser, S.B., "Some Realism About Orphism" (1984-85) 79 Nw. U.L.R. 869: 56
Prince, Harry G., "Perfecting the Third Party Beneficiary Standing Rule Under Section 302 of the Restatement (Second) of Contracts" 25 B.C.L.Rev. 919 (1957): 177
Raz, "Promises and Obligations" in *Law, Morality, and Society* eds Hacker & Raz (London: 1977): 150
Raz, "Voluntary Obligations and Normative Powers" Proceedings of the Aristotelian Society (1972) Supp'y Vol XLVI 59: 150
Reich, Charles, "The New Property" 73 Yale L. J. 733 (1964): 325
Reynolds, F., "Himalaya Clauses Resurgent" (1974) 90 L.Q.R. 301: 295
Reynolds, F., "Contract and Tort: The View from the Contract Side of the Fence" (1993) 5 Canta. L. R. 280: 299
Reynolds, F., *Bowstead and Reynolds on Agency* (16th ed., 1996): 269
Robertson, A., "Reliance and Expectation in Estoppel Remedies" (1998) 18 L.S. 360: 118

Rose, C., "Trust in the Mirror of Betrayal" (1995) 75 Boston University Law Review 531: 212

Rubin, G., "The County Courts and the Tally Trade, 1846-1914" in G. Rubin and D. Sugarman (eds), *Law, Economy and Society, 1750-1914: Essays in the History of English Law* (Abingdon, 1984): 211

Samuels, G., "Contracts for the Benefit of Third Parties" (1968) 8 U.W.A.L.R. 378: 33

Scamell, E.H., "Privity of Contract" (1955) 8 C.L.P. 131: 39

Schwartz, Gary T., "Economic Loss in American Tort Law: The Examples of J'Aire and of Products Liability" 23 San Diego L.Rev. 37 (1986): 180

Seddon, N., "Australian Contract Law: Maelstrom or Measured Mutation?" (1994) 7 Journal of Contract Law 93: 199

Shatwell, K.O., "The Doctrine of Consideration in the Modern Law" (1954) 1 Syd. L. Rev. 289: 79

Simpson, A.W.B., "Innovation in Nineteenth Century Contract Law" (1975) 91 Law Quarterly Review 247: 205

Simpson, A.W.B., "The Horwitz Thesis and the History of Contracts" (1979) 46 University of Chicago Law Review 533: 205

Simpson, A.W.B., *A History of the Land Law* (2nd ed., 1986): 263, 279

Simpson, A.W.B., *A History of the Common Law of Contract*, Clarendon Press, 1987: 87, 89, 325

Smith, Robert P., Recent Case, 31 Tex.L.Rev. 210 (1952): 183

Smith, Stephen A., "Contracts for the Benefit of Third Parties: In Defence of the Third-Party Rule" (1997) 17 O.J.L.S. 643: 90, 105, 128, 249, 320, 322, 330

Smith, Stephen A., "Rights, Remedies and Normal Expectancies in Tort and Contract" (1997) 113 L.Q.R. 426: 119, 148

Smith, Stephen A., "Concurrent Liability in Contract and Unjust Enrichment" (1999) 115 L.Q.R. 245: 164

Spence, "Australian Estoppel" (1997) 11 J.C.L. 1: 161

Standen, J.A., "Critical Legal Studies as an AntiPositivist Phenomenon" (1986) 72 Va. L.R. 983: 56

Stapleton, "The Normal Expectancies Measure in Tort Damages" (1997) 113 L.Q.R. 257: 148

Steyn, Lord, "Contract Law: Fulfilling the Reasonable Expectations of Honest Men" (1997) 113 L.Q.R. 433: 3, 123

Stoljar, S.J., *A History of Contract at Common Law* (1975): 273

Street, T.A., *The Foundations of Legal Liability*, Edward Thompson Company, Long Island 1906: 39, 324

Summers, David M., Note, "Third Party Beneficiaries and the Restatement (Second) of Contracts" 67 Cornell L.Rev. 880 (1982): 177

Sweet, Justin, *Legal Aspects of Architecture, Engineering and the Construction Process* (4th ed. 1989): 193

Symposium, "The Informal Economy" (1994) Yale Law Journal 2119: 209

Symposium, "Law, Economics, Norms" (1996) 144 University of Pennsylvania Law Review 1643: 209

Symposium, "Formalism Revisited (Formalism in Commercial Law)" (1999) 66 University of Chicago Law Review 710: 209

Transformation Thesis, "The, and the Ascription of Contractual Responsibility" in *Perspectives of Critical Contract Law* ed. T. Wilhelmsson (Aldershot: Dartmouth, 1993): 122

Treitel, G., "Damages in Respect of a Third Party Loss" (1998) 114 L.Q.R. 527: 116

Vincent-Jones, P., "Contract Litigation in England and Wales 1975-1991: A Transformation in Business Disputing?" (1993) 12 Civil Justice Quarterly 337: 210

Waddams, S.M., "Privity of Contract in the Supreme Court of Canada" (1993) 109 L.Q.R. 349: 299

Waters, A.J., "The Property in the Promise: A Study of the Third Party Beneficiary Rule" (1985) 98 Harv. Law Rev. 1109: 46, 311, 312, 314, 316, 317

Watson, A., *Legal Origins and Legal Change* (London, 1991): 203

Weir, "A *Damnosa Hereditas*" (1995) 111 L.Q.R. 357: 158

Wheeler, S., "Capital Fractionalized: The Role of Insolvency Practitioners in Asset Distribution" in M. Cain and C. Harrington (eds), *Lawyers in a Postmodern World* (New York, 1994): 220

Whitman, J., "The Moral Menace of Roman Law and the Making of Commerce: Some Dutch Evidence" (1996) 105 Yale Law Journal 1841: 232

Whittaker, S., "The Third-Party Rule of Contract and the Law of Tort: the French Experience" (1995) 15 O.J.L.S. 327: 152

Whittaker, S., "The Third-Party Rule of Contract and the Tort of Negligence: Future Directions" (1996) 16 O.J.L.S. 191: 147, 260

Williams, G., "Contracts for the Benefit of Third Persons" (1944) 7 M.L.R. 123: 45

Wright, Lord, "Ought the Doctrine of Consideration to be Abolished from the Common Law?" (1936) 49 Harv.L.R. 1225: 28

Zimmermann, R., *The Law of Obligations, Roman Foundations of the Civilian Tradition* (1990): 262

Zweigert, Konrad, and Hein Kötz, *Introduction to Comparative Law* (Oxford: Clarendon Press, 3rd revised ed., translated from the German by Tony Weir, 1998): 141, 152

# Cases

# Statutes

# Index